Adolescence

Development, Diversity, and Context

Series Editor

Richard M. Lerner
Tufts University

A Garland Series

Series Contents

The Editors of this series are grateful to the several colleagues who facilitated our work on this series. Foremost, we are grateful to the authors of the selections reprinted in this volume. Their scholarship has shaped the study of adolescent development and we appreciate greatly their allowing us to include their work in this book.

We are especially grateful to Sofia T. Romero, Editor at the Boston College Center for Child, Family, and Community Partnerships, and to Imma De Stefanis, Graduate Research Assistant at the Center, for all their many contributions. Ms. Romero provided us with sage and professional editorial advice. Her wisdom, judgment, and skills enhanced the quality of our work and made it much more productive. Sr. De Stefanis collaborated extensively with us in the selection and organization of the scholarship included in the series. Her knowledge of and enthusiasm for the study of adolescence was an invaluable asset in our work.

We appreciate as well the excellent work of Carole Puccino, Editor at Garland Publishing. Her productivity and organizational skill enabled the volume to be produced with efficiency and quality. Finally, we thank Leo Balk, Vice President of Garland, for his enthusiasm for this project and for his support, encouragement, and guidance.

Social Interactions in Adolescence and Promoting Positive Social Contributions of Youth

Edited, with an introduction by

Richard M. Lerner
Tufts University

Daniel F. Perkins
University of Florida

GARLAND PUBLISHING, INC.
A MEMBER OF THE TAYLOR & FRANCIS GROUP
New York & London
1999

Library of Congress Cataloging-in-Publication Data

Social interactions in adolescence and promoting positive social contributions of youth / edited, with an introduction by Richard M. Lerner and Daniel F. Perkins.

p. cm. — (Adolescence : development, diversity, and context 6)

Includes bibliographical references.

ISBN 0-8153-3295-5 (alk. paper)

1. Teenagers—United States—Social networks. 2. Social interaction in adolescence—United States. 3. Interpersonal relations in adolescence—United States. 4. Teenagers—Services for—United States. 5. Adolescence—United States. I. Lerner, Richard M. II. Perkins, Daniel F. III. Series: Adolescence (New York, N.Y.) ; 6.

HQ796.S5634 1999

305.235'0973—dc21 99-33728

CIP

Printed on acid-free, 250-year-life paper

Manufactured in the United States of America

Contents

Introduction

Issues in Studying Social Interactions In, and Promoting the Positive Development of, Adolescents

**Richard M. Lerner, **Daniel F. Perkins*

Adolescent life is grounded in a complex developmental system involving dynamic, reciprocal relations between diverse youth and the variations in the multiple levels of the ecology of human development (Bronfenbrenner and Morris, 1998; Lerner, 1998). Adolescents contribute to changes in this developmental system through the influence of their individual attributes — involving characteristics such as pubertal level, personality, and cognitive stage — and the levels of their ecology (e.g., family, peers, school, work). The person-context relations involved in this system is the basic process of development across life.

This relational, developmental systems view of adolescent development is represented in both of the two main sections in this volume. The first section includes articles depicting the key domains of relations adolescents have with their social world: Interactions with parents and peers, including romantic interactions, and in regard to the world of work are reviewed. If person-context relations constitute the basic process of development, then both positive and healthy development, on the one hand, and problematic or unhealthy development, on the other, must derive from particular histories of such relations.

In turn, then, the second section of the volume presents scholarship that seeks to promote the positive development of youth though embedding them in supportive person-context relations. Such relations help inculcate in adolescents the personal strength — and provide young people with the contextual (family or community) assets — needed to live healthy lives and to grow into successful adults.

Adolescents' Interactions with Their Social Ecology

In adolescence there is redefining of social roles and an expansion into new roles. The interpersonal exchanges of adolescents with peers, including romantic relationships, their continuing relationships with parents, and their transitions to work are important features of adolescents' social interactions.

Accordingly, articles in this section describe the structure, function, and developmental course in adolescence of peer group relations (Cairns et al., 1995; Hartup, 1993), and discuss the nature of, changes in, and effects of the broader context on psychosocial behavior and development in adolescence (Cauce et al., 1992; Larson and Richards, 1991). The articles highlight the malleable character of friendships during adolescence, adolescents' conceptions of romantic relations, and the influences of friendships, leisure contextual settings, and relationships with siblings (that is, of peer relationships within the family) on adolescent sexual behaviors and adjustment (Bingham and Crockett, 1996; Feiring, 1996; Silbereisen et al., 1992). Other familial influences — involving the types of parenting behaviors shown to youth by their mothers and fathers — are seen also to be significantly related to peer group relations among adolescents (Brown et al., 1993).

Finally, the world of work, and of experiences designed particularly to enhance the transition of young people to the work setting, are seen as crucial components of the social interactions of adolescents (Hamilton and Lempert, 1996). Indeed, programs facilitating successful transition to a productive adult role are significant instances of interventions into youth development that may promote positive development. Such programs are discussed as part of the articles included in the second section of this volume.

Promoting Positive Societal Contributions of Youth

The second section discusses how societal institutions and, as well, public policies and intervention programs, may foster positive youth development. These articles demonstrate how an integration of basic and applied research knowledge can be used to inform policy and programs for youth. The articles provide examples of the importance of the individual-context relationships discussed in the first section. The articles demonstrate how the multiple contexts of adolescents may be structured in order to enhance the likelihood of promoting positive youth development while, simultaneously, decreasing the risks linked to problem behaviors. Examples include policies and programs pertinent to health care (Earls et al., 1989; Hurrelmann, 1990); secondary school, peer counseling projects (Hamburg and Varenhorst, 1977); community-based interventions (Wagenaar and Perry, 1994; Weissberg et al., 1991); community service opportunities for youth (Yates and Youniss, 1996); and systems changes involving the integration of governmental and non-governmental organizations in the service of promoting positive youth development (Hamburg and Takanishi, 1996).

Together, these articles speak to the importance of integrating the assets of youth, institutions, and the people involved in nurturing the healthy development of the young in ways that create, across adolescence, a system of events that support and guide them to healthy outcomes (Lerner, 1995; Masten et al., 1994). Through such integration the social capital of communities may be directed to improving the life chances of even those youth most at risk for problematic development (Weissberg et al., 1991).

A consistent theme in these articles is the need to match features of the policies or programs designed for either the prevention of negative behavior or for the promotion of positive behavior with the specific and unique needs of the specific population of adolescents (Lerner, 1995). In essence, then, the articles in this section depict attempts to use policies or programs to enhance the developmental assets of, and the resources for, diverse youth (Benson, 1997). Based on the idea that prevention of problems does not constitute the provision of resources needed to promote desired outcomes (Pittman, 1996), the objective of such asset-based interactions between the adolescent and his or her social ecology is to promote healthy and successful youth development.

Using the knowledge drawn from "outreach scholarship" (i.e., scholarship addressing community-defined issues and needs), Lerner (1995) provides a summary of the necessary ingredients of such youth programs, including intensive and individualized attention to the diversity of program participants, responsivity to the individual needs of the people most at risk, and a program structure that integrates the levels of the youth's ecology. That is, Lerner stresses that a key foundation for developing successful youth programs is the integration of multiple features of the context of human development. Thus, promoting positive youth development occurs in concert with transforming the developmental system in which a youth is embedded.

Conclusion

Clearly, the message across the volume is one of hope about the possibility of enriching the lives of adolescents through promoting systematic interpersonal and institutional relations that meet the developing needs of diverse youth. Amid the enormous changes associated with this period of adolescence, and in the face of the great variability in both positive and negative dimensions of youth behavior, there is the potential that policies and programs can improve the life chances and enhance the development of all adolescents. Indeed, recent research provides evidence that in communities where the citizens and institutions focus their attention on increasing both competencies of youth and external supports at all levels of the ecology, there is a great likelihood for successfully creating conditions enabling the development of strong and resourceful youth (Furstenberg and Hughes, 1995; Keith and Perkins, 1995; Scales and Leffert, 1999).

This volume affords the opportunity to witness how theory informs practice and how practice informs theory and research. The volume suggests that, in many instances, we know what to do to serve adolescents. It leaves us with the issue of whether we have the will to do it.

*Richard M. Lerner holds the Bergstrom Chair inApplied Developmental Science at Tufts University. A developmental psychologist, Lerner received a Ph.D. in 1971 from the City University of New York. He has been a fellow at the Center for Advanced Study in the Behavioral Sciences and is a fellow of the American Association for the Advancement of Science, the American Psychological Association, the American Psychological Society, and the American Association of Applied and Preventive Psychology. Prior to joining Tufts University, he was on the faculty and held administrative posts at Michigan State University, Pennsylvania State University, and Boston College, where he was the Anita L. Brennan Professor of Education and the director of the Center for Child, Family, and Community Partnerships. During the 1994–95 academic year Lerner held the Tyner Eminent Scholar Chair in the Human Sciences at Florida State University. Lerner is the author or editor of 40 books and more than 275 scholarly articles and chapters, including his 1995 book, *America's Youth in Crisis: Challenges and Options for*

Programs and Policies. He edited Volume 1, on "Theoretical models of human development," for the fifth edition of the *Handbook of Child Psychology.* He is known for his theory of, and research about, relations between life-span human development and contextual or ecological change. He is the founding editor of the *Journal of Research on Adolescence* and of the new journal, *Applied Developmental Science.*

** Daniel F. Perkins is an assistant professor and extension specialist of family, youth, and community sciences at the University of Florida. A human ecologist, he received a Ph.D. in Family and Child Ecology in 1995 from Michigan State University. He received his M.S. in Human Development and Family Studies and B.S. in psychology from the Pennsylvania State University. His research examines factors related to positive youth development and youth engagement in risky behaviors. He has published several articles on youth service, leadership, positive youth development, and youth engagement in risky behaviors. Currently, Dr. Perkins is examining the issue of positive youth development as it relates to: 4-H Youth Development programs, adolescent suicide, and bulimia. He is also evaluating several prevention programs aimed at families and youth at risk. As specialist for the Florida Cooperative Extension Service, he has designed innovative training programs for developing community collaboration and for promoting positive youth development.

References[1]

Benson, P. (1997). *All our kids are our kids: What communities must do to raise caring and responsible children and adolescents.* San Francisco: Jossey-Bass Publishers.

Bronfenbrenner, U., and Morris, P.A. (1998). The ecology of developmental process. In R.M. Lerner (Ed.), *Theoretical models of human development.* Volume 1 of the *Handbook of child psychology* (5th ed., pp. 993–1028). Editor in chief: W. Damon. New York: Wiley.

Keith, J.G., and Perkins, D.F. (1995). *13,000 Adolescents speak: A profile of Michigan youth.* East Lansing, MI: Institute for Children, Youth, and Families.

Lerner, R.M. (1998). Theories of human development: Contemporary perspectives. In R.M. Lerner (Ed.), *Theoretical models of human development.* Volume 1 of the *Handbook of child psychology* (5th ed., pp. 1–24). Editor in chief: W. Damon. New York: Wiley.

Pittman, K. (1996). Community, youth, and development: Three goals in search of connection. *New Designs for Youth Development,* Winter, 4–8.

Scales, P.C., and Leffert, N. (1999). *Developmental assets: A synthesis of the scientific research on adolescent development.* Minneapolis: Search Institute.

Footnote

[1]This list provides reference only to citations not included in this volume.

The Company They Keep: Friendships and Their Developmental Significance

Willard W. Hartup
University of Minnesota

HARTUP, WILLARD W. *The Company They Keep: Friendships and Their Developmental Significance.* CHILD DEVELOPMENT, 1996, **67**, 1–13. Considerable evidence tells us that "being liked" and "being disliked" are related to social competence, but evidence concerning friendships and their developmental significance is relatively weak. The argument is advanced that the developmental implications of these relationships cannot be specified without distinguishing between *having friends, the identity of one's friends,* and *friendship quality.* Most commonly, children are differentiated from one another in diagnosis and research only according to whether or not they have friends. The evidence shows that friends provide one another with cognitive and social scaffolding that differs from what nonfriends provide, and having friends supports good outcomes across normative transitions. But predicting developmental outcome also requires knowing about the behavioral characteristics and attitudes of children's friends as well as qualitative features of these relationships.

On February 16, 1995, in the small Minnesota town of Delano, a 14-year-old boy and his best friend ambushed and killed his mother as she returned home. The circumstances surrounding this event were described in the next edition of the *Minneapolis Star Tribune* (February 18, 1995): The boy had "several learning disabilities—including attention deficit disorder." He had been "difficult" for a long time and, within the last year, had gotten in trouble with a step-brother by wrecking a car and carrying a gun to a movie theater. The mother was described as having a wonderful relationship with her daughter but having "difficulties" with her son. The family dwelling contained guns.

Against these child, family, and ecological conditions is a significant social history: The boy was " . . . a lonely and unliked kid who was the frequent victim of schoolmates' taunts, jeers, and assaults. He had trouble with school work and trouble with other kids. . . . He was often teased on the bus and at school because of his appearance and abilities. . . . He got teased bad. Every day, he got teased. He'd get pushed around. But he couldn't really help himself. He was kind of skinny. . . . He didn't really have that many friends."

The boy actually had two good friends: One appears to have had things relatively well put together. But with this friend, the subject " . . . passed [a] gun safety course for hunting; they took the class together." The second friend (with whom the murder was committed) was a troublesome child. These two boys described themselves as the "best of friends," and spent much time together. The boys have admitted to planning the ambush (one saying they had planned it for weeks, the other for a few hours). They were armed and waiting when the mother arrived home from work. One conclusion seems relatively certain: this murder was an unlikely event until these two antisocial friends reached consensus about doing it.

An important message emerges from this incident: Child characteristics, intersecting with family relationships and social setting, cycle through peer relations in two

Presidential address to the biennial meetings of the Society for Research in Child Development, April 1, 1995, Indianapolis, IN. The author is grateful to W. Andrew Collins, Rosemary K. Hartup, Gary W. Ladd, Brett Laursen, and Andrew F. Newcomb for their comments on this manuscript. Requests for reprints may be sent to Willard W. Hartup, Institute of Child Development, University of Minnesota, 51 E. River Road, Minneapolis, MN 55455-0345.

[*Child Development*, 1996, **67**, 1–13. © 1996 by the Society for Research in Child Development, Inc. All rights reserved. 0009-3920/96/6701-0011$01.00]

ways to affect developmental outcome: (*a*) through acceptance and rejection by other children in the aggregate, and (*b*) through dyadic relationships, especially with friends. Considerable evidence now tells us that "being liked" by other children (an aggregate condition) supports good developmental outcome; conversely, "being disliked" (another aggregate condition) is a risk factor (Parker & Asher, 1987). But the evidence concerning friendships and their developmental significance is weak—mainly because these relationships have not been studied extensively enough or with sufficient differentiation.

On the too-rare occasions in which friendships are taken into account developmentally—either in diagnosis or research—children are differentiated merely according to whether or not they have friends. This emphasis on having friends is based on two assumptions: First, making and keeping friends requires good reality-testing and social skills; "having friends" is thus a proxy for "being socially skilled." Second, friendships are believed to be developmental wellsprings in the sense that children must suspend egoism, embrace egalitarian attitudes, and deal with conflict effectively in order to maintain them (Sullivan, 1953). On two counts, then, having friends is thought to bode well for the future.

Striking differences exist, however, among these relationships—both from child to child and companion to companion. First, enormous variation occurs in who the child's friends are: Some companions are outgoing and rarely get into trouble; others are antisocial; still others are good children but socially clumsy. These choices would seem rather obviously to contribute to socialization—not only by affecting reputations (as the adage admonishes) but through what transpires between the children. Knowing that a teenager has friends tells us one thing, but the identity of his or her friends tells us something else.

Second, friendships differ from one another qualitatively, that is, in their *content* or normative foundations (e.g., whether or not the two children engage in antisocial behavior), their *constructiveness* (e.g., whether conflict resolution commonly involves negotiation or whether it involves power assertion), their *closeness* (e.g., whether or not the children spend much time together and engage in many different activities), their *symmetry* (e.g., whether social power is vested more or less equally or more or less unequally in the two children), and their *affective substrates* (e.g., whether the relationship is supportive and secure or whether it is nonsupportive and conflict ridden). Qualitative differences in these relationships may have developmental implications in the same way that qualitative variations in adult-child relationships do (Ainsworth, Blehar, Waters, & Wall, 1978).

This essay begins, then, with the argument that one cannot describe friendships and their developmental significance without distinguishing between *having friends*, *the identity of the child's friends* (e.g., personality characteristics of the child's friends), and *friendship quality*. In the sections that follow, these relationship dimensions are examined separately and in turn. Three conclusions emerge: First, having friends is a normatively significant condition during childhood and adolescence. Second, friendships carry both developmental advantages and disadvantages so that a romanticized view of these relationships distorts them and what they may contribute to developmental outcome. Third, the identity of the child's friends and friendship quality may be more closely tied to individual differences than merely whether or not the child has friends.

Having Friends

Measurement Issues

Children's friends can be identified in four main ways: (*a*) by asking the children, their mothers, or their teachers to name the child's friends and determining whether these choices are reciprocated; (*b*) by asking children to assess their liking for one another; (*c*) by observing the extent to which children seek and maintain proximity with one another; and (*d*) by measuring reciprocities and coordinations in their social interaction. Concordances among various indicators turn out to be substantial, but method variance is also considerable; the "insiders" (the children themselves) do not always agree with the "outsiders" (teachers) or the observational record (Hartup, 1992; Howes, 1989).

Some variation among measures derives from the fact that social attraction is difficult for outsiders to know about. Method variance also derives from special difficulties connected with self-reports: First, children without friends almost always can name "friends" when asked to do so (Furman, in press). Second, friendship frequently seems to investigators to be a dichotomous condition (friend vs. nonfriend), whereas variation is more continuous (best friend/good friend/occasional friend/not friend). Third, whether these categories form a Guttman scale has not been determined, although researchers sometimes assume that they do (see Doyle, Markiewicz, & Hardy, 1994). Fourth, the status of so-called unilateral or unreciprocated friendship choice is unclear. Sometimes, when children's choices are not reciprocated, social interaction differs from when friendship choices are mutual; in other respects, the social exchange does not. Unilateral friends, for example, use tactics during disagreements with one another that are different from the ones used by mutual friends but similar to those used by nonfriends (e.g., standing firm). Simultaneously, conflict *outcomes* among unilateral friends (e.g., whether interaction continues) are more similar to those characterizing mutual friends than those characterizing nonfriends (Hartup, Laursen, Stewart, & Eastenson, 1988).

Developmental Significance

The developmental significance of having friends (apart from the identity of the child's friends or the quality of these relationships) has been examined in three main ways: (*a*) comparing the social interaction that occurs between friends and between nonfriends, (*b*) comparing children who have friends with those who don't, and (*c*) examining the extent to which having friends moderates behavioral outcomes across certain normative transitions.

Behavior with friends and nonfriends.—Behaviors differentiating friends from nonfriends have been specified in more than 80 studies (Newcomb & Bagwell, 1995); four are cited here. In the first of these (Newcomb & Brady, 1982), school-aged children were asked to explore a "creativity box" with either a friend or a classmate who was not a friend. More extensive exploration was observed among the children with their friends; conversation was more vigorous and mutually oriented; the emotional exchange was more positive. Most important, when tested individually, the children who explored the box with a friend remembered more about it afterward.

Second, Azmitia and Montgomery (1993) examined problem solving among 11-year-olds (mainly their dialogues) working on "isolation of variables" problems either with friends or acquaintances (the children were required to deduce which pizza ingredients caused certain characters in a series of stories to get sick and die). Friends spontaneously justified their suggestions more frequently than acquaintances, elaborated on their partners' proposals, engaged in a greater percentage of conflicts during their conversations, and more often checked results. Most important, the children working with friends did better than children working with nonfriends—on the most difficult versions of the task only. Clearly, "a friend in need is a friend indeed." The children's conversations were related to their problem solving through engagement in transactive conflicts. That is, task performance was facilitated to a greater extent between friends than between nonfriends by free airing of the children's differences in a cooperative, task-oriented context.

Third, we recently examined conversations between friends and nonfriends (10-year-olds) in an inner-city magnet school while the children wrote stories collaboratively on a computer (Hartup, Daiute, Zajac, & Sholl, 1995). Stories dealt with the rain forest—subject matter that the children had studied during a 6-week science project. Baseline story writing was measured with the children writing alone; control subjects *always* wrote alone. Results indicate that friends did not talk more during collaboration than nonfriends but, nevertheless, (*a*) engaged in more mutually oriented and less individualistic utterances; (*b*) agreed with one another more often (but did not disagree more readily); (*c*) repeated their own and the other's assertions more often; (*d*) posed alternatives and provided elaborations more frequently; (*e*) spent twice as much time as nonfriends talking about writing content, the vocabulary being used, and writing mechanics; and (*f*) spent less time engaged in "off-task" talk. Principal component analyses confirm that the structure of friends' talk was strongly focused on the task (i.e., the text) and was assertively collaborative—reminiscent of the dialogs used by experts and novices as discovered in other social problem-solving studies (Rogoff, 1990). Our stories themselves show that, overall, the ones collaboratively written by friends were better than the ones written by nonfriends, a difference that seems to rest on better use of Standard English rather than the narrative elements included in the text. Results suggest, overall, that the affordances of "being friends" differ from the affordances of "being acquaintances" in social problem solving (Hartup, in press).

Fourth, we examined conflict and competition among school-aged children playing a board game when they had been taught different rules (Hartup, French, Laursen, Johnston, & Ogawa, 1993). Disagreements occurred more frequently between friends than between nonfriends and lasted longer. Conflict resolution, however, differed by friendship and sex: (*a*) boys used assertions *without rationales* more frequently than girls—but only when friends were observed; (*b*) girls, on the other hand, used assertions *with rationales* more frequently than boys but, again, only with friends. Sex differences in conflict talk, widely cited in the literature (see Maccoby, 1990), thus seem to be relationship manifestations rather than manifestations of individual children.

Based on these and the other available data sets, a recent meta-analysis identified significant friend versus nonfriend effects across four broad-band categories (Newcomb & Bagwell, 1995): *positive engagement* (i.e., talk, smiling, and laughter); *conflict management* (i.e., disengagement and negotiation vs. power assertion); *task activity* (i.e., being oriented to the task as opposed to being off task); and *relationship properties* (i.e., equality in the exchange as well as mutuality and affirmation). Behaviorally speaking, friendships clearly are "communal relationships" (Clark & Mills, 1979). Reciprocity constitutes their deep structure.

Existing data suggest that four cognitive and motivational conditions afford these distinctive interactions: (*a*) friends know one another better than nonfriends and are thus able to communicate with one another more efficiently and effectively (Ladd & Emerson, 1984); (*b*) friends and nonfriends have different expectations of one another, especially concerning assistance and support (Bigelow, 1977); (*c*) an affective climate more favorable to exploration and problem solving exists between friends than between nonfriends—namely, a "climate of agreement" (Gottman, 1983); and (*d*) friends more readily than nonfriends seek ways of resolving disagreements that support continued interaction between them (Hartup & Laursen, 1992).

Unfortunately, the developmental significance of these differences is not known. Only fragmentary information tells us about short-term consequences in problem solving and behavioral regulation. Recalled events (Newcomb & Brady, 1982), deductive reasoning (Azmitia & Montgomery, 1993), conflict rates (Hartup et al., 1988), creative writing (Hartup et al., 1995), and social/moral judgments (Nelson & Aboud, 1985) are better supported by transactions with friends than by transactions with nonfriends. But only a small number of investigations exists in each case—sometimes only one. The bottom line: Process-outcome studies are badly needed to tell us whether friends engage in better scaffolding than nonfriends, or whether it only seems like they do. Once process/outcome connections are established, we can then—and only then—conclude that friendships have normative significance (i.e., that children employ their friends adaptively on a daily basis as cognitive and social resources).

Having friends versus not having friends.—Does having friends contribute to developmental differentiation (i.e., contribute to individual differences)? For the answer to this question to be affirmative, children who have friends must differ from those who do not.

Cross-sectional comparisons show that, first, children who have friends are more socially competent and less troubled than children who do not; they are more sociable, cooperative, altruistic, self-confident, and less lonely (Hartup, 1993; Newcomb & Bagwell, in press). Second, troubled children (e.g., clinic-referred children) are more likely to be friendless than nonreferred control cases (Rutter & Garmezy, 1983). Friendlessness is not always assessed in the same manner in these studies, but the results are consistent: Not one data set suggests that children with friends are worse off than children who do not have them.

Although friended/friendless comparisons are consistent across data sets, the results are difficult to interpret. First, having friends in these studies usually means having good supportive friends; thus having friends is confounded with friendship quality. Second, causal direction is impossible to establish: Friendship experience may contribute to self-esteem, for example, but self-confident children may make friends more readily than less confident children.

Longitudinal studies can be more convincing concerning developmental significance. Unfortunately, few exist. Short-term studies suggest that certain benefits accrue across school transitions: First, attitudes toward school are better among kindergartners

(5-year-olds) who have friends at the beginning and who maintain them than those who don't. Making new friends also predicts gains in school performance over the kindergarten year (Ladd, 1990). Second, with data collected from 10-year-olds across a 1-year interval, friendship experience enhanced self-esteem (Bukowski, Hoza, & Newcomb, 1991). Third, psychosocial disturbances have been reported less frequently when school changes occur in the company of good friends than when they don't (Berndt & Hawkins, 1991; Simmons, Burgeson, & Reef, 1988). Having friends thus seems to contribute specifically to affective outcomes across normative school transitions.

One long-term investigation (Bagwell, Newcomb, & Bukowski, 1994) raises questions, however, about "having friends" as a developmental predictor: Eleven-year-old children were identified as either friended or friendless on two separate occasions; subjects were re-evaluated at 23 years of age. Having friends and sociometric status (i.e., social acceptance) *together* predicted school success, aspirations, trouble with the law, and several other outcomes. Unique contributions to adult adjustment, however, were verified only for sociometric status. And even then, when stability in the childhood adjustment measures was taken into account, neither sociometric status nor friendship predicted adult outcomes.

Comment

Overall, the developmental significance of having friends is far from clear. Social interaction between friends differs from social interaction between nonfriends, but this does not tell us much more than that these relationships are unique social entities. Correlational studies are difficult to interpret because the effects of having friends are difficult to disentangle from the effects of friendship quality. Short-term longitudinal studies suggest that having friends supports adaptation during normative transitions, but more substantial evidence is needed concerning these effects. Child differences may interact with friendship experience in relation to developmental outcome rather than being main effects. Having friends, for example, may differentiate mainly among children who are vulnerable in some way prior to the transition. Stress associated with developmental transitions is known to accentuate differences among vulnerable children to a greater extent than among nonvulnerable ones (Caspi & Moffitt, 1991). Similarly, developmental interventions often have greater effects on vulnerable than on nonvulnerable individuals (see Crockenberg, 1981).

The Identity of the Child's Friends

We turn now to the identity of the child's friends. Several questions can be asked: With whom does the child become friends? Can the identity of a child's friends be forecast from what we know about the child? What is the developmental significance of the company a child keeps?

Who Are Children's Friends?

Consider, first, that children make friends on the basis of common interests and common activities. Common ground is a sine qua non in friendship relations throughout childhood and adolescence, suggesting that friends ought to be similar to one another in abilities and outlook. Folklore sometimes suggests that "opposites attract," but this notion has not found general support in the empirical literature. The weight of the evidence suggests that, instead, "Beast knows beast; birds of a feather flock together" (Aristotle, *Rhetoric*, Book 11).

Similarities between friends, however, vary from attribute to attribute, in most cases according to *reputational salience* (i.e., according to the importance of an attribute in determining the child's social reputation). Considerable evidence supports this "reputational salience hypothesis": Behavior ratings obtained more than 60 years ago by Robert Challman (1932) showed that social cooperation (an attribute with considerable reputational salience) was more concordant among friends than nonfriends; intelligence (an attribute without reputational salience among young children) was not. Among boys, physical activity (reputationally salient among males) was more similar among friends than nonfriends. Among girls, attractiveness of personality and social network size (both more reputationally salient among females than among males) were more similar among friends than nonfriends.

More recent data also suggest that behavioral concordances among school-aged children and their friends are greater than among children and nonfriends (Haselager, Hartup, Van Lieshout, & Riksen-Walraven, 1995). Peer ratings were obtained in a large number of fifth-grade classrooms centering on three constructs: prosocial behavior, antisocial behavior, and social withdrawal (shyness). First, friends were more similar to one another than nonfriends within each construct cluster (i.e., mean difference scores were significantly smaller). Second, correlations between friends were greater for antisocial behavior (i.e., fighting, disruption, and bullying) than for prosocial behavior (i.e., cooperation, offering help to others) or social withdrawal (i.e., shyness, dependency, and being victimized). These differences may reflect differences among these three attributes in reputational salience: Fighting, for example, is more consistently related to reputation than either cooperation or shyness (Coie, Dodge, & Kupersmidt, 1990). Our results also show important sex differences: (*a*) Friends were more similar to one another among girls than among boys in both prosocial and antisocial behavior (see also Cairns & Cairns, 1994), and (*b*) friends were more similar among boys than among girls in shyness. These gender variations are consistent with the reputational salience hypothesis, too: Being kind to others and being mean to them have greater implications for girls' social reputations than boys', whereas shyness/withdrawal has more to do with boys' reputations than girls' (Stevenson-Hinde & Hinde, 1986).

Concordance data from other studies are consistent with the reputational salience notion: Among adolescents, friends are most similar to one another in two general areas: (*a*) school-related attitudes, aspirations, and achievement (Epstein, 1983; Kandel, 1978b) and (*b*) normative activities such as smoking, drinking, drug use, antisocial behavior, and dating (Dishion, Andrews, & Crosby, 1995; Epstein, 1983; Kandel, 1978b; Tolson & Urberg, 1993). Sexual activity among adolescents is also consistent with the reputational salience hypothesis. Among girls (both African-American and white) in the United States, friends have been found to be similar in sexual behavior and attitudes, even when age and antisocial attitudes are taken into account. Among boys, however, sexual activity (especially engaging in sexual intercourse) was not concordant (Billy, Rodgers, & Udry, 1984). The authors argue that sexual activity is more closely related to social reputation among adolescent girls than it is among boys, thus accounting for the gender differences in the results.

Still other investigators, employing the social network as a unit of analysis, have discovered that members of friendship networks are concordant on such salient dimensions as sports, academic activities, and drug use (Brown, 1989). Antisocial behavior also distinguishes social networks from one another beginning in middle childhood (Cairns, Cairns, Neckerman, Gest, & Garieppy, 1988).

Friendship Concordances: Sources and Developmental Implications

Similarities between friends are one thing, but where do they come from and where do they lead? Developmental implications cannot be specified without understanding that these similarities derive from three sources: (*a*) *sociodemographic conditions* that bring children into proximity with one another; (*b*) *social selection* through which children construct relationships with children who are similar to themselves rather than different; and (*c*) *mutual socialization* through which children become similar to their friends by interacting with them.

Sociodemographic conditions.—Demographic conditions determine the neighborhoods in which children live, the schools in which they enroll, and the classes they attend. Concordances among children and their friends in socioeconomic status, ethnicity, and chronological age thus derive in considerable measure from social forces that constrain the "peer pool" and the child's access to it. One should not underestimate, however, the extent to which some of these concordances derive from the children's own choices. Among children attending schools that are mixed-age, mixed-race, and mixed socioeconomically, friends are still more similar to one another in these attributes than nonfriends are (Goldman, 1981; McCandless & Hoyt, 1961).

Selection.—Some similarities among friends derive from the well-known tendency among human beings (not alone among the various species) for choosing close associates who resemble themselves. Recent studies confirm that the similarity-attraction hypothesis applies to children: Among elementary school children who began an experimental session as strangers, differential attraction was evident in some groups (40%). Within them, more social contact occurred between preferred than between nonpreferred partners, and correlations were higher between preferred than nonpreferred partners in sociability and the cognitive maturity of their play (Rubin, Lynch, Coplan, Rose-Krasnor, & Booth, 1994).

But friendship selection is embedded in assortative processes occurring in larger social networks. Dishion and his colleagues (Dishion, Patterson, & Griesler, 1994) believe that these network concordances emerge through a process called "shopping" in which children and adolescents construct relationships that maximize interpersonal payoffs. Children are not believed to choose friends who are similar to themselves on a rational basis so much as on an experiential one. Accordingly, relationships become established when they "feel right." Similar individuals cleave to one another more readily than dissimilar individuals because they are more likely to find common ground in both their activities and their conversations. Antisocial children are thus most likely to make friends with other antisocial children and, in so doing, their common characteristics merge to create a "dyadic antisocial trait." Similarly, soccer players or musicians make friends, merge themselves dyadically, and set the stage for becoming even more similar to one another.

Selection thus acts simultaneously to determine the identity of the child's friends through two interlocking processes: (*a*) similarity and attraction occurring within dyads, and (*b*) assortative network formation occurring within groups. These processes undoubtedly combine differently from child to child in affecting developmental outcome: Cooperative, friendly, nonaggressive children can choose friends resembling themselves from a wide array of choices; antisocial children can also choose their friends on the basis of similarity and attraction—but frequently from a more restricted range of social alternatives.

Mutual socialization.—What behavioral outcomes stem from mutual socialization? The weight of the evidence suggests, first, that children and their friends who ascribe to conventional norms move further over time in the direction of normative behavior (Ball, 1981; Epstein, 1983; Kandel & Andrews, 1986). But does antisocial behavior increase over time among children in antisocial networks? Does troublesome behavior escalate among children—especially into criminal activity—through membership in these networks? Answers to these questions have been surprisingly difficult to provide, especially since children perceive their friends as exerting more pressure toward desirable than toward undesirable conduct (Brown, Clasen, & Eicher, 1986). Nevertheless, increases in undesirable behavior through antisocial friends among children who are themselves at risk for antisocial behavior is now relatively well documented (Ball, 1981; Berndt & Keefe, 1992; Dishion, 1990; Dishion et al., 1994). Conversely, "desisting" is forecast as strongly by a turning away from antisocial friends as by any other variable (Mulvey & Aber, 1988).

What occurs on a day-to-day basis between aggressive children and their friends? Jocks and their friends? "Brains" and their friends? One guesses that children model normative behaviors *for* their friends and simultaneously receive reinforcement *from* them. Antisocial children, for example, are known to engage in large amounts of talk with their friends—talk that is deviant even when the children are being videotaped in the laboratory (Dishion et al., 1994, 1995). Ordinary children talk a lot with their friends, too, but the content is not generally as deviant (Newcomb & Bagwell, 1995). Antisocial children use coercion with one another (Dishion et al., 1995); ordinary children, on the other hand, are freewheeling with their criticisms and persuasion but are less likely to be coercive (Berndt & Keefe, 1992; Hartup et al., 1993). Finally, one guesses that friends support one another in seeking environments that support their commonly held worldviews, although not much is known about this.

Other results show that selection *combines* with socialization to effect similarity between friends. Kandel (1978a) studied changes over the course of a year in drug use, educational aspirations, and delinquency in early adolescence, discovering that similarity stemmed from both sources in approximately equal amounts. Relative effects, however, vary according to the norms and the children involved (see Hartup, 1993).

Comment

Children and their friends are similar to one another, especially in attributes with reputational salience. One must acknowledge that effect sizes are modest and that friends are not carbon copies of one another. One must also acknowledge that the reputational salience hypothesis has never been subjected to direct test and it needs to be. Nevertheless, the identity of the child's friends is a significant consideration in predicting developmental outcome. Friends may be generally intimate, caring, and supportive, thus fostering good developmental prognosis. At the same time, the activities in which they support one another (the relationship *content*) may be extremely deviant, suggesting an altogether different prognosis.

Friendship Quality

Conceptual and Measurement Issues

Qualitative assessment of child and adolescent friendships currently involves two main strategies: (*a*) *dimensional analysis* through which one determines whether certain elements are present or absent in the social interaction between friends (e.g., companionship, intimacy, conflict, or power asymmetries), and (*b*) *typological* or *categorical* analysis through which one identifies patterns in social interaction believed to be critical to social development and adaptation (Furman, in press).

Dimensional assessment.—Most current dimensional assessments are based on "provisions" or "features" that children mention when talking about these relationships (Berndt & Perry, 1986; Bukowski, Hoza, & Boivin, 1994; Furman & Adler, 1982; Furman & Buhrmester, 1985; Parker & Asher, 1993); most instruments tap five or six domains. Domain scores, however, are correlated with one another (Berndt & Perry, 1986; Parker & Asher, 1993), and most factor analyses yield two-factor solutions. Both Berndt (in press) and Furman (in press) argue that "positive" and "negative" dimensions adequately describe most dimensional assessments, although some data sets suggest that more elaborate solutions are warranted (e.g., Ladd, Kochenderfer, & Coleman, in press).

Typological assessment.—Typological assessment is evolving slowly since the functional significance of friendships remains uncertain. Can one, for example, regard friendships as attachments? Probably not. No one has demonstrated that "the secure base phenomenon," so common among children and their caregivers, constitutes the functional core of children's friendships. Friends have been shown to be secure bases in one or two instances (Ipsa, 1981; Schwartz, 1972), but one is not overwhelmed with the evidence that children and their friends are bound to one another as attachment objects. Children describe their relationships with friends differently from their relationships with their caregivers—as *more* companionable, intimate, and egalitarian and, simultaneously, as *less* affectionate and reliable (Furman & Buhrmester, 1985). For these reasons, some writers describe friendships as affiliative relationships rather than attachments (Weiss, 1986). The challenge, then, is to describe what good-quality affiliative relationships are.

One new classification system has been devised on the basis of family systems theory (Shulman, 1993). Well-functioning friendships are considered to be balanced between closeness and intimacy, on the one hand, and individuality, on the other. The family systems model suggests three friendship types: *interdependent* ones, with cooperation and autonomy balanced; *disengaged* ones, in which friends are disconnected in spite of their efforts to maintain proximity with one another; and *consensus-sensitive* or *enmeshed* relationships, in which agreement and cohesion are maximized. Empirical data are based largely on children's interactions in a cooperative task adapted from family systems research (Reiss, 1981) and document the existence of interdependent and disengaged relationships—a promising beginning. Once again, however, caution should be exercised: Friendship networks may not revolve around the same equilibrative axes as families do.

Developmental Significance

Cross-sectional studies.—Among the various qualitative dimensions, *support* (positivity) and *contention* (negativity) have been examined most extensively in relation to child outcomes. Support is positively correlated with school involvement and achievement (Berndt & Hawkins, 1991; Cauce, 1986) and negatively correlated with school-based problems (Kurdek & Sinclair, 1988); positively correlated with popularity and good social reputations (Cauce, 1986); positively correlated with self-esteem (Mannarino, 1978; McGuire & Weisz, 1982; Perry, 1987) and psychosocial adjustment (Buhrmester, 1990) as well as negatively correlated with identity problems (Papini, Farmer, Clark, Micke, & Barnett, 1990) and depression—especially among girls (Compas, Slavin, Wagner, & Cannatta, 1986). Results are thus consistent but, once again, impossible to interpret. We cannot tell whether supportive relationships contribute to the competence of the individual child or vice versa.

Longitudinal studies.—Longitudinal studies dealing with friendship quality (positive vs. negative) emphasize school attitudes, involvement, and achievement. Studying children across the transition from elementary to junior high school, Berndt (1989) measured the size of the friendship network, friendship stability, and self-reported friendship quality (positivity) as well as popularity, attitudes toward school, and achievement. First, network size was negatively related to friendship support as reported by the children, suggesting that children recognize what researchers have been slow to learn, namely, that friendships are not all alike. Second, several nonsignificant results are illuminating: Neither number of friends nor friendship stability contributed to changes in school adjustment—either across the school transition or across the first year in the new school. School adjustment was relatively stable across the transition and was related to friendship stability cross-sectionally but not with earlier adjustment factored out. Third, the self-rated supportiveness of the child's friends, assessed shortly after entrance to the new school, predicted increasing popularity and increasingly positive attitudes toward classmates over the next year, suggesting that positive qualities in one's friendship relations support a widening social world in new school environments.

Other investigations focus on friendship qualities as predictors of school adaptation within the school year. Among 5-year-olds enrolled in kindergarten (Ladd et al., in press), for example, those having friendships characterized by "aid" and "validation" improved in school attitudes over the year with initial attitudes toward school factored out. Perceived conflict in friendships, on the other hand, predicted increasing forms of school maladjustment, especially among boys, including school loneliness and avoidance as well as school liking and engagement.

One other investigation (Berndt & Keefe, 1992) focused on both positive and negative friendship qualities and their correlations across time with school adjustment and self-esteem among adolescents (Berndt & Keefe, 1992). Students with supportive, intimate friendships became increasingly involved with school, while those who considered their friendships to be conflict-ridden and rivalrous became increasingly disruptive and troublesome. Friendship quality was not correlated with changes in self-esteem, possibly because self-esteem was relatively stable from the beginning to the end of the year. Additional analyses (Berndt, in press) suggest that developmental prediction is better for the negative dimensions in these relationships than the positive ones.

Other investigators have examined the interactions between stress and social support as related to behavioral outcome. With elementary school children, increases in peer support over several years predict both increasingly better adaptation and better grade point averages (Dubow, Tisak, Causey, Hryshko, & Reid, 1991). Other results, however, suggest that support from school personnel was associated with decreases in distress across a 2-year period but not support from friends (controlling for initial adjustment). Regression models showed that, actually, school grades predicted changes in friends' support rather than the reverse (DuBois, Felner, Brand, Adan, & Evans, 1992). Among adolescents, however, results are more complex: Windle (1992) reported that, among girls, friend support is positively correlated with alcohol use but negatively correlated with depression (with initial adjustment levels factored out). Among boys, friendship support is associated with outcome depending on stress levels: When stress is high, friend support encourages both alcohol use and depression; when stress is low or moderate, both alcohol use and depression are associated with having *nonsupportive* friends.

The dissonances encountered in these results would be reduced considerably were the identity of the children's friends to be known. Children and adolescents with behavior difficulties frequently have friends who themselves are troublesome (Dishion et al., 1995). These friends may provide one another with emotional support, but the interactions that occur between them may not be the same as those occurring between nontroubled children and their friends. Knowing who the child's friends are might account for the empirical anomalies.

Other difficulties in accounting for these results derive from the fact that the referents used in measuring social support in these studies (except in Berndt's work) consisted of friendship networks (the child's "friends") rather than a "best friend." And still other complications arise from the use of one child's assessments of relationship qualities (the subject's) when the evidence suggests that discrepancies between partners may correlate more strongly with adjustment difficulties than the perceptions of either partner alone (East, 1991). Nevertheless, these studies provide tantalizing tidbits suggesting that friendship quality bears a causal relation to developmental outcome.

Comment

What kinds of research are needed to better understand the developmental implications of friendship quality? One can argue that we are not urgently in need of cross-time studies narrowly focused on friendships and their vicissitudes. Rather, we need comprehensive studies in which interaction effects rather than main effects are emphasized and that encompass a wide range of variables as they cycle through time: (*a*) measures of the child, including temperament and other relevant early characteristics; (*b*) measures of early relationships, especially their affective and cognitive qualities; (*c*) measures of early success in encounters with relevant institutions, especially the schools; (*d*) status and reputation among other children (sociometric status); *and*, (*e*) friendship measures that simultaneously include whether a child has friends, who the child's friends are, and what these relationships are like.

Coming close to this model are recent studies conducted by the Oregon Social Learning Center (e.g., Dishion et al., 1994; Patterson, Reid, & Dishion, 1992). Child characteristics and family relations in early childhood have not been examined extensively by these investigators, but their work establishes linkages between coerciveness and monitoring within parent-child and sibling relationships, on the one hand, and troublesomeness and antisocial behavior among school-aged boys on the other. These studies also establish that poor parental discipline and monitoring predict peer rejection and academic failures, and that these conditions, in turn, predict increasing involvement with antisocial friends. Among children with these early histories, the immediate connection to serious conduct difficulties in adolescence now seems to be friendship with another deviant child. Exactly these conditions existed in the social history of that Minnesota teenager who, together with his best friend, killed his mother early in 1995.

Conclusion

Friendships in childhood and adolescence would seem to be developmentally significant—both normatively and differentially. When children have friends, they use them as cognitive and social resources on an everyday basis. Normative transitions and the stress carried with them seem to be better negotiated when children have friends than when they don't, especially when children are at risk. Differential significance, however, seems to derive mainly from the identity of the child's friends and the quality of the relationships between them. Supportive relationships between socially skilled individuals appear to be developmental advantages, whereas coercive and conflict-ridden relationships are developmental disadvantages, especially among antisocial children.

Nevertheless, friendship and its developmental significance may vary from child to child. New studies show that child characteristics interact with early relationships and environmental conditions, cycling in turn through relations with other children to determine behavioral outcome (Hartup & Van Lieshout, 1995). The work cited in this essay strongly suggests that friendship assessments deserve greater attention in studying these developmental pathways than they are currently given. These assessments, however, need to be comprehensive. Along with knowing whether or not children have friends, we must know who their friends are and the quality of their relationships with them.

References

Ainsworth, M. D. S., Blehar, M. C., Waters, E., & Wall, S. (1978). *Patterns of attachment: A psychological study of the Strange Situation*. Hillsdale, NJ: Erlbaum.

Azmitia, M., & Montgomery, R. (1993). Friendship, transactive dialogues, and the development of scientific reasoning. *Social Development*, **2**, 202–221.

Bagwell, C., Newcomb, A. F., & Bukowski, W. M. (1994). *Early adolescent friendship as a predictor of adult adjustment: A twelve-year follow-up investigation*. Unpublished manuscript, University of Richmond.

Ball, S. J. (1981). *Beachside comprehensive*. Cambridge: Cambridge University Press.

Berndt, T. J. (1989). Obtaining support from friends during childhood and adolescence. In D. Belle (Ed.), *Children's social networks and social supports* (pp. 308–331). New York: Wiley.

Berndt, T. J. (in press). Exploring the effects of friendship quality on social development. In W. M. Bukowski, A. F. Newcomb, & W. W. Hartup (Eds.), *The company they keep: Friendships in childhood and adolescence*. Cambridge: Cambridge University Press.

Berndt, T. J., & Hawkins, J. A. (1991). *Effects of friendship on adolescents' adjustment to junior high school*. Unpublished manuscript, Purdue University.

Berndt, T. J., & Keefe, K. (1992). Friends' influence on adolescents' perceptions of themselves in school. In D. H. Schunk & J. L. Meece (Eds.), *Students' perceptions in the classroom* (pp. 51–73). Hillsdale, NJ: Erlbaum.

Berndt, T. J., & Perry, T. B. (1986). Children's perceptions of friendship as supportive relationships. *Developmental Psychology*, **22**, 640–648.

Bigelow, B. J. (1977). Children's friendship expectations: A cognitive developmental study. *Child Development*, **48**, 246–253.

Billy, J. O. G., Rodgers, J. L., & Udry, J. R. (1984). Adolescent sexual behavior and friendship choice. *Social Forces*, **62**, 653–678.

Brown, B. B. (1989). The role of peer groups in adolescents' adjustment to secondary school. In T. J. Berndt & G. W. Ladd (Eds.), *Peer relationships in child development* (pp. 188–215). New York: Wiley.

Brown, B. B., Clasen, D. R., & Eicher, S. A. (1986). Perceptions of peer pressure, peer conformity dispositions, and self-reported behavior among adolescents. *Developmental Psychology*, **22**, 521–530.

Buhrmester, D. (1990). Intimacy of friendship, interpersonal competence, and adjustment during preadolescence and adolescence. *Child Development*, **61**, 1101–1111.

Bukowski, W. M., Hoza, B., & Boivin, M. (1994). Measuring friendship quality during pre- and early adolescence: The development and psychometric properties of the Friendship Qualities Scale. *Journal of Personal and Social Relationships*, **11**, 471–484.

Bukowski, W. M., Hoza, B., & Newcomb, A. F. (1991). *Friendship, popularity, and the "self" during early adolescence.* Unpublished manuscript, Concordia University (Montreal).

Cairns, R. B., & Cairns, B. D. (1994). *Lifelines and risks.* Cambridge: Cambridge University Press.

Cairns, R. B., Cairns, B. D., Neckerman, H. J., Gest, S., & Garieppy, J.-L. (1988). Peer networks and aggressive behavior: Peer support or peer rejection? *Developmental Psychology*, **24**, 815–823.

Caspi, A., & Moffitt, T. E. (1991). Individual differences are accentuated during periods of social change: The sample case of girls at puberty. *Journal of Personality and Social Psychology*, **61**, 157–168.

Cauce, A. M. (1986). Social networks and social competence: Exploring the effects of early adolescent friendships. *American Journal of Community Psychology*, **14**, 607–628.

Challman, R. C. (1932). Factors influencing friendships among preschool children. *Child Development*, **3**, 146–158.

Clark, M. S., & Mills, J. (1979). Interpersonal attraction in exchange and communal relationships. *Journal of Personality and Social Psychology*, **37**, 12–24.

Coie, J. D., Dodge, K. A., & Kupersmidt, J. B. (1990). Peer group behavior and social status. In S. R. Asher & J. D. Coie (Eds.), *Peer rejection in childhood* (pp. 17–59). Cambridge: Cambridge University Press.

Compas, B. E., Slavin, L. A., Wagner, B. A., & Cannatta, K. (1986). Relationship of life events and social support with psychological dysfunction among adolescents. *Journal of Youth and Adolescence*, **15**, 205–221.

Crockenberg, S. B. (1981). Infant irritability, mother responsiveness, and social support influences on the security of mother-infant attachment. *Child Development*, **52**, 857–865.

Dishion, T. J. (1990). The peer context of troublesome child and adolescent behavior. In P. Leone (Ed.), *Understanding troubled and troublesome youth.* Newbury Park, CA: Sage.

Dishion, T. J., Andrews, D. W., & Crosby, L. (1995). Anti-social boys and their friends in early adolescence: Relationship characteristics, quality, and interactional process. *Child Development*, **66**, 139–151.

Dishion, T. J., Patterson, G. R., & Griesler, P. C. (1994). Peer adaptations in the development of antisocial behavior: A confluence model. In L. R. Huesmann (Ed.), *Current perspectives on aggressive behavior* (pp. 61–95). New York: Plenum.

Doyle, A. B., Markiewicz, D., & Hardy, C. (1994). Mothers' and children's friendships: Intergenerational associations. *Journal of Social and Personal Relationships*, **11**, 363–377.

DuBois, D. L., Felner, R. D., Brand, S., Adan, A. M., & Evans, E. G. (1992). A prospective study of life stress, social support, and adaptation in early adolescence. *Child Development*, **63**, 542–557.

Dubow, E. F., Tisak, J., Causey, D., Hryshko, A., & Reid, G. (1991). A two-year longitudinal study of stressful life events, social support, and social problem-solving skills: Contributions to children's behavioral and academic adjustment. *Child Development*, **62**, 583–599.

East, P. L. (1991). The parent-child relationships of withdrawn, aggressive, and sociable children: Child and parent perspectives. *Merrill-Palmer Quarterly*, **37**, 425–444.

Epstein, J. L. (1983). Examining theories of adolescent friendship. In J. L. Epstein & N. L. Karweit (Eds.), *Friends in school* (pp. 39–61). San Diego: Academic Press.

Furman, W. (in press). The measurement of friendship perceptions: Conceptual and methodological issues. In W. M. Bukowski, A. F. Newcomb, & W. W. Hartup (Eds.), *The company they keep: Friendships in childhood and adolescence.* Cambridge: Cambridge University Press.

Furman, W., & Adler, T. (1982). *The Friendship*

Questionnaire. Unpublished manuscript, University of Denver.

Furman, W., & Buhrmester, D. (1985). Children's perceptions of the personal relationships in their social networks. *Developmental Psychology*, **21**, 1016–1022.

Goldman, J. A. (1981). The social interaction of preschool children in same-age versus mixed-age groupings. *Child Development*, **52**, 644–650.

Gottman, J. M. (1983). How children become friends. *Monographs of the Society for Research in Child Development*, **48**(3, Serial No. 201).

Hartup, W. W. (1992). Friendships and their developmental significance. In H. McGurk (Ed.), *Childhood social development* (pp. 175–205). Gove, UK: Erlbaum.

Hartup, W. W. (1993). Adolescents and their friends. In B. Laursen (Ed.), *Close friendships in adolescence* (pp. 3–22). San Francisco: Jossey-Bass.

Hartup, W. W. (in press). Cooperation, close relationships, and cognitive development. In W. M. Bukowski, A. F. Newcomb, & W. W. Hartup (Eds.), *The company they keep: Friendships in childhood and adolescence*. Cambridge: Cambridge University Press.

Hartup, W. W., Daiute, C., Zajac, R., & Sholl, W. (1995). *Collaboration in creative writing by friends and nonfriends*. Unpublished manuscript, University of Minnesota.

Hartup, W. W., French, D. C., Laursen, B., Johnston, K. M., & Ogawa, J. (1993). Conflict and friendship relations in middle childhood: Behavior in a closed-field situation. *Child Development*, **64**, 445–454.

Hartup, W. W., & Laursen, B. (1992). Conflict and context in peer relations. In C. H. Hart (Ed.), *Children on playgrounds: Research perspectives and applications* (pp. 44–84). Albany: State University of New York Press.

Hartup, W. W., Laursen, B., Stewart, M. I., & Eastenson, A. (1988). Conflict and the friendship relations of young children. *Child Development*, **59**, 1590–1600.

Hartup, W. W., & Van Lieshout, C. F. M. (1995). Personality development in social context. In J. T. Spence (Ed.), *Annual Review of Psychology*, **46**, 655–687.

Haselager, G. J. T., Hartup, W. W., Van Lieshout, C. F. M., & Riksen-Walraven, M. (1995). *Friendship similarity in middle childhood as a function of sex and sociometric status*. Unpublished manuscript, University of Nijmegen.

Howes, C. (1989). Peer interaction of young children. *Monographs of the Society for Research in Child Development*, **53**(Serial No. 217).

Ipsa, J. (1981). Peer support among Soviet day care toddlers. *International Journal of Behavioral Development*, **4**, 255–269.

Kandel, D. B. (1978a). Homophily, selection, and socialization in adolescent friendships. *American Journal of Sociology*, **84**, 427–436.

Kandel, D. B. (1978b). Similarity in real-life adolescent pairs. *Journal of Personality and Social Psychology*, **36**, 306–312.

Kandel, D. B., & Andrews, K. (1986). Processes of adolescent socialization by parents and peers. *International Journal of the Addictions*, **22**, 319–342.

Kurdek, L. A., & Sinclair, R. J. (1988). Adjustment of young adolescents in two-parent nuclear, stepfather, and mother-custody families. *Journal of Consulting and Clinical Psychology*, **56**, 91–96.

Ladd, G. W. (1990). Having friends, keeping friends, making friends, and being liked by peers in the classroom: Predictors of children's early school adjustment? *Child Development*, **61**, 1081–1100.

Ladd, G. W., & Emerson, E. S. (1984). Shared knowledge in children's friendships. *Developmental Psychology*, **20**, 932–940.

Ladd, G. W., Kochenderfer, B. J., & Coleman, C. C. (in press). Friendship quality as a predictor of young children's early school adjustment. *Child Development*.

Maccoby, E. E. (1990). Gender and relationships: A developmental account. *American Psychologist*, **45**, 513–520.

Mannarino, A. P. (1978). Friendship patterns and self-concept development in preadolescent males. *Journal of Genetic Psychology*, **133**, 105–110.

McCandless, B. R., & Hoyt, J. M. (1961). Sex, ethnicity and play preferences of preschool children. *Journal of Abnormal and Social Psychology*, **62**, 683–685.

McGuire, K. D., & Weisz, J. R. (1982). Social cognition and behavior correlates of preadolescent chumship. *Child Development*, **53**, 1478–1484.

Mulvey, E. P., & Aber, M. S. (1988). Growing out of delinquency: Development and desistance. In R. Jenkins & W. Brown (Eds.), *The abandonment of delinquent behavior: Promoting the turn-around*. New York: Praeger.

Nelson, J., & Aboud, F. E. (1985). The resolution of social conflict between friends. *Child Development*, **56**, 1009–1017.

Newcomb, A. F., & Bagwell, C. (1995). Children's friendship relations: A meta-analytic review. *Psychological Bulletin*, **117**, 306–347.

Newcomb, A. F., & Bagwell, C. (in press). The developmental significance of children's friendship relations. In W. M. Bukowski, A. F. Newcomb, & W. W. Hartup (Eds.), *The company they keep: Friendship in childhood and adolescence*. Cambridge: Cambridge University Press.

Newcomb, A. F., & Brady, J. E. (1982). Mutuality in boys' friendship relations. *Child Development*, **53**, 392–395.

Papini, D. R., Farmer, F. F., Clark, S. M., Micke, J. C., & Barnett, J. K. (1990). Early adolescent age and gender differences in patterns of emotional self-disclosure to parents and friends. *Adolescence*, **25**, 959–976.

Parker, J. G., & Asher, S. R. (1987). Peer relations and later personal adjustment: Are low-accepted children at risk? *Psychological Bulletin*, **102**, 357–389.

Parker, J. G., & Asher, S. R. (1993). Friendship and friendship quality in middle childhood: Links with peer group acceptance and feelings of loneliness and social dissatisfaction. *Developmental Psychology*, **29**, 611–621.

Patterson, G. R., Reid, J. B., & Dishion, T. J. (1992). *Antisocial boys*. Eugene, OR: Castalia.

Perry, T. B. (1987). *The relation of adolescent self-perceptions to their social relationships*. Unpublished doctoral dissertation, University of Oklahoma.

Reiss, D. (1981). *The family's construction of reality*. Cambridge, MA: Harvard University Press.

Rogoff, B. (1990). *Apprenticeship in thinking*. New York: Oxford University Press.

Rubin, K. H., Lynch, D., Coplan, R., Rose-Krasnor, L., & Booth, C. L. (1994). "Birds of a feather . . . ": Behavioral concordances and preferential personal attraction in children. *Child Development*, **65**, 1778–1785.

Rutter, M., & Garmezy, N. (1983). Developmental psychopathology. In E. M. Hetherington (Ed.), P. H. Mussen (Series Ed.), *Handbook of child psychology: Vol. 4. Socialization, personality, and social development* (pp. 775–911). New York: Wiley.

Schwartz, J. C. (1972). Effects of peer familiarity on the behavior of preschoolers in a novel situation. *Journal of Personality and Social Psychology*, **24**, 276–284.

Shulman, S. (1993). Close friendships in early and middle adolescence: Typology and friendship reasoning. In B. Laursen (Ed.), *Close friendships in adolescence* (pp. 55–72). San Francisco: Jossey-Bass.

Simmons, R. G., Burgeson, R., & Reef, M. J. (1988). Cumulative change at entry to adolescence. In M. Gunnar & W. A. Collins (Eds.), *Minnesota symposia on child psychology* (Vol. **21**, pp. 123–150). Hillsdale, NJ: Erlbaum.

Stevenson-Hinde, J., & Hinde, R. A. (1986). Changes in associations between characteristics and interaction. In R. Plomin & J. Dunn (Eds.), *The study of temperament: Changes, continuities and challenges* (pp. 115–129). Hillsdale, NJ: Erlbaum.

Sullivan, H. S. (1953). *The interpersonal theory of psychiatry*. New York: Norton.

Tolson, J. M., & Urberg, K. A. (1993). Similarity between adolescent best friends. *Journal of Adolescent Research*, **8**, 274–288.

Weiss, R. S. (1986). Continuities and transformations in social relationships from childhood to adulthood. In W. W. Hartup & Z. Rubin (Eds.), *Relationships and development* (pp. 95–110). Hillsdale, NJ: Erlbaum.

Windle, M. (1992). A longitudinal study of stress buffering for adolescent problem behaviors. *Developmental Psychology*, **28**, 522–530.

Friendships and Social Networks in Childhood and Adolescence: Fluidity, Reliability, and Interrelations

Robert B. Cairns, Man-Chi Leung, Lisa Buchanan, and Beverley D. Cairns

University of North Carolina at Chapel Hill

CAIRNS, ROBERT B.; LEUNG, MAN-CHI; BUCHANAN, LISA; and CAIRNS, BEVERLEY D. *Friendships and Social Networks in Childhood and Adolescence: Fluidity, Reliability, and Interrelations.* CHILD DEVELOPMENT, 1995, **66**, 1330–1345. Social networks and friendships were tracked over a 3-week period for 132 students enrolled in fourth- and seventh-grade classrooms. Individual interviews were employed to collect data on friendships. Social group membership was determined by the composite social-cognitive map (SCM) procedure and by self-reports. Considerable overlap was found among the methods for establishing relational patterns (i.e., friendships, self-reported groups, composite social-cognitive maps). When loose criteria for stability were employed, high stability was found in friendships (p = .56–.75) and social group membership (p = .90) over a 3-week period. But when stringent criteria were employed, only modest social relationship stability was observed in both methods, suggesting that there is much greater fluidity in peer bonds than has been generally recognized. The relationship between friendship and social network measures, the distinctive information yielded by social networks, and gender and age differences in group structure, fluidity, and friendships are discussed.

The idea that individuals are tied together by invisible bonds into groups and networks of relationships has been a recurrent theme in social and developmental psychology (Baldwin, 1902). There remains much to be learned about the nature of social bonds and their stability over time. One premise of this investigation is that social relations do not depict static structures so much as they represent changing and adaptive processes (Cairns, Neckerman, & Cairns, 1989). Contemporary research suggests that the friends and peer groups of childhood and adolescence are dynamic in organization and identification (Brown, 1990). Over time, specific social relationships of persons may fade into the background or become thrust into the foreground, depending upon the contemporary quality and contextual salience of the relationship. To the extent that such dynamic processes are operative, they may be clarified by short-term longitudinal investigation.

A second and related premise is that analyses of friendship dyads and peer groups should extend beyond the individual as the focus of analysis. In this regard, Bronfenbrenner and Crouter (1983) have argued that precise identification of the effective social ecology is necessary to clarify how social influences are mediated in the lives of children and adolescents. According to this view, information about the person's "social address" or social status is not sufficient (i.e., socioeconomic or sociometric) to understand social processes. To clarify the dynamics of social influence, reciprocity, and change, techniques are required which identify the actual relationships that children form.

Following the early classic studies by Moreno (1934) and Sherif and Sherif (1953), the effects of social groups have been identified in diverse areas of childhood and adolescent adaptation, including:

1. *Deviance.*—Peer group membership has been viewed as an important factor in male and female adolescent delinquency (Elliott, Huizinga, & Menard, 1989; Giordano, Cernkovich, & Pugh, 1986), drinking (Stattin, Gustafson, & Magnusson, 1989), and drug use (Kandel, 1978; Zank, 1988).

2. *Developmental psychobiology.*—Girls tend to affiliate with other girls who are similar in terms of pubertal onset, and

Work on this study was supported by funds from R01-HD-23302-04, R01-MH-45532, and P50-MH52429-01. Correspondence should be sent to Robert B. Cairns, Center for Developmental Science, CB No. 8115, University of North Carolina, Chapel Hill, NC 27599-8115.

early maturing girls tend to form relationships with older girls and boys (Caspi & Moffitt, in press; Stattin & Magnusson, 1990).

3. *Personality development.*—Children and adolescents tend to affiliate in groups with others who are similar to themselves in multiple characteristics, including aggressive behaviors (Cairns, Cairns, Neckerman, Gest, & Gariépy, 1988) and school affiliations and aspirations (Cohen, 1977; Eder, 1985).

4. *Gender development.*—From early childhood through adolescence, there is a tendency for girls and boys to form same-sex peer groups (e.g., Benenson, 1990; Cairns, Perrin, & Cairns, 1985; Hallinan, 1980; Lagerspetz, Björkqvist, & Peltonen, 1988).

5. *School dropout.*—School dropout before the eleventh grade is associated with earlier peer group membership in elementary school, presumably because children who have failed a grade tend to form groups with others who have also failed (Cairns, Cairns, & Neckerman, 1989).

Despite such demonstrations, several questions remain on the properties of natural social groups. For example, Hallinan (1980) reported that 18% of the naturally formed peer groups in middle school classes remained stable over the school year, while Cohen (1977) reported that 76% of the peer groups in high school remained stable from the fall to the spring semesters. Because the two investigations differed on several factors relevant to stability—age of subjects, criteria for identifying groups, methods for assessing stability—the reason for the difference in findings could not be determined.

This discrepancy illustrates the general failure of published investigations of peer social groups to specify linkages between different methods, analyses, and constructs. The methods of collecting data have ranged from self-reports (e.g., Benenson, 1990; Giordano et al., 1986) and parental nominations of their child's social networks (Feiring & Lewis, 1987), to direct observations (e.g., Cairns, Perrin, & Cairns, 1985; Ladd, Price, & Hart, 1988; Strayer & Noël, 1986) and ethnographic reports (Dunphy, 1963; Eder, 1985; Savin-Williams, 1979). It seems reasonable to expect that these data collection procedures differ not only in economy and accessibility but, as well, in the extent they reflect biases in reporting.

In addition, diverse techniques have been employed to analyze social networks. The procedures range from quantitative solutions (e.g., Craven & Wellman, 1973; Shrum & Cheek, 1987) and rater judgments of social group size, cohesiveness, and membership (Salzinger, Kaplan, & Artemyeff, 1983) to the graphic depiction of groups (Moreno, 1934) and accounts of the average or modal qualities of persons or groups with whom the subject interacts (Cairns et al., 1985; Ladd, 1983). Comparative studies suggest that the analyses differ in economy, sampling requirements, and efficiency, as well as the nature of information that they yield about a person and members of her or his social group.[1]

Differences in methods have become interwoven with differences in theoretical orientation. In this regard, studies of personality development and developmental psychopathology have employed peer nomination techniques to identify individual differences in sociometric status (e.g., Asher & Coie, 1990; Coie, Dodge, & Coppotelli, 1982). This method focuses upon the child's social status rather than upon the child's network of relationships. One important hypothesis to grow out of this work is that children who have been classified "popular" will have more stable relationships and will show higher levels of adjustment than those who have been classified as "rejected" (Ladd, 1990).

Social network studies, by contrast, have focused on the relationships that children form with particular peers and the influences that these individuals have upon each other (e.g., Cairns et al., 1985; Cohen, 1977; Giordano et al., 1986). Recent studies of Kupersmidt and her colleagues (Kupersmidt, Courtney, DeRosier, & Patterson, 1991) suggest that children tend to associate with others who are similar to themselves in sociometric status (e.g., "rejected" children tend to form friendships with other "rejected" children). In support of this proposal, it has been reported that aggressive children (many of whom are unpopular in their classrooms) tend to form friendships and social groups with other aggressive chil-

[1] It is beyond the present paper to offer a detailed comparison of the advantages and limitations of these analytic methods; such comparisons are offered elsewhere (e.g., Cairns, Gariépy, & Kindermann, 1989; Hallinan, 1980).

dren (Cairns et al., 1988; Cohen, 1977; Giordano et al., 1986). More generally, at least some of the discrepancies in the empirical literature seem to reflect differences in how constructs of peer association and peer status have been operationally defined and analyzed.

In the light of these issues, one aim of the present investigation was to obtain information on the short-term stability of social groups and friendships of children and young adolescents. It was anticipated that evidence would be found for both continuity and fluidity of social relationships in a period as short as 3 weeks. A second aim was to cross-validate measures of social relationships by obtaining separate measures of dyadic friendships, social networks, and social centrality. In the light of the discrepancies in the empirical literature, it seems important to clarify the linkages that exist between different techniques of measurement, specifically self-report and peer reports of social group membership. A third aim was to obtain preliminary information on age-related and gender differences in relationship fluidity and stability. Prior work on age-related differences in relationship stability (e.g., Berndt, 1982; Horrocks & Bucker, 1951) suggests that both friendships and groups should become increasingly stable with age.

Dyadic friendships and social groups were assessed in the peer social networks of fourth-grade and seventh-grade classrooms over a 3-week period. In this investigation, peer social network is an inclusive concept, referring to the social relations among all students and groups of students in a specific context (classroom, grade, school). Social group refers to subsets of persons (cliques or clusters) within the network. Not all persons in the network necessarily belong to a social group, and some persons may belong to two or more groups.

Method

Subjects

Subjects were enrolled in the fourth or seventh grades of two schools located in the same suburban district. Five fourth-grade classrooms in an elementary school and four seventh-grade classrooms in a middle school participated in the study. Only students who agreed to participate and whose parents consented to their participation served as respondents and were individually interviewed. A total of 132 respondents, including 54 subjects in the fourth grade (26 girls, 28 boys) and 78 subjects in the seventh grade (35 girls, 43 boys), participated in the study. There was a 45% participation rate in the fourth-grade classrooms and 74% participation in the seventh-grade classrooms. Seven percent of the fourth-grade students and 21% of the seventh-grade respondents were of minority racial status (overwhelmingly African American). The data were collected in the spring semester (March–April 1990) after the classes had been together since the preceding August. In these schools, the average age at mid-year was 10.2 years in the fourth grade and 13.2 years in the seventh grade. The mean revised Duncan scale SES index for the sample was 32 (Stevens & Featherman, 1981), on a scale that ranged from 11 to 88. (The national average was 34.5, according to an analysis of the 1980 census data [Stevens & Cho, 1985].) The schools were situated in a suburban metropolitan area, according to the 1980 United States Census.

Measures

Friendship nomination.—Friends of subjects were identified from tape-recorded interviews conducted with each subject individually. The interviewer asked, "Some people have a number of close friends, but others have just one 'best friend,' and still others don't have a best friend. What about you?" Subjects were free to nominate any number of friends. No class lists or photographs were provided to assist the respondents: the method involved the free recall of persons. Similarly, respondents were free to name persons outside the classroom and outside the school.

Whether or not individuals are classified as friends can be determined in two different ways. The inclusive method employs information only from the individual nominator, without regard to whether the person named as a friend reciprocates the nomination. The exclusive method requires mutuality of choice. To determine mutuality, information is required from two persons: the individual who nominates as well as the individual who is nominated. The inclusive/exclusive methodological distinction is nontrivial because the results may differ, depending on whether mutuality is required in friendship judgments or whether one person's judgment is deemed sufficient.

Social groups and networks.—Subjects were also asked a set of questions about social networks, beginning with the inquiry: "Are there people who hang around together a lot at school? Who are they?" Depending on the subject's response, certain follow-up probes were employed. If the subject nominated only groups of one sex, he or she was asked, "Are there any boys' groups/girls' groups?" If subjects failed to nominate themselves, they were asked, "What about you? Do you hang around together a lot with a group?" To determine whether persons were left out by accident or design, the question was asked, "Are there any people who don't have a group?" Once again, respondents were not presented with any class lists or photographs to prompt memory or recall. By combining information across subjects, a composite social-cognitive map (SCM) of the network of groups was obtained for each school and each grade, following the technique described in previous publications (e.g., Cairns et al., 1985; Cairns et al., 1988). A computer program was used to assist in the computation.[2] Details of the social network identification procedure were reported in Cairns, Gariépy, and Kindermann (1989).

Network centrality/status.—It is possible to identify from nomination frequency the centrality of each group within the social network and the centrality of each person within his or her social group. Once the groups are identified (Cairns, Gariépy, & Kindermann, 1989), the steps are easy to follow. Accordingly, frequency of nomination to a group was summarized for each person. The centrality index (CI) for each group was simply the average of the two persons within that group who received the highest number of nominations from peers. Given this CI cluster index for all groups in the network, the status of each group was identified. "High" centrality groups referred to those groups that had a CI index which fell within the range of $\geq(0.7 \times CI_h)$, where CI_h was the highest-ranking group in the network. "Medium" centrality groups had a CI index that fell within the range defined by $>(0.3 \times CI_h)$ and $<(0.7 \times CI_h)$. "Low" centrality groups had a CI index that was equal to or below $(0.3 \times CI_h)$.[3]

Parallel classification criteria are employed to identify the status of persons within groups. Individuals are considered to have "high" centrality in the group if their frequency-of-nomination scores are $\geq(0.7 \times CI_i)$, where CI_i is the CI index of the group of which the person is a member. Persons have "medium" centrality in the group if their frequency-of-nomination scores fall between $>(0.3 \times CI_i)$ and $<(0.7 \times CI_i)$. "Low" centrality members have frequency-of-nomination scores $\leq(0.3 \times CI_i)$. If individuals are not nominated for group membership, they are regarded as "isolated" in the network.

The two measures of centrality (i.e., group relative to network and person relative to group) may be combined to describe the overall status of persons in the social network (Cairns, Gariépy, & Kindermann, 1989). In sum, nuclear network status meant the person was a high centrality member of a high centrality group. Peripheral network status meant the person was a low centrality member of any group or belonged to a low centrality group. Isolate network status meant the person was not nominated for membership in any group. Secondary network status consisted of those students with intermediate centrality (i.e., the remaining members of the network).

Criteria for stability of groups.—The primary criterion for stability was whether at least half (i.e., ≥50%) of the members of the original group remained together in the second wave. The designation of stable was used for those groups whose membership was identical or modified on the two observations. The remaining groups were considered to be unstable (i.e., groups whose membership was fragmented or dissolved). More precisely, "identical" refers to occasions where there was an exact duplication of the members of the group in the two assessments, with no new members added or old members lost; "modified" indicates that the criterion for overlap was met; "fragmented" indicates that the criterion was not met, but at least two persons in the original group remained together in the second assessment; "dissolved" indicates that no two persons from the original group remained together in the second assessment.

Procedure

Students were interviewed individually. The interviews were tape-recorded,

[2] Our thanks to Haldor Julliusson for creating the "Moreno" program. A new program that is capable of efficiently analyzing large data sets has recently been completed by Man-Chi Leung and employed in the analyses of this article.

[3] In applications to date, the centrality measures have been computed separately for male and female clusters within network units because girls show a consistent tendency to nominate more persons than boys (e.g., Lagerspetz, Björkqvist, & Peltonen, 1988).

TABLE 1

MEAN NUMBER OF "NOMINATED FRIENDS" BY INCLUSIVE METHOD (by Gender, Grade, and Time)

	MALE		FEMALE	
GRADE	Time 1	Time 2	Time 1	Time 2
Grade 4	3.84	4.76	3.50	3.19
Grade 7	3.29	4.05	4.24	4.87

TABLE 2

PROPORTION OF MUTUAL FRIENDS AS A FUNCTION OF GRADE, GENDER, AND TEST

	Time 1	Time 2
Grade 4:		
Male	.47 (18/38)[a]	.21 (8/39)
Female	.47 (20/43)	.37 (12/33)
Grade 7:		
Male	.28 (16/58)	.34 (30/89)
Female	.44 (40/91)	.30 (32/107)

[a] "(18/38)" means that there were 38 instances where subjects in this sex-grade cell nominated as a friend other persons who also participated in the research, and 18 occasions where the choice was reciprocated. Mutuality or nonmutuality was thus computed only where both individuals (i.e., subject and friend) participated in the research. The remaining cells may be interpreted similarly.

and the information was subsequently transcribed verbatim into written transcripts. Subjects were seen twice. The second interview was 3 weeks after the first interview (±5 days). The same questions on social affiliations and social networks were asked in both sessions. Four interviewers participated in Time 1 data collection, and six interviewers participated in Time 2 (three of whom had been involved as interviewers in Time 1). Subjects were seen by different interviewers in the two assessment waves.

Results

The findings are presented in three sections: (1) friendships, (2) social networks, and (3) interrelations among measures.

Friendships

Features.—The friendship patterns as a function of gender and grade were determined over the two assessment waves. Table 1 contains information on the number of friends named by subjects, regardless of whether the choices were reciprocated by the persons named as friends (i.e., the inclusive method). A mean of 3.81 friends were named in the fourth grade, and a mean of 4.09 friends were named in the seventh grade. Analysis by a MANOVA within-subjects model [gender × grade × time (within)] indicated a significant gender × grade interaction for number of friends, $F(1, 125) = 4.47$, $p < .05$. Boys named more friends than girls in grade 4, but the pattern was reversed in grade 7. No other effects were reliable.

Friendship choices were reciprocated (i.e., the exclusive method) in slightly over one-third of the nominations. (Note that reciprocation could be determined only for those pairs where both persons participated as respondents.) Across eight sex-grade-time cells, the percent reciprocated ranged from 21% to 47%, with a median of 36%. The weighted mean percentage reciprocation across the test periods, grades, and genders was 35%. There were no reliable effects of gender, grade, or test occasion (Table 2).

Fluidity.—Even close friendships are fluid. If two subjects were mutual friends in Time 1, their chances of being mutual friends again 3 weeks later were $p = .32$ and $p = .46$ in the fourth grade and seventh grade, respectively. But this does not mean that the relationship was entirely ruptured. There was a high probability that at least one subject in a mutual friendship would again nominate the other subject as a friend 3 weeks later, even when the choice was not reciprocated in the second assessment ($p = .74$ and $p = .89$ in the fourth grade and seventh grade, respectively). These results are summarized in Table 3. Compared to nonreciprocated friendships, individuals who were named mutual friends in the first assessment were more likely to be mutual friends in the second assessment, $F(1, 30) = 10.71$, $p < .01$. The general picture that emerges from these data is that friendship nominations are relatively stable when more inclusive (i.e., less stringent) methods for determining friendships were employed. But when strict criteria were applied, mutual friendships were maintained in less than half of the cases over a 3-week period.

There is also evidence for an age difference in short-term stability. When Time 1 friendship nominations of the subjects were considered, without regard to mutuality or nonmutuality, the probability of renaming a friend in Time 2 was higher in the seventh grade ($p = .75$) than in the fourth grade ($p = .56$). This grade difference was statistically reliable, $F(1, 86) = 4.09$, $p < .05$. Subjects

TABLE 3

Stability of Friendship Nominations over Two Assessments as a Function of the Initial Mutuality or Nonmutuality of the Nomination

Given Friendship at Time 1	N	Conditional Probability of Time 2 Status: Mutual Friendship	Nonmutual Friendship	Mutual or Nonmutual Friendship
Grade 4:				
Mutual	38[a]	.32 (12/38)	.42 (16/38)	.74 (28/38)
Nonmutual	43[b]	.02 (1/43)	.37 (16/43)	.39 (17/43)
Total	81[c]	.16 (13/81)	.40 (32/81)	.56 (45/81)
Grade 7:				
Mutual	56[a]	.46 (26/56)	.43 (24/56)	.89 (50/56)
Nonmutual	93[b]	.17 (16/93)	.50 (46/93)	.67 (62/93)
Total	149[c]	.28 (42/149)	.47 (70/149)	.75 (112/149)

[a] The number of instances a friendship nomination was reciprocated.

[b] The number of instances a friendship nomination was not reciprocated, given that the person being nominated was also in the study.

[c] The total number of instances that a friend was nominated, given that the person being nominated was also in the study.

were also somewhat more liberal in naming friends on the second occasion—the average nominations increased from 3.71 to 4.25 from Time 1 to Time 2—but the difference was not significant.

Social Networks

Similar numbers of social groups were identified in the two observations in the fourth grade: there were 24 groups in Time 1 and 23 groups in Time 2. In addition, the distributions of high, medium, and low centrality groups were similar in the two observations (see Table 4).

Seventh-grade network findings paralleled those of the fourth grade in that similar numbers of social groups were identified in the two observations: 28 groups in Time 1 and 31 groups in Time 2. The distributions of group centrality were also similar in the two observations (see Table 4). There is one notable difference in the two grades; namely, the appearance of mixed-gender groups in early adolescence (i.e., 7% in Time 1 and 12% in Time 2 in the seventh grade vs. 0% at both times in the fourth grade). No mixed-gender groups were identified in the fourth grade.

TABLE 4

Number of Social Groups as a Function of Gender, Time of Assessment, and Centrality of Group (Shown Separately for Fourth and Seventh Grades)

	Time 1 Centrality: High	Medium	Low	Sum	Time 2 Centrality: High	Medium	Low	Sum
Grade 4:								
Male	6	6	0	12	6	4	3	13
Female	7	4	1	12	6	3	1	10
Mixed	0	0	0	0	0	0	0	0
Sum Fourth	13	10	1	24	12	7	4	23
Proportion	.54	.42	.04	1.00	.52	.30	.17	1.00
Grade 7:								
Male	4	5	3	12	5	5	4	14
Female	4	8	2	14	6	6	1	13
Mixed	2	0	0	2	1	0	3	4
Sum Seventh	10	13	5	28	12	11	8	31
Proportion	.36	.46	.18	1.00	.39	.35	.26	1.00

TABLE 5

STABILITY OF SOCIAL GROUPS FROM TEST 1 TO TEST 2 (Combined Grades)
(Shown for 50%, 75%, or 100% Criteria for Stability)

	Proportion of Overlap		
Stability	≥50%	≥75%	100%
1. Identical	.02 (1/42)	.02 (1/42)	.02 (1/42)
2. Modified	.88 (37/42)	.60 (25/42)	.24 (10/42)
3. Fragmented	.05 (2/42)	.33 (14/42)	.69 (29/42)
4. Dissolved	.05 (2/42)	.05 (2/42)	.05 (2/42)
Sum	1.00	1.00	1.00
Stable Sum (1) + (2)	.90 (38/42)	.62 (26/42)	.26 (11/42)
Unstable Sum (3) + (4)	.10 (4/42)	.38 (16/42)	.74 (31/42)
Sum	1.00	1.00	1.00

Group size was analyzed as a dependent variable in a 2 × 2 × 2 ANOVA (grade × gender × time). (In contrast with other analyses in this paper where time is a within-subject factor, time is considered in this analysis to be a between-subjects factor. The composition of virtually all groups changed and the number of groups that were observed differed over the two time periods.) The mean size of groups varied as a function of their network centrality. The high centrality groups had more members ($M = 6.89$) than medium centrality groups ($M = 4.39$) and low centrality groups ($M = 2.50$), $F(2, 78) = 38.34$, $p < .001$. Moreover, fourth-grade groups were somewhat smaller than seventh-grade groups: $M_{\text{fourth}} = 5.02$ vs. $M_{\text{seventh}} = 5.46$, $F(1, 78) = 7.76$, $p < .01$. In addition, the average size of groups in the two test periods differed reliably: $M_{\text{Wave1}} = 4.86$ vs. $M_{\text{Wave2}} = 5.66$, $F(1, 78) = 5.27$, $p < .05$. Male and female groups did not differ in size. (Mixed-sex groups were not included in the male-female group size comparisons.) It should also be noted that the sheer number of nominations offered by respondents differed in the two assessment waves. More persons were named members of social groups in Test 2 than in Test 1, $M_{\text{Nominations Test1}} = 8.51$, $M_{\text{Nominations Test2}} = 9.95$, $F(1, 126) = 9.13$, $p < .01$.

Stability of groups.—When the group is employed as the unit of analysis, 52 groups were identified in the network analysis in Time 1, and 54 groups were identified in Time 2. What proportion of the original 52 groups remained sufficiently intact to be considered stable in Time 2? When the ≥50% criterion was employed to determine group stability, a high proportion of the groups (90%; 38/42) were identified as stable.[4] Only 10% were unstable (i.e., two groups fragmented, and two disintegrated). As noted in the procedure section, 50% overlap with Time 1 members was the primary criterion for determining stability. For comparison purposes, the results obtained with more stringent criteria for stability are also shown in Table 5 (i.e., ≥75% or 100% of the members of the original group remained together in the second wave). When stringent criteria are employed to define stability, the proportion of groups designated as stable drops sharply.

To illustrate the changes that occurred in group composition, we show in Figure 1 the shifts observed in four of the nine classrooms. It should be noted that members of groups could be within the classroom, outside the classroom, or outside the school. That is, the method for identifying group membership did not exclude persons who were outside the class. Two of the classrooms (A and H) show a rather uncomplicated pattern of stability, and two other classrooms indicate mergers and cross-group membership from Time 1 to Time 2. In Classroom B, the presence of a person who shared membership in two groups foreshadowed the merger of these two groups into a single group on the second assessment. The illustrations represent the patterns of stability and fluidity seen in the remaining classrooms.

[4] Ten of the 52 clusters had only two members. We considered these two-members clusters as dyads for the following analyses, and they are not included in Table 5 and related analyses.

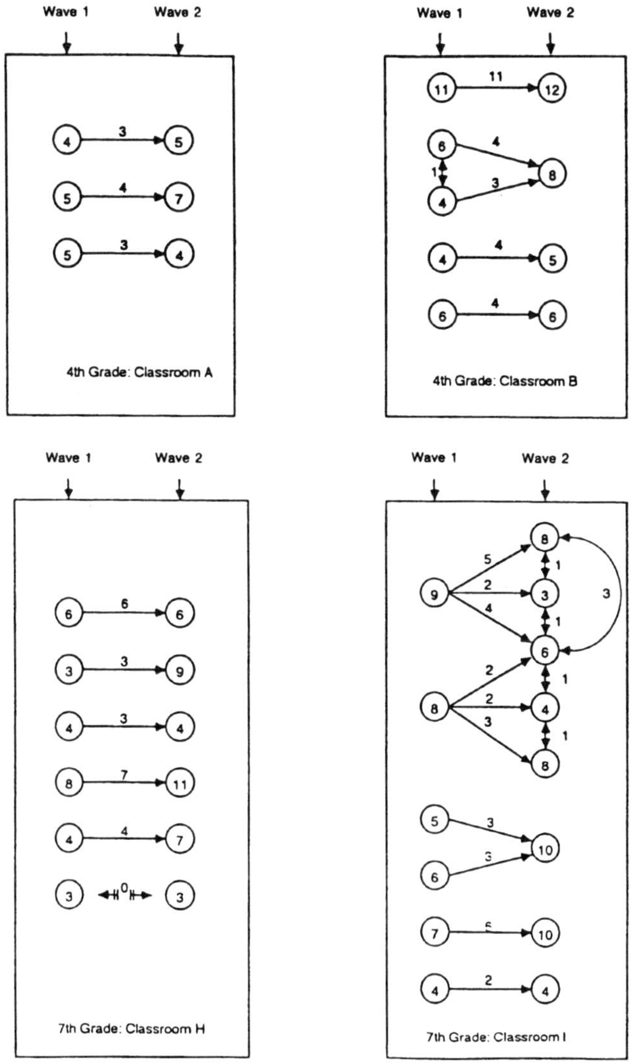

FIG. 1.—Illustrations of social group fluidity over 3 weeks in two fourth-grade classrooms (*A*, *B*) and two seventh-grade classrooms (*H*, *I*). The circles represent social groups, and the numbers within the circles indicate group size. All groups identified in the first test (Wave 1) are shown on the left side of each box, and all groups identified in the second test in the right side. A line is drawn between groups (circles) that meet the criteria for remaining intact in the two tests. The numbers above the connecting lines show the number of persons who were found in the group over the two tests. A break in the line from Wave 1 to Wave 2 indicates that there was no overlap in membership (i.e., the group dissolved). Within each column, the connecting lines indicate overlapping group membership. The numbers by the connecting lines indicate how many persons overlapped.

Stability as a function of centrality.—Two separate but related analyses may be made of the association between relationship stability and social status. One procedure employs the group as the unit of analysis and addresses the question of whether high centrality groups are more likely to remain intact than low centrality groups. No reliable differences in group stability were identified when the group was employed as the unit of analysis. High centrality groups were not necessarily high stability groups.

Even if a group × centrality stability difference had been identified, the interpretation would have been ambiguous. The ambiguity would arise because employment of "group" as the unit might obscure a possible differential stability of members within groups as a function of their centrality. For example, low centrality members (i.e., "hangers-on") of high centrality groups may be less secure in their continued membership than high centrality members (i.e., "leaders"). To address this matter, we asked whether high centrality members were more stable than low centrality members of the same group. A stability index was computed for high, medium, and low centrality members, respectively, holding the centrality of the group constant. This stability index was simply the proportion of persons in Time 1 who were identified in the same group in Time 2. This analysis required within-group comparisons (i.e., high, medium, and low centrality subjects who were members of the same group were compared to each other). Only the high centrality groups provided a sufficient distribution of high, medium, and low centrality subjects to permit within-group comparisons.

The findings indicate some support for the proposal of differential stability. The higher the centrality of an individual within a group, the more likely she or he would be relocated in the same group on the second test wave (Table 6). Hence high centrality members of the high centrality groups are most likely to remain within that identifiable group. As shown in Table 6, these individual status-based differences in stability were found in both grades, $F(2, 12) = 4.73$, $p < .05$, and $F(2, 12) = 15.35$, $p < .001$, for fourth and seventh grades, respectively.

Stability of individual status within the social network.—A final perspective on social continuity is provided when we divorce individual status from specific group membership. Here we focus upon individual status measures in the general network. Two types of such network measures are suggested by the social map procedure. One is simply the number of nominations that persons receive for membership in any group. A second network status measure is the assignment of persons as nuclear, secondary, peripheral, or isolated in the social network (following the criteria described in the method section). Because of the small number of subjects in the isolated and peripheral categories, they were combined for the following analyses.

TABLE 6

STABILITY OF GROUP MEMBERSHIP FROM TIME 1 TO TIME 2 AS A FUNCTION OF WITHIN-GROUP CENTRALITY (Shown Only for Stable High Centrality Groups)

Centrality of Individual	Grade 4	Grade 7
High	.88	1.00
Medium	.85	.66
Low	.52	.25

Consider first the number of nominations that an individual received in the two assessment waves. To control for differences in classroom size and respondents, Pearson product-moment correlations were computed separately within each classroom (the scores correlated membership nominations for each person in Time 1 and Time 2). The resultant correlations ranged from $r = .52$ to $r = .91$ in the fourth grade and from $r = .65$ to $r = .93$ in the seventh grade. These correlations were transformed into Fisher z scores and averaged across classes within each grade. The average z scores correspond to average Pearson product-moment correlations of $r = .74$, $t(106) = 9.50$, $p < .001$, and $r = .84$, $t(94) = 12.30$, $p < .001$, for the fourth and seventh grades, respectively.

The nuclear, secondary, peripheral/isolate network status of students was also reasonably stable over 3 weeks. Individual network status in Time 1 was closely associated with individual network status in Time 2 in both grades (Table 7). When the groups were combined across grades, nuclear members in Time 1 had a conditional probability of $p = .73$ of being nuclear members again in Time 2 (Fig. 2). The comparable conditional probability was $p = .56$ for secondary members and $p = .59$ for peripheral/isolate members. The likelihood that there would be a large shift in category (i.e., from nuclear

TABLE 7

STABILITY OF INDIVIDUAL STATUS IN THE SOCIAL NETWORK

Status in Time 1	Individual Network Status in Time 2			
	Nuclear	Secondary	Peripheral/ Isolate	Total
Grade 4:				
Nuclear	.76 (22/29)	.21 (6/29)	.03 (1/29)	1.00 (29/29)
Secondary	.22 (11/49)	.55 (27/49)	.22 (11/49)	1.00 (49/49)
Peripheral/isolate	.09 (4/43)	.30 (13/43)	.60 (26/43)	1.00 (43/43)
Total	.31 (37/121)	.38 (46/121)	.31 (38/121)	1.00 (121/121)
Grade 7:				
Nuclear	.69 (18/26)	.31 (8/26)	.00 (0/26)	1.00 (26/26)
Secondary	.26 (11/42)	.57 (24/42)	.17 (7/42)	1.00 (42/42)
Peripheral/isolate	.03/(1/38)	.39 (15/38)	.58 (22/38)	1.00 (38/38)
Total	.28 (30/106)	.44 (47/106)	.27 (29/106)	1.00 (106/106)

NOTE.—Fourth grade χ^2 = 53.64, $p < .001$, and lambda = .39; seventh grade χ^2 = 48.96, $p < .001$, and lambda = .29.

to peripheral/isolate or vice versa) was very low, regardless of direction (see Table 7 and Fig. 2).

Overlap between Self-Reports and SCM Measures of Relationships

Composite social-cognitive maps and self-reports.—One way to identify a person's social group was through peer social-cognitive maps, using information from all peer respondents in the social network. A second way was by the person's own self-report of his or her companions. To what extent do the self-reports and the SCM procedure yield the same or different information? In general, the number of persons in the social-cognitive map groups (SCM) was reliably larger than the self-reported

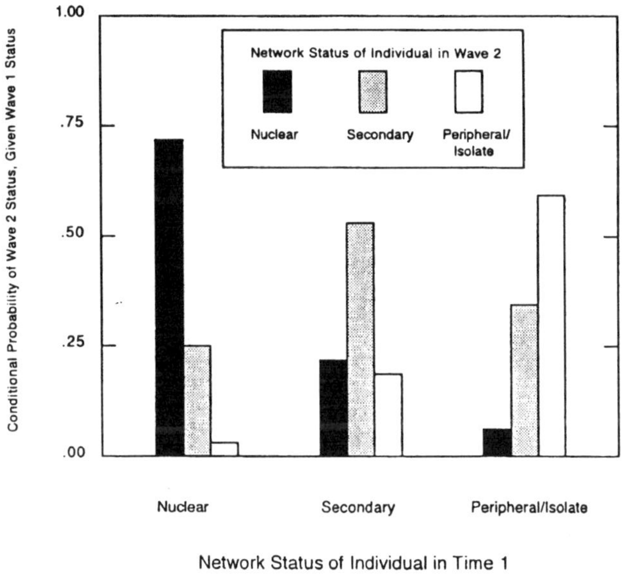

FIG. 2.—The stability of individual status in the network across 3 weeks. The columns represent the conditional probability that, for a given status in Time 1, the person will be in one of three status categories in Time 2 (data combined across grades and over genders). (See text and Table 7 for further explanation.)

groups, SCM_{mean} = 5.94 and $Self\text{-}report_{mean}$ = 3.72, $F(1, 57) = 12.45$, $p < .001$. Correspondence between these two methods for identifying social groups may be assessed by the proportion of members of the self-reported group who were also members of the composite social-cognitive map group. The proportion of overlap of self-reports of groups with the SCM computation was high ($p = .79$). There were few discrepancies of overinclusion in self-reports (i.e., few self-reports included persons in the subject's group when the composite social-cognitive map indicated that these persons were not in the subject's group). There was, however, frequent underrepresentation (i.e., self-reports that omitted persons from the subject's group when the composite social-cognitive map indicated that these persons were in the subject's group).

Friendship and group membership.— Correspondence between friendship and social group could be seen as the proportion of "friends" who were also in the subject's social group (as defined by the SCM procedure). An index of friendship/group overlap was computed as $F/G_{overlap} = F_g/F_n$ where F_g was the number of friends in the network who were also in the same group with the subject, and F_n was the total number of friends in the network the subject nominated. The overall correspondence between self-reports of friends and SCM group membership was $F/G_{overlap} = .57$ in wave 1 and $F/G_{overlap} = .82$ in wave 2. Chance overlap was also computed for each subject on the basis of such variables as the size of the network, group, and number of friends who were named.[5] The overlap between friends and SCM social group was greater than chance in all grade/gender comparisons in the two assessments, $F(1, 76) = 129.89$, $p < .001$. To sum up, persons named as "friends" by the subject were also likely to have been identified by peers as being members of the subjects' SCM social group, but there were typically fewer friends than group consorts.

Discussion

The present findings suggest that most social relationships among peers in schools endure over the short term, but even close relationships and coherent social groups are likely to wax and wane in strength. The persistence of dyadic relationships is underscored by the high stability of mutual friendships when relaxed criteria of friendship are employed in the second assessment (i.e., $p = .74$ and $p = .89$ stability indices in the two grades). Fluidity in the strength of relationships is shown, however, in the same data when stringent criteria of friendship are employed (i.e., $p = .32$ and $p = .46$ stability indices in the two grades). Similar conclusions may be reached when the unit of analysis was the group rather than the dyad. Almost all groups (90%) remained stable when a moderate criterion for stability was adopted in the second assessment. Only one group (2%) was stable when an exact duplication of membership was required in the two observations.

The present data may help explain the difference between the 76% group stability estimate of Cohen (1977) and the 18% stability estimate of Hallinan (1980). The studies differed on at least two factors that seem relevant to stability. Beyond the difference in age of subjects in the two studies, there was a major difference between the Cohen and Hallinan investigations in the criterion adopted for stability. In Cohen's investigation, at least 50% of the fall group's members had to be members of the same group in the spring (or vice versa), and there was a single reassessment. For Hallinan (1980), a "stable clique was defined as one that retains at least three of its members for an entire year" (p. 335). In Hallinan's work, at least three members had to be represented in all successive assessments over the school year (there was a minimum of six assessments for each classroom). In recognition of the severity of this criterion, Hallinan (1980) concluded, "This phenomenon [low stability] may be an artifact of the definition of clique employed in the analysis: a weaker definition is likely to result in more stable cliques" (p. 337). Table 5 provides data relevant to this speculation, illustrating the effects upon group stability of a relatively lenient or firm criterion for cluster membership. A strict criterion yields an estimate consistent with the low stability reported by Hallinan (1980); a relaxed criterion is consistent with the high stability estimate reported by Cohen (1977).

At first blush, the most compelling methodological problem in the present investigation would appear to be the less-than-complete subject participation in both Time

[5] The formulas for the computation of the chance correspondence took into account variations in size of the network and the group as well as the number of friends who were named, and the gender of the subjects and the cluster members.

1 and Time 2. Fewer than one-half of the potential fourth-grade subjects participated in both assessments, although approximately three-fourths of potential seventh-grade subjects participated. In any case, the differential participation rate should not have influenced the proportion or stability of the mutual friendships. The method adopted for determining mutual friendships was designed to eliminate such a "participation bias." In calculating reciprocal friendships (and the stability of mutual friendships), only pairs where both persons had participated were employed in the computation (i.e., subject as well as friend). This correction has been adopted in other investigations (e.g., Berndt & Hoyle, 1985). This correction also explains why the fourth-grade and seventh-grade findings could be similar, despite marked differences in participation rate. Furthermore, the rates of mutual friendships observed in this sample are wholly consistent with those observed in a companion investigation where the participation rate was very high (i.e., 89% of all possible subjects in the entire subject pool; Neckerman, 1992).

One puzzling observation is the apparent inconsistency of these findings on the stability of mutual friendships with the earlier report of Berndt and Hoyle (1985). Although the rates of mutual friendship were approximately the same as those observed in the present study, Berndt and Hoyle (1985) report considerably higher stability over a longer period, using a strict criterion for mutuality in the second assessment, i.e., $p = .32$ and $p = .46$ in the present study versus $p = .69$ and $p = .75$ in Berndt and Hoyle (1985) for the fourth and seventh grades, respectively. This outcome is curious because the same conventions seem to have been employed in collecting data in the two studies (i.e., individual interviews, free recall with no class lists) and analysis. A clue to the solution to this apparent discrepancy is suggested by the similarity that emerges when a more relaxed criterion of stability is employed (i.e., $p = .74$ and $p = .89$ in the two grades of this study). These stability outcomes indicated that the mutual friendships have been maintained at some level, and evidence for persistence may be found in at least one of the members of the relationship.[6]

Despite the shifts that occurred in reciprocal friendships, there was nonetheless substantial consistency in inclusive friendships over the two assessments. The changes that occurred in friendship status were in a direction that made sense on a priori grounds (i.e., mutual friendships were demoted to nonmutual friendships, but rarely vice versa). Friendships may change in salience and strength, but relationships tend to endure. The exploration of different criteria is useful—and perhaps necessary—to determine whether shifts in the intensity of relationships occur over time.

Measuring Friendships and Groups

Friendships constitute only part of the picture of peer relationships in childhood and adolescence. A broader view would include the pool of relationships from which friendships emerge and submerge; namely, the social network in which children are embedded and the specific groups of which they are members. Within the network, the social status of subjects was rather consistent over a 3-week period. This stability was reflected both in the stability correlations ($r = .74$ and $r = .84$ in the fourth and seventh grades, respectively) and in the nature of the status shifts that occurred. Most subjects did not shift in status category, and those who shifted tended to be adjacent to their original placement (e.g., secondary to nuclear or peripheral to secondary as opposed to peripheral to nuclear). Similar levels of stability were observed in social group membership. The more central the group and the more nuclear the member, the more likely it was that the person would continue to be a member of the group. High levels of status continuity were observed despite changes in group composition and network organization.

These data are consistent with a picture of social networks as constantly changing, dynamic systems rather than static entities. The flux and flow of social group organization and relationship strength indicated it was rare that social groups remained identi-

[6] In personal communication, Dr. Berndt (July 1991) has suggested a possible reason for the higher level of stability for mutual friendships in Berndt and Hoyle (1985). Subjects in that research had also participated in other research activities as friendship pairs in the first and second tests. Such exogenous support in the context of the investigation could have heightened the salience of the original relationship. More generally, the strength of a relationship can be reinstated by locating an old friend in a new context.

cal and unchanged, even over a period as short as 3 weeks. Nonetheless, virtually all of the groups could be readily identified after 3 weeks when a relaxed criterion was employed.

It should be noted that certain theoretical considerations played a role in the design of the present measures. No external prompts were employed in the collection of information on group membership and friends (i.e., subjects generated the names by free recall, and no class lists or photographs were provided). The objective was to encourage subjects to describe only those domains of the social system about which they were most confident. In large schools and classrooms, this methodological feature was of special importance. It seemed reasonable to expect that subjects would be most knowledgeable about group composition in the local domains that they themselves defined. It was also our goal to obtain free-recall information from subjects on their current friends, with minimal cues to prompt linkages or promote earlier ties.

Considerable overlap appeared among measures of (*a*) friendship, (*b*) self-nominated social groups, and (*c*) the SCM technique for analysis of social networks. But if self-reported friendships and social groups overlap with network measures, why bother with peer social-cognitive maps? Certain advantages may be mentioned. Perhaps most important, the SCM procedure permits the researcher to identify the individual's specific relationships and role in the social system, even without all members of a classroom participating in the research. The amount of information obtained is increased by permitting each respondent to describe groups and isolates in the whole network, rather than restricting descriptions to her or his own group. Given that permission/consent is usually less than complete in most schools, this is a nontrivial advantage over methods that require virtually unanimous cooperation (e.g., Shrum & Cheek, 1987). It may be especially significant for applications to emotionally disturbed children (Farmer & Cairns, 1991).

The SCM procedure also provides a comprehensive picture of the individual's associates and relationships. The groups derived by the social-cognitive maps are larger and more inclusive than those derived from self-reports. The self-reported groups may also be biased by cognitive constructions. In this regard, the recent work of Hawkins and his colleagues (Gillmore, Hawkins, Day, & Catalano, in press) suggests that elementary school children are aware of which peers are considered to be less desirable associates. The upshot is that aggressive and unpopular children may be selectively omitted in the individual self-reports of groups.

The linkages between sociometric status assessments and SCM measures of social status have not yet been broadly explored (but see the work of Kupersmidt et al., 1991, and Leung, 1993). It seems reasonable to expect that these procedures will provide complementary information. Specifically, the SCM procedure provides information about (*a*) groups of persons within the network, (*b*) the names (identity) of individuals with whom the child associates and the closeness of that association, or whether the person is socially isolated from the network, (*c*) the status of groups in the network, and (*d*) the status of the individual within the group and within the network. Sociometric status measures normally provide information about individual sociometric status (i.e., popular, average, controversial, neglected, and rejected) as well as distinctive information about the individual's likability and social reputation in the social network (Asher & Dodge, 1986). Further research is needed on the extent to which information obtained from these procedures overlaps, and the extent to which distinctive information is yielded by one procedure that may be unavailable in the other.

Age, Gender, and Context

Significant age-related increases in the stability of relationships were observed on virtually all of the measures employed in this study. Most effects were statistically reliable, and the remainder were in the direction of an age-related increase in the stability of relationships. These findings are consistent with prior reports in the literature. When broader age ranges have been sampled, significant differences have been shown in the stability of friendships and in the composition and size of social groups (e.g., Horrocks & Bucker, 1951; Shrum & Cheek, 1987).

Only modest gender differences in relationships were identified in this study. In the absence of supporting gender × grade interactions on the other measures of relationships, the interpretation of the grade × gender interaction in number of friends named is unclear. The interaction is especially interesting because it reverses the widely held assumption that the sex differences in relationships emerge, rather than diminish, with the onset of adolescence. More generally, the present results depict considerable overlap between males and females on several basic structural features of social relationships in childhood and adolescence, such as the mutuality of friendships, number of friends, and group organization. It would be a mistake, however, to conclude there are no gender differences in social group functioning over this age range. To the contrary, significant gender differences emerge when more dynamic measures of relationships or interpersonal actions have been employed (see, e.g., Eder, 1985, and Cairns, Cairns, Neckerman, Ferguson, & Gariépy, 1989).

The settings in which observations are made potentially influence both short-term and long-time relationship stabilities. In this regard, it has been demonstrated that new and intense group relationships may be rapidly established in short-term summer camps (Edwards, 1990; Savin-Williams, 1979; Sherif & Sherif, 1953) and residential schools (Farmer & Cairns, 1991). The rapid establishment of these groups underscores the ease with which new structures may be formed and old ones modified. In addition, the social context may promote or diminish stability. Observations conducted over a year (seventh to eighth grade) in a small, self-contained private middle school (Cairns et al., 1985) indicate higher network stabilities than those observed over a year in public middle schools (Neckerman, 1992). Not only were the public middle schools larger than the private school, they tended to redistribute students into new class configurations each school year. The private school remained virtually intact as a social unit, and the social groups were identifiable after 1 year (Cairns et al., 1985).

To conclude, fluidity in the strength of friendships and group membership appears to capture an important feature of normal social relationships. While the fluidity of affiliations may seem at first blush to be a threat to personal integrity and social continuity, we may speculate that there are good reasons for shifts. Close relationships that are productive and supportive in one set of circumstances can diminish in relevance—and create problems for adaptation—if they are rigidly maintained. When new needs and new contexts emerge, so should the strength and relevance of personal relationships. In everyday life, stability and constancy in personal relationships seem to be balanced with the dynamics of social adaptation and growth.

References

Asher, S. R., & Coie, J. D. (Eds.). (1990). *Peer rejection in childhood.* New York: Cambridge University Press.

Asher, S. R., & Dodge, K. A. (1986). Identifying children who are rejected by their peers. *Developmental Psychology*, **22**, 444–449.

Baldwin, J. M. (1902). *Social and ethical interpretations in mental development: A study in social psychology.* 3d ed. New York: Macmillan. (Originally published in 1897)

Benenson, J. F. (1990). Gender differences in social networks. *Journal of Early Adolescence*, **10**, 472–495.

Berndt, T. J. (1982). The features and effects of friendship in early adolescence. *Child Development*, **53**, 1447–1460.

Berndt, T. J., & Hoyle, S. G. (1985). Stability and change in childhood and adolescent friendships. *Developmental Psychology*, **21**, 1007–1015.

Bronfenbrenner, U., & Crouter, A. C. (1983). The evolution of environmental models in devellopmental research. In William Kessen (Ed.), P. H. Mussen (Series Ed.), *Handbook of child psychology: Vol. 1. History, theory, and methods* (pp. 357–414). New York: Wiley.

Brown, B. B. (1990). Peer groups and peer cultures. In S. S. Feldman & G. R. Elliott (Eds.), *At the threshold: The developing adolescent* (pp. 171–196). Cambridge, MA: Harvard University Press.

Cairns, R. B., Cairns, B. D., & Neckerman, H. J. (1989). Early school dropout: Configurations and determinants. *Child Development*, **60**, 1437–1452.

Cairns, R. B., Cairns, B. D., Neckerman, H. J., Ferguson, L. L., & Gariépy, J-L. (1989). Growth and aggression: I. Childhood to early adolescence. *Developmental Psychology*, **25**, 320–330.

Cairns, R. B., Cairns, B. D., Neckerman, H. J., Gest, S., & Gariépy, J-L. (1988). Social networks and aggressive behavior: Peer support or peer rejection? *Developmental Psychology*, **24**, 815–823.

Cairns, R. B., Gariépy, J-L, & Kindermann, T. (1989). *Identifying social groups in natural settings.* Unpublished manuscript, University of North Carolina at Chapel Hill.

Cairns, R. B., Neckerman, H. J., & Cairns, B. D. (1989). Social networks and the shadows of synchrony. In G. R. Adams, T. P. Gullota, & R. Montemayor (Eds.), *Advances in adolescent development* (pp. 275–305). Beverly Hills, CA: Sage.

Cairns, R. B., Perrin, J. E., & Cairns, B. D. (1985). Social structure and social cognition in early adolescence: Affiliative patterns. *Journal of Early Adolescence,* **5,** 339–355.

Caspi, A., & Moffitt, T. E. (in press). The continuity of maladaptive behavior: From description to understanding in the study of antisocial behavior. In D. Cicchetti & D. Cohen (Eds.), *Manual of developmental psychopathology.* New York: Wiley.

Cohen, J. M. (1977). Sources of peer group homogeneity. *Sociology of Education,* **50,** 227–241.

Coie, J. D., Dodge, K. A., & Coppotelli, H. (1982). Dimensions and types of social status: A cross-age perspective. *Developmental Psychology,* **18,** 557–570.

Craven, E., & Wellman, B. (1973). The network city. *Sociological Inquiry,* **43,** 57–88.

Dunphy, D. C. (1963). The social structure of urban adolescent peer groups. *Sociometry,* **26,** 230–246.

Eder, D. (1985). The cycle of popularity: Interpersonal relations among female adolescents. *Sociology of Education,* **58,** 154–165.

Edwards, C. A. (1990). *Leadership, social networks, and personal attributes in school age girls.* Unpublished doctoral dissertation, University of North Carolina.

Elliott, D. S., Huizinga, D., & Menard, S. (1989). *Multiple problem youth: Delinquency, substance use, and mental health problems.* New York: Springer-Verlag.

Farmer, T. W., & Cairns, R. B. (1991). Social networks and social status in emotionally disturbed children. *Behavioral Disorders,* **16,** 288–298.

Feiring, C., & Lewis, M. (1987). The child's social network: Sex differences from three to six years. *Sex Roles: A Journal of Research,* **17,** 621–636.

Gillmore, M. R., Hawkins, J. D., Day, L. E., & Catalano, R. F. (in press). Friendship and deviance: New evidence on an old controversy. *Journal of Early Adolescence.*

Giordano, P. C., Cernkovich, S. A., & Pugh, M. D. (1986). Friendship and delinquency. *American Journal of Sociology,* **91,** 1170–1201.

Hallinan, M. T. (1980). Patterns of cliquing among youth. In H. C. Foot, A. J. Chapman, & J. R. Smith (Eds.), *Friendship and social relations in children* (pp. 321–342). New York: Wiley.

Horrocks, J. E., & Bucker, M. E. (1951). A study of the friendship fluctuations of preadolescents. *Journal of Genetic Psychology,* **78,** 131–144.

Kandel, D. B. (1978). Homophily, selection, and socialization in adolescent friendships. *American Journal of Sociology,* **84,** 427–436.

Kupersmidt, J. B., Courtney, M. L., DeRosier, M. E., & Patterson, C. P. (1991, April). *Similarity as the basis for friendship among school-aged children.* Paper presented in J. Kupersmidt & S. Hymel (Chairs), Factors influencing children's dyadic and group relationships, at the Society for Research in Child Development, Seattle.

Ladd, G. W. (1983). Social networks of popular, average, and rejected children in school settings. *Merrill-Palmer Quarterly,* **29,** 283–307.

Ladd, G. W. (1990). Having friends, keeping friends, making friends, and being liked by peers in the classroom: Predictors of children's early school adjustment? *Child Development,* **61,** 1081–1100.

Ladd, G. W., Price, J. M., & Hart, C. H. (1988). Predicting preschoolers' peer status from their playground behaviors. *Child Development,* **59,** 986–992.

Lagerspetz, K. M. J., Björkqvist, K., & Peltonen, T. (1988). Is indirect aggression typical of females? Gender differences in aggressiveness in 11- to 12-year-old children. *Aggressive Behavior,* **14,** 403–414.

Leung, M-C. (1993). *Social cognition and social networks of Chinese school children in Hong Kong.* Unpublished doctoral dissertation, University of North Carolina at Chapel Hill.

Moreno, J. L. (1934). *Who shall survive? A new approach to the problem of human interrelations.* Washington, DC: Nervous and Mental Disease Publishing Co.

Neckerman, H. J. (1992). *A longitudinal investigation of the stability and fluidity of social networks and peer relationships of children and adolescents.* Unpublished doctoral dissertation, University of North Carolina at Chapel Hill.

Salzinger, S., Kaplan, S., & Artemyeff, C. (1983). Mothers' personal social networks and child maltreatment. *Journal of Abnormal Psychology,* **92,** 68–76.

Savin-Williams, R. C. (1979). Dominance hierarchies in groups of early adolescents. *Child Development,* **50,** 923–935.

Sherif, M., & Sherif, C. W. (1953). *Groups in harmony and tension.* New York: Harper.

Shrum, W., & Cheek, N. H. (1987). Social structure during the school years: Onset of the degrouping process. *American Sociological Review,* **52,** 218–223.

Stattin, H., & Magnusson, D. (1990). *Pubertal development in girls.* Hillsdale, NJ: Erlbaum.

Stattin, H., Gustafson, S. B., & Magnusson, D. (1989). Peer influences on adolescent drinking: A social transition perspective. *Journal of Early Adolescence,* **9,** 227–246.

Stevens, G., & Cho, J. H. (1985). Socioeconomic indexes and the new 1980 census occupational classification scheme. *Social Science Research,* **14,** 142–168.

Stevens, G., & Featherman, D. C. (1981). A re-

vised sociometric index of occupational status. *Social Science Research*, **10**, 364–395.
Strayer, F. F., & Noel, J. M. (1986). The prosocial and antisocial functions of preschool aggression: An ethological study of triadic conflict among young children. In C. Zahn-Waxler, E. M. Cummings, & R. Iannotti (Eds.), *Altruism and aggression: Biological and social origins* (pp. 107–131). Cambridge: Cambridge University Press.
Zank, S. (1988). *Zur Entwicklung des Lösungsmittelschnüffelns bei Jungendlichen und jungen Erwachsenen.* Berlin: Berlin Verlag Arno Spitz.

Daily Companionship in Late Childhood and Early Adolescence: Changing Developmental Contexts

Reed Larson

University of Illinois, Urbana-Champaign

Maryse H. Richards

Loyola University of Chicago

LARSON, REED, and RICHARDS, MARYSE H. *Daily Companionship in Late Childhood and Early Adolescence: Changing Developmental Contexts.* CHILD DEVELOPMENT, 1991, **62**, 284–300. The study employs time-sampling data to examine age differences in the quantity and quality of children's and young adolescents' daily experience with their families, friends, and alone. Participants (ages 9–15) carried electronic pagers for 1 week and reported their companionship, location, and affect at random times when signaled by the pagers. Findings show a dramatic decline in amount of time spent with family, with older students reporting half as much time with their families as younger students. Among boys, this family time was replaced by time spent alone; among girls, by time alone and with friends. Affect reported when with family became less positive between the fifth and seventh grade, but was more positive again in the ninth grade for boys. Affect with friends became more favorable across this age period; affect when alone did not vary. These age differences suggest changes in adolescents' daily opportunities for cognitive growth, emotional development, and social support.

The objective of this article is to chart age differences in the quantity and quality of time children and young adolescents spend with different companions. Theorists contend that individuation from parents and deepening of relationships with peers are central developmental projects of adolescence (Blos, 1967; Gilligan, 1982; Havighurst, 1984). Therefore, we expect adolescents to spend less time with their families and more time with their friends than preadolescents. Accompanying age changes in emotional states experienced when with family and friends might also be expected. This article evaluates these age trends in daily interaction with family, with friends, and also alone, employing time-sampling data from Midwestern fifth to ninth graders.

A large body of research substantiates theorists' predications that entry into adolescence is accompanied by a shift in the relative importance of family and friends. Age changes include: (*a*) a shift in "associative orientation" from family to friends (Bowerman & Kinch, 1959); (*b*) increased emotional detachment from parents, with changes occurring somewhat earlier for girls (Steinberg & Silverberg, 1986); (*c*) increased conflict with and emotional distance from parents, particularly around the occurrence of puberty (Steinberg, 1981, 1987); (*d*) increased behavioral independence from parents (Feldman & Quatman, 1988; Simmons & Blyth, 1987; Smetana, 1988); (*e*) increased influence of peers over certain domains of daily life (Berndt, 1979, 1989; Hartup, 1983); and (*f*) increased intimacy with friends, especially among girls (Berndt, 1982; Hunter & Youniss, 1982), and decreased intimate disclosure to parents (Buhrmester & Furman, 1987). Closeness and mutual valuation in relationships with parents do not necessarily decline in adolescence (Blyth, Hill, & Thiel, 1982; Hunter & Youniss, 1982; Smetana, 1988); nonetheless, this research clearly shows that closeness with friends increases and emotional autonomy from parents increases, with the timing of these trends varying somewhat by gender.

This research was supported by NIMH grant 1 R01 MH38324, awarded to the authors. We are grateful to Mary Chandler for assistance with the data analyses. Correspondence should be addressed to Reed Larson, Division of Human Development and Family Studies, University of Illinois, 1105 W. Nevada, Urbana, IL 61802.

[*Child Development*, 1991, **62**, 284–300. 0009-3920/91/6202-0003$01.00]

Little research, however, evaluates how these psychological and emotional changes are manifested in a child's hour-to-hour experience with family and friends. A time-budget study by Montemayor and Brownlee (1987) found a decline between sixth to seventh grade and eighth to twelfth grade in amount of time spent with fathers, but not mothers. In a questionnaire study by Buhrmester and Furman (1987), eighth graders rated their frequency of interactions with mothers, fathers, and teachers as lower than did fifth graders, and rated their frequency of interaction with same-sex friends (girls only) and opposite-sex friends as greater; ratings of time with grandparents and a closest sibling did not differ by age. In another questionnaire study, Crockett, Losoff, and Petersen (1984) found eighth-grade girls to report much more time talking on the phone than sixth-grade girls. These limited findings suggest a shift in time from family members to friends but do not provide precise information on the overall trends or on the quality of affect experienced with these different companions.

There is little research regarding the time young adolescents spend by themselves. Being alone is a frequent alternative for adolescents to being with family members and friends (Montemayor, 1982) and may present distinct liabilities and opportunities for development (Larson, 1990). Projective data collected by Coleman (1974) and questionnaire data obtained by Marcoen, Goossens, and Caes (1987) suggest that adolescents may find being alone less frightening than do children, although Marcoen et al. did not find that adolescents reported any greater desire to be alone than did children.

The present study employs time-sampling data obtained using the Experience Sampling Method (ESM) in which participants carry electronic pagers and report on their activities, companionship, and internal states at random times when signaled by the pagers (Csikszentmihalyi & Larson, 1987; Larson & Csikszentmihalyi, 1983). In an earlier set of papers on these data, we focused on age differences in the activities these youths reported (Larson & Richards, 1989). It was found that older participants—the adolescents—spent less time playing, watching TV, and participating in sports than preadolescents and spent more time talking (particularly girls) and listening to music. Within many activities, age trends in companionship were noted, with older participants reporting doing the activity less often with family members and more often alone or with friends.

In this article, we reanalyze these data with the focus on companionship. Two central hypotheses are tested: first, that early adolescence is associated with decreased time with family and increased time with friends, and second, that average affect with family becomes more negative and affect with friends more positive across this age period. Since past theory and research suggest gradual, cumulative age changes, we test the hypotheses by evaluating linear age trends. Also, since sex differences have been found frequently in the work cited above and in many other studies of adolescent relationships (e.g., Gilligan, 1982; Montemayor & Van Komen, 1980; Savin-Williams, 1979; Youniss & Smollar, 1985), we decided that boys and girls should not be grouped in the same analyses but rather should be considered separately. By making this choice, we elect not to evaluate the comparison between sexes but rather to focus on the trends within each sex.

In addition to testing the two hypotheses, we include exploratory analyses aimed at providing fuller understanding of the age differences. First, we conduct tests of quadratic age trends along with tests of linear trends in order to detect nonmonotonic age patterns. Family relationships, for example, have sometimes been found to show nonlinear age trends across this period (Hill & Holmbeck, 1986; Steinberg, 1981). Second, we evaluate age differences in time with specific subcategories of companions, such as mothers, extended family members, and same-sex chums, since prior research suggests that patterns may vary for each. Last, we examine whether trends in time with family and friends are related to shifts in where adolescents spend time. We expected that youth might spend more time away from home across this age period and that this might be interrelated with changes in companionship (see Montemayor & Van Komen, 1980).

Method

Sample

The participants in this study were 483 randomly selected fifth to ninth graders (ages 9–15) from four suburban Chicago school neighborhoods. Two of the neighborhoods were in a working-class suburb, two in a middle- and upper-middle-class suburb. All four were composed almost exclusively of people of European ancestry. The school systems these youths attended did not subject them to major changes in school structure or cohort until ninth grade, at which point students from several schools were brought together in large high schools.

Participants took part in one of eight waves, occurring over a period of 2 years. Sample selection was stratified to obtain equal numbers of (*a*) boys and girls, (*b*) from each neighborhood, (*c*) in each season of the year between the beginning of the fifth grade and the winter of the ninth grade.

The final sample of 483 includes 70% of the 688 randomly selected individuals initially invited to participate. Twenty-four percent of those invited decided not to participate or failed to obtain permission from their parents. Six percent began the study but failed to provide usable data. The overall participation rate was higher during the school year (75%, compared to 53% for the summer). Sample loss was approximately equal among boys and girls but was somewhat greater for boys in the older grades (fifth to ninth: 24%, 23%, 33%, 42%, 37%). A survey of the entire fifth to eighth grade in two of the schools indicated that students who declined to participate did not differ in self-esteem or in the socioeconomic prestige of their parents' jobs. Participation rates were somewhat higher among students in single-parent families and somewhat lower among students with remarried parents. A complete description of the sample is provided in Larson (1989a).

Procedures

At the beginning of the week of participation, each student was given an electronic pager and a booklet of self-report forms. Their instructions were to carry the pager and booklet with them for a week and fill out one self-report form immediately after receipt of each pager signal. Seven signals were sent each day, with one at a random time within every 2-hour block between 7:30 A.M. and 9:30 P.M. Nearly all participants started the study on a Tuesday or Wednesday. At the end of the 7-day period, the pagers and booklets were collected; the students were asked to take part in an interview and fill out a series of questionnaires, and they were paid $8.00 for their participation.

In total, the students responded to 18,022 signals, providing an average of 37.3 self-reports per person. To calculate the students' rate of response to the pager signals, we discounted times when the students went to bed early or slept late since they had been encouraged to turn the pager off in such instances. We also estimated that approximately 6% of the pager signals were not received due to mechanical failure of the pager. Discounting these factors, the students filled out self-reports for approximately 86% of the signals sent to them. Analyses of additional data indicated that missed reports occurred across a wide range of activities and situations, but may have been more common during sports, church services, family trips, and socializing away from home. Larson (1989a) calculated adjusted estimates of the students' allocation of time to different activities, taking these differential rates of loss into account, and found that the adjustments made only slight differences in estimates of how time was spent. Hence, the missed self-reports appear to have only a minor influence on the time budget estimates.

Measures

On each self-report form, participants responded to a series of items asking about their situation and state just before they received the signal.

Companionship.—Companionship was determined by responses to a fixed-response item asking, "Who were you with (or talking to on the phone)?" Fifteen nonexclusive choices could be checked. Responses have been coded into four superordinate categories—family, friends, alone and other—which are composed of 13 subcategories. *Family* includes times the student marked being with: (1) family group (any constellation of nuclear family members that includes at least one parent), (2) mother only, (3) father only, (4) sibling(s) only, and (5) extended family (one or more extended relatives with or without the presence of nuclear family members). *Friends* includes times with: (6) same-sex friend, (7) same-sex group, (8) mixed-sex group (two or more friends, of whom at least one is not of the respondent's sex), (9) opposite-sex friend, and (10) friends and family (any combination of people that includes at least one friend and one family member). This last subcategory was included with friends because analyses from this and a previous ESM study of adolescents (Csikszentmihalyi & Larson, 1984) suggest that friends typically set the activity and tone in these situations: activities and moods more closely resemble times with friends than times with family. *Alone* includes: (11) alone, others nearby (student marked "alone, other people nearby"), and (12) all alone (student marked "alone, no one around"). Instances when a person reported talking on the phone, but marked being alone, were coded according to the phone companion because mood states in this situation suggest they should be coded as such (see Larson, 1979, 1990). *Others* is composed of only one subcategory: (13) others (includes teachers, coaches, and other adults, as well as co-workers at a job and children being cared for by the student; also includes times when students were talking on the phone and failed to indicate with whom and times when they were with friends and others). Data for an additional category, times when the students marked that they were "in class," are excluded from the analyses for reasons explained in the analysis section below.

The reliability of the students' companionship reports is demonstrated by consistency in individuals' reports from the first to the last half of the week. Each person's sequence of self-reports was split at the midpoint in the week and the percentage of time reported in each companionship category computed separately for the first and second half. These percentages were highly correlated (time alone: $r[483] = .51$; time with family: $r[483] = .53$; time with friends: $r[483] = .49$), suggesting that individuals were quite stable in patterns of social companionship across the week.

Location.—On the ESM self-report form, students were asked the open-ended question, "Where were you?" Responses to this item were coded into 68 categories (interrater agreement = 99%). For the purposes of this report, these categories have been collapsed into three: (*a*) at home, not in bedroom; (*b*) at home, in bedroom; (*c*) away from home. Bedroom is considered a separate category because previous findings show it to have particular importance as a refuge of privacy for adolescents (Parke & Sawin, 1979).

Activity.—On the ESM form, students reponded to a question asking what they were doing. Responses were coded into 127 categories, with an interrater agreement of 94%. For analyses here, we have grouped these into 11 categories.

Affect.—Students rated their mood at each signal on a set of 7-point semantic differential items. A factor analysis study indicated that three of these items (happy-unhappy, cheerful-irritable, friendly-angry) form a scale of affect, which has strong internal reliability (*alpha* = .75) and construct validity (Larson, 1989b). Since there were substantial differences in individuals' mean responses to these items, including a decline in mean affect with age (Larson & Lampman-Petraitis, 1989), we have standardized values on this scale so that differences between contexts can be examined considering only within-individual variation. This standardization was computed by the equation, $z_{ij} = (X_{ij} - \text{mean}_j)/\text{SD}_j$, in which x_{ij} was the raw score for a given self-report, mean_j was the person's mean for the scale, and SD_j was the person's standard deviation for the scale. Hence, each person's *z*-scores are distributed around a mean of 0.0 with a standard deviation of 1.0, with positive scores indicating affect that is more positive.

Data Analyses

Exclusion of class time.—In order to control for summer/school year differences and focus on discretionary time, we have excluded occasions when students reported being "in class" (times in school when students were not in class *were* included). For participants during the school year, class time constituted an average of 30.7% of their self-reports, a percentage that did not vary as a function of grade or sex, $F(9,391) = 1.15$, $p = .32$. Class time accounted for only .9% of the summer participants' time.

Season and social class.—With this exclusion, summer participants did not differ in the proportion of time they reported spending with family, friends, or alone. A three-way MANOVA with grade, sex, and season as the factors indicated significant differences in the percentage of time individuals reported being in each of these three superordinate companionship categories, $F(9,1134) = 2.08$, $p = .03$. These seasonal differences, however, were quite small, attributable to slightly more time (4%) spent with friends and less time spent with family in the spring. There also were no significant interactions of season with grade and sex. Hence, season was not included in the main analyses of the article. Preliminary analyses comparing students from the working-class and middle-class communities showed no significant main effects or interactions, hence this social class variable was also not included in the analyses reported below.

Analysis strategy.—The hypotheses are tested using aggregate scores for each person as the unit of analysis, following the recommendations of Larson and Delespaul (1990). For analyses of quantity of time, these scores are percentages (e.g., the percentage of time spent alone); for the investigation of affect, these scores are means (e.g., mean affect when alone). These scores were analyzed using multivariate analysis of variance (MANOVA). Planned univariate two-tailed *t*-tests, evaluating the significance of linear and quadratic polynomial grade trends, are examined only when the multivariate *F* is significant. For evaluation of the hypotheses, we employ an alpha of .05; for the exploratory analyses (which include evaluation of the quadratic terms) we use an alpha of .01.

Results

Age Differences in Daily Companionship

Our first hypothesis predicted a shift in allocation of time from family to friends across this age period. We evaluated this hypothesis by conducting MANOVAs in which the percentages of time a student spent with family, friends, and alone were the dependent variables and grade was the factor. A highly significant effect for grade was found for both boys, $F(12,708) = 3.79$, $p < .001$, and girls, $F(12,711) = 4.17$, $p < .001$.

These findings show a dramatic decline in time with family across this age period (Fig. 1). In fifth grade, both genders spent close to half (47.8%) of their nonclass waking hours with their families. In ninth grade, this figure was closer to one-quarter (28.1% for boys and 26.5% for girls). The univariate linear grade trend for family time was highly significant for both boys, $t = 6.04$, $p < .001$, and girls, $t = 5.37$, $p < .001$. A significant quadratic term for girls, $t = 2.86$, $p = .005$, reflected a steeper drop for them in family time between the fifth and sixth grades.

Diminished time with family among older students was replaced, not by time with peers, but by time spent alone, particularly among boys. The amount of time boys spent with friends did not differ significantly across this age period, while the amount of time they spent alone increased by 16.4% between the fifth and ninth grades, linear $t = 4.79$, $p < .001$. With age, boys spent less time with their families and more time alone.

Girls spent more time with friends *and* alone with age. The amount of time girls spent with friends increased by 13.5% from the fifth to ninth grades, linear $t = 3.29$, $p < .001$. Amount of time spent alone showed both a linear trend, $t = 2.18$, $p = .03$, and a quadratic trend, $t = 2.87$, $p = .004$, indicating that amount of time alone for girls increased substantially between the fifth and seventh grade and then leveled off in the subsequent grades. As is evident in Figure 1, the time that older girls no longer spent with their families was spent alone in the sixth and seventh grade and then was increasingly devoted to friends in the eighth and ninth grades.

Variations by specific companions.—We next evaluated whether these age trends could be attributed to specific companionship subcategories by recomputing the MANOVAs employing the percentages of time in the first 12 of the 13 subcategories as the dependent variables. Since the distributions of these percentages were skewed toward 0, a square-root transformation was used to normalize them for the MANOVAs. As before, these MANOVAs yielded a significant effect for grade both for boys, $F(48,908) = 1.72$, $p = .002$, and girls, $F(48,924) = 1.83$, $p < .001$. In examining the univariate trends, we employ an alpha of $p < .01$, since these analyses are exploratory and not hypothesis driven.

The univariate significance tests indicate that the decline with age in amount of time with family can be attributed to differences in specific family subcategories (Table 1). In particular, both boys and girls in the older grades spent much less time with family groups. A significant linear age difference also occurred in amount of time spent with siblings for boys and in the amount of time spent with extended relatives, particularly for girls. It is notable that no age difference occurred in the amount of time participants spent with their mothers or fathers only.

These univariate tests also suggest why net amount of time with friends did not increase with age for boys and does increase for girls. Boys in the older grades reported significantly more time with one person of the opposite sex (Table 2). This trend, however, is counteracted by a close-to-significant age decrease in amount of time with friends and family jointly. For girls significant and close-to-significant linear age increases occurred for all subcategories of friends, except friends and family together. The most dramatic trend was in amount of time spent in mixed-sex groups, which was more than double in the ninth grade.

The increase in time alone across this age period appears to be most attributable to age differences in amount of time spent "all alone." For boys, time alone with no one else nearby is more than three times greater

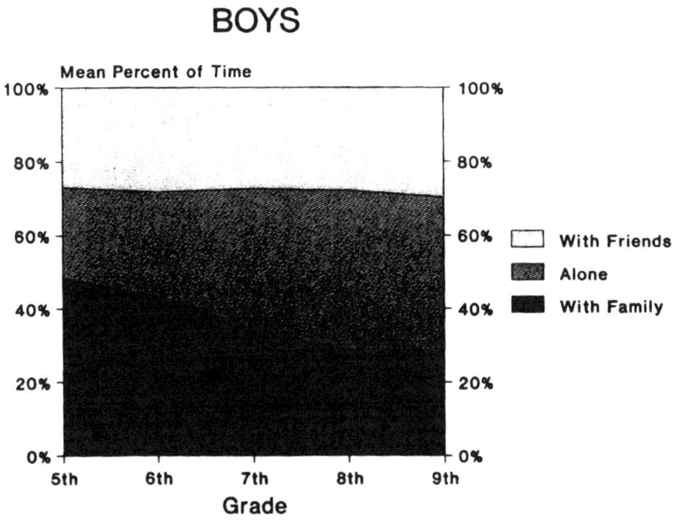

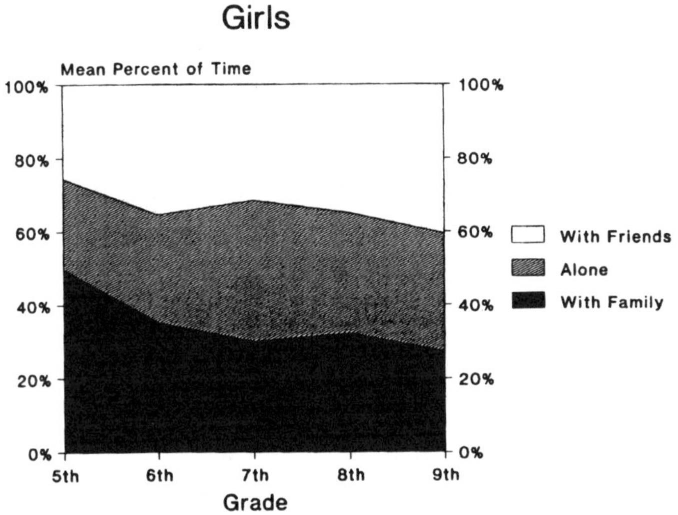

FIG. 1.—Daily companionship × grade (note that time in class and a small percentage of time spent with others are excluded).

in the ninth grade, as compared to the fifth, a trend that is highly significant. For girls, this trend is close to significant. The linear trend for time spent "alone others nearby" was also significant for boys, but not for girls, who showed a close-to-significant quadratic trend, $t = 2.17$, $p = .03$, reflecting a peak in this category in the seventh grade.

Variations related with location.—It was also anticipated that age trends in companionship might vary as a function of location; adolescents were expected to spend less time with their families as a correlate of spending less time at home. The data, however, do not support this interpretation.

First, we examined age trends in the amount of time spent in the three locations, irrespective of companionship. MANOVAs were conducted using the percent of time in two of the locations ("not at home" and "at

TABLE 1

PERCENTAGE OF TIME SPENT WITH DIFFERENT COMPANIONS BY GRADE

	Boys' Grade					Significance of Linear Trend		Girls' Grade					Significance of Linear Trend	
	5	6	7	8	9	t	p	5	6	7	8	9	t	p
N	52	53	51	49	36	...	...	50	54	53	48	37	...	...
Family:														
Family group	24.0	18.7	13.0	11.8	12.9	−4.45	.000	23.5	14.9	12.4	13.0	11.8	−3.73	.000
Mother only	4.5	3.2	5.0	3.8	4.8	.21	.835	5.0	3.6	5.6	5.8	4.0	.34	.734
Father only	2.7	1.7	2.9	2.6	2.4	.16	.874	1.6	1.6	1.3	2.2	1.7	.68	.500
Siblings only	9.1	12.0	8.6	5.2	5.0	−2.78	.006	8.4	6.9	4.9	6.4	5.2	−1.61	.108
Extended family	7.5	6.6	3.7	5.0	3.0	−2.50	.013	9.3	6.8	4.9	4.0	3.8	−2.84	.005
Friends:														
Same-sex friend	6.7	5.6	7.1	6.8	6.8	.25	.805	5.7	10.7	7.5	8.6	10.5	1.84	.066
Same-sex group	8.6	6.9	7.1	6.4	9.7	.61	.542	5.2	6.5	7.2	6.8	7.2	2.04	.042
Mixed group	7.2	7.5	8.1	8.5	8.9	.93	.353	6.1	10.4	9.1	12.4	14.4	4.24	.000
Opposite-sex friend	.0	.7	.3	1.3	1.4	2.97	.003	.8	.1	.4	1.7	1.9	2.49	.014
Friends and family	4.0	6.6	3.9	4.0	2.1	−2.52	.013	6.8	6.2	6.3	4.4	4.1	−1.76	.079
Alone:														
Others nearby	19.2	19.1	26.3	26.0	24.3	2.64	.009	17.6	20.3	27.7	19.8	21.3	.69	.487
All alone	4.9	8.4	11.1	16.0	16.2	5.78	.000	5.8	7.9	9.4	12.0	9.7	−2.59	.011
Others:														
Others:	1.8	3.2	3.0	2.6	2.5	...	...	4.4	4.2	3.3	3.2	4.4	...	...

NOTE.—Table displays mean percentage of time in each social context.

TABLE 2

COMPANIONSHIP AND LOCATION BY GRADE

	Boys' Grade					Significance of Linear Trend		Girls' Grade					Significance of Linear Trend	
	5	6	7	8	9	t	p	5	6	7	8	9	t	p
At home, not bedroom:														
Family	33.4	29.4	23.1	20.8	20.9	−4.34	.000	31.1	22.6	19.2	21.3	18.5	−3.79	.000
Friends	5.9	7.4	5.3	4.6	3.1	−2.82	.005	5.7	8.5	7.4	8.0	7.1	.19	.846
Alone	12.9	16.7	19.5	18.7	19.9	2.79	.006	11.6	13.1	19.4	16.2	13.0	1.31	.191
Other	.2	.4	.5	.3	.5	. . .	. . .	.4	.8	.2	.4	.9	. . .	. . .
Total	52.4	53.9	48.4	44.4	44.4			48.8	45.0	46.2	45.9	39.5		
At home, in bedroom:														
Family	3.5	3.8	2.7	2.1	1.4	−2.78	.006	4.4	3.3	2.3	1.7	1.9	−3.65	.000
Friends	.7	.6	.6	1.7	1.3	1.03	.306	.9	1.5	2.1	2.0	2.5	2.09	.038
Alone	4.8	6.8	9.5	15.7	11.9	5.02	.000	6.8	8.8	10.8	11.3	13.7	3.55	.000
Other	.0	.1	.1	.1	.0	. . .	. . .	.0	.1	.0	.0	.4	. . .	. . .
Total	9.0	11.3	12.9	19.6	14.6			12.1	13.7	15.2	15.0	18.5		
Not at home:														
Family	10.8	8.9	7.3	5.5	5.7	−4.24	.000	12.3	7.9	7.5	8.2	6.2	−3.69	.000
Friends	19.8	19.2	20.6	20.7	24.5	1.19	.234	17.9	23.9	21.0	23.7	28.4	2.70	.007
Alone	6.4	4.0	8.4	7.6	8.8	2.63	.009	5.0	6.3	6.9	4.2	4.2	−.52	.602
Other	1.6	2.6	2.4	2.2	2.0	. . .	. . .	4.0	3.3	3.1	2.8	3.2	. . .	. . .
Total	38.6	34.7	38.7	36.0	41.0			39.2	41.3	38.5	38.9	42.0		

NOTE.—Table displays the mean percentage of time in each context.

home, in bedroom") as the dependent variables and grade as the factor. Age trends in amount of time spent in the third location, "at home, not in bedroom," can be inferred from age trends for the other two, since amount of time in the three location categories adds to 100%. An alpha of .01 is used throughout this section, since we did not have specific hypotheses.

For boys, the multivariate grade effect was significant, $F(8,470) = 3.24$, $p < .001$. It was not, however, attributable to univariate age differences in time away from home; the test for this term was not significant. Rather, it was due to amount of time spent in the bedroom, which increased from 9.0% in fifth grade to 19.5% in the eighth and 14.6% in the ninth grades (linear $t = 3.36$, $p < .001$). For girls, the MANOVA did not yield a significant effect for grade, $F(8,476) = 1.47$, $p = .16$. This absence of age differences in location rules out the possibility that the age differences in companionship could be explained in terms of changes in where adolescents spend their time. The one exception is the age increase in time alone for boys, which might be a correlate of their greater time in their bedrooms.

In order to test this possibility and also to identify the locations in which the other age differences in companionship occurred, we conducted a second set of MANOVAs evaluating age differences in companionship within each of the three location categories. It was decided that these MANOVAs would be most informative if they considered amount of time in the nine major companionship × location combinations as separate variables. These MANOVAs, then, had nine dependent variables, corresponding to the amount of time spent in each of the three locations with family, friends, and alone. A square root transformation was used to normalize the distributions of these percentages prior to conducting the analyses. These MANOVAs yielded significant main effects for grade, both for boys, $F(36,920) = 2.43$, $p < .001$, and girls, $F(36,932) = 2.31$, $p < .001$.

Examination of the univariate statistics shows where the age differences in companionship occur (Table 2). Significant linear trends indicate declines in amount of time boys and girls spent with family in all three settings—home, bedroom, and away from home. Time alone shows a significant linear age increase in all three settings for boys, indicating that their increased aloneness is not merely a result of more time in the bedroom. For girls the linear age trend in time alone is significant only in the bedroom; they are not more often alone elsewhere in the home or in public places. In addition, for girls the amount of time spent alone at home outside the bedroom had a significant quadratic relation with grade, $t = 3.43$, $p < .001$, reflecting more time spent alone at home in the middle grades.

Age differences in amount of time with friends showed the most complex relations. For boys, time spent with friends at home declined significantly across this age period, with no other significant univariate relations. For girls, there was a close-to-significant linear increase in time spent with friends in the bedroom. Examination of location subcategories revealed that this was due partly to an increase in the amount of time spent in the bedroom talking to friends on the phone (fifth to ninth grade, respectively: .1, .1, .6, .7, 1.0). Girls also show a significant linear increase in the amount of time spent with friends away from home. Examination of the subcategories of location suggests that this is due to an increase in time spent at friends' homes (fifth to ninth: 3.5, 5.9, 3.9, 4.7, 7.7) and indoor public locations (2.3, 3.9, 2.5, 4.3, 4.8). It is worth noting that both girls and boys report less time with friends outdoors in the local neighborhood (girls: 3.0, 3.7, .6, 1.3, .7; boys: 4.7, 4.1, 3.0, 2.6, 1.5), suggesting that neighborhood friends are being replaced by friends known through school or organizations.

Age Differences in Affect with Companions

Our second hypothesis predicted that average affect with family would become more negative and affect with friends would become more positive across this age period. For example, it was expected that the lesser time adolescents spend with their families would be reflective of more frequent negative feelings when with their families. To evaluate this hypothesis, we tested whether the students' daily affect when they were with their families, friends, and alone differed by age. In the following analyses, we examine whether these age trends were interrelated with the students' daily locations and activities.

Overall trends for affect with family, friends, and alone.—To test the hypothesis, we computed average affect scores for each person for all times he or she was with family, with friends, and alone. Since we were using z scores, standardized according to

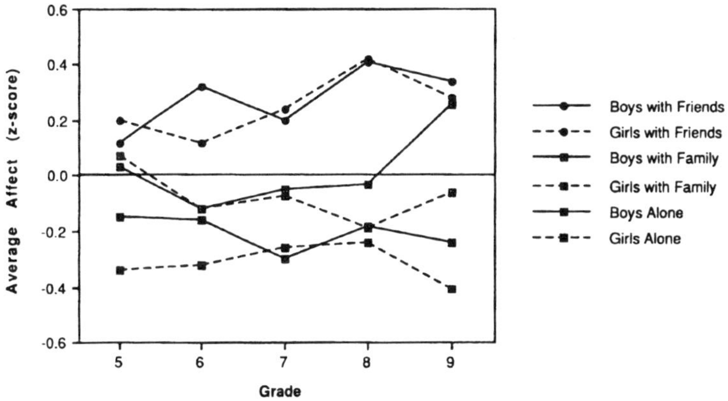

FIG. 2.—Average affect by companionship

each person's mean and standard deviation, values for these averages reflect a person's mean rating relative to the total distribution of his or her ratings for the week of self-reporting. These values for average affect in each context were then entered into MANOVAs as the dependent variables with grade constituting the independent factor. Because they had not filled out a report in one or more of the social contexts, 41 boys and 17 girls had to be dropped from the analyses.[1] A significant multivariate effect for grade was found both for boys, $F(12,582) = 2.10$, $p = .02$, and girls, $F(12,657) = 1.91$, $p = .03$.[2]

Univariate tests indicated that affect experienced in daily interactions with friends and with family, but not alone, differed across this age period (Fig. 2). For both genders, affect with friends was relatively positive in the fifth grade and became even more positive by the ninth grade. This linear trend was significant for girls, $t = 2.06$, $p = .04$, but only suggested for boys, $t = 1.79$, $p = .08$. In contrast, affect experienced with the family showed a quadratic age trend. For both boys and girls, feelings with the family were most positive in the fifth and the ninth grades, with more negative affect reported in the intervening sixth- to eighth-grade pe-

[1] Seventeen people never reported being with friends, 16 never reported being alone, 7 were never with their families, 8 were never in two of these contexts, and 10 were excluded because the overall quality of their affect ratings was poor. The boys who were dropped had significantly lower average affective states, $t(232) = 2.32$, $p = .02$, higher scores on Kovacs's (1985) Child Depression Inventory, $t(197) = 2.83$, $p = .005$, lower school GPAs, $t(231) = 4.38$, $p < .001$, and spent less time with friends, $t(240) = 5.91$, $p < .001$. The girls who were dropped were not significantly different from other girls on any of these measures.

[2] We repeated these MANOVAs using means based on the raw (unstandardized) affect ratings. For boys, analyses showed lower affect in all three social contexts with age. There were close-to-significant linear grade trends for affect with family, $t = 1.66$, $p = .10$, and with friends, $t = 1.66$, $p = .10$, and a significant linear relation for time alone, $t = 2.66$, $p = .008$. For girls, this analysis revealed the same linear grade trends for affect with the family, $t = 3.15$, $p = .002$, and alone, $t = 3.21$, $p < .001$, as well as a close-to-significant quadratic effect for family, $t = 2.16$, $p = .03$, similar to that displayed in Figure 2. These findings indicate that the increase in affect experienced with friends is only a relative increase. They also show that the overall linear declines in average affect from fifth to ninth grade (Larson & Lampman-Petraitis, 1989) occur across contexts and are not fully due to greater time spent in the more dysphoric context of solitude. Among girls, overall affect declines in spite of the fact that older girls spend more time in the relatively happier context of friends. In addition, we conducted similar MANOVAs with an item from the ESM reports that asked, "How much choice did you have about your current activity?" Raw mean responses to this item when with family, friends, and alone did not differ significantly by grade for either boys or girls. This suggests that age differences in companionship are not attributable to major changes in restrictive or coercive environmental forces acting on the adolescent.

riod. This quadratic trend was significant for boys, $t = 3.11$, $p = .002$, and close-to-significant for girls, $t = 1.96$, $p = .05$. A child's experience of his or her family appears to become less positive with entry into the early adolescent years, but then becomes more positive again in the ninth grade.

MANOVAs could not be used to examine these age trends for the finer subcategories of companionship since nearly all individuals were missing self-reports for one or more of the 13 categories. Therefore, we conducted univariate ANOVAs separately for each of the 13 including only those individuals with at least one self-report in that category. Out of a total of 26 ANOVAs, only two yielded a significant linear trend at the .01 level. Boys showed an increase in affect with one person of the opposite sex, $F(1,19) = 11.25$, $p = .003$, and girls showed a decrease in affect with their extended families, $F(1,110) = 8.27$, $p = .005$. Given the danger of Type I error, these trends should be interpreted with caution.

Interrelationship with activity and locations.—As with our findings for the first hypothesis, we evaluated whether findings for the second might be interrelated with other contextual variables. Might the age differences in affect with family and friends be related to age differences in the activities performed with these companions or the location in which the interactions took place?

In order to evaluate interrelations with these contextual variables, we performed ANOVAs in which activity and location were included as factors along with grade and companionship. Because of the large number of cells involved, it was necessary to test each of these two moderator variables in separate three-way ANOVAs. We also found it conceptually simpler to conduct these analyses using the self-report rather than the person as the unit of analysis (see Larson & Delespaul, 1990).

In these ANOVAs, the main effects for activity and location were significant (Table 3). Participants reported more positive affect when away from home and during active leisure. However, the interactions of these variables with companionship (and with companionship and grade) were not significant. In other words, there was no evidence of an interrelation between the age trends for companionship and these other contextual variables. The only significant interactions were the expected ones between grade and companionship from Figure 2. In sum, the greater positive affect older students reported with friends was not attributable to an age difference in the activities carried out with friends or to an age difference in affect during only one or a few activities. Rather, they reflect greater positive affect across all contexts of interaction with friends.

Discussion

Time with family.—The findings of this study confirm the hypothesis that the family recedes as a major context of daily interactions across this age period. Ninth graders reported being with family members half as often as did fifth graders. The older students spent less time with their families both at home and away from home. A study of older adolescents, which employed the same methodology, shows that time with family continues to recede during the senior high school years (Csikszentmihalyi & Larson, 1984). The family has been found to be a context that reinforces adult values, promotes school success, provides self-esteem support, and even increases security in relationships with peers (Hoffman, Ushpiz, & Levy-Shiff, 1988; Larson, 1983; Ryan & Lynch, 1989). This shrinkage of adolescents' contact time with the family may give it fewer opportunities to perform these functions.

Certain parts of family experience, however, recede more than others. It is time with family as a congregate unit, as well as time with siblings and extended relatives, that diminishes most across this age period. The amount of time youths spend with mother alone and father alone does not differ between fifth and ninth grade, and a separate analysis of these data showed that amount of time spent talking with parents does not decline over this age period (Raffaelli & Duckett, 1989). This suggests that mothers and fathers continue to have one-on-one opportunities to interact with, influence, and support young adolescents. In sum, while the congregate unit of the family may be receding as a major segment of daily experience, direct contact with parents remains intact, at least for many teenagers.

Furthermore, the subjective quality of family time does not show a net difference across this age period. Ninth graders did not experience less happiness or more distress when with their families than did fifth graders. This finding supports the position that the age changes in adolescent-parent relationships are best characterized as a process of "transformation" rather than emotional alienation (Grotevant & Cooper, 1986). In the intervening sixth- to eighth-grade period, however, the average affective states reported with the family *were* less positive than in fifth grade. This finding is consistent with past research suggesting the occurrence of an early adolescent transitional period during which hour-to-hour conflict with the family is heightened (Hill & Holmbeck, 1986; Steinberg, 1981).

Time with friends.—It is commonly assumed that, as the centrality of family recedes in adolescence, friends take its place. Our data did not provide unequivocal support for this hypothesis and indicate a need to qualify this assumption. Both boys and girls in the study did report more positive relative affect with friends in the older than younger grades, suggesting that interactions with friends have become more rewarding. However, the age trends in amount of time spent with friends were not very dramatic and certainly did not match the age decline in amount of time spent with the family. For boys, no significant age difference occurred across this period in amount of time spent with friends, at least during the 7:30 A.M. to 9:30 P.M. period covered by this study.[3] For girls, there was a net increase with age in amount of time with friends, but this occurred mostly after an intervening fifth- to seventh-grade period during which the amount of time spent alone increased substantially.

The unexpected smallness of age differences in time with friends can be understood by recognizing that the older students did not spend more time away from home than younger students and were not more likely to socialize with friends in their homes; in fact, older boys interacted less with friends at home than did younger boys. Older girls in the study achieved greater contact with friends in two ways: they spent a greater proportion of their time in public with friends (e.g., they went shopping with their friends rather than with siblings or parents), and they talked with their friends more often on the phone (Raffaelli & Duckett, 1989; see also Crockett et al., 1984). Data from high school students suggest that in middle adolescence, amount of time with friends increases substantially, along with time away from home (Csikszentmihalyi & Larson, 1984)—trends that may be related to easing of parental restrictions (see Feldman & Quatman, 1988) and access to cars in this later age period.

Time alone.—Amount of time alone increased both for boys and girls. When at home, young adolescents more often retired to their bedrooms or sought some unoccupied part of the house, rather than hanging out with their families as they did during the elementary school years. Parke and Sawin (1979) showed that within the home there is a large increase at this age in privacy-seeking behavior, such as closing one's bedroom door and expecting others to knock before entering. Boys in our study also spent more of their time away from home by themselves, reflecting greater independence. The absence of this trend in girls, we speculate, might be attributable to their greater vulnerability to sexual harassment (Shipman, 1968).

This increase in time spent alone presents a puzzle, given that this time is associated with less positive affect. Other research evidence suggests that this solitary age trend may be due to adolescents' increasing ability to use time alone in an instrumental fashion (Larson, 1990). Prior ESM research indicates that adolescents feel better after being alone, and that those individuals who spend some time alone show indications of better psychological well-being (Larson & Csikszentmihalyi, 1978, 1980). The cognitive changes associated with this age period may give young adolescents the capacity to deliberately employ solitude for relaxation, self-renewal, and exploration of a newly discovered private self (Broughton, 1981).

Adolescents who spend large amounts of time alone, however, show poorer well-being (Larson, 1990; Larson & Csikszentmihalyi, 1978, 1980). Indeed, spending too much time alone is a defining symptom of depression and a warning sign for suicidal behavior (American Psychiatric Association, 1987). Therefore, this shift to spending more time alone may be constructive for some, but a sign of increasing alienation for others—a

[3] The fifth graders reported an average bedtime of 9:25 P.M. on weekdays and 10:35 P.M. on weekends; hence we missed little of their waking experience. The ninth graders, however, reported an average bedtime of 10:25 P.M. on weekdays and 11:50 P.M. on weekends. Self-reports for the 8:30–9:30 P.M. period and retrospective questioning of students suggest that some of the older participants' waking time after 9:30 P.M. was spent with friends, particularly on weekends.

TABLE 3

AFFECT × COMPANIONSHIP × LOCATION AND ACTIVITY

	Means (and Cell Counts)					
	Boys			Girls		
	Family	Friends	Alone	Family	Friends	Alone
Location:						
Home (excluding bedroom)	−.05 (1436)	.18 (325)	−.13 (992)	−.13 (1534)	.11 (515)	−.25 (956)
Bedroom	−.15 (153)	.24 (58)	−.30 (548)	−.26 (178)	.01 (114)	−.25 (628)
Away from home	.00 (470)	.23 (1317)	−.04 (396)	.17 (593)	.27 (1602)	−.11 (327)
Activity:						
Schoolwork	−.31 (99)	−.07 (58)	−.47 (178)	−.23 (146)	.06 (90)	−.53 (185)
Eating	.07 (219)	.31 (147)	−.05 (117)	.08 (248)	.34 (169)	−.04 (88)
Transportation	.12 (98)	.28 (120)	−.05 (90)	.05 (119)	.17 (167)	−.23 (87)
Personal maintenance	−.25 (179)	−.12 (80)	−.40 (368)	−.28 (216)	.17 (140)	−.35 (524)
Chores and errands	−.03 (130)	.18 (27)	−.15 (97)	−.03 (172)	.13 (42)	−.22 (98)
Media use	−.04 (661)	.21 (104)	−.03 (508)	−.12 (599)	.16 (189)	−.20 (453)
Creative activities	−.05 (79)	.15 (38)	−.17 (118)	−.08 (103)	.19 (50)	−.06 (150)
Socializing	.06 (181)	.26 (296)	.40 (4)[a]	−.03 (280)	.22 (592)	.32 (7)[a]
Playing games	.03 (122)	.32 (154)	.12 (126)	.08 (108)	.31 (147)	−.20 (72)
Sports	−.06 (96)	.25 (442)	.19 (93)	.43 (56)	.35 (261)	−.12 (71)
Other	−.14 (197)	.20 (236)	−.21 (238)	−.04 (259)	.19 (380)	−.23 (177)

	ANOVAs					
	Boys			Girls		
	df	*F*	*p*	*df*	*F*	*p*
Location:						
Who with	2	34.44	.000	2	42.21	.000
Location	2	8.53	.000	2	33.41	.000
Grade	4	.28	.891	4	1.56	.182
Who × location	4	.83	.505	4	2.01	.090
Who × grade	8	1.98	.045	8	2.82	.003
Location × grade	8	.44	.899	8	.91	.509
Who × location × grade	44	1.27	.208	44	1.48	.094
Residual	5650	...	...	6400	...	...
Activity:						
Who with	2	31.56	.000	2	68.03	.000
Activity	10	10.79	.000	10	7.81	.000
Grade	4	.49	.745	4	1.48	.207
Who × activity	20	1.19	.141	20	1.02	.431
Who × grade	8	2.10	.033	8	2.29	.019
Activity × grade	40	1.15	.240	40	1.08	.329
Who × activity × grade	79	.94	.622	79	.79	.934
Residual	5531	...	...	6282	...	...

[a] Letter writing.

change in life-style that, unfortunately, puts them further from the reach of family and peers who might provide positive support.

Conclusion.—These age differences in time with family, friends, and alone, we believe, represent significant changes in teenagers' daily opportunities for cognitive growth, emotional development, and social support (Whiting & Edwards, 1988). The adolescent who is spending much of his or her time alone or with friends is participating in a different experiential world than the preadolescent who spends half of his or her time with family. It is important to recognize, however, that this research has not fully answered the complex question of why these age differences in daily companionship occur. We discounted the possibility that they were simply a correlate of age changes in daily locations or activities, but we could not isolate all the elements of environmental press (e.g., parental demands on their time, pressure from friends) and personal disposition (e.g., desire for autonomy) that might be involved. Future research might fruitfully examine the correlation of age changes in daily companionship with differences between teenagers in these environmental and personal factors.

It is also important to recognize that these findings come from a limited Midwestern American sample and may not apply to other groups. Separate analyses examining differences between subgroups within this sample indicate only small variations in patterns of companionship and affect related to maternal employment (Richards & Duckett, 1990), parental marital status (Asmussen, 1989), and depression (Larson, Raffaelli, Richards, Ham, & Jewell, 1990). Time-budget data from other cultures, however, suggest larger cultural variations in the amount of time adolescents spend with different companions (Saraswathi & Dutta, 1988; Zuzanek, 1980). Further work might consider how such intra- and intercultural differences in daily exposure to family, friends, and being alone influence development and socialization to adulthood.

References

American Psychiatric Association (1987). *Diagnostic and statistical manual of mental disorders* (rev. 3d ed.). Washington, DC: APA.

Asmussen, L. A. (1989). *Adolescents' daily experience and emotional well-being: A comparison of youth in single-parent and married-parent families.* Unpublished master's thesis, University of Illinois, Urbana-Champaign.

Berndt, T. J. (1979). Developmental changes in conformity to peers and parents. *Developmental Psychology*, **15**, 608–616.

Berndt, T. J. (1982). The features and effects of friendship in early adolescence. *Child Development*, **53**, 1447–1460.

Berndt, T. J. (1989). Friendship in childhood and adolescence. In W. Damon (Ed.), *Child development today and tomorrow* (pp. 332–348). San Francisco: Jossey-Bass.

Blos, P. (1967). The second individuation process of adolescence. *Psychoanalytic Study of the Child*, **22**, 162–186.

Blyth, D. A., Hill, J. P., & Thiel, K. S. (1982). Early adolescents' significant others: Grade and gender differences in perceived relationships with familial and nonfamilial adults and young people. *Journal of Youth and Adolescence*, **11**, 425–450.

Bowerman, C. E., & Kinch, J. W. (1959). Changes in family and peer orientation of children between the fourth and tenth grades. *Social Forces*, **37**, 206–211.

Broughton, J. (1981). The divided self in adolescence. *Human Development*, **24**, 13–32.

Buhrmester, D., & Furman, W. (1987). The development of companionship and intimacy. *Child Development*, **58**, 1101–1113.

Coleman, J. C. (1974). *Relationships in adolescence.* London and Boston: Routledge & Kegan Paul.

Crockett, L., Losoff, M., & Petersen, A. C. (1984). Perceptions of the peer group and friendship in early adolescence. *Journal of Early Adolescence*, **4**, 155–181.

Csikszentmihalyi, M., & Larson, R. (1984). *Being adolescent: Conflict and growth in the teenage years.* New York: Basic.

Csikszentmihalyi, M., & Larson, R. (1987). Validity and reliability of the experience-sampling method. *Journal of Nervous and Mental Disease*, **175**(9), 526–536.

Feldman, S. S., & Quatman, T. (1988). Factors influencing age expectations for adolescent autonomy: A study of early adolescents and parents. *Journal of Early Adolescence*, **8**, 325–343.

Gilligan, C. (1982). *In a different voice.* Cambridge, MA: Harvard University Press.

Grotevant, H. D., & Cooper, C. R. (1986). Individuation in family relationships. *Human Development*, **29**, 82–100.

Hartup, W. W. (1983). Peer relations. In E. M. Hetherington (Ed.), P. H. Mussen (Series Ed.), *Handbook of child psychology: Vol. 4. Socialization, personality, and social development* (pp. 103–196). New York: Wiley.

Havighurst, R. J. (1984). *Developmental tasks and education.* New York: David McKay.

Hill, J., & Holmbeck, G. (1986). Attachment and

autonomy during adolescence. In G. Whitehurst (Ed.), *Annals of child development* (Vol. 3, pp. 145–189). Greenwich, CT: JAI.

Hoffman, M. A., Ushpiz, V., & Levy-Shiff, R. (1988). Social support and self-esteem in adolescence. *Journal of Youth and Adolescence*, **17**, 307–316.

Hunter, F. T., & Youniss, J. (1982). Changes in functions of three relations during adolescence. *Developmental Psychology*, **18**, 806–811.

Kovacs, M. (1985). The Children's Depression Inventory: A self-rated depression scale for school-aged youngsters. *Psychopharmacology Bulletin*, **21**, 995–998.

Larson, R. (1979). *The significance of solitude in adolescents' lives.* Unpublished doctoral dissertation. University of Chicago.

Larson, R. W. (1983). Adolescents' daily experience with family and friends: Contrasting opportunity systems. *Journal of Marriage and the Family*, **45**, 739–750.

Larson, R. (1989a). Beeping children and adolescents: A method for studying time use and daily experience. *Journal of Youth and Adolescence*, **18**, 511–530.

Larson, R. (1989b). *The factor structure of moods and emotions in a sample of young adolescents.* Unpublished manuscript, University of Illinois, Urbana-Champaign.

Larson, R. W. (1990). The solitary side of life: An examination of the time people spend alone from childhood to old age. *Developmental Review*, **10**, 155–183.

Larson, R., & Csikszentmihalyi, M. (1978). Experiential correlates of time alone in adolescence. *Journal of Personality*, **46**, 677–693.

Larson, R., & Csikszentmihalyi, M. (1980). The significance of solitude in adolescents' development. *Journal of Current Adolescent Medicine*, **2**(8), 33–40.

Larson, R., & Csikszentmihalyi, M. (1983). The experience sampling method. In H. T. Reis (Ed.), *Naturalistic approaches to studying social interaction: New directions for methodology of social and behavioral science, no. 15* (pp. 41–56). San Francisco: Jossey-Bass.

Larson, R., & Delespaul, P. (1990). Analyzing experience sampling data: A guidebook for the perplexed. In M. deVries (Ed.), *The experience of psychopathology*. Cambridge: Cambridge University Press.

Larson, R., & Lampman-Petraitis, C. (1989). Daily emotional states as reported by children and adolescents. *Child Development*, **60**, 1250–1260.

Larson, R., Raffaelli, M., Richards, M. H., Ham, M., & Jewell, L. (1990). The ecology of depression in late childhood and early adolescence: A profile of daily states and activities. *Journal of Abnormal Psychology*, **99**, 92–102.

Larson, R., & Richards, M. H. (1989). The changing life space of early adolescence [special issue]. *Journal of Youth and Adolescence*, **18**, 501–626.

Marcoen, A., Goossens, L., & Caes, P. (1987). Loneliness in pre- through late adolescence: Exploring the contributions of a multidimensional approach. *Journal of Youth and Adolescence*, **16**, 561–578.

Montemayor, R. (1982). The relationship between parent-adolescent conflict and the amount of time adolescents spend alone and with parents and peers. *Child Development*, **53**, 1512–1519.

Montemayor, R., & Brownlee, J. R. (1987). Fathers, mothers, and adolescents: Gender-based differences in parental roles during adolescence. *Journal of Youth and Adolescence*, **16**, 281–291.

Montemayor, R., & Van Komen, R. (1980). Age segregation of adolescents in and out of school. *Journal of Youth and Adolescence*, **9**, 371–381.

Parke, R. D., & Sawin, D. B. (1979). Children's privacy in the home: Developmental, ecological, and child-rearing determinants. *Environment and Behavior*, **11**, 87–104.

Raffaelli, M., & Duckett, E. (1989). "We were just talking . . .": Conversations in early adolescence. *Journal of Youth and Adolescence*, **18**, 567–582.

Richards, M., & Duckett, E. (1990). *Maternal employment and young adolescents' daily experience of family and parents.* Manuscript submitted for publication.

Ryan, R. M., & Lynch, J. H. (1989). Emotional autonomy versus detachment: Revisiting the vicissitudes of adolescence and young adulthood. *Child Development*, **60**, 340–356.

Saraswathi, T. S., & Dutta, R. (1988). *Invisible boundaries: Grooming for adult roles.* New Delhi: Northern Book Center.

Savin-Williams, R. C. (1979). Dominance hierarchies in groups of early adolescents. *Child Development*, **50**, 923–935.

Shipman, G. (1968). The psychodynamics of sex education. *Family Coordinator*, **17**, 3–12.

Simmons, R. G., & Blyth, D. A. (1987). *Moving into adolescence: The impact of pubertal change and school context.* New York: Aldine De Gruyter.

Smetana, J. G. (1988). Adolescents' amd parents' conceptions of parental authority. *Child Development*, **59**, 321–335.

Steinberg, L. (1981). Transformations in family relations at puberty. *Developmental Psychology*, **17**, 833–840.

Steinberg, L. (1987). The impact of puberty on

family relations: Effects of pubertal status and pubertal timing. *Developmental Psychology*, 23, 451–460.

Steinberg, L., & Silverberg, S. B. (1986). The vicissitudes of autonomy in early adolescence. *Child Development*, 57, 841–851.

Whiting, B. B., & Edwards, C. P. (1988). *Children of different worlds: The formation of social behavior*. Cambridge, MA: Harvard University Press.

Youniss, J., & Smollar, J. (1985). *Adolescent relations with mothers, fathers, and friends*. Chicago: University of Chicago Press.

Zuzanek, J. (1980). *Work and leisure in the Soviet Union: A time-budget analysis*. New York: Praeger.

Parenting Practices and Peer Group Affiliation in Adolescence

B. Bradford Brown
University of Wisconsin—Madison

Nina Mounts
University of Illinois at Urbana-Champaign

Susie D. Lamborn
University of West Florida

Laurence Steinberg
Temple University

Brown, B. Bradford; Mounts, Nina; Lamborn, Susie D.; and Steinberg, Laurence. *Parenting Practices and Peer Group Affiliation in Adolescence.* Child Development, 1993, **64**, 467–482. Social scientists have often assumed that parental influence is sharply curtailed at adolescence because of the rising counterinfluence of peer groups, over which parents have little control. The present study tested a conceptual model that challenged this view by arguing that parents retain a notable but indirect influence over their teenage child's peer associates. Data from a sample of 3,781 high school students (ages 15–19) indicated that specific parenting practices (monitoring, encouragement of achievement, joint decision making) were significantly associated with specific adolescent behaviors (academic achievement, drug use, self-reliance), which in turn were significantly related to membership in common adolescent crowds (jocks, druggies, etc.). Findings encourage investigators to assess more carefully parents' role in adolescents' peer group affiliations.

Among the many transformations in family relationships expected to occur as a child enters adolescence, one of the most worrisome for adults is the shift in reference group orientation from parents to the peer group (Gecas & Seff, 1990). Parents often express concern that their adolescent child will "fall into the wrong crowd" and be persuaded by peer pressure to engage in behaviors that are self-destructive and/or counter to parental expectations. Such concern may seem justified by studies indicating that, across early adolescence, susceptibility to peer pressure increases while reliance upon parents' opinions and advice seems to decline (Berndt, 1979), as well as by research indicating that association with deviant peers is one of the strongest predictors of adolescent deviant activity (Elliott, Huisinga, & Ageton, 1985).

There is, however, evidence that parents do retain a substantial measure of influence over the attitudes and activities of

A version of this paper was presented at the biennial meeting of the Society for Research in Child Development, Seattle, 1991. The study on which this report is based was supported by grants to B. Bradford Brown from the Spencer Foundation through the Wisconsin Center for Education Research, University of Wisconsin—Madison; to B. Bradford Brown and Laurence Steinberg from the U.S. Department of Education through the National Center on Effective Secondary Schools, Wisconsin Center for Educational Research, University of Wisconsin—Madison; and to Sanford M. Dornbusch and P. Herbert Leiderman from the Spencer Foundation through the Center for the Study of Families, Youth, and Children at Stanford University. The opinions expressed in this paper are those of the authors and do not necessarily reflect the opinions of the funding agencies. The authors gratefully acknowledge the helpful comments of three anonymous reviewers on earlier versions of this paper, as well as the assistance of Bih-Hui Huang in data analyses and Lori Folgert in preparing the manuscript. Address correspondence to the first author at the Department of Educational Psychology, University of Wisconsin—Madison, 1025 West Johnson Street, Madison, WI 53706.

[*Child Development*, 1993, **64**, 467–482. 0009-3920/93/6402-0008$01.00]

their teenage offspring. We believe this evidence is key to demonstrating the significant role that parents play in their child's choice of peer group associates during adolescence. The present study tests a conceptual model in which parenting behaviors affect adolescents' peer group affiliations significantly but indirectly, through their influence on adolescent behavior patterns.

The Traditional View and Contemporary Counterevidence

At mid-century, social scientists promoted a perspective that emphasized the competitive or combative role that parents and peers play in the lives of teenagers. Parsons (1942) portrayed the adolescent social system as a monolithic youth culture whose value system is clearly at odds with adult expectations. Riesman (1961) contended that parents had abdicated much of their authority over adolescent offspring to the school and the peer group. Thus, it was common to portray parents and peers as competitors for teenagers' allegiance, with parents relatively powerless—in many domains, at least—to countermand the influence of peer group pressures (Bowerman & Kinch, 1959; Brittain, 1963; Coleman, 1961; Floyd & South, 1972).

More recent studies, however, have provided a very different image of parent and peer group influences on adolescents. In the first place, investigators have found that parental influence on children's behavior remains extensive in adolescence. Through particular child-rearing practices, parents can have a substantial impact on adolescent behaviors of major concern to adults, such as school achievement patterns, drug use and deviance, and self-concept. For example, outside of the child's intellectual ability, parental expectation for achievement is one of the strongest predictors of adolescents' academic achievement levels (Featherman, 1980; Seginer, 1983). Parental monitoring has a particularly powerful influence on adolescent delinquency and drug use (Coombs & Landsverk, 1988; Loeber & Dishion, 1983) as well as on academic achievement (Dornbusch, Ritter, Leiderman, Roberts, & Fraleigh, 1987). Parental efforts to engage their adolescent in joint decision making seem to foster self-confidence and self-reliance (Baumrind, 1991b; Grotevant & Cooper, 1986; Hauser et al., 1984), enhance academic performance (Dornbusch et al., 1987; Yee & Flanagan, 1985), and discourage excessive or abusive use of drugs (Glynn, 1984) or delinquent activities (Dornbusch & Ritter, 1991).

Second, in contrast to the mid-century image of a unified peer culture, ethnographers have consistently discovered a diverse array of peer groups in American high schools (Buff, 1970; Eckert, 1989; Eder, 1985; Larkin, 1979; Schwendinger & Schwendinger, 1985). An elite group similar to Coleman's (1961) "leading crowd" is always found, although it is often divided into two somewhat different crowds. "Populars" are portrayed as socially competent individuals with a strong commitment to academic achievement but also moderate involvement in delinquent behavior and illicit drug use. "Jocks" are quite similar but less academically oriented and more focused in their drug use on alcohol, which they sometimes use to excess. Counterposed against these crowds is a more alienated group—"druggies," "burnouts," "greasers," etc.—that is not only heavily involved in drug use and deviant activities but also inattentive to schoolwork and often hostile toward school adults; yet, group members seem to maintain a fairly strong self-image. Balanced between these groups are the "normals," average, or "in-between" students who seem to avoid deviant activities but otherwise are not clearly distinctive on any particular trait. In most studies there is also a group of high achievers, the "brains" or "eggheads" or "intellectuals," who thrive on academics, forge close relationships with school adults, and studiously avoid drugs and deviant activities. Their self-confidence is bolstered by academic achievements but also eroded by their marginal standing in the peer status system. Most schools also feature a socially inept crowd—"loners" or "nerds"—whose members are generally low in social status and, consequently, self-esteem. Their academic achievement levels are variable, but they seem to shy away from deviant activities.

The ethnographic studies not only emphasize the diversity of life-styles that adolescents pursue with peers, they also emphasize the limits of peers' ability to direct teenagers' behavior. Adolescents do not haphazardly fall into one crowd or another and then fall victim to the normative pressures of that crowd. Instead, they are "selected into" a particular crowd by virtue of the reputation they establish among peers (Brown, 1990). One does not become a jock by quirk of fate or even simply by honing one's athletic skill and making the basketball team. One must be perceived by peers as acting primarily in "jock-like" ways: being interested in sports, getting adequate but not outstanding grades, exuding self-confidence but remaining compliant with adult authority, shying away from drugs except for alcohol, and so on. There is, to be sure, pressure to conform to crowd norms (Clasen & Brown, 1985) and to select friends from fellow crowd members (Eckert, 1989; Eder, 1985), but these do not direct adolescents to new behaviors as much as they reinforce existing dispositions—dispositions that helped direct the adolescent to a particular crowd in the first place.

In sum, parents retain substantial influence over their child's behavior in adolescence, and peer influences are not predominantly antisocial but quite variable, contingent on the norms of the peer crowd to which the adolescent belongs. Further, crowd affiliation is not a matter of chance association but a function of the reputation one establishes among peers by virtue of one's background and behavior.

Linking Parenting Practices to Peer Group Affiliations

Ethnographers have provided a detailed analysis of the characteristics of adolescent crowds but have been remarkably inattentive to the family characteristics of crowd members. By the same token, researchers who have detailed associations between parenting strategies and adolescent behaviors usually have not concerned themselves with adolescents' peer group relationships. This fosters the impression that the family and peer group are quite separate worlds for teenagers, perhaps because by this age parents have lost their ability to affect peer associations. Recent studies of adolescent deviance counter this impression, but they also raise questions about the *way* in which parents influence peer group affiliations. Some investigators have found that if parents model deviant behavior or fail to maintain close relationships with their teenager, the child is more likely to drift into deviant peer groups and, as a consequence, be more involved in drug use (Kandel & Andrews, 1987; Oetting & Beauvais, 1987) or delinquency (Marcos, Bahr, & Johnson, 1986; Massey & Krohn, 1986). Others have suggested a different causal arrangement of these variables: parental detachment from early adolescents promotes antisocial behaviors, and youngsters with such behaviors seem to band together in antisocial cliques (Cairns, Cairns, Neckerman, Gest, & Gariepy, 1988; Dishion, 1990). To date, however, such studies have been largely confined to deviant behavior and deviantly oriented peer groups.

The intent of this study was to expand consideration of parental influences on adolescent peer group affiliation to a broader array of peer groups and to consider both antisocial and prosocial behaviors. The assumption that parenting behaviors have a *direct* effect on teenagers' peer relationships follows neatly from similar research on younger age groups (e.g., Parke & Bhavnagri, 1989). Nevertheless, the evidence reviewed above, indicating that parents influence many behaviors by which adolescents are assigned to crowds, seems to favor a conceptual model in which parents play a significant but *indirect* role in adolescent peer group affiliations (see Fig. 1). According to this model, specific parenting behaviors are significantly associated with specific adolescent characteristics, which in turn predict the peer group with which the adolescent is associated. Peer group pressures serve to reinforce behavior patterns by which adolescents come to be associated with a particular crowd. By fostering certain traits in their children, parents essentially direct a child toward a particular peer group, and thus exercise some control over the type of peer group influences to which their child is exposed.

To test the conceptual model, we focused on three parenting practices—emphasis on academic achievement, moni-

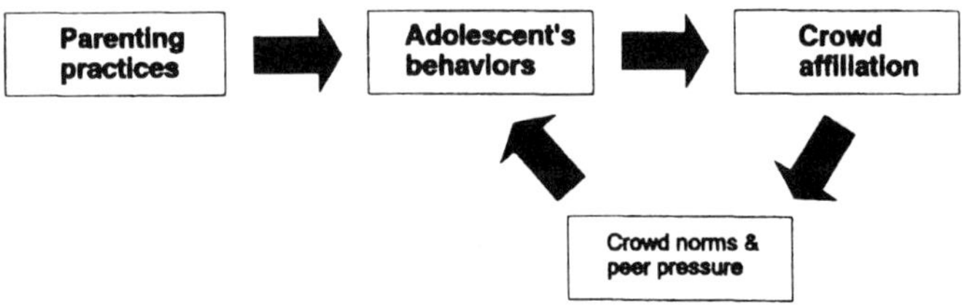

FIG. 1.—Conceptual model of the connections between parenting behaviors, peer group influences, and adolescent behavior.

toring, and efforts to engage the child in joint decision making—that have been shown in previous studies to be significant parental influences on adolescent behavior. We also selected three adolescent behaviors—academic achievement, drug use, and self-reliance—that are not only highly salient to researchers, educators, and parents, but also instrumental in defining adolescent peer groups. We relied upon adolescents' own descriptions of their social system to define the crowds to be studied. Because the study's basic intent was to examine the manner in which parents influence peer group affiliation, the portion of the conceptual model specifying peer group influences on adolescent behavior patterns (the "feedback loop" in Fig. 1 from peer group affiliation to adolescent behavior) was not included in our analyses.

Method

Sample and Procedures

Six public, 4-year high schools—three in the Midwest and three on the West Coast—participated in the study. These included a small, rural school that drew its 400 students (98% European-American) primarily from farm or working-class families; a school whose more ethnically diverse student body (only 70% of the 1,500 students were European-Americans) hailed from working- and middle-class neighborhoods of a moderate-sized city; a mid-sized school (1,000 students) located in a pervasively European-American, upper-middle-class suburb; a large, ethnically diverse school (45% of the 2,500 students were African-American or Hispanic) located in a predominantly upper-middle-class community but also drawing from less economically privileged families in neighboring towns; a school whose 1,300 students were largely bifurcated between working- and upper-middle-class families, with Asian-American and Hispanic students collectively outnumbering European-Americans; and a large inner-city school with an ethnically diverse student body—African-Americans formed the largest single racial/ethnic group (40%)—from a broad range of socioeconomic backgrounds. Collectively, the schools comprised a diverse sample in terms of size, location, socioeconomic background, and ethnic composition.

All students in participating schools were invited to complete a self-report questionnaire that focused on school-related behaviors (academic achievement, engagement in classes, extracurricular participation) but also included measures of family relationships and parenting behaviors, peer relationships, deviant activities, and psychological well-being. Because of its length, the questionnaire was divided into two sections, which were administered on separate days. Students also received peer ratings of crowd affiliation, based on the Social Type Rating (STR) procedure (Brown, 1989) that is explained in the next section. STR ratings were obtained for all students in the Midwestern schools but, because of time constraints, only freshmen and sophomores in the West Coast schools.

Analyses in the present study were confined to the 3,781 students who received STR ratings and also successfully completed both portions of the self-report questionnaire, from which measures of parenting practices and adolescent behaviors were derived. This constituted 72% of the combined student bodies of the participating schools (excluding the California upperclassmen not included in STR ratings). Of the remainder, 4% refused or were denied permission by parents to participate in the study, 6% failed to fill out a questionnaire completely or credibly, and 18% were absent from class on one or both questionnaire administration dates. The sample ranged in age from 14 to 19 (M = 15.5) and was fairly evenly divided by sex (52% female). Although a majority (61%) of the sample was European-American, there were also substantial numbers of African-Americans (12%), Asian-Americans (12%), and Hispanic youth (13%).

Peer-rated Crowd Affiliation

The Social Type Rating (STR) procedure (Brown, 1989) is an efficient mechanism for identifying adolescents' peer group affiliation, based on their reputation among peers. It is somewhat similar to sociometric ratings by which younger children are classified into comparison groups (popular, rejected, neglected, etc.; see, e.g., Terry & Coie, 1991), except that the STR ratings take advantage of the more sophisticated social system of adolescents in which there are commonly shared labels for particular peer groups.

Derived from earlier studies of adolescent peer groups (Clasen & Brown, 1985; Poveda, 1975; Schwendinger & Schwendinger, 1985), the STR procedure was a two-step process. In the first step, school administrators were asked to identify a set of boys and girls (within each ethnic group in multiethnic schools) in each grade who represented a good cross-section of the school's student body. These students were interviewed in small groups composed of students of the same gender, same grade level, and same ethnic group. Through group discussion, each group derived a list of the school's major crowds; then each participant listed two boys and two girls in his or her grade who were the leaders or most prominent members of each crowd. From these lists a stratified sample was drawn in each grade (stratified by crowd type, gender, and ethnicity, but with preference given to the most frequently listed students) to become "STR raters" in the second step. Each rater, accompanied by a friend of her or his own choosing, was individually interviewed. The raters were presented with the list of crowds derived from the earlier group interviews, then asked to place each student in their grade level into one of the crowds. Raters could indicate that they did not know a student well enough to assign to a crowd. STR ratings continued until each student had been rated by at least 10 STR raters. Because raters could only deal with about 300 names in the time allotted for STR interviews, class lists in the larger schools had to be partitioned and the number of raters increased to ensure that all students received the required number of ratings.

There are several ways of using the STR ratings to describe students' crowd affiliation. One is to create categorical assignments, that is, to place each student in the crowd to which a majority of STR raters assigned him or her. While useful for many analyses, categorical assignments mask the fact that few students are placed in the same crowd by all raters; they also give the same score to marginal crowd members (those rated into a particular crowd by a bare majority of raters) and central crowd members (those associated with the crowd by virtually all raters). An alternative strategy, which was employed for this study, is to create a series of proportion scores representing the percentage of raters (excluding those who did not know a student well enough to assign to any crowd) who placed the student in a given crowd. Thus, respondents received a score from 0 to 1.00 for each of their school's major crowds. Defining the outcome measures as continuous rather than categorical variables also permitted us to use standard regression procedures for assessing the direct and mediated effects of our dependent measures (parenting behaviors).

Analyses in the present study were confined to proportion scores for six major crowds: populars, jocks, brains, normals, druggies, and outcasts.[1] These six crowds were widely recognized by raters in all participating schools. In fact, they comprised the bulk of STR crowd assignments (70%, on average). They are also the crowds on which most studies of adolescent peer groups have focused. Means, standard deviations, and intercorrelations among the crowd proportion scores are provided in Table 1.

As would be expected with the scoring procedure we used, crowd proportion scores were negatively skewed and negatively intercorrelated.[2] The comparatively low intercorrelation between proportion scores for

[1] The outcast group combined two crowds that were sometimes differentiated by STR raters: loners and nerds. Although distinctive in some ways, these groups share the same basic image among peers, especially regarding the behaviors of interest in this study: limited social skills, low self-image, low involvement in deviant behavior, and average or above average academic achievement levels. Thus, they appear to be different factions of the same major crowd (Brown, Lohr, & Trujillo, 1990). In fact, some STR raters confessed that calling someone a "loner" was basically a "nice" way of acknowledging that the person was a nerd. It may seem odd to consider outcasts (or at least loners) as a crowd because their label implies a lack of social interaction. Nevertheless, it is a widely recognized social category with a distinctive normative image (Brown et al., 1990) and pattern of peer pressures (Clasen & Brown, 1985). Thus, it clearly fits with our conceptual orientation toward crowds as reputation-based entities.

[2] Crowd proportion scores are not independent; collectively, all of them (including those for crowd types not included in these analyses) must add to 1.00. Thus, as the number of crowd types increases the average score expected for each type diminishes. Crowd proportion scores in this study were low because of the substantial number of crowd types employed by STR raters. Further, as the proportion of assignments to a specific crowd increases, the proportion of assignments to other crowds must diminish; this explains the preponderance of negative correlations among crowd proportion scores. The negative skew of crowd proportion scores prompted us to repeat the major analyses using log transformations of the scores. Because results were substantively equivalent with both sets of scores we decided to retain the analyses based on the original scores.

TABLE 1

MEANS, STANDARD DEVIATIONS, AND INTERCORRELATIONS OF CROWD PROPORTION SCORES

			Intercorrelations				
Variable	Mean	SD	Popular	Jock	Brain	Normal	Druggie
Popular	.11	.20	...				
Jock	.07	.16	.02	...			
Brain	.09	.18	−.09	−.09	...		
Normal	.19	.23	−.11	−.10	−.07	...	
Druggie	.06	.16	−.11	−.08	−.14	−.14	...
Outcast	.18	.25	−.24	−.18	−.02	−.10	−.11

the populars and jocks and for the brains and outcasts suggests that these pairs of crowds are more compatible and closely aligned than other possible pairs; the relatively high negative correlation between proportion scores for populars and outcasts suggests that this pair of crowds is quite incompatible. Previous research on adolescent crowds confirms these patterns (see Brown, Mory, & Kinney, in press), thus bolstering the validity of the STR procedure.

Other Measures

Apart from crowd affiliation (which was based on peer ratings), all other measures were derived from students' responses to self-report questionnaire items. These measures fell into three basic sets: demographic characteristics, respondents' report of parents' child-rearing practices, and scores on three measures of adolescent behavior. Each of these sets is described below.

Demographic characteristics.—Students provided information on their background and current family situation. Specifically, they indicated their *sex*, *ethnic affiliation*, *family structure* (classified as intact, single-parent, stepparent, or other), and family *socioeconomic status* (SES), based on parents' level of education.

Parenting practices.—Investigators have taken a variety of approaches to measuring parenting behaviors. Some have attempted to identify global parenting styles that reflect an adult's child-rearing values and orientations (Baumrind, 1991a). Bronfenbrenner (1991), however, has cautioned that a given parenting style is not necessarily translated into the same behaviors by all parents. Thus, in view of our model, we chose to measure parenting practices directly rather than inferring them from parenting styles. There is also some controversy about the best way to measure parenting behaviors: observations of parent-child interactions (usually in contrived situations), parents' self-report, or reports from children. Each approach has strengths and limitations; observations lack ecological validity, and both parents and children seem to distort reality somewhat in their reports of parenting behavior. Because of the size of our sample, we were forced to rely exclusively on adolescents' report of parenting behaviors. To minimize distortions in their responses, we focused on measures of concrete parenting behaviors, rather than asking respondents to make more general (subjective) judgments about their parents' child-rearing practices.

From the wider set of variables on the questionnaire relating to parent attitudes and behaviors, we selected several that met our operational criteria (i.e., assessed concrete behaviors) and defined constructs that were especially pertinent to the questions on which this study focused. The first construct was *parental emphasis on achievement*. Included in this 15-item measure were answers to the following questions: "How often does each of your parents (*a*) help you with homework when asked, (*b*) know how you're doing in school, (*c*) go to school programs for parents, (*d*) watch you in sports or activities, and (*e*) help you in choosing your courses?"; "What is the lowest semester grade you could get in each of these subject areas without your parents getting upset? (*a*) English, (*b*) math, (*c*) science, (*d*) social studies"; "How important is it to your parents or guardians that you work hard on your schoolwork?" All items were answered on a 5-point Likert scale. The items formed a scale with acceptable internal consistency (alpha = .84); scores represented the mean of item responses (1 = low, 5 = high).[3]

Students also completed a five-item parental *monitoring* scale similar to ones that have been used in previous studies (Dishion, 1990; Dornbusch et al., 1985; Patterson & Stouthamer-Loeber, 1984). On a three-point scale (don't know, know a little, know a lot) they indicated how much their parents *really* knew about who their friends were, how they spent their money, where they were after school, where they went at night, and what they did with their free time. The scale had an internal consistency alpha of .80; scale scores (mean item score) ranged from 1.00 (low) to 3.00 (high).

The third measure indicated the degree to which parents engaged their child in *joint decision making* rather than making unilateral decisions for the child or allowing the child to decide things completely by himself or herself. This measure was based on a 13-item scale in which respondents indicated, on a 5-point scale (from "my parents decide this without discussing it with me" to "I decide this without discussing it with my parents"), how they and their parents arrived at a decision about a variety of issues commonly faced by high school students: school classes, curfew times, spending patterns, use of alcohol, and so on (Dornbusch et al., 1985; Steinberg, 1987). The scale's alpha was .82. Scale scores, ranging from 0 to 1.00, indicated the proportion of items on which decisions were derived jointly as opposed to unilaterally (by parents only or the adolescent only).[4]

Adolescent behaviors.—Three measures assessed adolescent behaviors that were expected to be related to parenting practices. Self-reported *grade-point average* (GPA), scored on the standard 4-point scale, was employed as a measure of academic achievement. Self-reported grades have been found to correlate highly (r = .75) with actual grades taken from student transcripts (Donovan & Jessor, 1985; Dornbusch et al., 1987). Respondents also completed a five-item *drug use* scale (alpha = .86), indicating, on a four-point scale (never, once or twice, several times, often), how often in the past 6 months they had used various controlled substances. Scale scores (the mean of item responses) ranged from 1.00 (low) to 4.00 (high). Similar measures in previous studies have been shown to be valid indicators of adolescent drug use (Needle, McCubbin, Lorence, & Hochhauser, 1983; O'Malley, Bachman, & Johnston, 1983; Polich, 1982). Finally, respondents completed the 10-item *self-reliance* subscale from Greenberger's Psychosocial Maturity Inventory (Form D; Greenberger, Josselson, Knerr, & Knerr, 1974). This scale measures adolescents' feelings of internal control and the ability to make decisions without extreme reliance upon others. Items are answered on a four-point Likert scale. Like the drug use measure, scale scores (the mean of item responses) ranged from 1.00 (low) to 4.00 (high). In this sample the scale's alpha was .81.

Plan of Analyses

Our conceptual model postulated that adolescent behaviors would mediate the association between parenting practices and crowd affiliation. Analyses followed a standard procedure for testing such mediating effects (Baron & Kenny, 1986). First, we examined the direct association between parenting practices and crowd affiliation. Then, we determined whether the significant direct effects of parenting practices diminished or disappeared when adolescent behaviors were introduced as mediating variables. Following this, we examined associations between parenting practices and adolescent behaviors and between adolescent behaviors and crowd affiliation. Separate analyses were conducted for each crowd affiliation score, using multiple regression techniques.

[3] Several other items were considered for this scale but dropped on the basis of initial factor analyses and reliability analyses. The omitted items seemed to focus on parental strategies in response to poor academic performance (e.g., "How often does your parent make sure you do your homework") rather than behaviors that underscore the value they attach to achievement.

[4] Previous studies have emphasized *joint* versus unilateral decision-making, without differentiating whether unilateral decisions are made by parents or the child (Yee & Flanagan, 1985). Those who have differentiated the two types of unilateral decisions have reported curvilinear effects, in which adolescent outcomes were highest in families practicing joint decision-making and not significantly different in families practicing "youth alone" or "parent alone" strategies (Dornbusch et al., 1985, 1989). Thus, the most appropriate usage of this measure for our analyses seems to be to calculate the proportion of joint decisions.

Results

Characteristics of Each Set of Variables

Table 2 presents the mean scores, standard deviations, and intercorrelations for the measures of parenting practices and adolescent behaviors. Within each set of measures correlations were positive but relatively low, suggesting (as expected) that the measures addressed distinctive aspects of parenting or adolescent behavior.

To determine the strength of association between student background characteristics and crowd affiliation, we correlated crowd affiliation scores with SES and also conducted a series of ANCOVAs (covarying for SES) that examined the independent effects of sex, grade level, ethnicity, family structure, and school on each crowd affiliation score. Results are summarized in Table 3. SES was positively correlated with membership in the popular (r = .13) and brain (r = .14) crowds but virtually uncorrelated (r's < .05) with other crowd scores. There were significant sex differences in scores for all crowds; girls had stronger associations than boys with the popular, brain, and normal crowds, but weaker associations with the jocks, druggies, and outcasts. Grade differences were significant for half of the crowds (jocks, brains, and outcasts), although there was no clear or consistent pattern to these differences. Being from an intact family seemed to enhance membership in the brain crowd and diminish membership in the druggie crowd. All crowd affiliation scores differed significantly by school, suggesting that there were substantial school- or community-based differences in the size of each crowd. Except for the absence of association between SES and druggie crowd scores, these demographic differences corresponded to ethnographers' observations about the crowds; ethnographers have portrayed the druggies as dominated by lower-class youth. Collectively, demographic variables accounted for between 7.3% and 13% of the variance in crowd affiliation scores (see Table 4). Because of these differences, we included demographic variables as control variables in all subsequent analyses.

Direct Associations between Parenting Practices and Crowd Affiliation

The first step in testing the conceptual model was to examine the direct effects of parenting practices on crowd affiliation. This was accomplished by regressing each crowd affiliation score on each parenting variable, after controlling for effects of the demographic variables noted above as well as the other two parenting variables. The paths in these analyses that were significant at p < .05 or better are reported in Figure 2. Parental emphasis on achievement was positively associated with membership in the popular, jock, and normal crowds and negatively associated with membership in the druggies. Parent monitoring was positively associated with membership in the brain crowd and negatively associated with membership in the druggies. Joint decision making was positively associated with membership in the brains and normals and negatively associated with membership in the druggies. There were no significant paths between parenting variables and membership in the outcast crowd.

Adolescent Behaviors as Mediating Variables

The next step in testing the conceptual model was to determine if the effects of par-

TABLE 2

Means, Standard Deviations, and Intercorrelations of Parenting and Psychosocial Adjustment Variables

			Intercorrelations				
Variable	Mean	SD	PEA	Mon	JDM	GPA	Drug Use
Parental emphasis on achievement (PEA) ..	3.12	.80					
Monitoring (Mon)	2.31	.49	.33*				
Joint decision making (JDM)	.49	.25	.34*	.36*			
GPA	2.76	.85	.26*	.17*	.17*		
Drug use	1.54	.72	−.12*	−.27*	−.20*	−.27*	
Self-reliance	3.04	.53	.13*	.10	.02	.19*	−.07*

* $p < .001$.

TABLE 3

DEMOGRAPHIC DIFFERENCES IN MEAN CROWD AFFILIATION SCORES

DEMOGRAPHIC GROUP	CROWD AFFILIATION SCORE					
	Popular	Jock	Brain	Normal	Druggie	Outcast
Sex:						
Male	.08	.09	.08	.16	.07	.22
Female	.16	.03	.10	.21	.05	.15
Grade level:						
Freshmen	.12	.05	.07	.19	.06	.22
Sophomores	.12	.07	.10	.19	.06	.15
Juniors	.11	.06	.09	.21	.07	.17
Seniors	.14	.06	.10	.19	.04	.18
Family structure:						
Intact	.12	.07	.10	.20	.05	.19
Single parent	.11	.06	.08	.18	.07	.18
Step-parent	.14	.04	.06	.19	.09	.16
Other	.10	.04	.06	.16	.10	.16
Ethnicity:						
African-American	.09	.08	.05	.19	.00	.11
Euro-American	.14	.06	.09	.20	.09	.14
Asian-American	.10	.03	.18	.13	.02	.21
Hispanic	.07	.04	.05	.18	.02	.12
School:						
A	.11	.10	.13	.24	.06	.13
B	.22	.10	.09	.12	.05	.22
C	.11	.06	.06	.25	.06	.14
D	.06	.06	.05	.19	.06	.19
E	.09	.02	.10	.16	.06	.13
F	.14	.05	.10	.18	.06	.23

NOTE.—Scores for each variable are adjusted for the effects of all other variables plus socioeconomic status. Schools are listed in the order in which they are described in the Method section. Students who did not belong to any of the four ethnic comparison groups were omitted from these analyses. Further details of the analyses are available from the first author.

enting practices on crowd affiliation were mediated by adolescent behaviors. Of the nine initially significant paths between parenting practices and crowd affiliation (Fig. 2), five were reduced to nonsignificance, three were reduced substantially in magnitude, and only one (the association between parental emphasis on achievement and membership in the jock crowd) remained significant at an equivalent level of magnitude when adolescent behaviors were included in the regression analyses (see Fig. 3). Thus, as expected, the effects of parenting practices were largely mediated by adolescent behaviors.

Collectively, parenting practices and adolescent behaviors accounted for between

TABLE 4

PROPORTION OF VARIANCE IN CROWD AFFILIATION SCORES ACCOUNTED FOR BY BACKGROUND VARIABLES, PARENTING PRACTICES, AND ADOLESCENT BEHAVIORS

Crowd	Background Variables	Parenting Practices (PP)	PP + Adolescent Behaviors	Total
Populars	.129	.009	.033	.162
Jocks	.073	.013	.016	.089
Brains	.088	.010	.139	.227
Normals	.070	.004	.007	.077
Druggies	.053	.026	.175	.230
Outcasts	.087	.001	.023	.111

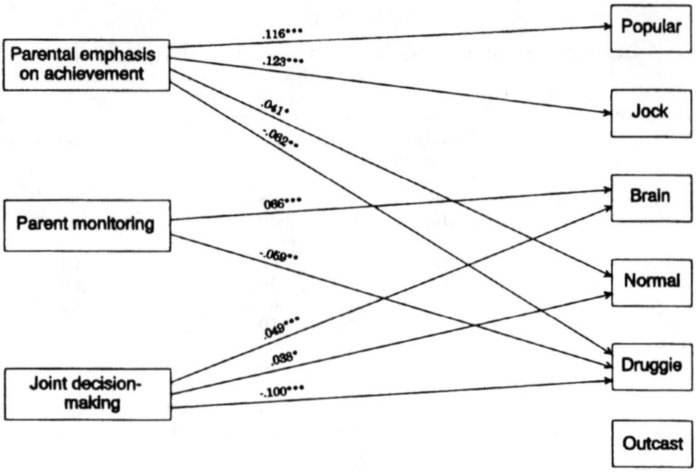

FIG. 2.—Observed direct associations between parenting practices and crowd affiliation. Standardized betas are shown for all paths significant at at least the .05 level. *$p < .05$; **$p < .01$; ***$p < .001$.

2% and 15% of the variance in crowd affiliation scores. Except for the jock and normal scores, this was a notable improvement over the initial regression analyses assessing the direct effects of parenting practices on crowd affiliation (see Table 4).

To further establish the mediating role of adolescent behaviors in our model, we examined the associations between parenting practices and adolescent behaviors and between adolescent behaviors and crowd affiliation. Results of these analyses are depicted in Figure 3, which shows all paths that were significant at $p < .05$ or better.

First, to assess the direct, independent effect of each parenting practice on each adolescent behavior, the score for each of the three adolescent behavior variables was re-

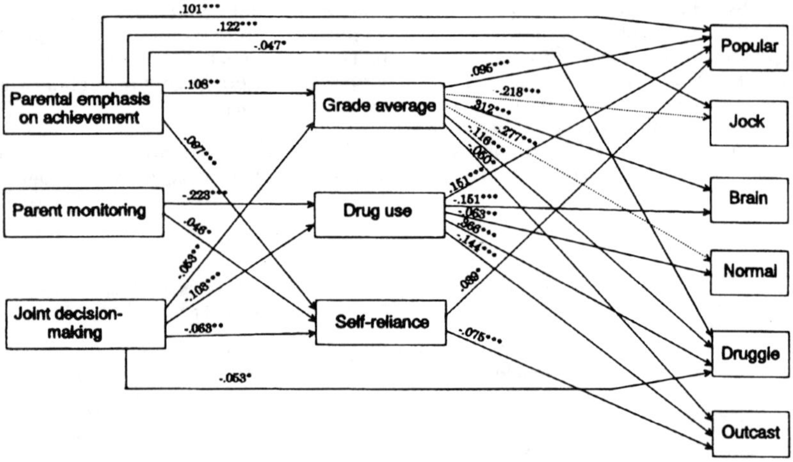

FIG. 3.—Observed associations between parenting practices, adolescent behaviors, and crowd affiliation. Standardized betas are shown for all paths significant at at least the .05 level. Dotted lines indicate curvilinear effects. *$p < .05$; **$p < .01$; ***$p < .001$.

gressed, in turn, on scores on the other two variables and the parenting measures (as well as demographic control variables). Parental emphasis on achievement was positively related to adolescents' reports of their self-reliance and grade-point average. Parental monitoring was inversely associated with drug use and directly associated with self-reliance. Also, higher rates of joint decision making were predictive of higher student grade-point averages and lower levels of drug use and self-reliance. These findings were consistent with results of previous studies except for (*a*) the tendency of joint decision making to depress, rather than enhance, self-reliance, and (*b*) the absence of a significant association between parent monitoring and student achievement.

Finally, regression analyses examined the relation between adolescent behaviors and peer crowd affiliation. In most cases, previous studies have suggested that crowd affiliation is directly enhanced or diminished by the behaviors we considered. In a few instances, however, the relation has been depicted as curvilinear, that is, jocks and normals have been depicted as moderate academic achievers, and brains and normals have been portrayed as harboring moderate levels of self-esteem or self-reliance. For these four instances, we tested for possible curvilinear as well as linear effects in the regression analyses. With few exceptions, the significant paths for these analyses, shown in Figure 3, confirmed the behavioral profiles of crowds that had been observed in previous studies. Membership in the popular crowd was predicted by high scores on all three behaviors, whereas membership in the outcasts was predicted by relatively *low* scores on these behaviors (the tendency for outcasts to have low GPAs was unexpected). Membership in the brains was related to high grades and low drug use but not to self-reliance (a curvilinear effect had been predicted). Membership in the druggies was associated with low grades and high drug use; the expected positive association with self-reliance was not significant. Academic achievement was the only behavior that predicted membership in the jock crowd; as expected, the relation was curvilinear. And as expected, drug use discouraged membership in the normals, whereas moderate GPA levels enhanced it, but the expected curvilinear association with self-reliance was not significant for this crowd. Each crowd affiliation score had a unique pattern of association with the adolescent behavior measures, which served to confirm ethnographers' observations that each crowd features a distinctive life-style.

Summary

Collectively, these analyses provided clear evidence of the mediating role that adolescent behaviors play between parenting practices and adolescent crowd affiliation. Parenting practices had a significant impact on adolescent behaviors, which in turn were significantly associated with crowd affiliation, such that each crowd score had a unique profile on these three behavioral measures. Even with the inclusion of adolescent behaviors as mediating variables, however, some direct associations between parenting behaviors and crowd affiliation scores remained significant.

Crowd affiliation scores also were modestly associated with adolescents' background characteristics, some of which (SES, family structure) reflected features of their family background. The ability of these three sets of variables—parenting practices, adolescent behaviors, and background characteristics—to account for variance in crowd affiliation scores differed considerably among the crowds. In most cases, the direct and indirect effects of parenting practices superseded the effects of background characteristics, but in all cases these variables explained a relatively modest proportion of variance in crowd affiliation scores.

Discussion

Researchers have clearly documented the powerful role parents play prior to adolescence in shaping children's social skills and directing their relationships with peers (Ladd, Muth, & Hart, in press; Parke & Bhavnagri, 1989; Putallaz, 1987); studies of how parental influences in this area continue through adolescence are much less extensive. By linking two sets of findings that have been pursued rather independently—examining the influence of parenting practices on adolescent behavior patterns, and showing how these behaviors differentiate members of various adolescent crowds—the study joins a number of investigations demonstrating that although parental influence over peer associations may diminish in adolescence, it is far from inconsequential.

Investigators have acknowledged that parents retain some control over their adolescent child's choice of peer associates through their selection of the neighborhood in which the family lives or the schools, churches, and community organizations in which family members participate (Rubin & Sloman, 1984). Our study confirmed this in the substantial differences among schools in the size of various crowds. In this respect, our findings relate to the "community studies" of several decades ago, in which the authors contended that the high school peer group system reflected characteristics of the community in which it was located (Coleman, 1961; Hollingshead, 1949; Lynd & Lynd, 1957). Often, however, these studies asserted that peer group membership was primarily a function of socioeconomic divisions within the community, whereas in our study socioeconomic status was a relatively poor predictor of crowd affiliation—and community (school) differences in crowd affiliation scores remained highly significant after controlling for students' socioeconomic background. These school-based differences remind us of the limitations of generalizing characteristics of the adolescent peer group system across contexts. They also underscore the need to consider contextual features when examining such questions as how parents influence teenagers' peer group affiliations. Parents' efforts to direct a child toward an athletically oriented crowd, for example, may be fruitless if such a crowd is virtually nonexistent—as appeared to be the case in school E (see Table 3).

Although ethnographers have emphasized family socioeconomic status as an important factor in adolescents' peer group affiliations (Eckert, 1989; Hollingshead, 1949; Larkin, 1979), we found other family background characteristics—family structure and ethnicity—to be more salient. Students from intact families appeared to be overrepresented among the brains and underrepresented among druggies, which was precisely the opposite pattern of students from stepparent families, who were also underrepresented in the jock crowd. It may be that the hostility that many teenagers harbor toward a stepparent (Fine, 1986) "spills over" to their relationship with school adults, thus constraining their ability to thrive in peer groups (such as jocks and brains) that feature close relationships with school staff.

The predominance of European-Americans in the druggie crowd was consistent with research evidence indicating that European-American teenagers are more involved in drug use than adolescents from other ethnic groups (McCord, 1990). In other respects, ethnic differences in crowd affiliation scores paralleled stereotypic orientations of ethnic groups: European-Americans were overrepresented among the high-status, popular crowd; Asian-Americans were overrepresented among brains; and African-American students were overrepresented in the jock crowd. Whether or not these patterns reflected ethnic differences in parental expectations or family reward structures is an important area for further research.

Family structural characteristics such as socioeconomic status, ethnic background, and marital arrangements reflect one important way in which parents retain some influence over teenagers' peer group associations, but our model was concerned primarily with process characteristics, namely, parenting practices. Our confidence in the causal relationships specified in the model are tempered by the fact that the findings are not based on longitudinal data. Hays and Revetto (1990) demonstrated that several causal arrangements can be supported in correlational data such as ours. There is, however, a growing body of research evidence, including some longitudinal work, that supports the causal arrangement of variables specified in our model. Feldman and Wentzel (1990) found that harsh discipline strategies affected early adolescent boys' sociometric status indirectly, through the boys' capacity to inhibit aggressive behavior. Whitbeck, Simons, Conger, and Lorenz (1989) found that parental values influenced the values of their teenage offspring, which, in turn, were significantly related to the teenagers' associations with deviant peers. Working with younger age groups (fourth through seventh graders), Dishion (1990; Dishion, Patterson, Stoolmiller, & Skinner, 1991) has reported both correlational and longitudinal evidence that parenting strategies (discipline and monitoring) predict child behaviors (academic performance and deviant activity), which in turn affect patterns of peer associations (sociometric status and involvement with deviant peers). Our causal ordering is also consistent with other longitudinal evidence that deviant behavior predicts association with deviant peers rather than the reverse (Magnusson, 1988).

This model contrasts sharply with ones proposing that parenting strategies affect peer group affiliations directly (Elliott et al., 1985; Kandel & Andrews, 1987). The consequences of these different perspectives are well illustrated by our findings with reference to the popular crowd. Had we applied a "direct effects" perspective to our data we might have argued that parents may "nudge" their child toward the popular crowd by encouraging academic achievement, a behavior further enhanced by popular crowd norms (considering the relatively high achievement levels of this crowd). Yet, in view of the absence of direct paths between other parenting behaviors and popular crowd affiliation, we probably would have concluded that peer group norms, rather than parenting behaviors, must be responsible for populars' propensity to engage in drug use. By contrast, our "mediated model" suggests that parents have a hand in shaping both the prosocial and antisocial behavior patterns that characterize the popular crowd. Parental emphasis on achievement inspires higher academic performance, which fosters association with the populars. Yet, when the emphasis on achievement is accompanied by efforts to monitor the child's behavior, the child is oriented more toward the brain crowd, whereas when parents fail to monitor the child and do not encourage joint decision making, the child is more likely to become associated with the popular crowd, whose desirable behaviors (academic achievement) are accompanied by undesirable ones (drug use).

In fact, our model proposes that peer groups are unlikely to countermand parental influences—for example, to lead an adolescent into deviant activities despite parents' efforts to orient the child toward prosocial values and behaviors. Instead, peer group norms serve primarily to reinforce behaviors and predispositions to which parents (through parenting strategies and/or family background characteristics) have already contributed. Although this contrasts with some traditional perspectives on deviance (Sutherland & Cressey, 1978), it is consistent with some more recent work in this area (e.g., Dishion et al., 1991; Snyder, Dishion, & Patterson, 1986). Of course, support for these suppositions awaits longitudinal data that examine the full conceptual model displayed in Figure 1, including the "feedback" loop of crowd norms and peer pressures. This study was simply a modest first step in this process, but the findings should encourage researchers to pursue the full model in earnest.

The findings make explicit what remains implicit in much of the research on deviant behavior: that whereas inadequate or undesirable parenting practices may contribute to the child's involvement in deviant peer groups and deviant activities, positive parenting fosters desirable behavior patterns and association with prosocial peer groups. Yet, in view of the amount of variance in crowd affiliation scores accounted for by our parenting variables, it may appear as if parents exert some modest influence over their child's associations with brains or druggies, but that otherwise parental influences on crowd affiliation are trivial. It may well be that parents have an impact on adolescents' affiliations with certain crowds more so than others, but, for several reasons, conclusions about the magnitude of parental influences seem premature. First, a skewed distribution of scores on outcome measures (as was the case here) typically depresses the amount of variance accounted for, so that parenting effects may be underestimated in our results. Second, adolescent crowds are differentiated on a much wider range of behaviors, which in turn are likely to be affected by a much broader array of parenting practices, than were examined in this study. Indeed, the variables we examined seem highly salient for the brains (academic performance, parental emphasis on achievement) and druggies (drug use, parental monitoring), which probably accounts for the fact that we explained more of the variance in scores for these crowds than other crowds.

Most important, our study was confined to measures of parenting practices and children's behavior in adolescence, whereas it is likely that parental influences on adolescent crowd affiliation operate on a more extended developmental timetable. Cairns et al. (1988) have shown that parenting characteristics contribute to the division of youngsters by middle childhood into clusters of deviant and nondeviant peers, which may be the forerunners of prosocial (e.g., brains, jocks) and antisocial (e.g., druggies) crowds in adolescence. Thus, a teenager's crowd affiliation may be influenced by parenting behaviors many years prior to adolescence. Snyder et al. (1986) found evidence that associations with deviant peers in adolescence seemed to be the result of a series of events across childhood and early adolescence. What is more, the parenting behaviors that contributed to this chain of events changed with age: in childhood, parents' effectiveness in teaching social skills and disciplining antisocial behavior were key factors; by early adolescence, parental monitoring of the child's behavior was more salient. In other words, our data did not consider the cumulative or lagged effects of parenting behaviors prior to adolescence, which may have as much if not more impact (as parenting practices in adolescence) on nurturing behaviors that help direct teenagers to particular peer groups. Researchers must now turn attention to the task of tracing the linkages between parents' efforts to monitor peer associates and foster social skills in childhood, the formation and metamorphosis of preadolescent cliques, and the emergence of adolescent peer groups and processes whereby teenagers become associated with a particular crowd.

There may be other facets of teenage peer relations in which parental influences operate rather directly, but as for adolescents' crowd affiliations, the results of this study suggest that parental influences are largely indirect, through their impact on behaviors by which teenagers become associated with a particular crowd. What is more, parents have the capacity to direct their child toward an essentially prosocial crowd (such as the brains) or an antisocial crowd (such as the druggies) or a peer group with mixed characteristics (such as populars or outcasts). To be sure, parenting practices and family background characteristics cannot *determine* a teenager's crowd affiliation, but their influence should not be discounted. In view of this, researchers are encouraged to pay more attention to the *joint* influences of parents and peers on adolescent behavior.

References

Baron, R. M., & Kenny, D. A. (1986). The moderator-mediator variable distinction in social psychological research: Conceptual, strategic, and statistical considerations. *Journal of Personality and Social Psychology*, **51**, 1173–1182.

Baumrind, D. (1991a). Parenting styles and adolescent development. In R. M. Lerner, A. C. Petersen, & J. Brooks-Gunn (Eds.), *Encyclopedia of adolescence* (Vol. **2**, pp. 746–758). New York: Garland.

Baumrind, D. (1991b). The influence of parenting style on adolescent competence and substance use. *Journal of Early Adolescence*, **11**, 56–95.

Berndt. T. J. (1979). Developmental changes in conformity to peers and parents. *Developmental Psychology*, **15**, 606–616.

Bowerman, C. E., & Kinch, J. W. (1959). Changes in family and peer orientation between the 4th and 10th grades. *Social Forces*, **37**, 206–211.

Brittain, C. V. (1963). Adolescent choices and parent-peer cross-pressures. *American Sociological Review*, **28**, 385–391.

Bronfenbrenner, U. (1991, April). Discussant's commentary. In S. Lamborn (Chair), *Authoritative parenting and adolescent development*. Symposium presented at the biennial meetings of the Society for Research in Child Development, Seattle.

Brown, B. B. (1989). *Social Type Rating Manual*. Madison: National Center on Effective Secondary Schools, University of Wisconsin—Madison.

Brown, B. B. (1990). Peer groups and peer cultures. In S. S. Feldman & G. R. Elliott (Eds.), *At the threshold: The developing adolescent* (pp. 171–196). Cambridge, MA: Harvard University Press.

Brown, B. B., Lohr, M. J., & Trujillo, C. (1990). Multiple crowds and multiple life-styles: Adolescents' perceptions of peer group stereotypes. In R. E. Muuss (Ed.), *Adolescent behavior and society*, 4th ed. (pp. 30–36). New York: McGraw-Hill.

Brown, B. B., Mory, M., & Kinney, D. (in press). Casting adolescent crowds in a relational perspective: Caricature, channel, and context. In R. Montemayor, G. R. Adams, & T. P. Gullotta (Eds.), *Advances in adolescent development: Vol.* **6**. *Personal relationships during adolescence*. Newbury Park, CA: Sage.

Buff, S. A. (1970). Greasers, dupers, and hippies: Three responses to the adult world. In L. Howe (Ed.), *The white majority* (pp. 60–77). New York: Random House.

Cairns, R. B., Cairns, B. D., Neckerman, H. J., Gest, S. D., & Gariepy, J.-L. (1988). Social networks and aggressive behavior: Peer support or peer rejection? *Developmental Psychology*, **24**, 815–823.

Clasen, D. R., & Brown, B. B. (1985). The multidimensionality of peer pressure in adolescence. *Journal of Youth and Adolescence*, **14**, 451–468.

Coleman, J. S. (1961). *The adolescent society*. New York: Free Press.

Coombs, R. H., & Landsverk, J. (1988). Parenting styles and substance use during childhood and adolescence. *Journal of Marriage and the Family*, **50**, 473–482.

Dishion, T. J. (1990). The peer context of troublesome child and adolescent behavior. In P. E. Leone (Ed.), *Understanding troubled and troubling youth* (pp. 128–153). Newbury Park, CA: Sage.

Dishion, T. J., Patterson, G. R., Stoolmiller, M., & Skinner, M. L. (1991). Family, school, and behavioral antecedents of early adolescent involvement with antisocial peers. *Developmental Psychology*, **27**, 172–180.

Donovan, J., & Jessor, R. (1985). Structure of problem behavior in adolescence and young adulthood. *Journal of Consulting and Clinical Psychology*, **53**, 890–904.

Dornbusch, S. M., Carlsmith, J. M., Bushwall, P.

L., Ritter, P. L., Leiderman, P. H., Hastorf, A. H., & Gross, R. T. (1985). Single parents, extended households, and the control of adolescents. *Child Development*, **56**, 326–341.

Dornbusch, S. M., & Ritter, P. L. (1991, April). *Family decision-making and authoritative parenting*. Paper presented at the biennial meetings of the Society for Research in Child Development, Seattle.

Dornbusch, S. M., Ritter, P. L., Leiderman, P. H., Roberts, D. F., & Fraleigh, M. J. (1987). The relation of parenting style to adolescent school performance. *Child Development*, **58**, 1244–1257.

Eckert, P. (1989). *Jocks and burnouts: Social categories and identity in the high school*. New York: Teachers College Press.

Eder, D. (1985). The cycle of popularity: Interpersonal relations among female adolescence. *Sociology of Education*, **58**, 154–165.

Elliott, D. S., Huisinga, D., & Ageton, S. S. (1985). *Explaining delinquency and drug use*. Beverly Hills, CA: Sage.

Featherman, D. L. (1980). Schooling and occupational careers: Constancy and change in worldly success. In O. Brim & J. Kagan (Eds.), *Constancy and change in human development* (pp. 675–738). Cambridge, MA: Harvard University Press.

Feldman, S. S., & Wentzel, K. R. (1990). The relationship between parenting styles, son's self-restraint, and peer relations in early adolescence. *Journal of Early Adolescence*, **10**, 439–454.

Fine, M. (1986). Perceptions of stepparents: Variation in stereotypes as a function of current family structure. *Journal of Marriage and the Family*, **48**, 537–543.

Floyd, H. H., & South, D. R. (1972). Dilemma of youth: The choice of parents or peers as a frame of reference for behavior. *Journal of Marriage and the Family*, **34**, 627–634.

Gecas, V., & Seff, M. A. (1990). Families and adolescents: A review of the 1980s. *Journal of Marriage and the Family*, **52**, 941–958.

Glynn, T. J. (1984). Adolescent drug use and the family environment: A review. *Journal of Drug Issues*, **14**, 271–295.

Greenberger, E., Josselson, R., Knerr, C., & Knerr, B. (1974). The measurement and structure of psychosocial maturity. *Journal of Youth and Adolescence*, **4**, 127–143.

Grotevant, H., & Cooper, C. R. (1986). Individuation in family relationships: A perspective on individual differences in the development of identity and role-taking skill in adolescence. *Human Development*, **29**, 82–100.

Hauser, S. T., Powers, S., Noam, G., Jacobsen, A., Weiss, B., & Follansbee, D. (1984). Familial contexts of adolescent ego development. *Child Development*, **55**, 195–213.

Hays, R. D., & Revetto, J. P. (1990). Peer cluster theory and adolescent drug use: A reanalysis. *Journal of Drug Education*, **20**, 191–198.

Hollingshead, A. B. (1949). *Elmtown's youth: The impact of social class on adolescents*. New York: Wiley.

Kandel, D. B., & Andrews, K. (1987). Processes of adolescent socialization by parents and peers. *International Journal of the Addictions*, **22**, 319–342.

Ladd, G. W., Muth, S., & Hart, C. H. (in press). Parents' management of children's peer relations: Facilitating and supervising children's activities in the peer culture. In R. D. Parke & G. W. Ladd (Eds.), *Family-peer relations: Modes of linkage*. Hillsdale, NJ: Erlbaum.

Larkin, R. W. (1979). *Suburban youth in cultural crisis*. New York: Oxford.

Loeber, R., & Dishion, T. J. (1983). Early predictors of male adolescent delinquency: A review. *Psychological Bulletin*, **94**, 68–99.

Lynd, R. S., & Lynd, H. M. (1957). *Middletown: A study in American culture*. New York: Harcourt, Brace, and World.

Magnusson, D. (1988). *Individual development from an interactional perspective*. Hillsdale, NJ: Erlbaum.

Marcos, A. C., Bahr, S. J., & Johnson, R. E. (1986). Test of a bonding/association theory of adolescent drug use. *Social Forces*, **65**, 135–161.

Massey, J. L., & Krohn, M. D. (1986). A longitudinal examination of an integrated social process model of deviant behavior. *Social Forces*, **65**, 106–134.

McCord, J. (1990). Problem behaviors. In S. S. Feldman & G. R. Elliott (Eds.), *At the threshold: The developing adolescent* (pp. 414–430). Cambridge, MA: Harvard University Press.

Needle, R., McCubbin, H., Lorence, J., & Hochhauser, M. (1983). Reliability and validity of adolescent self-reported drug use in a family-based study: A methodological report. *International Journal of the Addictions*, **18**, 901–912.

Oetting, E. R., & Beauvais, F. (1987). Peer cluster theory, socialization characteristics, and adolescent drug use: A path analysis. *Journal of Counseling Psychology*, **34**, 205–213.

O'Malley, P. M., Bachman, J. G., & Johnston, L. D. (1983). Reliability and consistency in self-reports of drug use. *International Journal of the Addictions*, **18**, 805–824.

Parke, R., & Bhavnagri, N. P. (1989). Parents as managers of children's peer relationships. In D. Belle (Ed.), *Children's social networks and social support* (pp. 241–259). New York: Wiley.

Parsons, T. (1942). Age and sex in the social structure of the United States. *American Sociological Review*, **7**, 604–616.

Patterson, G. R., & Stouthamer-Loeber, M. (1984). The correlation of family management practices and delinquency. *Child Development*, **55**, 1299–1307.

Polich, J. M. (1982). The validity of self-reports in alcoholism research. *Addictive Behaviors*, **7**, 123–132.

Poveda, T. G. (1975). Reputation and the adolescent girl: An analysis. *Adolescence*, **37**, 127–136.

Putallaz, M. (1987). Maternal behavior and children's sociometric status. *Child Development*, **58**, 324–340.

Riesman, D. (1961). *The lonely crowd*. New Haven, CT: Yale University Press.

Rubin, Z., & Sloman, J. (1984). How parents influence their children's friendships. In M. Lewis (Ed.), *Beyond the dyad* (pp. 115–140). New York: Plenum.

Schwendinger, H., & Schwendinger, J. S. (1985). *Adolescent subcultures and delinquency*. New York: Praeger.

Seginer, R. (1983). Parents' educational expectations and children's academic achievements: A literature review. *Merrill-Palmer Quarterly*, **29**, 1–23.

Snyder, J., Dishion, T. J., & Patterson, G. R. (1986). Determinants and consequences of associating with deviant peers during preadolescence and adolescence. *Journal of Early Adolescence*, **6**, 20–34.

Steinberg, L. (1987). Single parents, step-parents, and the susceptibility of adolescents to antisocial peer pressure. *Child Development*, **57**, 269–275.

Sutherland, E. W., & Cressey, D. R. (1978). *Criminology* (10th ed.). Philadelphia: Lippincott.

Terry, R., & Coie, J. D. (1991). A comparison of methods for defining sociometric status among children. *Developmental Psychology*, **27**, 867–880.

Whitbeck, L. B., Simons, R. L., Conger, R. D., & Lorenz, F. O. (1989). Value socialization and peer group affiliation among early adolescents. *Journal of Early Adolescence*, **9**, 436–453.

Yee, D. K., & Flanagan, C. (1985). Family environments and self-consciousness in early adolescence. *Journal of Early Adolescence*, **5**, 59–68.

American Journal of Community Psychology, Vol. 20, No. 6, 1992

Brief Reports

Life Stress, Social Support, and Locus of Control During Early Adolescence: Interactive Effects[1]

Ana Mari Cauce[2]
University of Washington

Keith Hannan
Auburn University

Marion Sargeant
University of Delaware

Examined the relationships between negative events, locus of control, social support, and psychological adjustment in an early adolescent sample. Of interest were the potential stress-buffering effects of social support and the conjunctive effects of social support and locus of control upon adjustment. Family support was positively related to adjustment in several domains, whereas school support was only related to school competence. Peer support was positively related to peer competence and anxiety, and negatively related to school competence. Examination of the buffering hypothesis suggested that both family and school support served to moderate the relationship between negative events and school competence. Conjunctive effects were also detected in that school support buffered number of negative events best for those individuals with an internal locus of control for successes.

After infancy, the preadolescent through early adolescent years are characterized as the period of most rapid biological, cognitive, and social growth

[1]We thank the three anonymous reviewers for their help in fine-tuning this manuscript.
[2]All correspondence should be sent to Ana Mari Cauce. Department of Psychology, NI-25, University of Washington, Seattle, Washington 98195.

0091-0562/92/1200-0787$06.50/0

(Lipsitz, 1972). In light of this, it is not surprising that Coddington's normative studies (1972a, 1972b) found that life stress increased with age throughout childhood, peaking most dramatically between the ages of 12 to 14. Yet, research addressing the effects of stressful life events before college age is rare and most of this has focused on either latency-aged children or older adolescents (Swearingen & Cohen, 1985b). The purpose of the present study was to better determine the relationship between stressful life events and psychological adjustment during early adolescence with a specific emphasis on the examination of the conjunctive effects of social support and locus of control as moderators of this relationship. A secondary goal was to explore whether such moderating relationships are, in part, dependent upon a "match" between the social and personal resources proposed as moderators and the specific aspect of adjustment examined.

Relatively few studies have examined the relationship between social support or locus of control and adjustment in child or adolescent populations, fewer still have explored the role of social support or locus of control as a stress buffer, and none have examined the role of locus of control in conjunction with social support. Those studies that have been conducted suggest that social support is positively related to adjustment and serves to buffer life stress (Dubow & Tisak, 1989; Sandler, Miller, Short, & Wolchik, 1989: Wolchik, Ruehlman, Braver, & Sandler, 1989), although some notable exceptions exist, especially when peer support is specifically examined (cf. Cauce, Felner, & Primavera, 1982; Wolchik et al., 1989). An internal locus of control has also been found to be positively related to adjustment and there is some support for its effects as a stress buffer (Findley & Cooper, 1983; Siddique & D'Arcy, 1984; Wiegel, Wertlieb, & Feldstein, 1989). However, while such results are promising, the magnitude of relationships reported have been disappointingly small, leading some researchers to believe that it may be a combination of such factors that is most important.

According to Roos and Cohen (1987), "One glaring weakness in the empirical literature is the relative failure to include both social support and personality variables in a model of life stress adjustment" (p. 576). They noted that recent theory and research suggests that it is the interaction between personal and environmental characteristics that may best explain an individual's reaction to negative life events. For example, individuals may not be able to effectively take advantage of social support while experiencing a stressful event unless they are personally disposed to view such events as controllable. Vinokur and Seltzer (1975) have suggested that people with an internal locus of control are less apt to accept negative events as factors outside of their control. As such, they are more likely to take action and utilize their supportive networks to alleviate such stressors. Indeed, those studies within the adult literature that have examined the interactive effects of social support and a personality factor have generally focused on variables that indicate instrumentality, such as locus of control, hardiness, and masculinity. Such studies have suggested that social support most effectively buffers the effects of life stress for individuals with an instrumental disposition (Kobasa, Maddi, & Courington, 1981; Roos & Cohen, 1987; Smith, Smoll, & Ptacek, 1989).

Alternatively, others have suggested that stress-buffering effects occur only when the personality style is appropriately matched to the type of stress or area of adjustment examined (S. Cohen & Edwards, 1989; Swindle, Heller, & Lakey, 1988). For example, S. Cohen and Edwards (1989) stated that elevated "(locus of) control in a specific domain (e.g., academics) is more likely to operate as a buffer in that domain" (p. 239). In a similar vein, it has been suggested that school personnel and peers may serve as support specialists, although family members have been considered support "generalists" (Bogat, Caldwell, Rogosch, & Kreigler, 1985). This schema received some support in terms of a simple effects model in childhood (Cauce, Reid, Landesman, & Gonzales, 1990), but has yet to be examined in a stress-buffering paradigm or during adolescence.

Given the lack of well-established relationships between social support, locus of control, life stress, and adjustment in this age group, we examined the simple relationships between these variables and adjustment in addition to stress-buffering and conjunctive effects. In line with previous research, we expected social support and a more internal locus of control to be positively related to adjustment and negative events to be negatively related to adjustment. We also expected social support to buffer the effects of negative life events. Drawing from the adult literature, we expected the buffering effects of social support to be strongest for those individuals with an internal locus of control. If simple or moderating effects exist predominantly within similar domains (e.g., school support serves as a buffer for school competence but not peer competence) support for the matching model will be attained.

In the examination of the interaction between life stress and social support, distinctions have been made between moderator and mediator variables. A variable can be said to function as a moderator if it either affects the direction *or* strength of the relationship between a simple predictor and the criterion (Baron & Kenny, 1986). Buffering effects refer to a specific pattern of moderation. In this study we conclude that buffering effects exist only if (a) the interaction between social support and negative events significantly increases the amount of variance accounted for in measures of adjustment *and* (b) the form of the relationship is such that the slope of the regression of adjustment on stress is higher for adolescents with high support than it is for adolescents with lower levels of support.

More recently, a further distinction has been drawn between conjunctive and disjunctive effects when examining the role of personality and environmental variables and how they *jointly* affect the relationship between life stress and adjustment (see Smith et al., 1989). In the most simple case, conjunctive effects could be said to exist if the relationship between the hypothesized stress buffer (usually social support) and life events is most noteworthy when a third variable (in this case, locus of control) is taken into account. In this study we conclude that a conjunctive effect exists only if (a) the three-way interaction adds unique variance to the prediction of adjustment after all one- and two-way interactions have been controlled *and* (b) the form or pattern of the effect is such that social support evidences buffering effects more dramatically for individuals with a more internal locus of control.

METHOD

Participants and Procedures

Participants were drawn from a sample of all sixth and eighth graders in two private suburban schools in the Northeast. After obtaining informed consent from parents and adolescents, 120 students (48% female) comprised the final sample, which represented approximately 80% of the parents/students contacted. Students were predominantly middle to upper-middle class and white. Paper-and-pencil measures were administered to students in their school by a graduate and advanced undergraduate student trained in all procedures.

Measures

Life Stress. To measure recent (within the last 6 months) stressful life changes, the Junior High Life Experience Survey (JHLES; Swearingen & Cohen, 1985a) was administered. The JHLES is a 39-item self-report scale developed specifically for use with young adolescents and used in numerous studies with this age group. We used a simple count of negative events (unit scores) in our analyses, as Swearingen and Cohen (1985b) found this the most efficient scoring strategy for life stress.

Social Support. Participants completed a modified version of the Social Support Rating Scale (SSRS: Cauce, et al., 1982) which lists 13 potential sources of support. These sources fall into three main subscales established via factor analysis: peer support (which includes similar-aged friends), family support (including support from adult relatives like mother, father, and grandparents), and school support (which includes school personnel such as teachers and coaches). Students rated their perception of helpfulness of each support source on a 5-point scale and subscale scores were derived by summing across all providers within each support category.

Locus of Control. This construct was measured using the Intellectual Achievement Responsibility Scale (IAR; Crandall, Katovsky, & Crandall, 1965). The IAR is a 35-item measure in which students report whether a hypothetical success or failure situation was due to their own qualities or to some outside force. Sample items are: "Suppose you study to become a teacher, scientist, or doctor and you fail. Do you think this would happen — a. because you didn't work hard enough, or b. because you needed help and other people didn't give it to you" and "When you do well on a test at school, is it more likely to be — a. because you studied for it, or b. because the test was easy." The IAR yields separate locus of control indices for success situations (IAR+, the second sample) and failure situations (IAR–, first sample). All items relate to school or academic situations. Although our initial interest was in generalized beliefs about control contingencies, we chose this measure rather than a more Rotter-like scale because of its simple language and suitability for group administration to an early adolescent sample. It is unclear whether control beliefs about school situations should be related to other domains of adjustment, a question that is addressed by this study.

Psychological Adjustment. Two widely used self-report measures were administered to assess general psychological adjustment: the Perceived Social Competence Scale for Children (PCSC; Harter, 1982, now called the Self-Perception Profile for Children) and the State Anxiety Inventory for Children (SAI; Spielberger, 1973). The SAI contains 20 items and was employed as a measure of general negative affect since most studies do not indicate good discrimination between anxiety, depression, and other dysphoric states among normal populations of children and adolescents (Wolfe et al., 1987). The PCSC taps domain-specific areas of perceived competence and yield scores on four subscales: Perceived school competence, perceived peer competence, perceived physical competence, and perceived general competence. The general competence scale is similar to other general self-worth or self-esteem measures. Previous studies have suggested that both peer and school competence are related to peer measures of these constructs. School competence has been found to be highly related to both grades in school and to achievement test scores (Cauce, 1986).

RESULTS AND DISCUSSION

In the initial phase of analysis, we examined means and standard deviations for all measures and found that they were similar to those obtained in previous studies of normal young adolescents. The mean number of negative events reported was 3.33, with about 20% of the sample reporting 6 or more negative events within the last 6 months. We also examined the internal reliabilities of measures using Cronbach's alpha and found that they were all adequate, ranging from a low of .65 on locus of control for successes to .86 on family support. Sex and grade differences, along with their interaction, were also examined and few differences were obtained. Boys reported higher levels of physical competence, $t(120) = 7.56, p < .01$, than girls. Eighth-grade girls reported lower levels of general competence than sixth-grade girls, whereas eighth-grade boys reported higher levels of general competence than sixth-grade boys, $F = 5.33, p < .05$. These few differences are consistent with previous research in the area.

Correlations between predictor variables (e.g., negative events, social support, and locus of control) were next examined, since theory suggests that conjunctive effects are best detected when different classes of predictor variables are uncorrelated with each other. These analyses indicated that measures of locus of control were uncorrelated with measures of social support (*r*s ranged from –.10 to .06, all *p*s = ns) and that neither locus of control nor support measures were correlated with negative events (*r*s ranged from –.13 to .14, all *p*s = ns).

To examine the direct relationships between predictor variables and adjustment simple correlations were examined. These are reported in Table I. As this table indicates, negative events were significantly correlated with anxiety and school competence in the expected direction, suggesting that adolescents experiencing more negative events also report more anxiety and lower levels of school competence. Relationships between negative events and other types of competence were not significant.

Social support analyses also yielded a mixed pattern of results. In line with previous studies and the generalist notion, family support evidenced the most consistent and strongest relationships with adjustment, correlating significantly and in the expected direction with general, peer, and physical competence. In keeping with the specialist notion, school support was

Table I. Correlations Between Psychological Adjustment and Negative Events, Social Support, and Locus of Control

Variable[a]	Anxiety	Competence General	School	Peer	Physical
Negative events	.27[c]	–.13	–.26[b]	.00	.07
IAR+	–.15[b]	.20[b]	.23[c]	.05	.20[b]
IAR–	–.06	.01	.07	.04	–.08
Family support	–.05	.23[c]	.04	.32[c]	.23[c]
Peer support	.18[b]	–.08	–.21[b]	.19[b]	.08
School support	–.04	–.06	.17[b]	–.01	–.05

[a] IAR+ = Locus of Control for Successes, IAR– = Locus of Control for Failures.
[b] $p < .05$.
[c] $p < .01$.

found to correlate only with school competence. In this same vein, peer support was positively correlated with peer competence, but, it was also positively related to anxiety and negatively correlated with school competence. The direction of the relationships with school competence and anxiety, while opposite to those expected, are consistent with other studies that have found support from peers to have negative as well as positive relationships to adjustment (Cauce & Srebnik, 1989).

As expected, higher scores on the locus of control scale for success, which are indicative of a more internal locus of control, were related to more positive adjustment in terms of anxiety, and general, school, and physical competence. In contrast, locus of control for failures was unrelated to all measures of adjustment. Such findings suggest that whereas taking personal responsibility for successes is adaptive, taking personal responsibility for failures is not. This is consistent with suggestions that it is not helpful for children to make internal, stable, and global attributions about failure experiences (Cicchetti & Schneider-Rosen, 1984).

Stress-buffering and conjunctive effects were examined using hierarchical multiple regressions. In these regressions, the simple effects of all predictor variables were entered into the first step of the hierarchy. All two-way interactions were examined next (e.g., Negative Events × Family Support), followed by an examination of all three-way interactions (e.g., Negative Events × Family Support × Locus of Control for Successes). A full-model least-squares solution was adopted and effects are only presented and discussed when they contributed a significant amount of unique variance. That is, all effects were examined when entered in the *last* step of their respective hierarchy. In all regressions we included

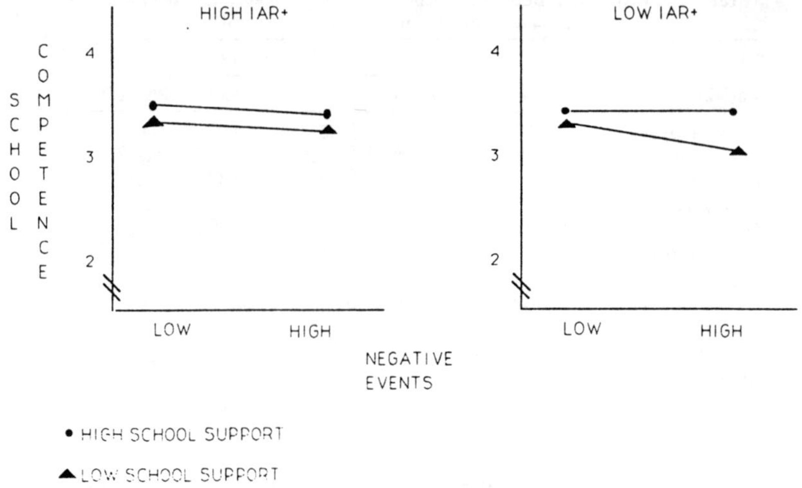

Fig. 1. Three-way interaction between negative events, locus of control for successes, and school competence.

a test of the parallelism of regression planes for gender and sex, but no significant effects were detected. As such, results presented are for the entire sample.

No significant two- or three-way interaction effects were evident in the analyses where peer competence, physical competence, global competence, or anxiety served as the criterion. When school competence was the criterion, two-way interactions between family support by negative events and school support by negative events both accounted for significant amounts of unique variance ($\Delta F = 4.24$, $\Delta r^2 = .14$, $p < .05$; $\Delta F = 5.29$, $\Delta r^2 = .13$, $p < .05$, respectively). The latter interaction was further qualified by a three-way interaction between negative events, school support, and locus of control for successes ($\Delta F = 4.91$, $\Delta r^2 = .09$, $p < .05$). As such, family and school support met the first criteria for a simple stress-buffering effect, and school support in combination with locus of control for successes met the first criteria for a conjunctive effect in that both contributed significantly and uniquely to school competence.

To determine whether they met the second criteria, which implies a particular "form" to the relationship, two- and three-way interactions were plotted by a technique suggested by Cohen and Cohen (1983) where separate equations are solved based on scores 1 standard deviation above and below the mean for predictor variables. Figure 1 illustrates the three-way interaction between school support, locus of control for success, and negative events. As this figure suggests, the form of the interaction is in keeping with the conjunctive hypothesis. The effects of school support as a stress buffer are most pronounced for adolescents with a more internal locus of control for success (e.g., high IAR+).

The two-way interaction between the family support and negative events was similar in form to the diagram on the right side of Fig. 1. In this case, the interaction was such that adolescents with higher levels of family support did not evidence lower school competence even when experiencing a relatively high number of negative events. Those with lesser family support did evidence lowered school competence when stress was high. As such, the form of the interaction was in keeping with the stress-buffering hypothesis.

CONCLUSIONS

As is so often the case in the life events and social support literature with children or adolescents, analyses suggested a somewhat mixed pattern of results and the magnitude of relationships found were modest, even when interactive effects were examined. Family support and internal locus of control for school successes came closest to demonstrating a generalized pattern of positive effects. Family support was correlated positively with general, peer, and physical competence and it also served to buffer the effects of negative events upon school competence. Locus of control for successes was positively related with general, school, and physical competence, and negatively related to anxiety. This is in stark contrast to the more domain-specific positive effects evidenced by school and peer support. Peer support was only positively related to peer competence, albeit negative relationships with adjustment, as noted previously, were also in evidence. School support was only related with school competence. It also buffered the effects of negative events upon school competence both directly and in conjunction with locus of control for successes, the only conjunctive effect detected.

The nature of this conjunctive effect further underscores the specificity of those relationships that were found. In this instance, *school* support was found to serve as a stress buffer upon school competence for adolescents with a more internal locus of control for school-related situations. This finding is similar to that of Sarason, Levine, Basham, and Sarason (1983) who, using an innovative laboratory design, found that college students with low perceived social support and an external locus of control performed most poorly (in terms of persistence and cognitive interference) on an insoluble problem. These studies in combination lend some credence to the oft-noted phenomenon observed by parents, teachers, and child clinicians, that concentration, and hence, school performance, is particularly sensitive to disturbances in the lives of children and adolescents. Indeed, impaired school performance is implicated in the early stages of various manifestations of childhood maladjustment, including depression, conduct disorders, and antisocial aggression (Achenbach, 1982). The fact that school support may be beneficial in buffering the negative effects of life stress upon school competence, whether alone or in conjunction with locus of control, should also encourage those working on prevention programs that mobilize school personnel as sources of support for children in stress.

In sum, this study provides some support for models suggesting that social support is most effective in buffering stress in conjunction with an instrumental personality style. Some support was also provided for models stressing that there should be a match between resources and areas of adjustment examined. Yet, conclusions are limited by the less than consistent pattern of results, by the self-report and cross-sectional nature of all the data, and by the homogeneous nature of the population. More conclusive evidence awaits replication, especially from studies using prospective designs and measurements of various aspects of adjustment from multiple perspectives (e.g., parent, peer, or teacher reports in addition to self-report) on at least two points in time. In addition, a better test of the matching hypothesis could be achieved by utilizing measures of different types of stress and a more varied array of personal resources.

It is clear that social support is not the elixir that cures all that ails you, whether alone or in combination with other potent potables. What we still need is a better understanding of what types of support, in combination with which personal resources, affect what types of stress upon which aspects of adjustment.

REFERENCES

Achenbach, T. M. (1982). *Developmental psychopathology (2nd ed.).* New York: Wiley.

Baron. R. M., & Kenny, D. A. (1986). The moderator—mediator variable distinction in social psychological research: Conceptual, strategic, and statistical considerations. *Journal of Personality and Social Psychology, 51,* 1173-1182.

Bogat, G. A., Caldwell. R. A., Rogosch. F., & Kriegler, J. A. (1985). Differentiating specialists and generalists within college students' social support networks. *Journal of Youth and Adolescence, 14,* 23-35.

Cauce, A. M., Felner, R. D., & Primavera, J. (1982). Social support in high-risk adolescents. *American Journal of Community Psychology, 10,* 417-428.

Cauce, A. M., Reid, M., Landesman, S., & Gonzales, N. (1990). Social support in young children: Measurement, structure, and behavioral impact. In B. Sarason, I. Sarason, & G. Pierce (Eds.), *Social support: An interactional view.* New York: Wiley.

Cauce, A. M., & Srebnik, D. (1989). Peer networks and social support: A focus for preventive efforts with youth. In L. Bond & B. Compas (Eds.), *Primary prevention in the schools.* New York: Sage.

Cichetti, D., & Schneider-Rosen, K. (1984). An organizational approach to childhood depression. In M. Rutter, C. Izard, & P. Read (Eds.), *Depression in children: Developmental perspectives.* New York: Guilford.

Coddington, R. D. (1972a). The significance of life events as etiologic factors in the diseases of children I. *Journal of Psychosomatic Research, 16,* 7-18.

Coddington, R. D. (1972b). The significance of life events as etiologic factors in the diseases of children II. *Journal of Psychosomatic Research, 16,* 205-213.

Cohen, J., & Cohen, P. (1983). *Applied multiple regression/correlation analysis for the behavior sciences (2nd ed.).* Hillsdale, NJ: Erlbaum.

Cohen, S., & Edwards, J. R. (1989) Personality characteristics as moderators of the relationship between stress and disorder. In R. W. J. Neufeld (Ed.), *Advances in the investigation of psychological stress.* New York: Wiley.

Crandall, V. C., Katkowsky, W., & Crandall, V. J. (1965). Children's belief in their own control of reinforcements in intellectual-academic achievement situations. *Child Development, 36,* 91-109.

Dubow, E. F., & Tisak, J. (1989). The relation between stressful life events and adjustment in elementary school children: The role of social support and social problem solving skills. *Child Development, 60,* 1412-1423.

Findley, M., & Cooper, H. M. (1983). Locus of control and academic achievement: A literature review. *Journal of Personality and Social Psychology, 9,* 13-16.

Harter, S. (1982). The perceived competence scale for children. *Child Development, 53,* 87-97.

Kobasa, S., Maddi, S., & Courington, S. (1981). Personality and constitution as mediators in the stress—illness relationship. *Journal of Health and Social Behavior, 22,* 368-378.

Lipsitz, J. (1977). *Growing up forgotten: A review of research and programs concerning early adolescence.* Lexington, MA: Lexington Books.

Roos, P. E., & Cohen, L. (1987). Sex roles and social support as moderators of life stress adjustment. *Journal of Personality and Social Psychology, 52,* 576-585.

Sandler, I. N., Miller, P., Short, J., & Wolchik, S. A. (1989). Social support as a protective factor for children in stress. In D. Belle (Ed.), *Children's social networks and social supports.* New York: Wiley.

Sarason, I., Levine, H., Basham, R., & Sarason, B. (1983). Assessing social support: The social support questionnaire. *Journal of Personality and Social Psychology, 44,* 127-139.

Siddique, C. M., & D'Arcy, C. (1984). Adolescence, stress, and psychological well being. *Journal of Youth and Adolescence, 13,* 459-473

Spielberger, C. (1973). *State-Trait Anxiety Inventory for Children.* Palo Alto, CA: Consulting Psychologists Press.

Smith, R. E., Smoll, F. L., & Ptacek, J. T. (1989). Conjunctive moderator variables in vulnerability and resiliency research. *Journal of Personality and Social Psychology, 58,* 360-370.

Swearingen, E. M., & Cohen, L. (1985a) Measurement of adolescents' life events: The Junior High Life Experiences Survey. *American Journal of Community Psychology, 13,* 69-85.

Swearingen, E. M., & Cohen, L. (1985b). Life events and psychological distress: A prospective study of young adolescents. *Developmental Psychology, 21,* xxx-xxx.

Swindle, R. W., Heller, K., & Lakey, B. (1988). A conceptual reorientation to the study of personality and stressful life events. In L. Cohen (Ed.), *Life events and psychological functioning.* New York: Sage.

Vinokur, A., & Selzer, M. L. (1975). Desirable versus undesirable life events: The relationship to stress and mental disorders. *Journal of Personality and Social Psychology, 32,* 329-337.

Weigel, C., Wertlieb, D., & Feldstein, M. (1989). Perceptions of control, competence, and contingency as influences on the stress-behavior symptom relation in school-age children. *Journal of Personality and Social Psychology, 56,* 456-464.

Wolchik, S. A., Ruehlman, L. S., Braver, S. L., & Sandler, I. N. (1989). Social support of children of divorce: Direct and stress buffering effects. *American Journal of Community Psychology, 17,* 485-501.

Wolfe, W., Finch, A. J., Saylor, C. F., Blout, R. L., Pallmeyer, T. P., & Carek, D. J. (1987). Negative affectivity in children: A multitrait-multimethod investigation. *Journal of Consulting and Clinical Psychology, 126,* 116-121.

JOURNAL OF RESEARCH ON ADOLESCENCE, 6(2), 181–200

Concepts of Romance in 15-Year-Old Adolescents

Candice Feiring
Institute for the Study of Child Development

Early romantic experiences are believed to play a central role in the development of the self and intimacy, although little work exists on the nature of romance in early to middle adolescence. This study examines White, middle class 15-year-olds' descriptions of their dating partners and romance. As expected, the majority of the sample had dating experiences that were brief in duration, although they were intense in terms of frequency of contact. Affiliative more than attachment qualities characterized these adolescents' conscious views of romance. Girls were more likely to mention interpersonal qualities, and boys were more likely to mention physical attraction when describing romantic relationships.

Early romantic experiences are believed to play a central role in the development of the self and the ability to be intimate with significant others. Interaction and relationships with the other sex are believed to influence the course of subsequent romantic involvements and marriage in adulthood (Erikson, 1968; Sullivan, 1953). Although romantic relationships presumably involve more than sexual encounters, the adolescent literature emphasizes the sexual aspects of emerging heterosexual relationships and patterns of dating.

Dating is viewed as the social processes through which adolescents practice and experiment with heterosexual relationships. In early adolescence, interest in other-sex friends increases and they become more likely partners for interaction and companionship (Blyth & Foster-Clark, 1987; Buhrmester & Furman, 1987; Epstein, 1986; Feiring & Lewis, 1991; Hallinan,

Requests for reprints should be sent to Candice Feiring, Institute for the Study of Child Development, Robert Wood Johnson Medical School, 97 Paterson Street, New Brunswick, NJ 08903.

1978–79; Schofield, 1981). This process appears to follow a progression from being in situations in which other-sex peers are likely to be present, to participation in mixed-sex group activities, to group dating in which couples see each other in a group context, to individual dyads going out alone (Blyth & Padgham, 1987; Dunphy, 1963). By 15 years of age, most teenagers have had some experience dating (Blyth, Hill, & Thiel, 1982; Buhrmester & Furman; Csikszentmihalyi, Larson, & Prescott, 1977; Hansen, 1977; Wright, 1982). For many adolescents, sexual activity takes place as part of dating. By 15 years of age, most girls and boys from the White middle class report having had at least some sexual experience (Smith & Udry, 1985; Zelnik & Shah, 1983).

Theories of dating focus on the development of sexual identity rather than the attachment, friendship, or caregiving aspects of heterosexual relationships (Feinstein & Ardon, 1973; McCabe, 1984). The earliest stages of adolescent sexual identity development involve first directing attention to, but minimal interaction with, other-sex peers. This is followed by numerous short-term relationships in which the practice of basic sexual relations and comfort with the other sex are achieved.

It is generally believed that social skills learned in maintaining and developing same-sex friendships, such as companionship and intimacy, are further developed in romantic relationships. Dating has been observed to serve diverse purposes, some of which overlap with friendship. These functions include recreation, autonomy seeking, status seeking, sexual experimentation, social skills practice, and courtship (Grinder, 1966; Hansen & Hicks, 1980; Husbands, 1970; McDaniel, 1969; Rice, 1975; Skipper & Nass, 1966; Smith, 1962).

The interpersonal nature of romantic relationships in early to middle adolescence has received limited attention (Furman & Wehner, 1994; Katchadourian, 1990; Savin-Williams & Berndt, 1990). The conceptualization of the qualitative, interpersonal nature of romance in this time period is problematic because most work on romantic relationships has been done in late adolescence or adulthood (e.g., Ainsworth, 1989; Hazan & Shaver, 1994; Lee, 1977, 1988; Sternberg, 1986). Some work on adult romance has focused on characterizing its components and functions. Sternberg's (1988) triangular theory of love emphasizes the structure of romance. He believes love comprises three components—intimacy, passion, and decision/commitment. Love is seen as derived from genetically transmitted instincts and socially learned role modeling (Sternberg, 1986). Lee (1988) proposed a typology of love with three love styles: Eros (powerful physical attraction), Storage (affection that develops slowly), and Ludus (multiple casual relationships).

The attachment view of adult heterosexual love relationships offers a developmental perspective of love relationships. As a result of hormone changes, adolescents shift the focus and nature of primary attachment relationships (Ainsworth, 1989). Typically, an other-sex partner becomes the new principal attachment figure, replacing the parental figures as primary in the attachment hierarchy. In contrast to infant attachment, which is typically complementary in caregiving, adult attachment relationships are usually reciprocal, with each partner being both a provider and recipient of care (Weiss, 1982). Adult romantic relationships are seen as an integration of the attachment, caregiving, and sexual reproductive behavioral systems (Hazan & Shaver, 1994). Differences in how romantic love is experienced and manifested are related to differences in past attachment histories, resulting in three types of adult love: secure, preoccupied, and dismissing (Hazan & Shaver, 1987; Shaver & Hazan, 1988). Although the attachment approach is appealing in terms of understanding the different types and origins of adult love relationships, it lacks sufficient explanation and emphasis on the nature and course of romance in adolescence.

The work of Sullivan (1953) and, more recently, Furman and Wehner (1994) suggests that peer relationships and the affiliative behavioral system are more critical for the development of adolescent romance than is indicated in the adult attachment approach. Sullivan asserted that intimacy experiences with friends provide the adolescent with consensual validation of self-worth and create the opportunity for learning sensitivity and caregiving. During adolescence, the mature type of intimacy is increasingly sought in heterosexual relationships. Sullivan proposed that the need for security, intimacy, and lustful satisfaction must all be coordinated in order for the adolescent to achieve satisfactory relations with the other sex. Close friendships with same-sex friends and romantic relationships share common attributes in adulthood (Davis & Todd, 1982). Intimacy, understanding, and enjoyment of each other's company are common attributes; fascination and exclusiveness distinguish romantic relationships from friendships. Essential features of romantic relationships, such as collaboration, affiliation, and reciprocal intimacy, are developed in friendships with peers (Berndt & Hoyle, 1985; Furman & Wehner, 1994; Sharabany, Gershoni, & Hofman, 1981; Youniss & Smollar, 1985).

In the theory of adolescent romantic relationships offered by Furman and Wehner (1992), close relationships involve the integration of affiliative, attachment, caregiving, and sexual reproductive behavioral systems. Mature attachments to romantic partners are seen as unlikely to emerge early on in romantic life when relationships are casual and short-lived. Rather, a number of short-term relationships may serve as the context for the development of affiliative and sexual behavioral systems in romantic encounters. It is not until the onset of more stable or committed relationships, usually in late adolescence or young adulthood, that the attachment and caregiving behavioral systems emerge as a central part of romantic relationships.

This study examines 15-year-olds' descriptions of their dating partners as well as romance in general. Of central concern is an understanding of these adolescents' conscious views of the benefits and costs of romantic relationships. Two major issues are addressed. The first issue involves the extent to which descriptions of dating partners and romance resemble characteristics of attachment and affiliative behavioral systems. Affiliative more than attachment qualities were expected to characterize descriptions of dating partners and romance. Contact with the other sex and dating appears to most often emerge within a group context of friends and peers (Blyth & Padgham, 1987; Dunphy, 1963; Feinstein & Ardon, 1973). Within this context, affiliative qualities and skills should be most important. In addition, as suggested by Furman and Wehner (1994), the attachment system should not become central until stable or committed relationships emerge. Because 15-year-old adolescents are more likely to be engaged in casual short-term relationships (Feinstein & Ardon, 1973), attachments to partners are less likely to develop.

The second issue of interest involves the nature of gender differences in descriptions of dating partners and romance. Society encourages women and men to have somewhat different attitudes toward the desire for intimacy, love, and sex. Women are socialized to be more relationship and caregiving oriented and expressive of love (Hatfield & Rapson, 1987b; Hazan & Shaver, 1994). Weak gender differences have been found in the frequency and intensity of adult passionate love, with women reporting higher scores than men (DeLamater, 1982; Hatfield & Rapson, 1987a; Peplau, 1983). Women also may be more anxious about being unloved and rejected (Bartholomew, 1991; Brennan, Shaver, & Tobey, 1991).

Research on the development of same-sex and other-sex friendships indicates that intimacy is more important and emerges earlier for girls than boys (Belle, 1989; Berndt, 1982; Bigelow & LaGaipa, 1975; Blyth & Foster-Clark, 1987; Buhrmester & Furman, 1987; Furman & Buhrmester, 1985; Rivenbark, 1971; Sharabany et al., 1981). Girls are more likely to base their friendships on mutual support and self-disclosure than are boys, who rely on joint activities and companionship. Work on older adolescents suggests that girls initially emphasize the interpersonal aspects of romantic relationships such as commitment and self-disclosure, whereas boys focus more on their partners' physical attractiveness and sexual relations (Maddock, 1973; McCabe, 1984). Consequently, girls were expected to emphasize intimacy more than boys. Boys were expected to emphasize physical attraction more than girls.

In summary, although romantic relationships are known to emerge in early to middle adolescence, little is known about the interpersonal nature of romantic involvements as they begin to develop. This study provides new information on the relationship qualities of romantic involvements as described by a sample of White, middle class 15-year-olds. The extent to which affiliative and attachment qualities characterize romantic relationships in this age group and the nature of gender differences are of primary interest.

METHOD

Study Participants

The sample consisted of 117 White, middle class 15-year-olds who have been participating in a longitudinal study from infancy.[1] Sixty of the adolescents were girls and 57 were boys. Fifty-nine were from upper middle and 58 were from middle socioeconomic status families (Feiring & Lewis, 1981). The large majority of adolescents were from two-parent families (94%), and all were White, of European descent, and residing in suburban communities.

Procedure

The participants were interviewed in their homes by a same-sex young adult concerning dating, volunteer and prosocial behavior, and friendships. Interviewers were trained to provide nonevaluative feedback to make the adolescents feel comfortable and encourage them to talk. Following the adolescents' initial responses to the interview questions, the interviewer probed for additional information without pressuring the participant to talk. In regard to dating, the participants were administered a structured

[1] Of 120 possible participants, only 3 completed questionnaire data and declined to be interviewed, citing lack of time or interest. The 117 adolescents on whom dating information is available at 15 years do not differ significantly from the original sample in the distribution of gender, socioeconomic status, family size, or development of secondary gender characteristics. It should also be noted that self-reported stage of secondary gender characteristics (using Petersen, Crockett, Richards, & Boxer, 1988) was not related to dating status or description of dating partners.

interview with specific questions that allowed for open-ended responses about these topics:

1. The duration of the relationship and frequency of contact (in person and on the phone) with their current or most recent girlfriend or boyfriend.
2. When going on dates, the type and frequency of activities they engaged in as part of a group and alone as a couple.
3. Their likes and dislikes about their current or most recent girlfriend or boyfriend.
4. The advantages and disadvantages of having a girlfriend or boyfriend.

The interviews were audiotaped, and the adolescents' comments transcribed for coding.

Coding, Reliability, and Limitations of Dating Data

For the interview questions concerning likes and dislikes and advantages and disadvantages of having a girlfriend or boyfriend, the transcripts were reviewed to determine what categories best described the data. The categories derived were as follows:

Likes about girlfriend or boyfriend: (a) positive personality (e.g., funny, outgoing, nice), (b) intimacy (e.g., open about feelings, can talk to each other about problems), (c) support (helps me, cares about me, there for me), (d) companionship (enjoy each other's company, have fun together), (e) physical attraction (e.g., cute, pretty), and (f) common interest (e.g., like same activities, have same attitudes)

Dislikes about girl or boyfriend: (a) negative personality traits (e.g., stubborn, obnoxious, bossy), (b) negative interpersonal relations (e.g., fights, hassles, breaks dates, nags), (c) jealousy, and (d) nothing (could not think of anything negative).

Advantages of having a girl or boyfriend: (a) intimacy, (b) support, (c) companionship, (d) friendship (e.g., having a good, close friend), (e) social status (e.g., image, being status quo), and (f) learn about the other sex (e.g., finding out how to be with girls or boys).

Disadvantages of having a girl or boyfriend: (a) too much commitment (e.g., cuts down on freedom, always tied down, too much time together), (b) negative interpersonal relations, (c) jealousy, (d) costs money, (e) worry about other's feelings, and (f) nothing (could not think of any disadvantages).

Using these categories, each participant's answers were coded according to whether they mentioned a given category in response to a particular question (e.g., likes about girlfriend or boyfriend). In order to establish interrater reliability on these categories, 20 transcripts (10 girls, 10 boys) were coded independently by two raters. Interrater reliability for each category was calculated using Cohen's Kappa. On all but three categories, agreement was perfect. The exceptions were companionship (for likes, κ = .77), negative personality traits (dislikes, κ = .88), and jealousy (dislikes, κ = .77).

The interview data used in this study are thus highly reliable and provide adolescents' own descriptions of romantic relationships rather than investigator-imposed ratings. Nevertheless, the data do not provide in-depth information about adolescents' feelings and thoughts about romantic relationships. The majority of adolescents did not answer each interview question with more than several sentences. The limited nature of adolescents' discussion is not unusual when they are interviewed by an unfamiliar friendly adult (W. Furman, personal communication, 1993; R. Kobak, personal communication, 1993). There also is the tendency to present socially desirable information and inhibit the discussion of negative or highly personal feelings or thoughts. This suggests that adolescents would be less likely to mention characteristics of relationships such as fights, jealousy, or sexual behavior.

RESULTS

This section begins with a discussion of the structure of dating in this adolescent sample, followed by a report of the positive (likes about partner and advantages of having a girlfriend or boyfriend) and negative (dislikes about partner and disadvantages of having a girlfriend or boyfriend) aspects of romantic relationships.

Structure of Dating

Table 1 presents data on the occurrence of dating, duration and frequency of contact, context of dates, and type of dating activities. Although the majority of the sample reports having had a girlfriend or boyfriend in the

TABLE 1
The Structure of Dating

Occurrence of Dating	*Total*		
Have dated	88%		
Currently dating	21%		
Never dated	12%		
Duration and Frequency	*M*	*SD*	*Median*
Length of relationships (weeks)	16.7	18.8	12
Frequency of contact (days per week)			
In person	5.6	2.1	7
By phone	5.5	2.2	7
Context (number of times per week)			
Group			
Total	7.5	7.5	4
Boys	5.4	4.9	4
Girls	9.4	8.7	8
Alone			
Total	4.9	4.9	4
Boys	5.4	5.9	4
Girls	4.6	3.8	4
Type of Date	*Group %*	*Alone %*	
Activities			
Movies	74	72	
Dinner	18	20	
Hang out	32	35	
Parties	30	6	
Home visits	0	30	

past 3 years, most of the teenagers interviewed were not currently dating. Girls and boys did not differ on whether they had dated.[2]

As expected, short-term relationships, averaging 4 months, characterized the majority of the sample. Only 8% of those adolescents with dating experience had a relationship for 1 year or longer. As a point of comparison, 97% of the adolescents have known their current same-sex best friend for 1 year or more.

Although the length of dating relationships is relatively brief, contact is very frequent. The adolescents report seeing each other in person and talking on the phone almost daily. There were no gender differences in length or frequency of contact.

[2]Eighty-eight percent of the sample answered the questions about dating partners because they had current or recent (past 3 years) experience dating. Of this sample, 53 were girls and 50 were boys; 49 were upper middle and 54 were of middle socioeconomic status.

Context. A repeated-measures analysis of variance was performed on the number of times per month that adolescents dated their partners in a group compared to a couples-alone context (between-subjects factor = sex; within-subject factor = context). Dating occurs more in a group than in a couples-alone context, context effect, $F(1, 103) = 7.9, p = .01$, and girls report a greater number of dates in a group context than boys, Sex × Context interaction, $F(1, 103) = 7.6, p = .01$. There are no gender differences in number of dates in a couples-alone context.

Activities. Adolescents were asked to describe what activities they engaged in with their dating partners and whether they had done this activity as part of a group or as a couple alone. Going out to movies, dinner, and hanging out at the mall or school are activities adolescents are equally as likely to report having done in a group or as a couple alone. Parties are more often reported as a group activity, whereas visiting each others' homes was only reported as a couples-alone activity.

Positive Aspects of Romantic Relationships

Likes about dating partner. Table 2 shows the types of qualities most often mentioned by the adolescents when asked to describe what they liked

TABLE 2
Positive Aspects of Romantic Relationships

Qualities	*Girls* %	*Boys* %	*Total* %
Likes about dating partner			
Positive personality traits	85	88	86
Physical attraction[a]	46	68	57
Intimacy[b]	42	26	34
Support[c]	44	14	29
Companionship	27	24	26
Common interests	6	10	8
Advantages of having a dating partner			
Companionship	71	60	66
Intimacy[d]	54	32	43
Support	36	23	30
Friendship	18	16	17
Social status[e]	18	7	12
Learn about opposite sex	9	16	12

[a] $\chi^2 = 4.11$, $p = .04$. [b] $\chi^2 = 3.01$, $p = .08$. [c] $\chi^2 = 9.51$, $p = .001$. [d] $\chi^2 = 4.73$, $p = .03$. [e] $\chi^2 = 3.05$, $p = .08$.

about their dating partners. Data are given for the total sample and by sex of adolescent. Chi-square analyses by sex of adolescent were performed to determine if there were gender differences in types of likes mentioned. Descriptions of positive personality traits (e.g., nice, funny) is the type of response most often given by the large majority of the sample. Physical attractiveness also is frequently mentioned, followed by intimacy, support, and companionship. Common interest is not mentioned very often. As expected, boys are more likely to mention physical attraction, whereas girls are more likely to mention support and intimacy when describing dating partners.

Advantages of having a dating partner. Table 2 also shows the types of qualities mentioned by the adolescents when asked to describe advantages of having a dating partner. Companionship was the advantage most frequently mentioned by the sample. Intimacy and support also were mentioned fairly frequently, followed by friendship, social status, and learning about the opposite sex. Chi-square analyses by sex of adolescent revealed that girls mentioned intimacy and social status more than boys as advantages.

Negative Aspects of Romantic Relationships

Dislikes about dating partner. Table 3 shows the types of qualities mentioned by the adolescents when asked to describe dislikes about dating

TABLE 3
Negative Aspects of Romantic Relationships

Qualities	*Girls* %	*Boys* %	*Total* %
Dislikes about dating partner			
Negative personality	43	40	42
Negative interpersonal relations	25	26	25
Nothing	30	44	37
Jealousy[a]	19	0	10
Disadvantages of having a dating partner			
Too much commitment	79	65	72
Negative interpersonal relations	34	21	17
Worried about other's feelings and well being	9	11	10
Jealousy	7	5	6
Costs money[b]	0	9	4
Nothing	9	11	10

[a] $\chi^2 = 8.41, p = .01$. [b] $\chi^2 = 5.14, p = .02$.

partners. These data are given for the total sample and by sex of adolescent. Negative personality traits (e.g., boring, stubborn) are mentioned most frequently as dislikes, followed by negative interpersonal relations (e.g., fights). Approximately one third of the sample had nothing negative to say about their dating partners. Jealousy was a dislike mentioned only by girls.

Disadvantages of having a dating partner. Table 3 also shows the types of characteristics mentioned by the adolescents as disadvantages of having a dating partner. Too much commitment (the adolescents often used this phrase), especially in terms of time, was mentioned by the majority of the sample. Negative interpersonal relations were mentioned fairly frequently, followed to a lesser extent by worried about other's feelings, jealousy, and costs money. A small percentage of the adolescents could not think of any disadvantages to having a dating partner. Only boys mentioned the disadvantage of having to spend money on dates.

Number of Comments About Romantic Relationships

In conducting the interviews, we noticed that girls appeared to have more to say than boys about positive and negative aspects of romantic relationships. Consequently, a multivariate analysis of variance was conducted on the number of different types of comments (likes, dislikes, advantages, disadvantages) made by the adolescents. Sex of adolescent was the between-subjects factor and type of comment (i.e., categories of likes, dislikes, advantages, and disadvantages) was the within-subject factor. Table 4 shows the mean number of comments for each type of comment by sex of adolescent. For each type of comment, girls had significantly more to say than boys. These findings cannot be explained by verbal fluency because covarying verbal IQ from the Wechsler Intelligence Scale for Children–Revised (Wechsler, 1974; available from the 13-year assessment of partici-

TABLE 4
Number of Comments About Partners by Type of Comment and Sex of Participant

	Girls		*Boys*			
Type of Comment	*M*	*SD*	*M*	*SD*	*F*	*p*
Likes	3.9	(2.3)	2.7	(1.3)	11.5	.001
Dislikes	1.6	(1.2)	.9	(1.8)	11.9	.001
Advantages	2.8	(1.4)	1.9	(.9)	13.4	.0001
Disadvantages	2.2	(1.2)	1.7	(1.1)	4.3	.04

Note. The F tests given are for sex differences. Also note, a significant measure effect with more positive than negative comments $F(1, 103) = 83.98$, $p = .0001$.

pants) did not change the results. For both sexes, there was also a significantly higher number of positive compared to negative comments.

DISCUSSION

Structure and Context of Early Romantic Relationships

Consistent with other findings, most 15-year-old adolescents from this study have had some experience with dating (Hansen, 1977; Offer, 1969; Wehner, 1992; Wright, 1982). For all but a small minority, these adolescents are in what has been described as the casual stage of dating, in which the duration of relationships is brief, lasting on average only a few months (Feinstein & Ardon, 1973; Furman & Wehner, 1992; McCabe, 1984). This is in contrast to best same-sex friendships, which are relatively stable during this period, with most adolescents maintaining friendships for 1 year or more (Berndt, 1982; Crockett, Losoff, & Petersen, 1984). Although stability in same-sex friendships is evident by preadolescence (Berndt, 1982, 1989), it is not common in romantic relationships until late adolescence (Blyth & Padgham, 1987; Feinstein & Ardon; Wright, 1982). Stable, supportive, same-sex friendships in early to middle adolescence are related to good social adjustment, especially during times of transition or environmental change (Berndt, 1989; Berndt & Hawkins, 1987). In contrast, stable romantic relationships in this period have been associated with subsequent emotional and school problems (Neeman, Kojetin, & Hubbard, 1992). Premature stability in romantic relationships may preclude healthy development of self-identity (Erikson, 1968).

The short-term nature of these adolescents' romantic relationships may merit the label *casual*, but this term does not capture the daily involvement with boyfriends and girlfriends. When dating, these 15-year-olds report seeing and talking to their partners on the phone almost daily. The average length of a phone conversation is reported to be 60 min! The quality of fascination has been used to differentiate romantic from friendship relationships in adolescents and adults (Davis & Todd, 1982; Hatfield & Rapson, 1987b). One adolescent used the expression "like a candle in the wind" to describe his current dating experiences. This statement captures the brief but intense nature of adolescent romance in this sample. Given the amount of attention focused on the dating partner, *short-term fascination* might best describe the initial stage of romance in adolescence.

Consistent with the work of Dunphy (1963) and Sullivan (1953), this study finds that adolescent romance emerges in a peer-group context. Group activities are much more frequent than activities engaged in alone as a couple. Both group and couple-alone activities are more likely to occur in public than in private settings. These findings indicate that it is the peer group that sets the stage to facilitate the transition to interactions and relationships with the other sex. It is not until late adolescence to young adulthood that dyadic dating is the norm (Dunphy, 1963, 1969; Padgham & Blyth, 1991). Dating in a group context appears to be more characteristic of girls than boys. For girls beginning to date, a group context may have the advantage of providing constraints on sexual activity with one's dating partner. It is interesting to note that the dyadic pairing more frequently observed in girls' friendships from childhood onward may prepare them for greater comfort in the dyadic romantic interactions more characteristic of late adolescence (Berndt, 1982; Hartup, 1983).

Characteristics of Romance in 15-Year-Olds

Models of dating and mate selection in late adolescence and early adulthood propose that partners are initially selected on the basis of stimulus characteristics (e.g., desirable personality and physical attractiveness). If the relationship continues, common interests and values, and then interpersonal compatibility, become important (Kerckhoff & Davis, 1962; Murstein, 1976). These results indicate that stimulus characteristics of the partner are particularly important for adolescents' newly formed relationships with the other sex. Positive personality traits and physical attractiveness are the most frequently reported likes about the dating partner. Physical attraction is obviously a distinctive characteristic of romantic relationships (Hatfield & Rapson, 1987b; Sternberg, 1988). In the adolescents' reports, it is most often described in general terms, such as cute, pretty, or handsome, rather than in terms of sexuality (e.g., a good kisser).

The failure to explicitly discuss sexual attraction was more than likely due to the adolescents' discomfort in talking about such personal feelings and behavior in a face-to-face interview with an unfamiliar adult. Because adolescents were not asked directly about the importance of sexuality, failure to mention it does not mean it was not important for romantic relationships. Research suggests that most of this sample would be expected to have experience with precoital sexual behavior (Katchadourian, 1990; Smith & Udry, 1985).

Interpersonal qualities of the relationship also play a central role in adolescents' conscious views of romance. Given the casual nature and group context of romance in early to middle adolescence, affiliative qualities were expected to characterize descriptions more than attachment qualities. Consistent with this prediction and the work of Furman and Wehner

(1994), the affiliative qualities of companionship, intimacy, and support were frequently mentioned as positive aspects of romantic relationships, whereas love and security were not. Companionship, a fundamental characteristic of friendship, is reported most frequently as an advantage of having a dating partner. Close same-sex friendships in adolescence also are characterized by intimacy, support, and extensive companionship (Youniss & Smollar, 1985). Developmentally, the emphasis on these characteristics in same-sex friendships emerges in early adolescence (Berndt, 1982; Bigelow & LaGaipa, 1975; Buhrmester & Furman, 1987). The results here indicate that these qualities—important for same-sex friendships—appear to provide the foundation for romantic relationships as well.

In general, adolescents were less likely to mention negative aspects compared to positive aspects of romantic relationships. Typical negative characteristics of close relationships, such as jealousy and fights, were not frequently mentioned. This may have been due to the adolescents' desire to make a positive impression during the interview or a tendency to conceptualize romantic relationships as being more of a positive than negative experience. The most frequently mentioned disadvantage of romantic relationships was too much commitment. The view of commitment as a negative characteristic rather than positive one by the majority of the sample suggests that the attachment system does not predominate for these adolescents engaged in casual relationships with the other sex. This finding is in direct contrast to research showing the central importance of loyalty and commitment in adolescents' same-sex friendships (Berndt, 1981; Bigelow & LaGaipa, 1975, 1980; Douvan & Adelson, 1966; Hartup & Overhauser, 1991; Youniss & Smollar, 1985).

The data presented here are obviously limited in their ability to capture attachment attributes, because the interview questions and analyses were not designed to assess working models of attachment expectations in describing dating partners. Nevertheless, the results do indicate that the affiliative system needs to be incorporated into any theory of adolescent romance (Furman & Wehner, 1994). Recent research has shown that, for 14-year-old to 18-year-old adolescents, the security of relationship style with romantic partners is more highly correlated with the security style for close friends compared with parents (Wehner, 1992). Furthermore, only relationship style with friends predicted relationship style with romantic partners. Adult attachment theory has focused on the association between parent–child and romantic relationships. The importance attributed to friendship relationships for newly forming romantic relationships has been limited. These results, and those of others, suggest that friendships may provide the most proximal basis for evolving romantic relationships.

Gender Differences

Girls' development of intimacy skills in same-sex friendships appears to accelerate in adolescence. Girls are more likely than boys to report sharing feelings, acceptance, and understanding of each other as the basis for same-sex friendships (Berndt, 1982; Bigelow & LaGaipa, 1975; Blyth & Foster-Clark, 1987; Buhrmester & Furman, 1987; Hill, Thiel, & Blyth, 1981). Girls have been found to value intimate conversations and intimate knowledge of friends as part of friendship more than boys (Berndt, 1982). This study finds that girls are more likely than boys to mention intimacy and support when describing romantic relationships. This suggests some degree of continuity in girls' perceptions of the importance of intimacy and support for close relationships with the same and other sex.

During adolescence, boys do not show strong developmental increases in intimacy with same-sex friends and they do not report reaching as high a level of disclosure as girls (Blyth & Foster-Clark, 1987; Buhrmester & Furman, 1987). It may be that shared activities, more so than interpersonal disclosure, are the means by which boys achieve intimacy in same-sex friendships (Buhrmester & Furman, 1987). This may be the case for newly emerging romantic relationships as well. However, research on adults indicates that men are more likely to use opposite-sex rather than same-sex friends or lovers as primary confidants (Antonucci & Akiyama, 1987; Wheeler, Reis, & Nezlek, 1983). Thus, intimacy as self-disclosure is probably more important to men's views of romance in late adolescence or early adulthood (Feiring, 1993; Sharabany et al., 1981). Fifteen-year-old boys also may be more reluctant to mention intimacy and support because traditional masculine stereotypes do not stress expressivity and disclosure. On the other hand, they do mention physical attraction more than girls, which is consistent with masculine stereotypes and research on how men decide who to date (Hinde, 1984; Huston & Ashmore, 1986; McCabe, 1984).

This study also finds that girls have more to say about the positive and negative aspects of romantic relationships than boys. Girls express interest in the other sex earlier than do boys (Blyth & Foster-Clark, 1987; Blyth et al., 1982; Feiring & Lewis, 1991, 1993). It has been argued that women's sense of self, to a greater extent than men's, is organized around being able to make and maintain affiliations and relationships (Archer, 1985; Gilligan, 1982; Miller, 1976). During adolescence, girls spend a significant amount of dyadic interaction time with their close same-sex friends analyzing interpersonal events and relationships. A topic that receives considerable attention is relationships and events with the other sex, including current or potential romantic partners (Parker & Gottman, 1989). Thus, girls may have more to say than boys because the interview questions focus on relationships, a topic of central concern and one that girls have had more practice thinking and talking about.

In interpreting these gender differences, it is important to remember that self-assessed tendencies by female and male participants often show stronger differences than observational measures (Deaux, 1987). Self-reported gender differences such as these may reflect the operation of demand characteristics, with participants describing gender stereotypes rather than accurately assessing their own behavior. Future research that includes observation of interactions as well as self-report techniques will help clarify this issue. It also is important to realize that the differences reported are relative ones with considerable agreement between girls and boys in their views of romantic relationships.

Early adolescence is believed to be a period of accelerated gender differential socialization (Hill & Lynch, 1983). Although socialization pressure from same-sex peers and parents, as well as the role of puberty, have been discussed as mechanisms for gender role development in adolescence, little work has focused on romantic relationships (Hill & Lynch; Simmons, Blyth, & McKinney, 1983; Steinberg, 1981). Examination of self-report and observational measures of romantic relationships in early to middle adolescence, as they are related to the development of gender related role expectations, behavior, and self-concept, is needed.

In conclusion, this study represents an initial step in understanding adolescents' conscious views of romance as they begin to date. Although theory and research on adult love provide a point of departure, they do not sufficiently address issues of importance during the adolescent period. Most notable is the importance of friendship and affiliative qualities in these adolescents' conceptions of romance. The challenge of adolescence is to integrate the sexual and social aspects of romantic relationships (Damon, 1983; Erikson, 1968; Sullivan, 1953). The sexual aspects of romantic relationships are, for the most part, first experienced in interactions with dating partners. Social aspects of romantic relationships should have a basis in relationships with parents and close friends. How skills and expectations learned in close relationships with family and friends influence the nature of romance in adolescence is an important topic for future investigation.

ACKNOWLEDGMENTS

Preparation of this article was made possible by a grant from the William T. Grant Foundation. I thank Roger Kobak, Stuart Hauser, and Barbara Louis for their thoughtful feedback.

REFERENCES

Ainsworth, M. D. S. (1989). Attachments beyond infancy. *American Psychologist, 44,* 709–716.

Antonucci, T. C., & Akiyama, H. (1987). An examination of sex differences in social support among older men and women. *Sex Roles: A Journal of Research, 17*(11/12), 737–749.

Archer, S. L. (1985). Identity and choice of social roles. In A. S. Waterman (Ed.), *Identity in adolescence: Processes and contents* (pp. 79–100). San Francisco, CA: Jossey-Bass.

Bartholomew, K. (1991). Attachment styles among young adults: A test of a four-category model. *Journal of Personality and Social Psychology, 61,* 226–244.

Belle, D. (1989). Gender differences in children's social networks and supports. In D. Belle (Ed.), *Children's social networks and social supports* (pp. 173–188). New York: Wiley.

Berndt, T. J. (1981). Age changes and changes over time in prosocial intentions and behavior between friends. *Developmental Psychology, 17,* 408–416.

Berndt, T. J. (1982). The features and effects of friendship in early adolescence. *Child Development, 53,* 1447–1460.

Berndt, T. J. (1989). Obtaining support from friends during childhood and adolescence. In D. Belle (Ed.), *Children's social networks and social supports* (pp. 308–331). New York: Wiley.

Berndt, T. J., & Hawkins, J. A. (1987). *The contribution of supportive friendships to adjustment after the transition to junior high school.* Unpublished manuscript, Purdue University.

Berndt, T. J., & Hoyle, S. G. (1985). Stability and change in childhood and adolescent friendships. *Developmental Psychology, 21,* 1007–1015.

Bigelow, B. J., & LaGaipa, J. J. (1975). Children's written descriptions of friendship: A multidimensional analysis. *Developmental Psychology, 11,* 857–858.

Bigelow, B. J. & LaGaipa, J. J. (1980). The development of friendship values and choice. In H. G. Foot, A. J. Chapman, & J. R. Smith (Eds.), *Friendship and social relations in children* (pp. 15–44). New York: Wiley.

Blyth, D. A., & Foster-Clark, F. S. (1987). Gender differences in perceived intimacy with different members of adolescents' social networks. *Sex Roles: A Journal of Research, 17* (11/12), 689–718.

Blyth, D. A., Hill, J. P., & Thiel, K. S. (1982). Early adolescents' significant others: Grade and gender differences with familial and non-familial adults and young people. *Journal of Youth and Adolescence, 11,* 425–450.

Blyth, D. A., & Padgham, J. J. (1987, August). *Stages of adolescent same- and other-sex peer relations.* Poster session presented at the meeting of the American Psychological Association, New York.

Brennan, K. A., Shaver, P. R., & Tobey, A. E. (1991). Attachment styles, gender, and parental problem drinking. *Journal of Social and Personal Relationships, 8,* 451–466.

Buhrmester, D., & Furman, W. (1987). The development of companionship and intimacy. *Child Development, 58,* 1101–1113.

Crockett, L., Losoff, M., & Petersen, A. C. (1984). Perceptions of the peer group and friendship in early adolescence. *Journal of Early Adolescence, 4,* 155–181.

Csikszentmihalyi, M., Larson, R., & Prescott, S. (1977). The ecology of adolescent activity and experience. *Journal of Youth and Adolescence, 6,* 181–194.

Damon, W. (1983). *Social and personality development.* New York: Norton.

Davis, K. E., & Todd, M. J. (1982). Friendship and love relations. In K. E. Davis & M. J. Todd (Eds.), *Advances in descriptive psychology, Vol. 2* (pp. 79–122). Greenwich, CT: JAI.

Deaux, K. (1987). Psychological constructions of masculinity and femininity. In J. M. Reinisch, L. A. Rosenblum, & S. A. Sanders (Eds.), *Masculinity/Femininity* (pp. 289–303). New York: Oxford University Press.

DeLamater, J. (1982, March). *Gender differences in sexual scenarios.* Paper presented at the meeting of the American Sociological Association, San Francisco, CA.
Douvan, E., & Adelson, J. (1966). *The adolescent experience.* New York: Wiley.
Dunphy, D. C. (1963). The social structure of urban adolescent peer groups. *Sociometry, 26,* 230–246.
Dunphy, D. C. (1969). *Cliques, crowds, and gangs.* Melbourne, Australia: Chesire.
Epstein, J. L. (1986). Friendship selection: Developmental and environmental influences. In R. C. Mueller & C. R. Cooper (Eds.), *Process and outcome in peer relationships* (pp. 129–160). New York: Academic.
Erikson, E. H. (1968). *Identity: Youth and crisis.* New York: Norton.
Feinstein, S. C., & Ardon, M. S. (1973). Trends in dating patterns and adolescent development. *Journal of Youth and Adolescence,* 2(2), 157–166.
Feiring, C. (1993, March). Developing concepts of romance from 15 to 18 years. In W. Furman (Chair), *Adolescent romantic relationships: A new look.* Symposium conducted at Society for Research in Child Development, New Orleans.
Feiring, C., & Lewis, M. (1981). Middle class differences in the mother–child interaction and the child's cognitive development. In T. Field (Ed.), *Culture and early interactions* (pp. 63–94). Hillsdale, NJ: Lawrence Erlbaum Associates, Inc.
Feiring, C., & Lewis, M. (1991). The transition from middle childhood to early adolescence: Sex differences in the social network and perceived self-competence. *Sex Roles, 24*(7/8), 489–509.
Feiring, C., & Lewis, M. (1993). Do mothers know their teenagers' friends? Implications for individuation in early adolescence. *Journal of Youth and Adolescence, 22*(4), 1–18.
Furman, W., & Buhrmester, D. (1985). Children's perceptions of the personal relationships in their social networks. *Developmental Psychology, 21,* 1014–1024.
Furman, W., & Wehner, E. A. (1994). Romantic views: Toward a theory of adolescent romantic relationships. In R. Montemayor, G. R. Adams, & T. P. Gullotta (Eds.), *Advances in adolescent development, Vol. 3: Relationships in adolescence* (pp. 168–195). Beverly Hills, CA: Sage.
Gilligan, C. (1982). *In a different voice.* Cambridge, MA: Harvard University Press.
Grinder, R. E. (1966). Relations of social dating attractions to academic orientation and peer relations. *Journal of Educational Psychology, 57,* 27–34.
Hallinan, M. T. (1978–79). The process of friendship formation. *Social Networks, 1,* 193–210.
Hansen, S. L. (1977). Dating choices of high school students. *The Family Coordinator, 26,* 133–138.
Hansen, S. L., & Hicks, M. W. (1980). Sex role attitudes and perceived dating-mating choices of youth. *Adolescence, 15,* 83–90.
Hartup, W. W. (1983). Peer relations. In E. M. Hetherington (Series Ed.) and P. H. Mussen (Vol. Ed.), *Handbook of child psychology, Vol. 4: Socialization, personality, and social development* (pp. 103–196). New York: Wiley.
Hartup, W. W., & Overhauser, S. (1991). Friendships. In R. M. Lerner, A. C. Petersen, & J. Brooks-Gunn (Eds.), *Encyclopedia of adolescence* (pp. 378–384). New York: Garland.
Hatfield, E., & Rapson, R. L. (1987a). Gender differences in love and intimacy: The fantasy vs. reality. In H. Gochros & W. Ricketts (Eds.), *Social work and love.* New York: Hayworth.
Hatfield, E., & Rapson, R. L. (1987b). Passionate love: New directions in research. In W. H. Jones & D. Pearlman (Eds.), *Advances in personal relationships, Vol. 1* (pp. 109–139). Greenwich, CT: JAI.
Hazan, C., & Shaver, P. (1987). Conceptualizing romantic love as an attachment process. *Journal of Personality and Social Psychology, 52,* 511–524.
Hazan, C., & Shaver, P. (1994). Attachment as an organizational framework for research in close relationships. *Psychological Inquiry, 5,* 1–22.

Hill, J. P., & Lynch, M. E. (1983). The intensification of gender-related role expectations during early adolescence. In J. Brooks-Gunn & A. C. Petersen (Eds.), *Girls at puberty: Biological and psychosocial perspectives* (pp. 201–228). New York: Plenum.

Hill, J. P., Thiel, K. S., & Blyth, D. A. (1981). *Grade and gender differences in perceived intimacy with peers among seventh to tenth grade boys and girls.* Unpublished manuscript, Boys Town Center for the Study of Youth Development, Omaha, NE.

Hinde, R. A. (1984). Why do the sexes behave differently in close relationships? *Journal of Social and Personal Relationships, 1,* 471–501.

Husbands, C. T. (1970). Some social and psychological consequences of the American dating system. *Adolescence, 5,* 451–462.

Huston, T. L., & Ashmore, R. D. (1986). Women and men in personal relationships. In R. D. Ashmore & F. K. Del Boca (Eds.), *The social psychology of female–male relations* (pp. 167–210). Orlando, FL: Academic.

Katchadourian, H. (1990). Sexuality. In S. S. Feldman & G. R. Elliott (Eds.), *At the threshold: The developing adolescent* (pp. 330–351). Cambridge, MA: Harvard University Press.

Kerckhoff, A. C., & Davis, K. E. (1962). Value consensus and need complementarity in mate selection. *American Sociological Review, 27,* 295–303.

Lee, J. A. (1977). A typology of styles of loving. *Personality and Social Psychology Bulletin, 3,* 172–182.

Lee, J. A. (1988). Love styles. In R. J. Sternberg & M. Barnes (Eds.), *The psychology of love* (pp. 38–67). New Haven, CT: Yale University Press.

Maddock, J. W. (1973). Sex in adolescence: Its meaning and its future. *Adolescence, 8*(31), 325–342.

McCabe, M. P. (1984). Toward a theory of adolescent dating. *Adolescence, 19*(73), 159–170.

McDaniel, C. O. (1969). Dating roles and reasons for dating. *Journal of Marriage and the Family, 31,* 97–107.

Miller, J. B. (1976). *Toward a new psychology of women.* Boston, MA: Beacon Press.

Murstein, B. I. (1976). *Who will marry whom? Theories and research in marital choice.* New York: Springer.

Neeman, J., Kojetin, B., & Hubbard, J. (1992, March). Looking for love in all the wrong places: A longitudinal study of adjustment and adolescent romantic relationships. In W. Furman (Chair), *Adolescent romantic relationships: Conceptualizations, characterizations, and functions.* Symposium conducted at the meeting of the Society for Research on Adolescence, Washington, DC.

Offer, D. (1969). *The psychological world of the teenager.* New York: Basic.

Padgham, J. J., & Blyth, D. A. (1991). Dating during adolescence. In R. M. Lerner, A. C. Petersen, & J. Brooks-Gunn (Eds.), *Encyclopedia of adolescence* (pp. 196–198). New York: Garland.

Parker, J. G., & Gottman, J. M. (1989). Social and emotional development in a relational context. In T. J. Berndt & G. W. Ladd (Eds.), *Peer relationships in child development* (pp. 95–131). New York: Wiley.

Peplau, L. A. (1983). Roles and gender. In H. H. Kelley, E. Berschied, A. Christensen, J. H. Harvey, T. L. Huston, G. Levinger, E. McClintock, L. A. Peplau, & D. R. Peterson (Eds.), *Close relationships* (pp. 220–264). New York: Freeman.

Petersen, A. C., Crockett, L., Richards, M., & Boxer, A. (1988). A self-report measure of pubertal status: Reliability, validity, and initial norms. *Journal of Youth and Adolescence, 17*(2), 117–133.

Rice, F. P. (1975). *The adolescent: Development, relationships and culture.* Boston: Allyn & Bacon.

Rivenbark, W. H. (1971). Self-disclosure patterns among adolescents. *Psychological Reports, 28,* 35–42.

Savin-Williams, R. C., & Berndt, T. J. (1990). Friendship and peer relations. In S. S. Feldman & G. R. Elliott (Eds.), *At the threshold: The developing adolescent* (pp. 277–307). Cambridge, MA: Harvard University Press.

Schofield, J. W. (1981). Complementary and conflicting identities: Images of interaction in an interracial school. In S. A. Asher & J. M. Gottman (Eds.), *The development of children's friendships* (pp. 53–90). New York: Cambridge University Press.

Sharabany, R., Gershoni, R., & Hofman, J. E. (1981). Girlfriend, boyfriend: Age and sex differences in intimate friendship. *Developmental Psychology, 17,* 800–808.

Shaver, P., & Hazan, C. (1988). A biased overview of the study of love. *Journal of Social and Personal Relationships, 5,* 473–501.

Simmons, R. G., Blyth, D. A., & McKinney, K. L. (1983). The social and psychological effects of puberty on White females. In J. Brooks-Gunn & A. C. Petersen (Eds.), *Girls at puberty: Biological and psychosocial perspectives* (pp. 229–272). New York: Plenum.

Skipper, J. K., & Nass, G. (1966). Dating behavior: A framework for analysis and an illustration. *Journal of Marriage and the Family, 28,* 412–420.

Smith, E. A. (1962). *American youth culture: Group life in teenage society.* New York: The Free Press of Glencoe.

Smith, E. A., & Udry, J. R. (1985). Coital and non-coital sexual behaviors of White and Black adolescents. *American Journal of Public Health, 75,* 1200–1203.

Steinberg, L. (1981). Transformations in family relationships at puberty. *Developmental Psychology, 17,* 833–840.

Sternberg, R. J. (1986). A triangular theory of love. *Psychological Review, 93*(2), 119–135.

Sternberg, R. J. (1988). Triangulating love. In R. J. Sternberg & M. Barnes (Eds.), *The psychology of love* (pp. 119–138). New Haven, CT: Yale University Press.

Sullivan, H. S. (1953). *The interpersonal theory of psychiatry.* New York: Norton.

Wechsler, D. (1974). *Wechsler Intelligence Scale for Children–Revised.* San Antonio, TX: Psychological Corporation.

Wehner, E. A. (1992, March). Characteristics of adolescent romantic relationships and links with parent–adolescent relationships and friendships. In W. Furman (Chair), *Adolescent romantic relationships: Conceptualizations, characterizations, and functions.* Symposium conducted at the meeting of the Society for Research on Adolescence, Washington, DC.

Weiss, R. S. (1982). Attachment in adults. In C. M. Parker & J. Stevenson-Hinde (Eds.), *The place of attachment in human behavior* (pp. 171–184). New York: Basic.

Wheeler, L., Reis, H., & Nezlek, J. (1983). Loneliness, social interaction, and sex roles. *Journal of Personality and Social Psychology, 45,* 945–953.

Wright, L. S. (1982). Parental permission to date and its relationship to drug use and suicidal thought among adolescents. *Adolescence, 17,* 409–418.

Youniss, J., & Smollar, J. (1985). *Adolescent relations with mothers, fathers, and friends.* Chicago: University of Chicago Press.

Zelnik, M., & Shah, F. K. (1983). First intercourse among young Americans. *Family Planning Perspectives, 15,* 64–70.

Received September 8, 1992
Revision received May 9, 1994
Accepted December 7, 1994

Adolescents' Development of Romantic Friendship and Change in Favorite Leisure Contexts

Rainer K. Silbereisen
University of Giessen
Peter Noack
University of Mannheim
Alexander von Eye
Pennsylvania State University

Hopes for successful dating for the year ahead, the actual state of romantic friendships, and preferred leisure contexts were assessed for a German sample of male and female students in early and middle adolescence. Data were collected twice, with a 1-year time interval. Using confirmatory prediction analyses, hypotheses concerning the association between transition to dating and change in preferred leisure contexts were tested. Novices in dating were expected to prefer home and neutral settings throughout the year or to change to public, development-enhancing places by the second time of measurement. More experienced adolescents were expected to prefer public, development-enhancing places throughout the year or to fall back on home and neutral settings. Results showed that frustrated hopes for romantic friendship led to a retreat from public contexts. A desire for romantic friendship increased the use of public contexts where one could meet members of the other sex. The use of public settings reflects adolescents' attempts to gain control over friendship development.

During the last decade, developmentalists have become increasingly aware of those patterns of change that may be conceived of as the result of a person's own goal-directed action (Brandtstädter, 1984; Lerner & Busch-

---

Portions of this paper were presented to the Second Biennial Meeting of the Society for Research on Adolescence, Old Town Alexandria, VA, March 1988. The research was supported in part by German Research Council Grants to R. K. Silbereisen (Si 296/1-1 through 6, coprincipal investigator K. Eyferth; Si 296/3-1). The paper was written while R. K. Silbereisen was a visiting scholar with the Department of Individual and Family Studies and the Center for the Study of Child and Adolescent Development, Pennsylvania State University. Special thanks are extended to Helfried T. Albrecht, Urie Bronfenbrenner, Lisa Crockett, Don Ford, and Fred W. Vondracek for their comments on an earlier version of this paper.

Journal of Adolescent Research, Vol. 7 No. 1, January 1992 80-93

Rossnagel, 1981; Silbereisen & Eyferth, 1986). Transition periods, such as adolescence, characterized by a multitude of changes both within the individual and within the social environment, mobilize an individual's adaptive capacities. Thus such periods are interesting for the study of self-regulation in development.

The present study focused on the development of heterosexual friendship, a paramount developmental task in adolescence (Erikson, 1968; Havighurst, 1952; Sullivan, 1953). Leisure contexts chosen by the young can be seen as a prominent way of promoting development, and change in friendship development in particular (Krauß & Tippelt, 1986; Van Vliet, 1983). Specifically, depending on the match between the actual state and the desired future state of romantic friendship, the settings adolescents prefer are expected to differ in potential for development. In short, transition in dating is related to change in context preference.

In earlier research, Silbereisen and Noack (1988; cf. Silbereisen, Noack, & Eyferth, 1986) used two approaches to investigate the role of leisure contexts in adolescent development. First, adolescents were interviewed when entering such everyday leisure settings as shopping centers, discotheques, or outdoor swimming pools. Making contacts with the other gender was found to be a typical goal of the visit. The strategies the adolescents reported showed the importance of differential opportunities available in different settings. Discotheques, for instance, offer—in the adolescents' view—all kinds of facilities. Examples include the dance floor which provides a stage for presenting oneself and legitimate ways to approach others and darker alcoves which help in initiating and making progress with more intimate contacts.

Second, systematic field observations in the same settings showed that such behaviors as looking around, chatting, and making physical contact can be interpreted as instrumental in starting new relationships and maintaining existing acquaintances. These results are consistent with other studies on the ecology of adolescents' activities (Csikszentmihalyi, Larson, & Prescott, 1977; Evans, 1989; Muchow & Muchow, 1935). Whereas many more new contacts were observed to take place between adolescents of the same sex, there was a fair amount of initiating contacts between males and females as well. Romantic relationships seemed to be most likely to develop on the basis of successful integration into a larger peer network. This finding parallels earlier results on peer group formation (Dunphy, 1963).

The evidence accumulated thus far is based on adolescents' interpretations and on observations of behavioral episodes. It remains to be shown that a change in the discrepancy between desired states and actual state in romantic friendship can be related to changes in preferences for leisure places that provide opportunities for promoting goals for development. This is the aim of the present research. Two cohorts of adolescent girls and boys were studied twice within a 1-year interval.

Hypotheses

Concerning change in friendship, adolescents were grouped based on their experience with heterosexual relations. "Novices" did not succeed across the time span observed, whereas "experts" gained at least some experience with romantic friendship. Although assessments were available on change in the discrepancy between actual state and desired state for the year ahead, further distinctions were addressed when analyzing the data.

Concerning the contexts adolescents attended, "private" places, such as the parental home, and "public" contexts, such as discotheques, are distinguished. Thus change in context preference can be described in terms of increase, decrease, or stable territorial range expressed. In supplementary analyses, the contexts are also characterized according to their potential for enhancing the development of romantic relations. "Neutral" places in this respect are compared with "development-enhancing" contexts.

The analysis of change in context as a consequence of dating transition is the prime focus of the present investigation. The following prediction is made. Adolescents who displayed the more advanced dating pattern (experts) either consistently favor public and development-enhancing places or shift back to private and neutral places. Those who show the less advanced dating pattern (novices) will be stable in their preference for private and neutral places or move toward public and development-enhancing places.

This main hypothesis was primarily based on the results from interviews and observations in leisure contexts as reported earlier in this paper (Silbereisen & Noack, 1988; Silbereisen, Noack, & Eyferth, 1986). A common thread in the goals and behaviors of adolescent visitors in places like discotheques, shopping malls, and ice-skating rinks was their interest in meeting people and making friends. Besides their potential for enhancing romantic friendship, the move away from the guidance and control of the parental home results in access to "loci of volitional learning" (Moore & Young, 1978). Facilitated by the anonymity they provide, public contexts allow more leeway for self-direction and, at the same time, offer opportunities for passive as well as active participation in social life.

One also has to bear in mind that privacy increasingly becomes an issue through adolescence (Laufer & Wolfe, 1977; Parke & Sawin, 1979). Interviews conducted with shop owners, guards, and maintenance personnel indeed revealed a tendency among older adolescent couples to withdraw from the public toward private contexts (Noack, 1990). Consequently, those showing the more advanced friendship pattern well may prefer to shift back in favor of home and neutral places.

The available data allow one to compare a sample aged 11.5 years (early adolescent cohort) with a sample aged 14.5 years (middle adolescent cohort) of girls and boys. Thus some additional hypotheses can be tested on age and gender effects. Sharabany, Gershoni, and Hofman (1981) reported more intimate other-gender friendships among females than among same-aged males and also observed a substantial increase between Grades 7 and 11. According to Feldman and Quatman (1988), the age of 14 or 15 is seen by adolescents as adequate for autonomy concerning "go to boy-girl parties at night with friends" or "go out on dates." Thus a higher proportion of adolescents with dating experience was expected among females and in the older cohort and a higher proportion of adolescents lacking dating experience was expected among males and in the younger cohort.

Finally, the younger cohort was expected to be more likely to reach out from home and neutral places or stay there across the time-span observed. Likewise, the older cohort should dominate the other patterns of change in context preference.

METHOD

Subjects

The subjects in the present study included the adolescents participating in the Berlin Youth Longitudinal Study (BYLS). The principal aim was to analyze the role of problem behavior in normal adolescent development in Berlin, West Germany (for short technical reference see Verdonik & Sherrod, 1984).

The median age of the younger, early adolescent cohort was 11.5 years, the median age of the older, middle adolescent cohort was 14.5 years. The first wave of annual data collection was conducted in 1982. A stratified random sampling procedure was used to obtain a sample of adolescents from more than 70 schools in Berlin. The sample was representative with respect to socioeconomic status and the track of secondary school followed by the students.

At the beginning of each school year, subjects in this sample completed questionnaires about various aspects of their psychosocial development, family and peer relations, leisure activities, and patterns of substance use. Attrition from 1982 to 1983 was 14%. From 1983 to 1984, 14% of the remaining sample dropped out (Boehnke & Scherrinsky, 1985; Reitzle,

1987). Sample size was further reduced because only 13 males in the early adolescence group were asked questions concerning heterosexual friendship at the first time of measurement. Also, the contextual preference questions were open-ended which led to some deliberate omissions. Only subjects with complete data were included.

When testing the main hypothesis on the prediction of change in leisure preferences as a consequence of transition in dating, subjects were included with complete data available for years 1982, 1983, and 1984. This three-wave data set consisted of 349 subjects; 122 in early adolescence (15 males, 107 females) and 227 in middle adolescence (111 males, 116 females). Concerning the other hypotheses, subjects with complete data for 1983 and 1984 were included in the analyses. This two-wave data set included 606 subjects; 328 in early adolescence (157 males, 171 females) and 278 in middle adolescence (136 males, 142 females).

Measures

State of dating. Adolescents were asked "Would you like to go steady with a boyfriend/girlfriend in the near future?" There were three alternative response categories given for this *desired state* for the year ahead: (a) "I don't care much about boyfriends (girlfriends)"; (b) "It's true I'd like to have a boyfriend (girlfriend), but that's not that important now"; (c) "I really would like to have a boyfriend (girlfriend) who I'm in love with."

In addition, adolescents were asked "Do you have a boyfriend (girlfriend) you are in love with?" There were three alternative responses possible in evaluating the *actual state* of heterosexual relations: (a) "not at this time"; (b) "I'm in love. I'm sure he'll (she'll) be my new boyfriend (girlfriend) because we have already gone out a few times together"; (c) "I've been going steady with a boyfriend (girlfriend) for a long time now. We are in love with each other."

The statements on intimate other-gender relations were part of a larger questionnaire that addressed 10 developmental issues including peer acceptance, autonomy from parents, and occupational preparation (Kindermann & Silbereisen, 1982).

Preferred leisure places. Adolescents were asked to report up to five of their most-frequented leisure places. Two aspects revealed in the reports were content-analyzed. The first aspect addresses *variation in the home range* as provided by the preferred places. Leisure preference is called private, if a subject named only his or her own, relatives', or friends' homes. This response type indicated a considerable restriction of opportunities to meet new people and to entertain self-controlled activities. If one or more of the places reported was accessible to the public, the subject's overall leisure preference was called public.

The second aspect of the content analysis of the most-frequented leisure places was their potential *impact on enhancing the development of romantic relations*. Results from earlier field research in leisure settings (Noack, 1990; Silbereisen & Noack, 1988) suggested labeling leisure places such as discotheques, outdoor swimming pools, or shopping malls as development enhancing because they provide opportunities for dating. If one or more of the places reported was categorized as development enhancing, the subject's overall leisure preference was called development enhancing. Otherwise the preference was labeled neutral.

Statistical Analyses

The measures of actual and future desired state were reduced by combining the two affirmative response categories. Thus intimate other-gender relations (actual or desired) were either realized (indicated by 1) or not (0). To assess *transition in dating*, patterns were established that describe the two waves of measurement as shown in Table 1. The resulting patterns depict developmental progression of aspirations and/or experience with the other sex. For instance, combination 1/0-1/1 characterizes adolescents ("gainers") who could not realize (0 following slash) strong desires for friendship (1 preceding slash) at Time 1, but have realized their aspirations at Time 2 (separated by dash). Of the 16 possible patterns, the comparison between novices (Patterns 1 through 4) and experts (Patterns 5 through 7) is most relevant for testing the hypotheses.

Similarly, *transition in context* was indicated by patterning the preferences in terms of home range and development – enhancing potential across the two waves of measurement. For instance, change from home (H) to public (P) is indicated by H-P; similarly, change from neutral (N) to development-enhancing places is indicated by N-D.

Hypotheses in this investigation specified covariations between categorical variables. Confirmatory *prediction analysis* (Hildebrand, Laing, & Rosenthal, 1977; von Eye & Brandtstädter, 1988a, 1988b) was used to assess the degree to which the hypothesized patterns of covariation account for the observed frequency distribution when compared with a chance distribution. The chance distribution assumes independence between predictors and criteria, and allows for any interaction both within predictors and within criteria. Hypothesized patterns of covariation are specified as patterns of "hit" and

TABLE 1: Patterns of Transition in Dating

	Year 2			
Year 1	*0/0*	*1/0*	*1/1*	*0/1*
0/0	1 Naives	2 Hopefuls	a	b
1/0	3 Frustrated	4 Isolated	5 Gainers	b
1/1	a	6 Losers	7 Fulfilled	b
0/1	b	b	b	b

NOTE: Figures preceding slash indicate desired future state of friendship, figures following slash indicate actual state of friendship. For instance, 1/0-1/1 characterizes adolescents ("gainers") who could not realize (0) strong desires for friendship (1) at Time 1, but have realized their aspirations at Time 2. Patterns 1 through 4 comprise the group of *novices*, Patterns 5 through 7 form the group of *experts*.
a. Abrupt change not included because of too few cases.
b. Excluded due to conceptual reasons; all cases in cells a and b together amount to less than 10% of the sample.

"error" cells in the contingency table. Specifically, higher frequencies than expected by chance were predicted for hit cells and lower frequencies for error cells. Thus, when predicting a higher prevalence of either "consistently favor public places" (P-P) or "shifting back home" (P-H) among adolescents experienced in dating, every instance of these relations is a hit; in contrast, the two other cases (H-H, H-P) would represent instances of prediction error.

The proportionate reduction in error-measure (PRE) describes the extent to which errors with regard to the observed data are avoided when assigning elements on the basis of the prediction model as compared to application of the chance hypothesis model. Multiplied by 100, the measure represents percentage reduction of errors and increases of hits, respectively. Statistical inference is based on a standard normally distributed z statistic (for details see von Eye & Brandtstädter, 1988b).

RESULTS

Because the predicted association between transition in dating and contextual change may be influenced by other variables like age cohort or gender, loglinear analyses were first conducted (Fienberg, 1980; Green, 1988; Kennedy, 1983). None of the higher than first-order interactions were necessary for accounting the observed data. Consequently, the following prediction analyses were performed on the two-way contingency tables relevant for the hypotheses.

Results on the import of age cohort and gender are reported first. In line with the hypothesis, more subjects of the middle adolescent cohort show patterns involving friendship experience (Patterns 5 through 7 in Table 1), and more subjects of the early adolescent cohort display lack of experience (Patterns 1 through 4). This prediction led to a significant decrease in errors: PRE = 12.1%, $p < .01$, thus confirming the hypothesis.

Concerning gender, a higher proportion of females was expected among the expert patterns, and a higher proportion of males was expected among the novices. The deviations from chance confirmed this hypothesis: PRE = 13.0%, $p < .001$. A closer inspection of where the prediction rule failed revealed more girls than expected displaying the "first hopes" pattern (0/0-1/0). In line with research on pubertal timing (Petersen, 1988), this may point to a subgroup of late-maturing female adolescents in the sample.

The hypothesis concerning the association between age cohort and context preference was confirmed. The statistics for territorial range were: PRE = 6.7%, $p < .05$; for developmental impact: PRE = 7.6%, $p < .05$. Thus, as predicted, more of the older cohort than expected by chance showed either a stable preference for public and development-enhancing places or shifted back to home and neutral places at Time 2. Likewise, more of the subjects in early adolescence showed stable preferences for home and neutral places, or changed at Time 2 to public and development-enhancing places. It should be noted, however, that only the frequency of change from development-enhancing to neutral contexts—not from public to home—was as pronounced as predicted.

Turning to the data on *home range*, Table 2 gives the observed and expected frequencies for the cross-classification of transition in dating with change in context preference. As the analyses rely on a time-lag between the assessment of friendship development and changes in preferred leisure contexts, the results will be crucial for causal interpretations.

The hypothesis was clearly confirmed: PRE = 10.3%, $p < .05$. Thus more novices than expected by chance preferred home and more experts preferred public places, at first measurement.

An inspection of the components of the overall statistic (last column in Table 2) revealed that adolescents who once had realized their hopes, but reported later on no friendship ("losers"; 1/1-1/0), actually show a preference pattern that is the reverse of the hypothesis. More of these adolescents than expected by chance spent their leisure time during the following year at home or changed in favor of public contexts.

TABLE 2: Cross-Tabulation of Transition in Dating 1982/1983 and Change in Leisure Context 1983/1984: Home Versus Public Places

	Change in Leisure Context 1983/84									
	H-H		*H-P*		*P-H*		*P-P*			
Transition in Dating 1982/1983	*Obs*	*Exp*	*Obs*	*Exp*	*Obs*	*Exp*	*Obs*	*Exp*	*Row Total*	*Row PRE*
	Hit cells				Error cells					
1. Naives	5	2.44	2	1.65	2	2.51	3	5.40	12	.37
2. Hopefuls	4	5.09	7	3.44	4	5.23	10	11.25	25	.15
3. Frustrated	8	2.64	0	1.79	3	2.72	2	5.85	13	.42
4. Isolated	33	28.48	15	19.26	33	29.28	59	62.98	140	.00
	Error cells				Hit cells					
5. Gainers	3	8.95	4	6.05	14	9.20	23	19.79	44	.53
6. Losers	8	7.93	10	5.36	7	8.16	14	17.54	39	–.35
7. Fulfilled	10	15.46	10	10.45	10	15.90	46	34.19	76	.23
Column total	71		48		73		157		349	

Total PRE = 10.3%, $p < .05$

NOTE: Contingency table refers to variables when assessed cross-lagged. The patterns of dating transition are those defined in Table 1. Leisure contexts are characterized by H = home and P = public. Obs = observed frequencies; Exp = expected frequencies. Observed frequencies in agreement with the hypotheses are underlined.

The same analysis was performed with the *developmental impact* of contexts as target. Although the prediction just failed significance, the trend in the earlier reported results was replicated: PRE = 8.8%, $p = .06$. The same pattern as in the prior analysis (1/1-1/0) has frequencies contradicting the expectation.

In both data sets, "hopefuls" (1/0-1/0) contributed little to the overall prediction accuracy (see right-hand column in Table 2). Fewer adolescents than expected started to prefer public places, while at the same time more than expected changed their preference for public places to home settings. This transitional pattern was also most prevalent among all patterns.

DISCUSSION

Studies of other-gender friendship and romantic relations in adolescence have characterized development by, for instance, change in the sociocognitive structure of friendship concepts (Selman, 1980), change in the number and import of dimensions such as intimacy (Bukowski, Newcomb, & Hoza, 1987), change in the people adolescents rely on to provide emotional support (Buhrmester & Furman, 1987), and change in variables like the involvement in dating (Hartup, 1983).

This study investigated change in the discrepancy between the desired and the actual state of adolescents' intimate relationships, mainly contrasting adolescents who did not succeed with intimate relationships (novices) with adolescents who gained at least some experience (experts). Adolescents' most favored leisure contexts were evaluated in regard to the variation in home range and whether they can be deemed conducive to the development of romantic friendship. The former aspect captures rather general contextual conditions of behavioral autonomy and the latter more directly addresses opportunities for the pursuit of romantic friendship. Considered together, the respective results allow for more subtle insights into person-environment interactions.

Results suggest that age and gender differences in dating transition were as predicted. In the early adolescence cohort and among the males transition patterns implying no experience with a girlfriend were prevalent. In the middle adolescence cohort and among the females, patterns implying experience with the other gender were prevalent.

Central to the study is the hypothesis that novices would prefer home contexts or shift during the course of the investigation to public places and expert adolescents would prefer public places, or show a renewed interest in home settings. This hypothesis clearly was confirmed. The same was true when comparing neutral with development-enhancing settings.

The sample comprised adolescents living in West Berlin, one of the largest cities in Europe. Although the quarters differ tremendously in terms of building structures and population density, varying from inner-city business districts to village-like recreational areas, caution is required concerning the generalizability of the results to other types of communities. In particular, the easy access to a variety of commercial leisure opportunities may ease the impact on dating transition, as found in the present study.

Development is a function of the interplay between attributes of the person and characteristics of the context. However, maintaining a dynamic, process-oriented perspective on both sides, person and context, is more often desired than realistic in developmental research (Bronfenbrenner, 1986, 1988). This study points to the behavioral relevance of change in the balance between hopes and reality of adolescent friendships with the other gender. Transition in friendship development was shown to influence consequent change in the contexts adolescents select for leisure activities. When youth want to establish heterosexual friendships, they go places that provide this possibility. Once they have established a close relationship they are more likely to seek out settings where the possibility of privacy is greatest. The same conclusions hold true concerning the development-enhancing potential. It should be kept in mind, however, that although these differences are statistically significant, there are still many adolescents who do not behave in this way.

A closer look at the results depicted in Table 2 reveals two transitional patterns that do not follow the general trend in context change. First, the adolescents who lost a friendship at second measurement ("losers"; 1/1-1/0) showed a pattern similar to agemates who did not report a friendship with the other gender at all. The main deviations from the predicted pattern are as follows: fewer adolescents than expected stayed in the public (P-P), and twice as many adolescents than predicted started anew reaching out for public leisure (H-P). The "hopefuls" (0/0-1/0), though less experienced, showed a similar pattern. Thus the mismatch between desire and actual state seems to be the root of change in contextual preferences.

Second, the prediction for adolescents who hoped all the time but never got a friend of the other gender was especially weak ("isolated"; 1/0-1/0). In contrast to the hypothesis, fewer than expected moved out to public settings, and more than expected changed "back home" from earlier preferences for public settings.

For adolescents who preferred private settings, there may be good reason to assume that staying at home might not be experienced as splendid isolation. Rather, earlier research using the same measure of dating transition points to problems the isolated adolescents have to face. As Silbereisen and Noack (1990) showed, self-esteem is low among adolescents not able to establish romantic friendships despite their strong desire to do so. According to Wissler (1990), overdrawn expectations concerning intimacy were common among male adolescents who later lost their intimate friendship. Only after having switched to more realistic hopes did they realize their desires and find a new friend.

According to Simmons, Burgeson, Carlton-Ford, and Blyth (1988), those adolescents are especially at risk who cannot maintain an "arena of comfort," that is, enjoy at least one domain of development where they can feel competent. A follow-up for the group of isolated adolescents, the most prevalent of all transitional patterns seems to be an interesting future step. One assumption is that this group consists of two kinds of adolescents – the shy ones who do not know the right strategies at all and never try and others who tried without success and hence fell back to preferring the home setting.

Further research on several issues seems necessary. The favorite leisure places' attributed home range and developmental impact depicts only a fraction of what could be important for shaping an adolescent's experience. Other aspects of places such as the selectivity in terms of socioeconomic factors, or the flexibility and controllability of activities as stressed by the adolescents, deserve no less attention.

The mutual importance of friendship influences on context preference and context influence on friendship development should be addressed. It is not so much the question of whether contexts "fire back"; rather, the relative strength of effects in both directions is under scrutiny. Research on this topic requires a psychologically more in-depth description of the potential impact of places as previously mentioned.

REFERENCES

Boehnke, K., & Scherrinsky, K. (1985). Die ersten zwei Erhebungswellen des Berliner Jugendlängsschnitts – Eine Bilanz der Stichprobenentwicklung [The first two waves of the Berlin Youth Longitudinal Study – The sampling process]. In R. K. Silbereisen & K. Eyferth (Eds.), *Berichte aus der Arbeitsgruppe Tudrop-Jugendforschung* (No. 49/85). Berlin: Department of Psychology, Technical University of Berlin.

Brandtstädter, J. (1984). Personal and social control over development: Some implications of an action perspective in life-span developmental psychology. In P. B. Baltes & O. G. Brim, Jr. (Eds.), *Life-span development and behavior* (Vol. 6, pp. 1-32). New York: Academic Press.

Bronfenbrenner, U. (1986). Recent advances in research on the ecology of human development. In R. K. Silbereisen, K. Eyferth, & G. Rudinger (Eds.), *Development as action in context: Problem behavior and normal youth development* (pp. 287-309). New York: Springer.

Bronfenbrenner, U. (1988). Ecological systems theory. In R. Vastsa (Ed.), *Annals of child development* (Vol. 6, pp. 187-249). Greenwich, CT: JAI.

Buhrmester, D., & Furman, W. (1987). The development of companionship and intimacy. *Child Development, 58*, 1101-1114.

Bukowski, W. M., Newcomb, A. F., & Hoza, B. (1987). Friendship conceptions among early adolescents: A longitudinal study of stability and change. *Journal of Early Adolescence, 7*, 143-152.

Csikszentmihalyi, M., Larson, R., & Prescott, S. (1977). The ecology of adolescent activity and experience. *Journal of Youth and Adolescence, 6*, 281-294.

Dunphy, D. C. (1963). The social structure of urban adolescent peer groups. *Sociometry, 26*, 230-246.

Erikson, E. (1968). *Identity: Youth and crisis*. New York: Norton.

Evans, S. T. (1989). *Nightclubbing: An exploration after dark*. Paper presented at the British Psychological Society Scottish Branch Annual Conference, University of Strathclyde, Glasgow.

Feldman, S. S., & Quatman, T. (1988). Factors influencing age expectations for adolescent autonomy: A study of early adolescents and parents. *Journal of Early Adolescence, 8*, 325-343.

Fienberg, S. E. (1980). *The analysis of cross-classified categorical data* (2nd ed.). Cambridge, MA: MIT Press.

Green, J. A. (1988). Loglinear analysis of cross-classified ordinal data: Applications in developmental research. *Child Development, 59*, 1-25.

Hartup, W. W. (1983). Peer relations. In E. M. Hetherington (Ed.), P. H. Mussen (Series Ed.), *Handbook of child psychology: Vol. 4. Socialization, personality, and social development* (pp. 103-196). New York: Wiley.

Havighurst, R. J. (1952). *Developmental task and education* (2nd ed.). New York: Plenum.

Hildebrand, D. K., Laing, J. D., & Rosenthal, H. (1977). *Prediction analysis of cross classifications*. New York: Wiley.

Kennedy, J. J. (1983). *Analyzing qualitative data*. New York: Praeger.

Kindermann, W., & Silbereisen, R. K. (1982). Individuelle Anspruchsetzungen gegenüber jugendtypischen Entwicklungsaufgaben [Differences in aspiration levels in adolescent developmental tasks] In R. K. Silbereisen & K. Eyferth (Eds.), *Berichte aus der Arbeitsgruppe TUdrop-Jugendforschung* (No. 14/82). Berlin: Department of Psychology, Technical University of Berlin.

Krauß, J., & Tippelt, R. (1986). Die Bedeutung der Wohngemeinde und der Bildung für das Freizeitverhalten junger Menschen [The impact of community life and education on young people's leisure activities]. *Neue Praxis, 3*, 236-248.

Laufer, R. S., & Wolfe, M. (1977). Privacy as a concept and a social issue. *Journal of Social Issues, 33*, 22-42.

Lerner, R. M., & Busch-Rossnagel, N. A. (Eds.). (1981). *Individuals as producers of their development. A life-span perspective*. New York: Academic Press.

Moore, R., & Young, D. (1978). Children outdoors. In I. Altman & J. F. Wohlwill (Eds.), *Children and the environment* (pp. 88-130). New York: Plenum Press.

Muchow, M., & Muchow, H. (1935). *Der Lebensraum des Großstadtkindes* [The life-space of children in big cities]. Hamburg: Martin Riegel Verlag.

Noack, P. (1990). *Jugendentwicklung im Kontext. Zum aktiven Umgang mit sozialen Entwicklungsaufgaben in der Freizeit* [Adolescent development in context. Coping with developmental tasks in leisure]. München: Psychologie Verlags Union.

Parke, R. D., & Sawin, D. B. (1979). Children's privacy in the home: Developmental, ecological, and child-rearing determinants. *Environment and Behavior, 11*, 87-104.
Petersen, A. C. (1988). Adolescent development. *Annual Review of Psychology, 39*, 583-607.
Reitzle, M. (1987). *Alkoholkonsum und Selbstbewertung Jugendlicher: Entwicklung, Funktion und Kontext des Alkoholgebrauchs in der frühen und mittleren Adoleszenz* [Alcohol use and self-appraisal in adolescents: Development, function, and context of alcohol use in early and middle adolescence]. Unpublished doctoral dissertation, Technical University of Berlin, Berlin (West).
Selman, R. L. (1980). *The growth of interpersonal understanding*. New York: Academic Press.
Sharabany, R., Gershoni, R., & Hofman, J. (1981). Girlfriend, boyfriend: Age and sex differences in intimate friendship. *Developmental Psychology, 17*, 800-808.
Silbereisen, R. K., & Eyferth, K. (1986). Development as action in context. In R. K. Silbereisen, K. Eyferth, & G. Rudinger (Eds.), *Development as action in context: Problem behavior and normal youth development* (pp. 3-16). New York: Springer.
Silbereisen, R. K., & Noack, P. (1988). On the constructive role of problem behavior in adolescence. In N. Bolger, A. Caspi, G. Downey, & M. Moorehouse (Eds.), *Person and context: Developmental processes* (pp. 152-180). Cambridge, MA: Cambridge University Press.
Silbereisen, R. K., & Noack, P. (1990). Adolescents' orientations for development. In S. Jackson & H. Bosma (Eds.), *Coping and self-concept in adolescence* (pp. 112-127). Berlin: Springer.
Silbereisen, R. K., Noack, P., & Eyferth, K. (1986). Place for development. In R. K. Silbereisen, K. Eyferth, & G. Rudinger (Eds.), *Development as action in context: Problem behavior and normal youth development* (pp. 87-107). New York: Springer.
Simmons, R. G., Burgeson, R., Carlton-Ford, S., & Blyth, D. A. (1988). The impact of cumulative change in early adolescence. *Child Development, 58*, 1220-1234.
Sullivan, H. S. (1953). *Conceptions of modern psychiatry*. New York: Norton.
Van Vliet, W. (1983). Exploring the fourth environment. *Environment and Behavior, 15*, 567-588.
Verdonik, F., & Sherrod, L. R. (1984). *An inventory of longitudinal research on childhood and adolescence*. New York: Social Science Research Council.
von Eye, A., & Brandtstädter, J. (1988a). Evaluating developmental hypotheses using statement calculus and nonparametric statistics. In P. B. Baltes, D. L. Featherman, & R. M. Lerner (Eds.), *Life-span development and behavior* (Vol. 8, pp. 61-97). Hillsdale, NJ: Lawrence Erlbaum.
von Eye, A., & Brandtstädter, J. (1988b). Application of prediction analysis to cross-classifications of ordinal data. *Biometrical Journal, 30*, 651-665.
Wissler, E. (1990). *Partnerschaftserfahrungen und Freundschaftskonzepte in der Jugend* [Dating and the development of friendship concepts]. Unpublished diploma thesis, University of Giessen, West Germany.

Requests for reprints should be addressed to Rainer K. Silbereisen at University of Giessen, Department of Psychology, D-6300 Giessen, Federal Republic of Germany.

Patricia L. East University of California, San Diego

Marianne E. Felice University of Maryland*

Maria C. Morgan University of California, San Diego

Sisters' and Girlfriends' Sexual and Childbearing Behavior: Effects on Early Adolescent Girls' Sexual Outcomes

This study examined three key issues related to the effects of sisters' and girlfriends' sexual and childbearing behavior on early adolescent girls' sexual outcomes. Subjects were 455 girls from predominantly minority racial backgrounds. Results indicated that number of sexually active girlfriends, number of sexually active sisters, and presence of an adolescent childbearing sister were positively associated with permissive sexual attitudes, positive intentions for future sexual activity, and a greater likelihood of being a nonvirgin. The strength of these relationships did not vary by race, but there was a greater presence of permissive social influences for African American girls than for nonblack girls. Results from multiple hierarchical regression analyses indicated that having both many sexually active girlfriends and an adolescent childbearing sister had particularly strong effects on permissive sexual attitudes and a nonvirgin status.

University of California, San Diego, Department of Pediatrics, 200 West Arbor Drive, Mail Code 8449, San Diego, CA 92103-8449.

*Department of Pediatrics, Division of Adolescent Medicine, University of Maryland, Baltimore, MD 21201.

There is increasing evidence that siblings and friends play a central role in the onset of adolescent sexual activity. For example, same-sex friendship dyads have been shown to share similar sexual attitudes and ages at first sexual intercourse (Billy, Rodgers, & Udry, 1984; Billy & Udry, 1985; Mirande, 1968; Rodgers, Billy, & Udry, 1984; Shah & Zelnik, 1981; Udry, 1988; Udry & Billy, 1987). Adolescent sibling pairs have also been shown to have correlated ages at sexual onset and extent of sexual permissiveness (Haurin & Mott, 1990; Rodgers & Rowe, 1988, 1990; Rodgers, Rowe, & Harris, 1992; Rowe, Rodgers, Meseck-Bushey, & St. John, 1989). In addition, the sisters of pregnant and childbearing adolescents appear to be at a twofold elevated risk of adolescent childbearing themselves (East & Felice, 1992; Friede et al.,1986; Goldfarb et al., 1977; Hogan & Kitagawa, 1985) and to have higher sexual activity rates and younger ages of coitarche than other girls of the same age, race, and socioeconomic status (Hogan & Kitagawa, 1985).

As socializing agents, both siblings and friends may set standards of conduct or serve as role models who shape the development of sexual attitudes and sexual norms. Once established, these norms may eventually guide early adolescents' sexual behavior. Hogan and Kitagawa

(1985) discussed this socialization process with regard to adolescent parenthood, proposing that girls who witness their sisters become teenage mothers are more likely to accept nonmarital, adolescent parenthood as normative. Such attitudinal changes are thought to precede an increased willingness to engage in early sexual activity and nonmarital childbearing. This may be especially likely for early adolescent siblings who are making formative decisions about school, employment, marriage, and family formation.

Given that siblings and friends can be powerful reference groups for shaping adolescents' sexual attitudes, it is interesting to consider whether the number of sexually active siblings and the number of sexually active friends are consequential for guiding adolescents' sexual attitudes, sexual initiation intentions, and sexual onset. It would seem reasonable to expect that a large number of sexually active siblings and friends would be associated with stronger and more pervasive pressures to conform. Indeed, whether or not an adolescent engages in cigarette smoking and drug use is highly related to the number of peers and friends who engage in such behaviors (Mosbach & Leventhal, 1988; Oetting & Beauvais, 1986).

Two studies have indirectly implicated the importance of siblings' sexual experience for adolescent sexual onset. Miller and associates (Miller, Higginson, McCoy, & Olson, 1987) found that sexual intercourse experience was less common among adolescents who had many younger siblings and that adolescents who held the most conservative sexual attitudes had more siblings, especially more younger siblings. Rodgers and Rowe (1988) found, in studying random sibling pairs within families, that younger siblings had systematically higher levels of sexual activity at a given age than their older siblings, even when controlling for various genetic, developmental, and historical effects. Even in these studies, however, investigators have examined sibling effects on adolescent sexual behavior principally by analyzing family size as a correlate of adolescent sexual activity, or by estimating the concordance of sexual status of one random sibling pair within the family. To our knowledge, no study to date has attempted to bridge these two types of studies by examining the relationship between adolescents' sexual outcomes and the sexual experience of all same-sex siblings within the family.

Similarly, with regard to friends' influence on adolescent sexual behavior, most research on friends' effects has examined concordance of sexual experience within friendship dyads and has omitted examining how the sexual experience within a friendship group could be consequential for adolescents' sexual attitudes and sexual intentions. Moreover, only one study to date has examined whether an association exists between adolescents' sexual attitudes and their friends' sexual behavior. In that study, Shah and Zelnik (1981) reported that 15- to 19-year-old women who believed that premarital sex was acceptable were likely to have friends who shared that view. Their data further showed that adolescents' views about sex before marriage were highly related to whether their friends had actually engaged in premarital sex.

The strength of the linkages between adolescents' sexual outcomes and their friends' and siblings' sexual behavior may also vary for different racial groups. For example, sisters' age at first intercourse was found to be more highly correlated among black women than among white women (Haurin & Mott, 1990). Similarly, Shah and Zelnik (1981) reported that the similarity of friends' sexual attitudes was higher for black women than for white women. However, Billy and Udry (1985) found a correspondence between female friends' intercourse status for white females only, with black females no more likely to have friends with the same intercourse status than two women chosen at random.

The study presented in this article addressed three key issues related to the linkages between sisters' and girlfriends' sexual and childbearing behavior and early adolescent girls' sexual outcomes. First, we examined whether the number of sexually active girlfriends and the number of sexually active sisters were associated with early adolescent girls' attitudes about premarital sex and with their sexual status (virgin vs. nonvirgin) and, for virginal girls, their sexual initiation intentions (that is, girls' intentions of initiating sexual relations in the near future). These relationships were also examined while controlling for number of sisters within the family to rule out the possibility that it was not simply the number of sisters per se that was consequential for girls' sexual outcomes. In addition, we examined sister and girlfriend linkages to adolescent sexual outcomes within racial group to determine whether the strength of the relationships varied by race. The current sample includes, in particular, a sizeable

Hispanic (Mexican American) subsample, allowing for an analysis of sister and girlfriend linkages to adolescent sexual outcomes within this and other (black, white, and Asian) populations. Second, in efforts to examine the precursors of the reported early childbearing and higher sexual activity rates among the sisters of childbearing adolescents, we compared the sexual attitudes, sexual initiation intentions, and sexual status of girls who had at least one adolescent childbearing sister with girls who had only nulliparous (nonchildbearing) adolescent sisters. Third, using a hierarchical regression model, we examined the unique contribution and possible interaction effects of each sister and girlfriend status variable in "predicting" early adolescent girls' sexual attitudes, sexual initiation intentions, and sexual status. This study deliberately focused on girls only, in an effort to identify the influences of friends and siblings on girls' sexual behavior, influences which may also ultimately influence girls' pregnancy and childbearing behavior.

Method

Subjects

Subjects were 455 early adolescent girls (ranging in age from 11 to 15 years, with a mean of 12.93 years) from predominantly minority racial backgrounds (30% Hispanic, 29% black, 16% white, 10% Asian, and 15% of other or not reported racial background). All subjects were attending sixth through eighth grades in public suburban junior high schools in Southern California. Subjects were predominantly of low socioeconomic status, with almost half of the subjects' families (48%) having a mean annual family income of less than $15,000 and with the modal family income between $8,000 and $14,999. Twenty-five percent of subjects' families were receiving Aid to Families with Dependent Children at the time this study was conducted, and 45% of subjects' families had received AFDC at least one time previously. Thirty-two percent of the subjects' mothers had less than a high school education; 25% had completed high school; 30% had completed some college; and 12% had a college or graduate degree. (Data on family income, AFDC status, and mothers' education were based on questionnaires completed by 72% of subjects' mothers.) To be eligible for the study, all girls had to have at least one older sister between 15 and 19 years of age who was living with them at the time of the study. The total number of sisters in subjects' families ranged from 1 to 8 and the mean family size was 2.5 siblings. Subjects were recruited by sending a letter to all eligible girls' parents requesting their daughters' participation in a study on sister and girlfriend influences on girls' development. Of all eligible participants (i.e., all sixth- through eighth-grade girls who had at least one 15- to 19-year-old sister), approximately 85% agreed to participate.

Measures

All subjects completed self-administered questionnaires about their sexual attitudes, sexual initiation intentions, and sexual intercourse experience. Subjects were also asked about their girlfriends' sexual status (e.g., How many of your girlfriends have had sex with a boy?). Response options were: 0 (none of my girlfriends have had sex), 1 (a few of my girlfriends), 2 (most of my girlfriends), and 3 (all of my girlfriends have had sex). A response option of "don't know" was available and used by 11% of respondents when reporting about their girlfriends' sexual status. Subjects also reported on their sisters' sexual and childbearing behavior (e.g., How many of your sisters have had sex with a boy [had a baby] when they were 19 years old or younger?). Response options for sisters' sexual and childbearing status were: 0 (none of my sisters have had sex [had a baby] while 19 years old or younger), 1 (one of my sisters), 2 (two of my sisters), and 3 (three or more of my sisters have had sex [had a baby] while 19 years old or younger). Because less than 5% of subjects (n = 22) had more than one adolescent childbearing sister, the presence or absence of at least one adolescent childbearing sister was used in the analyses of this study, coded respectively as 1 and 0. Nine percent of subjects reported not knowing the sexual status of one or more of their sisters, and 4% of subjects reported not knowing if their sister had had a baby while still a teenager. Subjects who did not know the sexual or childbearing status of their sisters or the sexual status of their girlfriends were omitted from those analyses respectively.

Subjects' sexual attitudes were assessed using the Revised Sexual Permissiveness Scale (RSPS; Sprecher, McKinney, Walsh, & Anderson, 1988), a revised version of Reiss' (1964) Sexual Permissiveness Scale. The scale includes questions about acceptance of sexual intercourse at five relationship stages (e.g., Is sexual intercourse acceptable when a couple: just met? is dating occasionally? is dating often [e.g., once a week]? is going steady? is engaged to be married?). Response options used in this study were 1 (yes, really okay), 2 (yes, sort of okay), 3 (no, sort of not okay), and 4 (no, really not okay). Scores from each relationship stage were reversed so that high scores indicated permissive sexual attitudes. The validity of this scale is supported by theoretically predicted associations between increasing acceptance of premarital sexual activity at increasingly committed relationship stages (Sprecher et al., 1988). For this study, subjects' sexual attitudes were indexed by adding scores of acceptance of sexual intercourse at the going steady and engaged relationship stages. These two levels were used because the other three relationship level scores had relatively low variability, with most girls (at least 77%) disapproving of sexual intercourse at the dating often, dating occasionally, and just met relationship stages.

Subjects' sexual initiation intentions were indexed using four items drawn from Olsen, Weed, Daly, and Jensen (1992) that ask respondents about their intentions of future sexual involvement. For two reasons, only virgins were included in analyses involving sexual intentions. First, we were interested primarily in the sexual onset behavior of young adolescents. Second, it is likely that the intentions to have sexual intercourse over the next year for nonvirgins would be disproportionately high relative to virgins. Items for the sexual initiation intention scale included: How likely is it that you will have sexual intercourse in the next year?, If someone tried to get you to have sex with him, what would you do?, How sure are you that you are ready to have sex?, and, Would you date someone who tried to get you to have sex with him? An item pertaining to intention to engage in sexual petting behavior, included in Olsen et al.'s original sexual intention scale, was deleted from the items used in this study because we were interested specifically in subjects' intention to engage in sexual intercourse. Response options for the sexual intention scale ranged from 1 (very unlikely or very unsure) to 5 (very likely or very sure) with high scores indicating positive sexual intention. Olsen et al. (1992) report high internal reliability (Cronbach alpha = .91) for their five-item scale. Using the current sample and the four items described above, the Cronbach alpha was .74.

Subjects' sexual status was assessed by the questionnaire item, Have you ever had voluntary sexual intercourse with a boy? Response options were yes or no, coded respectively as 1 and 0. This question was asked twice on the questionnaire packet to detect inconsistencies in girls' responses. Both responses for all subjects were consistent.

Procedure

Testing was conducted in a small, private room in the subjects' schools (e.g., a conference room or the library) during the fall of 1991. Two adult women administered the questionnaire packet to four or five students at one time so that students' questions about the survey could be answered fully and individually. Subjects were instructed to be quiet and not to discuss their responses with each other either during or after the testing session. Subjects were able to complete the survey in about 1 hour. All questionnaires were coded using only an identification number, and all subjects were assured of the confidentiality of their responses. The subjects' mothers completed a short questionnaire about basic demographic information at their homes; their daughters delivered the forms to their mothers the day of the testing. Mothers were then instructed to return their forms within 1 week to the investigator, either by mail (a stamped, self-addressed envelope was provided) or by having their daughters return the form to the school's main office. Seventy-two percent of subjects' mothers (n = 328) completed and returned the surveys. Subjects whose mothers participated did not differ from subjects whose mothers did not participate on such sociodemographic characteristics as age, race, family size, religiosity, religion, sexual status, or presence or absence of an adolescent childbearing sister.

Results

Before addressing the main analyses of the study, the descriptive data associated with the measures used in this study are briefly presented. Within the current sample, most adolescents had at least a few sexually active girlfriends, with 39% of girls responding that a few of their girlfriends had had sex and 20% of girls responding that most or all of their girlfriends had had sex. Regarding sisters' sexual status, exactly half of the sample responded that none of their sisters were sexually active, while 41% reported that at least one of their sisters was sexually active while 19 years old or younger. Twenty percent of the subjects

($n = 91$) reported that at least one of their sisters had had a baby while still a teenager.

Regarding subjects' sexual attitudes, subjects as a whole were quite conservative, with most girls not accepting sexual intercourse at the just met, dating occasionally, dating often, or going steady stages. It was only at the engaged to be married stage that sexual intercourse was accepted by a majority of the respondents (70%). Twelve percent of this sample of 11- to 15-year-old girls were nonvirgins ($n = 55$), a figure in line with other data gathered on national samples (Hofferth, Kahn, & Baldwin, 1987; Smith & Udry, 1985). When analyzed separately by race, the nonvirgin rate of blacks (18%) was significantly higher than that of Hispanics (10%; $\chi^2 = 4.27$, $p < .05$), Asians (4%; $\chi^2 = 5.34$, $p < .05$), and whites (4%; $\chi^2 = 8.71$, $p < .01$). The nonvirgin rates for Hispanics, whites, and Asians were all comparable.

Relations Between Subjects' Sociodemographic Characteristics and the Variables Used in This Study

Prior to presenting the main analyses of this study, we wished to determine whether background characteristics of the adolescent (e.g., age, religiosity, socioeconomic status, number of siblings, number of brothers, and number of sisters) might be related to subjects' sexual attitudes, sexual intentions, and sexual behavior. Previous research has been inconsistent, with some studies showing that adolescent sexual activity is related to subjects' socioeconomic status (Haurin & Mott, 1990; Kantner & Zelnik, 1972; Miller & Bingham, 1989), religiosity (Haurin & Mott, 1990; Miller et al., 1987), number of brothers (Rodgers, 1983), and number of sisters (Miller et al., 1987), while other studies have found no relation among these sociodemographic variables and subjects' sexual behavior or attitudes (Miller et al., 1987; Shah & Zelnik, 1981). Thus, to determine whether subjects' sexual outcomes were related to their sociodemographic characteristics, we computed correlations among subjects' age, race, religiosity, socioeconomic status (SES), number of siblings, number of brothers, number of sisters and girls' sexual attitudes, sexual intentions, and sexual status (coded dichotomously as 0 = virgin and 1 = nonvirgin). Race was coded dichotomously as black and nonblack (0 = nonblack, 1 = black), given that the nonvirgin rate for blacks was significantly higher than that for girls of other races and that the sexual activity rates for all nonblack girls (i.e., Hispanics, whites, and Asians) were all comparable. Religiosity was indexed by subjects' reports of their frequency of attending religious services, with five response options ranging from never attend to attend weekly or more often. Subjects' socioeconomic status was indexed by the highest level of education completed by subjects' mothers (with eight response options ranging from did not finish grade school to Master's degree or beyond) and by reported annual family income (with six response options ranging from under $8,000 to over $45,000), both of which were assessed by subjects' mothers' reports.

Results indicate that age is significantly associated with virginal girls' sexual intentions ($r = .14$, $p < .01$), with older girls having more permissive sexual intentions. Sexual status, or being a nonvirgin, is significantly associated with being black ($r = .13$, $p < .01$). None of the other sociodemographic variables correlate significantly with girls' sexual outcomes.

Correlations were also computed between the six subject sociodemographic variables (age, race, religiosity, SES, number of sisters, number of brothers, and number of siblings) and number of sexually active girlfriends, number of sexually active sisters, and the presence of at least one adolescent childbearing sister (coded as 0 = no adolescent childbearing sisters and 1 = one or more adolescent childbearing sisters). Results indicate that subjects' age correlates significantly with number of sexually active girlfriends ($r = .31$, $p < .001$), number of sexually active sisters ($r = .17$, $p < .01$), and presence of an adolescent childbearing sister ($r = .11$, $p < .05$). Race (coded as 0 = nonblack and 1 = black) also correlates significantly with number of sexually active girlfriends ($r = .17$, $p < .01$), number of sexually active sisters ($r = .15$, $p < .01$), and presence of an adolescent childbearing sister ($r = .15$, $p < .01$). None of the other correlations reached significance. Thus, older and black subjects are more likely to have sexually active girlfriends, sexually active sisters, and an adolescent childbearing sister. Given these relationships, subjects' age and race (black versus nonblack) were used as control variables in all analyses.

As further preliminary analyses, correlations were also computed among girlfriend and sister status variables (number of sexually active girlfriends, number of sexually active sisters, and presence of an adolescent childbearing sister).

Results show that number of sexually active girlfriends is significantly related to number of sexually active sisters ($r = .37$, $p < .001$) and the presence of an adolescent childbearing sister ($r = .28$, $p < .001$). Thus, early adolescent girls who have sexually active sisters and an adolescent childbearing sister are likely to also have sexually active girlfriends. As would be expected, number of sexually active sisters is significantly associated with having a teenage childbearing sister ($r = .52$, $p < .001$). Controlling for number of sisters within the family had little effect on these correlations. The interrelations of the dependent variables of this study, namely girls' sexual attitudes, sexual intentions, and sexual status, were also calculated. Consistent with previous research (e.g., Shah & Zelnik, 1981), girls' sexual attitudes are significantly related to virgins' intentions to initiate sex ($r = .39$, $p < .001$) and all girls' sexual status ($r = .23$, $p < .001$). These significant relationships partially substantiate the validity of this study's measures of sexual attitude and sexual intention.

Correlations Among Number of Sexually Active Girlfriends and Number of Sexually Active Sisters and Girls' Sexual Outcomes

The correlations among number of sexually active girlfriends and sisters and girls' sexual attitudes, sexual initiation intentions, and sexual status are shown in Tables 1, 2, and 3. Pearson's *r* was used for all correlational analyses and Bonferroni-adjusted probability values were used to gauge statistical significance. Coefficients for the total sample are partial correlations controlling for subjects' age and race (black versus nonblack). This was done given the significant relationships among age, race, and the independent and dependent variables of this study. Using the total sample, results indicate that number of sexually active girlfriends and number of sexually active sisters are significantly associated with girls' sexual attitudes and sexual status and virgins' sexual initiation intentions. Thus, the more sexually active friends and sisters early adolescent girls have, the more permissive they are with regard to their attitudes about premarital sex, their sexual behavior and, for virginal girls, their intentions to have sex. Controlling for number of sisters within the family did not diminish the significance levels of any of the correlations with sister status when using the total sample. Thus, it is the number of sexually active sisters, specifically, that appears to be

TABLE 1. CORRELATIONS AMONG NUMBER OF SEXUALLY ACTIVE GIRLFRIENDS AND SISTERS AND GIRLS' SEXUAL ATTITUDES

	Number of Sexually Active		
Sexual Attitudes[a]	Girlfriends	Sisters	Sisters[b]
Total ($n = 455$)	.28***	.19***	.22***
Hispanic ($n = 137$)	.31***	.24**	.29***
Black ($n = 132$)	.33***	.16	.19
White ($n = 73$)	.33**	.31**	.26*
Asian ($n = 46$)	.54***	.42**	.44***

[a]Coded such that high scores indicate permissive sexual attitudes.

[b]Partial correlations controlling for subjects' age, race (when computed for the total sample), and number of sisters in the family.

*$p < .05$. **$p < .01$. ***$p < .001$.

TABLE 2. CORRELATIONS AMONG NUMBER OF SEXUALLY ACTIVE GIRLFRIENDS AND SISTERS AND GIRLS' SEXUAL INTENTIONS

	Number of Sexually Active		
Sexual Intentions[a]	Girlfriends	Sisters	Sisters[b]
Total ($n = 400$)	.45***	.32***	.26***
Hispanic ($n = 123$)	.33***	.21*	.20*
Black ($n = 108$)	.31***	.27**	.19
White ($n = 70$)	.38***	.51***	.45***
Asian ($n = 44$)	.23	.38*	.38*

[a]Coded such that high scores indicate positive intention to initiate. Includes virgins only.

[b]Partial correlations controlling for subjects' age, race (when computed for the total sample), and number of sisters in the family.

*$p < .05$. **$p < .01$. ***$p < .001$.

TABLE 3. CORRELATIONS AMONG NUMBER OF SEXUALLY ACTIVE GIRLFRIENDS AND SISTERS AND GIRLS' SEXUAL STATUS

	Number of Sexually Active		
Sexual Status[a]	Girlfriends	Sisters	Sisters[b]
Total ($n = 455$)	.33***	.25***	.27***
Hispanic ($n = 137$)	.23**	.13	.16
Black ($n = 132$)	.27**	.18	.20
White ($n = 73$)	.23*	.16	.20
Asian ($n = 46$)	.48***	.29*	.29*

[a]Coded such that 0 = virgin and 1 = nonvirgin.

[b]Partial correlations controlling for subjects' age, race (when computed for the total sample), and number of sisters in the family.

*$p < .05$. **$p < .01$. ***$p < .001$.

TABLE 4. MEANS, STANDARD DEVIATIONS, AND *F* VALUES OF GIRLS' SEXUAL ATTITUDES, SEXUAL INTENTIONS, AND SEXUAL STATUS BY SISTERS' ADOLESCENT CHILDBEARING STATUS

Sexual Outcome	Nonchildbearing Sisters (n = 346)	Childbearing Sisters (n = 91)	F	(df)
Attitudes[a]	1.86	2.31	12.99**	(3,429)
SD	1.05	1.14		
Intentions[b]	6.35	7.46	4.20*	(3,377)
SD	3.91	4.32		
Status[c]	0.07	0.26	28.60**	(3,428)
SD	0.26	0.44		

[a]High scores indicate permissive sexual attitudes.
[b]High scores indicate positive intention to initiate. Includes virgins only.
[c]Coded as 0 = virgin and 1 = nonvirgin.
*$p < .05$. **$p < .001$.

important for girls' sexual outcomes and not the number of sisters in adolescents' families per se.

When analyzed separately by race, correlations were controlled for subject's age only. The significant correlations found with the total sample are replicated in all but six cases: number of sexually active sisters did not correlate significantly with black girls' sexual attitudes, black girls' sexual intentions (when controlling for total number of sisters), black girls' sexual status, Hispanic girls' sexual status, and white girls' sexual status. In addition, number of sexually active girlfriends did not correlate significantly with Asian girls' sexual intentions. When testing for differences in magnitude of the within-race correlations (using Fisher's procedure and the chi-square test for homogeneity as described in Cohen and Cohen, 1983), none of the correlation contrasts were significant. Thus, the strength of the relationships between sisters' and girlfriends' sexual status and girls' sexual outcomes did not differ significantly among black, Hispanic, white, or Asian girls.

Presence of an Adolescent Childbearing Sister and Girls' Sexual Outcomes

To determine whether sisters' childbearing status was associated with early adolescent girls' sexual outcomes, three separate analyses of covariance were computed using the presence or absence of an adolescent childbearing sister as the independent variable and using girls' sexual attitudes, sexual initiation intentions, and sexual status as the three dependent variables. Three separate ANCOVAs were computed because analyses involving subjects' sexual initiation intentions used virgins only. To compute a MANCOVA on all three dependent variables, using virgins only, would have biased the results. The two sister groups (i.e., girls with a teenage childbearing sister and girls without a teenage childbearing sister) were similar with regard to socioeconomic status, number of sisters, number of brothers, number of siblings, and family type (one-parent vs. two-parent families). However, because girls with an adolescent childbearing sister tended to be older and were more likely to be black than of another race, subjects' age and race (coded dichotomously as 0 = nonblack and 1 = black) were used as control variables in each of the ANCOVAs. Results shown in Table 4 indicate that, when compared to girls with nonchildbearing adolescent sisters, girls with at least one adolescent childbearing sister have more permissive attitudes about premarital sex. When analyzing virgins only, girls with an adolescent childbearing sister have more positive intentions to initiate sexually in the near future than do girls with only nonchildbearing sisters. When examining all subjects' sexual status, girls with at least one adolescent childbearing sister were almost 4 times more likely to be nonvirgins (M = 0.26) than were girls with only nonchildbearing sisters (M = 0.07).

Regression Analyses

To explore further the relations among girlfriends' and sisters' sexual and childbearing behavior and girls' sexual outcomes, a series of hierarchical regression analyses were computed. The three dependent variables were girls' sexual attitudes, sexual intentions, and sexual status (coded as 0 = virgin and 1 = nonvirgin). Subjects' age, race, and number of sisters within the family were entered on the first step. Race was coded dichotomously as 0 = nonblack and 1 = black. Number of sexually active girlfriends, number of sexually active sisters, and presence of an adolescent childbearing sister (coded as 0 = no adolescent childbearing sisters and 1 = at least one adolescent childbearing sister) were entered on the second step. The three 2-way interaction terms were entered on the third step, and the one 3-way interaction term was entered on the final step. These analyses allowed for a determination of the unique contribution and relative strength of each status variable in "predicting" girls' sexual outcomes, as well as an analysis of their possible interaction effects due to the joint contribution of two or three girlfriend and sister status scores beyond their independent contributions alone. For example, it may be that having both sexually active girlfriends and sexually active sisters enhances the likelihood of an adolescent being sexually active beyond having either influence alone. Or, similarly, having sexually active sisters and an adolescent childbearing sister may interact to increase girls' likelihood of having sex. These analyses test for such effects.

Results shown in Table 5 indicate that, after subjects' sociodemographic characteristics have been accounted for, number of sexually active girlfriends, the presence of an adolescent childbearing sister, and their interaction make a unique contribution to the variance in girls' sexual attitudes, accounting for 19% of the variance. Regarding subjects' sexual intentions, number of sexually active girlfriends and number of sexually active sisters uniquely predict virginal girls' sexual intentions. None of the interaction terms significantly predict girls' sexual intentions. Results of the regression analysis for girls' sexual status show that number of sexually active girlfriends, presence of an adolescent childbearing sister, and their interaction uniquely contribute to the variance associated with girls' sexual behavior. All variables and their interactions are positively associated with girls' sexual outcomes, indicating that the significant predictor variables are associated with permissive sexual attitudes, positive intention for future sexual activity, and the likelihood of being a nonvirgin. All variables contribute significant amounts of the variance in sexual outcome, with 20%, 24%, and 17% of the variance accounted for in girls' sexual attitudes, sexual intentions, and sexual status, respectively.

Discussion

As a whole, the results of this study suggest the significance of siblings and friends as potentially important reference groups and socializing agents

Table 5. Girlfriends' and Sisters' Sexual and Childbearing Behavior as Predictors of Girls' Sexual Attitudes, Sexual Intentions, and Sexual Status

	Attitudes[a]			Intentions[b]			Status[c]		
Predictor	β	t	Cumulative R^2	β	t	Cumulative R^2	β	t	Cumulative R^2
Age	.02	—	.01	.09	—	.04	.04	—	.04
Race[d]	.27	—	.01	.17	—	.04	.04	—	.05
Number of sisters	.07	—	.01	.08	—	.04	−.03	—	.06
Number sexually active girlfriends	.43	5.57***	.13	.47	6.02***	.17	.13	3.99***	.13
Number sexually active sisters	.02	—	.13	.18	2.79**	.23	−.01	—	.13
Childbearing sister[e]	.38	2.54*	.16	.16	—	.23	.24	2.88**	.15
Sexually active girlfriends × sexually active sisters	.05	—	.16	.04	—	.23	.09	—	.15
Sexually active girlfriends × childbearing sister	.36	2.22*	.19	.22	—	.24	.44	1.97*	.17
Sexually active sisters × childbearing sister	−.07	—	.19	.24	—	.24	−.05	—	.17
Sexually active girlfriends × sexually active sisters × childbearing sister	−.24	—	.20	.14	—	.24	−.02	—	.17
$F(df)$	$F(11,438) = 5.63$***			$F(11,397) = 9.04$***			$F(11,423) = 8.27$***		
Total R^2	.20			.24			.17		

[a]Coded such that high scores indicate permissive sexual attitudes.
[b]Coded such that high scores indicate positive intention to initiate. Includes virgins only.
[c]Coded as 0 = virgin and 1 = nonvirgin.
[d]Coded as 0 = nonblack and 1 = black.
[e]Coded as 0 = only nonchildbearing adolescent sisters and 1 = at least one adolescent childbearing sister.
*$p < .05$. **$p < .01$. ***$p < .001$.

for early adolescent girls' sexual outcomes. Girlfriends' sexual behavior and sisters' sexual and childbearing behavior may set standards of conduct that shape early adolescent girls' sexual attitudes and guide their sexual behavior. Girlfriend and sister influence, however, varies by outcome. Results from correlational analyses indicate that having many sexually active girlfriends and having many sexually active sisters are significantly related to permissive attitudes about premarital sex. When all three girlfriend and sister status variables are considered conjointly in the regression analysis—which is, of course, how they are actually experienced in life—number of sexually active girlfriends, presence of a childbearing adolescent sister, and their interaction are associated with girls' sexual attitudes. This is also the case with girls' sexual status, with number of sexually active girlfriends, presence of an adolescent childbearing sister, and their interaction significantly associated with nonvirgin status. It appears, then, that once sisters' adolescent childbearing status is taken into account, number of sexually active sisters is not a significant factor for girls' sexual attitudes or sexual status. Or, put another way, having an adolescent childbearing sister has a stronger effect on permissive sexual attitudes and nonvirgin status than does having many sexually active sisters.

The significance of these findings is twofold. First, they highlight the importance of the sibling group and the friendship group, in terms of the groups' sexual and childbearing behavior, for early adolescent girls' sexual outcomes. Most previous research has focused, instead, on the behavioral and attitudinal similarity within sibling and friendship dyads. Second, these results are important because they suggest that girlfriend and sister influences interact together to direct girls' sexual attitudes and sexual behavior. Siblings and friends appear not to present the adolescent with contradictory or inconsistent influences but, rather, they appear to expose the adolescent to consistent role models who serve to act together in heightening adolescents' permissive sexual attitudes and sexual behavior.

A somewhat different picture emerges when examining virginal girls' sexual intentions. Intention to initiate sexually for virginal girls is related to having many sexually active girlfriends and many sexually active sisters. Presence of an adolescent childbearing sister has no relationship to virginal girls' sexual intentions. This finding may be partially explained by the fact that very few virgins (only 17%) have a teenage childbearing sister. Thus, number of sexually active girlfriends and number of sexually active sisters appear to be most important for virginal girls' sexual intentions, with presence of an adolescent childbearing sister not contributing significantly beyond that already accounted for by sisters' sexual status.

When the correlations were computed separately within racial group, the strength of the relationships among sisters' and girlfriends' sexual status and girls' sexual outcomes did not differ significantly across the various racial groups studied. Thus, contrary to other studies that have found that sibling and friend effects vary for black adolescents and for white adolescents (e.g., Billy & Udry, 1985; Haurin & Mott, 1990; Shah & Zelnik, 1981), the results of the current study indicate that having many sexually active girlfriends and many sexually active sisters is associated with equally permissive sexual outcomes for girls of all of the racial groups studied. However, it is important to note that although the linkages are not stronger for blacks than for nonblacks, black girls in the sample are more likely to have more sexually active girlfriends, more sexually active sisters, and to have an adolescent childbearing sister than are nonblack girls. Thus, there appears to be a greater presence of permissive social influences for African American girls, influences that are not present for girls from the other racial backgrounds.

Our findings also indicate that, when compared to girls with only nonchildbearing adolescent sisters, girls with an adolescent childbearing sister have more permissive sexual attitudes and more positive intentions for future sexual activity, and are more likely to be nonvirgins. To our knowledge, this is the first study to examine having an adolescent childbearing sister vis-à-vis adolescents' sexual attitudes and sexual intentions. All studies to date examining sisters' childbearing status have focused only on sibling outcomes of pregnancy or childbearing (Friede et al., 1986; Goldfarb et al., 1977) and only one study has shown an earlier age at coitarche for the sisters of childbearing teens (Hogan & Kitagawa, 1985). Thus, it may be that having an adolescent childbearing sister alters girls' sexual attitudes, attitudes which, over time, shape their sexual intentions and, ultimately, change their sexual behavior. Or, considering our criterion of adolescent childbearing sisters (i.e., we selected out households that were more accepting of teenage births, as opposed to abortions), perhaps girls with adolescent childbearing sisters grow up in families and social climates where teenage sexuality and childbearing are condoned or even encouraged, making both sisters equally susceptible to early parenthood (East & Felice, 1992; Haurin & Mott, 1990). In either case, further longitudinal research is needed to substantiate these processes of influence.

Several limitations of this study warrant specific comment. Perhaps the most significant limitation was that girlfriend and sister sexual and childbearing behavior were assessed using subjects' reports. Certainly, reporter bias may have inflated the correlational measures of association. Indeed, although sisters' and girlfriends' sexual data are subject to perceptual bias, the childbearing data are presumably quite reliable. In any case, it should be emphasized that this study assessed girls' perceptions of others' sexual activity and did not attempt to capture the true sexual status of specific girlfriends or sisters.

The results of this study should also be placed in the proper context, recognizing that there exist other, perhaps more powerful, influences on adolescent sexual behavior. For example, many studies have demonstrated pubertal and hormonal influences on adolescents' age at coitarche (Udry, 1988; Udry & Billy, 1987; Udry, Halpern, & Campbell, 1991). Preliminary evidence also exists that indicates an indirect biological path between mother's menarcheal age and daughter's sexual behavior (Newcomer & Udry, 1984). Such familial-biological processes of influence certainly warrant further consideration in explaining the covariation between sisters' sexual status as found in this study.

The single-occasion design of the study was also a limitation. For example, we believe that girlfriends' and sisters' sexual behavior shape early adolescent girls' sexual attitudes and intentions, which, in turn, guide their sexual behavior. This process of influence cannot, however, be tested using the current correlational design. It is equally plausible that girls with liberal sexual attitudes and permissive sexual intentions and behavior seek out friends who share these predispositions. Of course, this would not be a possible explanation within sister relationships because sisters cannot select or deselect one another. Thus, at the very least, we can interpret our findings as evidence that exposure to sexually active sisters and adolescent childbearing sisters may enhance early adolescent girls' permissiveness with regard to their own sexual attitudes and behavior. Recall, too, that girls in our sample who had sexually active sisters and adolescent childbearing sisters were likely to also have sexually active girlfriends. Again, because siblings cannot select one another, girls are likely to be choosing friends who match the sexual experience of their siblings. This interpretation places the origins of adolescent sexual activity within the immediate family context, with friends and peers as more indirect, distal influences. We caution, however, as have others (e.g., Jessor & Jessor, 1975; Rodgers & Rowe, 1990; Udry & Billy, 1987), that a far more complex picture likely exists with regard to the etiology of adolescent sexual activity.

Despite these limitations, however, the results of the current study point to the risk of early sexual initiation among young adolescent girls who have many sexually active girlfriends and sisters and at least one adolescent childbearing sister. It follows, then, that such individuals would be a strategic population to target in a pregnancy prevention program (cf. East & Felice, 1992). The present findings also call for further research on the specific components of the sister and girlfriend relationships that make a difference in early adolescent girls' sexual outcomes. Rodgers and Rowe (1988) have proposed a sibling interaction hypothesis that holds much promise in predicting sibling similarity in adolescent sexual behavior (see also Rodgers et al., 1992; Rowe et al., 1989). With further research into such mechanisms, these findings could be used to better understand, and, ultimately, to reduce, the reported elevated sexual activity and pregnancy rates among the sisters of sexually active and childbearing adolescents.

Note

This research was supported by grants awarded to Patricia East by the Office of Adolescent Pregnancy Programs (U.S. Public Health Service #APH-000344) and by the National Institute of Child Health and Human Development R29-HD29472. The work of Dr. Felice was supported by grant MCJ980 from the Maternal and Child Health Bureau. The authors are grateful to Carolyn Bushman, Beth Blaustein, Maria Lara, Marla Becker, Sharon Simpson, Grace Barca, and Katy Engelhorn for their time and effort in data collection and data management. We also appreciate the gracious cooperation of the San Diego and Sweetwater Unified School Districts, particularly Horace Mann, Roosevelt, Standley, and Southwest Junior High Schools. Requests for reprints should be addressed to Patricia East.

References

Billy, J. O. G., Rodgers, J. L., & Udry, J. R. (1984). Adolescent sexual behavior and friendship choice. *Social Forces, 62,* 653–678.

Billy, J. O. G., & Udry, J. R. (1985). Patterns of adolescent friendship and effects on sexual behavior. *Social Psychology Quarterly, 48,* 27–41.

Cohen, J., & Cohen, P. (1983). *Applied multiple regression/correlation analysis for the behavioral sciences* (2nd ed.). Hillsdale, NJ: Lawrence Erlbaum.

East, P. L., & Felice, M. E. (1992). Pregnancy risk among the younger sisters of pregnant and childbearing adolescents. *Journal of Developmental and Behavioral Pediatrics, 13,* 128–136.

Friede, A., Hogue, C. J. R., Doyle, L., Hammerslough, C. R., Sniezek, J. E., & Arrighi, H. (1986). Do the sisters of childbearing teenagers have increased rates of childbearing? *American Journal of Public Health, 76,* 1221–1224.

Goldfarb, J. L., Mumford, D. M., Schum, D. A., Smith, P. B., Flowers, C., & Schum, C. (1977). An attempt to detect "pregnancy susceptibility" in indigent adolescent girls. *Journal of Youth and Adolescence, 6,* 127–144.

Haurin, R. J., & Mott, F. (1990). Adolescent sexual activity in the family context: The impact of older siblings. *Demography, 27,* 537–557.

Hofferth, S. L., Kahn, J. R., & Baldwin, W. (1987). Premarital sexual activity among U.S. teenage women over the past three decades. *Family Planning Perspectives, 19,* 46–53.

Hogan, D. P., & Kitagawa, E. M. (1985). The impact of social status, family structure, and the neighborhood on the fertility of black adolescents. *American Journal of Sociology, 90,* 825–855.

Jessor, S. L., & Jessor, R. (1975). Transition from virginity to nonvirginity among youth: A social-psychological study over time. *Developmental Psychology, 11,* 473–484.

Kantner, J. F., & Zelnik, M. (1972). Sexual experience of young unmarried women in the United States. *Family Planning Perspectives, 4,* 9–18.

Miller, B. C., & Bingham, C. R. (1989). Family configuration in relation to the sexual behavior of female adolescents. *Journal of Marriage and the Family, 51,* 499–506.

Miller, B. C., Higginson, R., McCoy, J. K., & Olson, T. D. (1987). Family configuration and adolescent sexual attitudes and behavior. *Population and Environment, 9,* 111–123.

Mirande, A. M. (1968). Reference group theory and adolescent sexual behavior. *Journal of Marriage and the Family, 30,* 572–577.

Mosbach, P., & Leventhal, H. (1988). Peer group identification and smoking: Implications for intervention. *Journal of Abnormal Psychology, 97,* 1–8.

Newcomer, S. F., & Udry, J. R. (1984). Mothers' influence on the sexual behavior of their teenage children. *Journal of Marriage and the Family, 46,* 477–485.

Oetting, E. R., & Beauvais, F. (1986). Peer cluster theory: Drugs and the adolescent. *Journal of Counseling and Development, 65,* 17–22.

Olsen, J., Weed, S., Daly, D., & Jensen, L. (1992). The effects of abstinence sex education programs on virgin versus nonvirgin students. *Journal of Research and Development in Education, 25,* 69–75.

Reiss, I. L. (1964). The scaling of premarital sexual permissiveness. *Journal of Marriage and the Family, 26,* 188–198.

Rodgers, J. L. (1983). Family configuration and adolescent sexual behavior. *Population and Environment, 6,* 73–83.

Rodgers, J. L., Billy, J. O. G., & Udry, J. R. (1984). A model of friendship similarity in mildly deviant behaviors. *Journal of Applied Social Psychology, 14,* 413–425.

Rodgers, J. L., & Rowe, D. C. (1988). Influence of siblings on adolescent sexual behavior. *Developmental Psychology, 24,* 722–728.

Rodgers, J. L., & Rowe, D. C. (1990). Adolescent sexual activity and mildly deviant behavior: Sibling and friendship effects. *Journal of Family Issues, 11,* 274–293.

Rodgers, J. L., Rowe, D. C., & Harris, D. F. (1992). Sibling differences in adolescent sexual behavior: Inferring process models from family composition patterns. *Journal of Marriage and the Family, 54,* 142–152.

Rowe, D. C., Rodgers, J. L., Meseck-Bushey, S., & St. John, C. (1989). Sexual behavior and nonsexual deviance: A sibling study of their relationship. *Developmental Psychology, 25,* 61–69.

Shah, F., & Zelnik, M. (1981). Parent and peer influence on sexual behavior, contraceptive use, and pregnancy experience of young women. *Journal of Marriage and the Family, 43,* 339–348.

Smith, E. A., & Udry, J. R. (1985). Coital and noncoital sexual behaviors of white and black adolescents. *American Journal of Public Health, 75,* 1200–1203.

Sprecher, S., McKinney, K., Walsh, R., & Anderson, C. (1988). A revision of the Reiss Premarital Sexual Permissiveness Scale. *Journal of Marriage and the Family, 50,* 821–828.

Udry, J. R. (1988). Biological predispositions and social control in adolescent sexual behavior. *American Sociological Review, 53,* 709–722.

Udry, J. R., & Billy, J. O. G. (1987). Initiation of coitus in early adolescence. *American Sociological Review, 52,* 841–855.

Udry, J. R., Halpern, C., & Campbell, B. (March, 1991). *Hormones, pubertal development and sexual behavior in adolescent females.* Paper presented at the biennial meetings of the Society for Research in Child Development, Seattle, WA.

Developmental Psychology
1996, Vol. 32, No. 4, 647–658

0012-1649/96/$3.00

Longitudinal Adjustment Patterns of Boys and Girls Experiencing Early, Middle, and Late Sexual Intercourse

C. Raymond Bingham
Michigan State University

Lisa J. Crockett
Pennsylvania State University

This study examined the association between psychosocial development and the timing of first sexual intercourse in a sample of White, rural adolescents. Two theoretical models were tested. The first model, derived from problem behavior theory, proposed that earlier timing of first sexual intercourse is associated with longitudinal patterns of transition proneness and poor psychosocial adjustment. The second model, the stage termination model, proposed that early first sexual intercourse interferes with subsequent development, thereby resulting in negative developmental outcomes. Problem behavior theory was supported. For both boys and girls, earlier timing of first sexual intercourse was associated with longitudinal patterns of greater transition proneness and poorer psychosocial adjustment. The stage termination model was not supported. No evidence was found suggesting that early timing of first sexual intercourse results in negative psychosocial outcomes.

During the current century, adolescents' sexual attitudes and behaviors have changed dramatically, resulting in an increased incidence of adolescent sexual intercourse and a decreased age at first intercourse for both boys and girls (Forrest & Singh, 1990; Zelnik & Kantner, 1980). Adolescents' increased participation in sexual intercourse places them at risk for a variety of undesirable physiological outcomes, including unintended pregnancy (Jones et al., 1986; Zelnik & Kantner, 1980), sexually transmitted disease, and AIDS (Bingham, 1989; Chilman, 1980; D'Augelli & Bingham, 1993; Zelnik & Kantner, 1980). The psychosocial consequences of adolescent sexual intercourse, however, are less well understood.

Research has provided consistent evidence of an association between adolescent sexual behavior and several aspects of psychosocial development. Generally, adolescents who initiate sexual intercourse early experience greater psychosocial risk, including more problem behavior and substance use, disrupted family and parental relationships, and poor school performance (Billy, Landale, Grady, & Zimmerle, 1988; Crockett, Bingham, Chopak, & Vicary, 1996; Day, 1992; Dorius, Heaton, & Steffen, 1993; R. Jessor, Costa, Jessor, & Donovan, 1983; S. L. Jessor & Jessor, 1977). However, current understanding of the associations between adolescent sexual intercourse and psychosocial development is limited by the cross-sectional nature of most of the research conducted to date. In particular, it is unclear whether timing of first sexual intercourse has psychosocial consequences or simply psychosocial correlates. The present research tests these alternatives and extends the existing literature in two ways. First, it moves beyond the prediction of first sexual intercourse by using a longitudinal design to investigate the antecedent–consequent relation between timing of first intercourse and subsequent psychosocial development. Second, whereas the majority of research on adolescent sexual behavior has used urban and suburban samples, the present research examines sexual behavior among rural adolescents.

Correlates of Adolescent Sexual Behavior

Problem Behavior

Research has consistently identified an association between adolescent sexual behavior and other socially proscribed behaviors. In general, adolescent involvement in deviance, alcohol use and abuse, and illicit drug use has been found to predict earlier first sexual intercourse, both cross-sectionally (Verner & Stewart, 1974) and longitudinally (Crockett et al., 1996; R. Jessor et al., 1983; S. L. Jessor & Jessor, 1977; Rosenbaum & Kandel, 1990). Longitudinal research has indicated that substance use predicts the transition to adolescent sexual involvement (R. Jessor et al., 1983; S. L. Jessor & Jessor, 1977); however, evidence regarding the temporal sequencing of problem behavior involvement and sexual intercourse is mixed, with some research suggesting that substance use precedes sexual intercourse (R. Jessor et al., 1983; S. L. Jessor & Jessor, 1977; Mott & Haurin, 1988; Rosenbaum & Kandel, 1990), other research suggesting that sexual intercourse precedes substance use (Dorius et al., 1993; Mott & Haurin, 1988), and still other evidence suggesting that the temporal ordering of substance use and sexual behavior varies by substance (Dorius et al., 1993).

C. Raymond Bingham, Department of Psychology, Michigan State University; Lisa J. Crockett, Department of Human Development and Family Studies, Pennsylvania State University.

This research was supported by Grant APR 000933-01, Contract 282-90-0047 awarded to J. R. Vicary by the Office of Adolescent Pregnancy Programs, and by grants from the College of Health and Human Development and the Center for the Study of Child and Adolescent Development at the Pennsylvania State University.

We acknowledge Pennsylvania State University for providing the facilities for this research, the students and school personnel who made data collection possible, and the reviewers of the manuscript who provided invaluable feedback.

Correspondence concerning this article should be addressed to C. Raymond Bingham, Department of Psychology, Michigan State University, 135 Snyder Hall, East Lansing, Michigan 48824-1117. Electronic mail may be sent via Internet to bingham@pilot.msu.edu.

Conventional Behaviors

Educational attitudes and behaviors are associated with adolescent sexual behavior (Billy et al., 1988; Dorius et al., 1993). Greater investment in educational and academic pursuits is related to later initiation (Billy et al., 1988; Hayes, 1987) and lower frequency of sexual intercourse (Ohannesian & Crockett, 1993). It has also been found that girls' academic aspirations and boys' grades in school decline following first sexual intercourse (Billy et al., 1988). The association between sexual intercourse and academic performance and attitudes may result either from sexually abstinent adolescents spending more time in school activities and less time with members of the opposite sex (Chilman, 1980) or from more educationally motivated students holding less stereotyped sex role images (Cvetkovich, Grote, Lieberman, & Miller, 1978).

The frequency of church attendance is inversely related to involvement in sexual intercourse (Bingham, Miller, & Adams, 1990; Crockett et al., 1996; R. Jessor et al., 1983; S. L. Jessor & Jessor, 1977; Miller, McCoy, Olson, & Wallace, 1986). Although some evidence suggests that adolescents who experience less religious commitment are more likely to be involved in sexual behavior (Crockett et al., 1996), it also appears that sexual involvement results in decreased religious commitment and less frequent church attendance (Billy et al., 1988).

Social Relationships

The quality of relationships between parents and their children predicts sexual intercourse. Poorer quality family relationships are associated with more adolescent involvement in sexual behaviors, including necking, petting (Wagner, 1980), and intercourse (Crockett et al., 1996; Rob, Reynolds, & Finlayson, 1990; Wagner, 1980). In addition, adolescent boys feel less close to their mothers, but not their fathers, following first sexual intercourse (Billy et al., 1988).

Very little is known about the association between the quality of peer relationships and the timing of first sexual intercourse. However, evidence indicates that, following first intercourse, adolescents are more likely to select friends who are also sexually active (Billy et al., 1988).

Psychological Characteristics

Sexually active adolescents commonly possess a variety of psychological characteristics distinguishing them from their less sexually experienced peers. A number of studies suggest an association between self-esteem and sexual intercourse. Among adults, there is evidence that low self-esteem interferes with involvement in sexual intercourse (Long, 1976). This is congruent with research indicating that nonvirgin adolescent boys report higher self-esteem than their virgin counterparts (S. L. Jessor & Jessor, 1977; Wade, 1989), but it does not explain the negative association found between sexual intercourse and the self-esteem of adolescent girls (Day, 1992).

Although some evidence suggests that self-esteem may predict the timing of first intercourse, it is not clear whether involvement in sexual intercourse results in further changes in self-esteem. In either case, it is important to understand the relation between self-esteem and sexual intercourse, because increasing self-esteem is the target of a variety of interventions into adolescent sexual and contraceptive behaviors (Watson & Kelly, 1989). Given the small amount of research on the topic, and the assumption that higher self-esteem is important in the intervention into adolescent sexual behavior, further research is merited.

Negative affect and depression predict less participation and interest in sexual intercourse among adults (Lief, 1986). However, the association between negative affect and adolescent sexual behavior is not well understood. When knowledge regarding adult depression and sexual intercourse is generalized to adolescents, it is anticipated that (a) depressed adolescents are less interested and less involved in sexual intercourse and/or (b) adolescents who begin sexual intercourse early are more likely subsequently to suffer from depression. Further research is needed on this topic.

Gender Issues

Society has historically maintained a sexual double standard (Reiss, 1960) suggesting that premarital sexual behavior is more permissible for males than for females. Although the sexual double standard has decreased in strength (Clement, 1989; Gagnon, 1977), it still influences sexual socialization, especially among adolescents. This influence is evidenced by gender differences in adolescents' reported age at first sexual intercourse, frequency of intercourse, contraceptive use, and number of sexual partners (Bingham et al., 1990; Zelnik & Kantner, 1980), as well as their emotional responses to first coitus (Koch, 1988). Because of the differences in socialization existing for adolescent boys and girls, we included gender in the present research so that its moderating effects on the association between timing of first sexual intercourse and psychosocial development could be examined.

Models of Timing and Psychosocial Development

There are currently no comprehensive theories of adolescent sexuality (Miller & Fox, 1987). However, *problem behavior theory* (R. Jessor et al., 1983; S. L. Jessor & Jessor, 1977) and the *stage termination model* (Peskin, 1967, 1973) provide direction for the present research.

Problem Behavior Theory

Problem behavior theory posits that a variety of adolescent problem behaviors and sexual intercourse occur together as a behavioral syndrome. This behavioral syndrome constitutes a state of transition proneness that provides adolescents with a means of achieving otherwise unattainable developmental objectives. Transition proneness is typified by poorer psychosocial adjustment (i.e., more problem behavior and less conventional behavior) and is associated with the timing of developmental transitions (S. L. Jessor & Jessor, 1977).

Problem behavior theory categorizes psychosocial variables into three domains: the *personality system*, including the individual's perceptions and feelings about themselves; the *perceived environment system*, consisting of parental and peer influences; and the *behavior system*, encompassing problem behaviors such as delinquency and conventional behaviors such as school performance (R. Jessor et al., 1983). In the present research, we examined variables measuring these three domains so that their antecedent–consequent association with the timing of first intercourse could be tested.

The Stage Termination Model

The stage termination model (Peskin, 1967, 1973) assumes that in each stage of development a minimum level of maturation is necessary in order for successful advancement into the next stage. This model suggests that when transitions occur too early, development is curtailed and negative individual consequences result (Erikson, 1968).

Where sexual intercourse and psychosocial development are concerned, the stage termination model suggests that earlier involvement in sexual activity increases the chances that subsequent development will be compromised. Although it is known that a variety of negative characteristics are associated with early first sexual intercourse (Chilman, 1980; Crockett et al., 1996; Dorius et al., 1993; R. Jessor et al., 1983; S. L. Jessor & Jessor, 1977; Mott & Haurin, 1988; Ohannesian & Crockett, 1993; Rosenbaum & Kandel, 1990), it is not known whether the timing of first sexual intercourse produces these characteristics or whether they are simply correlates of the timing of first sexual intercourse.

Hypotheses

The first hypothesis was derived from problem behavior theory, which suggests that transition proneness is associated with poorer psychosocial adjustment and earlier timing of developmental transitions. Hence, the first hypothesis was that longitudinal patterns indicative of poorer psychosocial development (i.e., more problem behavior, less conventional behavior, poorer family and peer relationships, and lower self-esteem and less positive affect [greater depression]) would be associated with earlier timing of first sexual intercourse.

The stage termination model posits that poorer outcomes result when developmental transitions are made too early and individuals are advanced beyond their developmental capability to cope positively. The second hypothesis was that earlier first sexual intercourse would be associated with negative psychosocial outcomes.

The third hypothesis was based on the sexual double standard (Reiss, 1960) and posited that the negative effects of early sexual debut would be greater for girls than for boys.

Method

Design

Using a cohort-sequential longitudinal design (Baltes, 1968; Schaie, 1965), we collected the data for the present research to measure three cohorts of adolescents: 7th, 8th, and 9th graders, initially. Each cohort was surveyed annually through 12th grade. Because only two cohorts had data collected before 9th grade, the longitudinal analyses used data collected when the students were in 9th through 12th grades; however, 7th- and 8th-grade data were used to assess psychosocial adjustment before first sexual intercourse, which was included as a covariate.

We pooled data from the three cohorts to maximize the sample size for each grade level; hence, each cohort's 9th-grade data were pooled together, as were their 10th-grade data, and so on through 12th grade. A few students repeated a grade during high school. To maintain the integrity of the design, we assigned the data to consecutive annual waves of the study as though no grade had been repeated. Tests for cohort effects in the pooled data were all nonsignificant, suggesting that the data were not biased by cohort differences.

Sample

The sample for this study consisted of Euro-American, rural adolescents from a single school district in a geographically contained, middle- to low-income (1980 median household income = $14,400; approximately 12% of all households were below the poverty level) rural community in the northeastern United States. At 9th grade, all participants considered together had a mean age of 14 years ($SD = 0.50$).

Data were collected during regular school hours, with trained research personnel surveying boys and girls in separate rooms. To ensure privacy and maintain confidentiality, we excluded teachers and school administrators from all aspects of the surveying process, identified surveys by a six-digit numerical code, and placed participants in noncontiguous seats while surveys were being filled out. Students who refused consent or whose parents refused consent were excluded from data collection (participation rate was about 95%).

The total longitudinal sample ($N = 505$; 251 girls and 254 boys) included students who participated in the first annual survey, students who completed at least three of the four annual surveys given between their 9th and 12th grades, and students for whom age at first sexual intercourse could be calculated. As a result of inconsistent reporting of sexual intercourse experience, age at first intercourse could not be calculated for 91 of the participants (35 girls and 56 boys). Because the psychosocial adjustment of these 91 adolescents did not differ from the adjustment of those who had complete and consistent sexual behavior data, the adolescents who were missing age at first intercourse data were dropped from analyses.

The remaining sample consisted of 414 participants (216 girls, 198 boys). Ninety-nine of these individuals (47 girls and 52 boys) were missing one of the four surveys given from 9th and 12th grade. Because these students were significantly less well adjusted than their peers who had complete longitudinal data, they were retained in the sample and their missing data were estimated using a method designed to estimate missing data in longitudinal data sets (Petersen, 1987; see also Galambos, Almeida, & Petersen, 1990). This method imputes missing data by using two components, one nomothetic and cross-sectional, and the other idiographic and longitudinal. The nomothetic component, $\bar{X}_j$, is an arithmetic mean obtained from each of the four times of measurement and is calculated as:

$$\bar{X}_j = \frac{1}{N_j} \sum_i x_{ij}, \qquad (1)$$

where i = the ith participant at longitudinal measurement point j who is missing data at a time-point other than j; j = time-points {1, 2, 3, . . .}; and, N_j = the number of participants at time j for which data are missing at time-points other than j.

The idiographic component, I_{x_i}, is the weighted average distance between each participant's data point and the nomothetic component, calculated as

$$\bar{I}_{x_i} = \frac{1}{K} \sum_j (x_{ij} - \bar{X}_j), \qquad (2)$$

where i = the ith participant at longitudinal time-point j who is missing data at a time-point other than j; j = time-points {1, 2, 3, . . .}; k = the number of longitudinal time-points with non-missing data for x_i.

As an example, consider a participant who is missing the third (S3) of four surveys (S1, S2, S3, S4). The nomothetic component is calculated as the mean of variable x_{i1} measured at S1 and is based on the subsample of participants who are missing data from a time point other than S1, and so forth for x_{i2} (S2) through x_{i4} (S4). The missing data point is then estimated by adding the idiographic component to the nomothetic component. Because of the prevalence of gender (6 out of 10 measures) and timing group (9 out of 10 measures) differences in psychosocial adjustment, missing data for the present research were estimated separately for boys and girls and for the three timing groups.

To assure that data imputation had not biased the sample, we used LISREL7 (Jöreskog & Sörbom, 1989) to compare the sample covariance structure before and after imputation in a stacked two-group (the covariance structures before and after imputation) design with all parameter estimates constrained to be invariant across the two groups (Jöreskog & Sörbom, 1989). Goodness of fit exceeded .990, indicating that the covariance structure of the data was not altered by the estimation procedure.

Measures

Timing of first sexual intercourse. The independent variable was the relative timing of first sexual intercourse. Annual surveys asked participants if they had ever had sex.[1] The annual data from this question were used, along with chronological age, to calculate each participant's age at first intercourse.

We used age at first sexual intercourse to assign participants to one of three timing groups: early, middle, or late. Timing groups were formed separately for boys and girls, because girls in the sample became sexually active an average of 10 months later than boys. Participants were assigned to the early timing group if they had sexual intercourse before 12th grade (n = 166) and their age at first intercourse was below the median age at first intercourse (*Mdn* girls = 15.5 years of age; *Mdn* boys = 14.75 years of age). Participants were assigned to the middle timing group (n = 156) if they had sexual intercourse before 12th grade and their age at first sexual intercourse was at or above the median. Determination of the median age at first intercourse was based on the subsample of adolescents who had sexual intercourse before 12th grade. Those who remained virgins at the beginning of 12th grade were assigned to the late timing group (n = 92).

The adolescents in the present sample reported a lower median age at first sexual intercourse than adolescents in several notable national samples of urban adolescents, namely, the National Longitudinal Study of Youth, the National Study of Family Growth, and the national surveys of young women and men conducted by Zelnik and Kantner (1980). These three studies show a median age at first sexual intercourse ranging from 17.0 to 17.2 years. This differs markedly from the present study, in which the median age at first sexual intercourse (considering the entire sample) was 16.1 and 15.1 years for female and male adolescents, respectively. However, these three national samples represented earlier cohorts of adolescents (birth years of 1959–1963) than did the sample used in the present research (birth years ranging from approximately 1970 to 1973).

Other evidence suggests that the median age of first sexual intercourse for the present sample does not differ from other samples of adolescents from more recent cohorts, which indicate that the age at first sexual intercourse continued to decline during the 1980s (Hofferth, 1987). In addition, 71% of the adolescents in the present sample reported having had intercourse at least once by the beginning of 12th grade. This is comparable with national statistics indicating that approximately 80% of adolescents experience first sexual intercourse by the end of 12th grade (Hayes, 1987). Finally, the age at first intercourse of adolescents in the present sample is comparable with that found in other samples of rural adolescents (Alexander et al., 1989). Taken together, this evidence suggests that the age at first sexual intercourse for adolescents in the present research is similar to those in other rural samples and does not differ greatly from more recent cohorts of nonrural adolescents.

We took several precautions to ensure the validity of the timing of first sexual intercourse measure. First, no age at first intercourse was assigned to participants who reported contradictory longitudinal information regarding their virginity status (e.g., reporting that they were virgins after indicating that they had previously been nonvirgins, or retrospectively reporting an age at first intercourse[2] that disagreed with their longitudinal reports of intercourse activity), and these participants were excluded from the present analyses. As mentioned previously, the participants who were missing age at first sexual intercourse (91 participants, including those whose longitudinal data were contradictory) did not differ from the remaining sample.

Second, as a check on construct validity, we used analysis of variance to examine the association between timing of first sexual intercourse and other sexual behaviors. Results showed that earlier timing was significantly associated with more necking and petting, $F(2, 291) = 57.26$, $p < .0001$ and $F(2, 291) = 50.96$, $p < .0001$. Further examination of the data indicated that adolescents in the late timing group were more likely than their nonvirgin age-mates to have never necked or petted, whereas all but 2 of the nonvirgins had necked or petted at least once. It is unlikely that adolescents who have had sexual intercourse would not have necked or petted. In addition, it is expected that adolescents who have had sexual intercourse would be more involved than their virgin age-mates in other sexual behaviors. The observation of these expected patterns of association in the present sample provides validity for the timing measure.

Psychosocial Outcomes

Problem behavior theory guided the selection of outcome measures for the present research. The measures represent the three conceptual systems of problem behavior theory (e.g., R. Jessor et al., 1983): the behavior system (conventional and problem behaviors); the perceived environment system (quality of family and peer relationships); and the personality system (self-esteem and level of affect).

Problem behaviors. Minor deviance was measured by an 11-item scale from the Primary Prevention Awareness, Attitudes and Usage Scale (PPAAUS; Swisher, Shute, & Bibeau, 1985). The PPAAUS assesses behaviors such as shoplifting, truancy, cheating on exams, staying out all night without parental permission, and fighting. Responses range from 1 = *never* to 5 = *almost every day*. Scores were computed so that higher scores reflected more minor deviance. On the basis of data from the annual surveys, coefficient alphas ranged from .75 to .81.

Substance use was measured by using two single-item measures that were also taken from the PPAAUS. These two items reflected how often

[1] The question regarding the occurrence of sexual intercourse asked the adolescents if they "had ever been sexually active (had sex)." Because of concerns within the participating school district regarding the sexual content of survey items, no more detailed or explicit question was allowed.

[2] The item added at the fourth survey was judged not to be appropriate as a sole indicator of first sexual intercourse for three reasons: (a) it was retrospective, making it inferior to the item measured longitudinally; (b) the retrospective item was asked at different grades in school for members of the three cohorts, making it impossible to use once the data were pooled (see Figure 1); and (c) data for the retrospective item were more frequently missing than were the data for the item asked year to year.

participants got drunk and got high on drugs, respectively. Responses to these items ranged from 1 = *never* to 5 = *almost every day*.

Conventional behaviors. Three single items measured conventional behaviors. The first item measured the frequency of church attendance. Responses ranged from 0 = *never* to 5 = *more than once per week*. The second item assessed academic expectations by asking participants how much education they planned to complete. Responses ranged from 1 = *some high school* to 6 = *beyond college*. Finally, the third item measured school performance by asking participants to report their average grades (e.g., marks) in school. Responses to this item ranged from 1 = *mostly F's* to 8 = *mostly A's*. On the basis of annual survey data, intercorrelations among these items ranged from .51 to .79.

Quality of relationships. Two multi-item subscales, taken from the Self-Image Questionnaire for Young Adolescents (SIQYA), were used to measure the quality of parent (17 items) and peer (9 items) relationships (Petersen, Schulenberg, Abramowitz, Offer, & Jarcho, 1984). Responses to the scale items ranged from 1 = *very strongly agree* to 6 = *very strongly disagree*. A sample item from the family relationships scale is, "I can count on my parents most of the time," and a sample item from the peer relationships scale is, "I do not have a particularly difficult time making friends." Scale scores were computed so that higher scores indicated more positive relationships. On the basis of the data from the annual surveys, coefficient alphas ranged from .82 to .91 for the family relationships scale and from .89 to .93 for the peer relationships scale. Instrument validity has been demonstrated in prior studies (Petersen et al., 1984).

Psychological adjustment. Psychological adjustment was measured by two multi-item scales assessing self-esteem and positive affect. Self-esteem was measured by the Rosenberg Self-Esteem Scale (Rosenberg, 1965). Items on this scale ranged from 1 = *strongly agree* to 4 = *strongly disagree*. A sample item from this scale is, "On the whole, I am satisfied with myself." Scale scores were computed so that higher scores indicated higher self-esteem. On the basis of data from the annual surveys, coefficient alphas ranged from .85 to .91. The validity of this widely used instrument has been previously established (Rosenberg, 1965).

Positive affect was measured by the Emotional Tone subscale of the SIQYA (Petersen et al., 1984). Emotional Tone measures positive affect and correlates negatively with depression. Item responses ranged from 1 = *very strongly agree* to 6 = *very strongly disagree*. An example item from this scale is, "Most of the time I am happy." Scale scores were computed so that a higher score depicted more positive affect. On the basis of data from the annual surveys, coefficient alphas ranged from .82 to .86. Instrument validity has been demonstrated in prior studies (Petersen et al., 1984).

Results

Descriptive sample statistics for the 9th- through 12th-grade outcome variables are reported in Table 1. Means broken down by gender and timing of first intercourse groups at each of the four grades are presented in Figures 1, 2, and 3.

The purpose of the present research was to compare two alternative developmental models explaining the association between the timing of first sexual intercourse and psychosocial development. First, assumptions of problem behavior theory were tested by comparing the longitudinal patterns of psychosocial development of adolescents from the timing of first intercourse groups: early, middle, and late. We examined data for the presence and consistency of timing group differences in psychosocial development beginning when the participants were in 9th grade, and continuing through 10th, 11th, and 12th grades. These analyses tested whether the timing of first intercourse was associated with longitudinal patterns of poorer psychosocial adjustment.

Table 1
Means, Standard Deviations, and Sample Sizes for Psychosocial Adjustment From 9th Through 12th Grades (N = 414)

Variable	Grade in school			
	9th	10th	11th	12th
Minor deviance				
M	1.68	1.68	1.70	1.68
SD	0.48	0.46	0.47	0.46
Drunkenness				
M	1.97	2.14	2.34	2.40
SD	1.04	1.06	1.06	1.05
Drug use				
M	1.21	1.25	1.39	1.44
SD	0.68	0.70	0.79	0.84
Church attendance				
M	2.77	2.51	2.26	2.05
SD	1.75	1.84	1.85	1.86
Academic plans				
M	4.26	4.14	4.16	4.03
SD	1.47	1.42	1.37	1.30
Marks in school				
M	6.16	6.03	6.11	6.18
SD	1.26	1.24	1.19	1.31
Family relationships				
M	4.55	4.57	4.50	4.53
SD	0.80	0.78	0.78	0.81
Peer relationships				
M	4.60	4.68	4.69	4.53
SD	0.72	0.73	0.71	0.73
Self-esteem				
M	3.19	3.21	3.24	3.22
SD	0.50	0.50	0.48	0.55
Positive affect				
M	4.41	4.52	4.51	4.58
SD	0.82	0.80	0.80	0.84

Second, the hypotheses suggested by the stage termination model were tested by examining the partial association between the timing of first sexual intercourse and psychosocial development measured at 12th grade. That is, we tested 12th-grade psychosocial functioning for timing group differences while controlling for the level of psychosocial adjustment before first intercourse. These analyses tested the effect of the timing of first intercourse on subsequent psychosocial adjustment.

In all analyses, gender was used as an independent variable, along with timing of first sexual intercourse, so that gender differences in the association between timing of first sexual intercourse and psychosocial development could be tested.

Longitudinal Patterns

Doubly multivariate analysis of variance (i.e., a repeated measures analysis of variance with multiple dependent variables; D-MANOVA) was used to test the first hypothesis. A 3 (timing group) × 2 (gender) × 4 (grade in school) design was used. Grade in school was the repeated within-subject variable. Analyses were conducted for each set of outcome variables: problem behaviors, conventional behaviors, quality of relation-

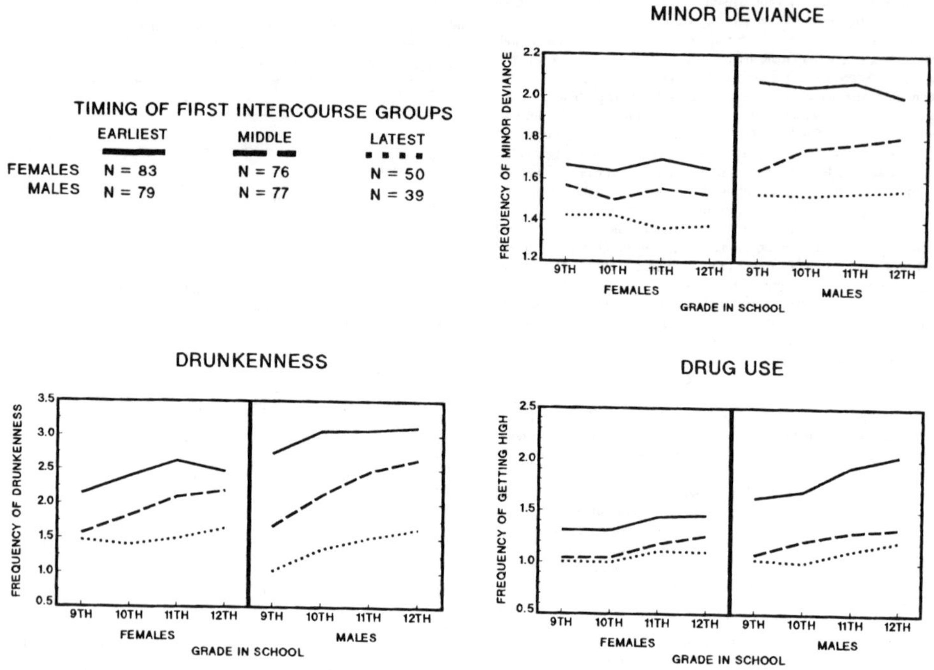

Figure 1. Frequency of involvement in minor deviance, drunkenness, and drug use from 9th to 12th grade by gender and timing group.

ships, and psychological adjustment. D-MANOVA results are reported in Table 2 and cell means are presented in Figures 1 through 3.

Problem behavior involvement. D-MANOVA resulted in significant multivariate main effects of gender and timing group, and a significant multivariate interaction of timing and gender (see Table 2). Univariate tests indicated that earlier timing of first sexual intercourse was associated with more minor deviance, drunkenness, and drug use (see Figure 1). The significant multivariate interaction resulted from boys in the earlier timing group consistently reporting more problem behaviors than any other group of girls or boys.

The D-MANOVA also resulted in a significant within-subjects main effect of grade for drunkenness and drug use and a significant within-subjects interaction of grade in school and timing group for drunkenness (see Table 2). Drunkenness and drug use increased from 9th to 12th grade for all three timing groups (see Figure 1).

Conventional behavior. D-MANOVA resulted in between-subjects main effects of gender and timing (see Table 2). Univariate effects showed one significant gender difference: Girls reported higher marks in school than boys (see Figure 2). Univariate timing group differences were found for church attendance, academic plans, and marks in school. For all three conventional behaviors, participation was greatest for the latest timing group, lower for the middle timing group, and lowest for the earliest timing group.

D-MANOVA also resulted in a significant multivariate within-subjects main effect of grade and a significant interaction of grade and gender. Academic plans increased and church attendance decreased from 9th to 12th grades for all gender and timing groups (see Figure 2). Girls' marks in school increased from 9th to 12th grade, whereas boys' marks remained constant across all four grades, resulting in the interaction of grade and gender (see Figure 2).

Quality of relationships. D-MANOVA resulted in a significant multivariate between-subjects main effect of timing for family relationships and peer relationships (see Table 2). The univariate tests indicated that the quality of family relationships increased and the quality of peer relationships decreased with later first intercourse (see Figure 3). Hence, members of the latest timing group reported the best family relationships, whereas early timing was associated with the best peer relationships.

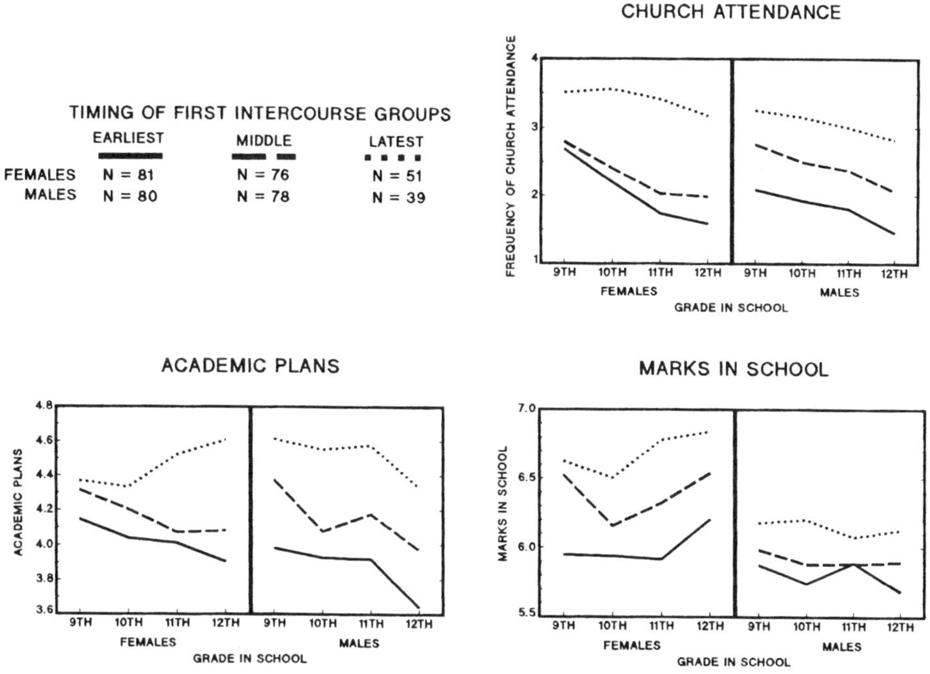

Figure 2. Frequency of church attendance, school aspirations, and marks in school from 9th to 12th grade by gender and timing group.

D-MANOVA also resulted in significant multivariate within-subjects interactions between grade and gender, and between grade and timing group for quality of relationships (see Table 2). Univariate tests indicated that family relationships increased in quality for girls and decreased for boys between 9th and 12th grades. In addition, the pattern of family relationships over time were different for the three timing groups, showing a strong cubic pattern for the middle group that was not evident for the other groups (see Figure 3).

Psychological adjustment. D-MANOVA resulted in a multivariate between-subjects main effect of gender. Univariate analyses indicated that boys reported significantly higher self-esteem and more positive affect compared with girls from 9th to 12th grades (see Table 2). No significant effects of timing group were found for self-esteem or positive affect.

D-MANOVA also resulted in a significant within-subjects interaction of grade and gender for self-esteem (see Table 2). Self-esteem for girls increased steadily from 9th to 12th grade, whereas the self-esteem of boys did not change significantly. A significant main effect of grade was found for positive affect, which increased significantly between 9th and 12th grades for both girls and boys.

Summary of the longitudinal analyses. The longitudinal analyses demonstrated consistent longitudinal patterns of development associated with the timing of sexual debut. The early timing group had a longitudinal trajectory of poor psychosocial development, whereas members of the middle and late timing groups demonstrated more positive longitudinal patterns of development. These results support the problem behavior theory and suggest that first sexual intercourse is associated with a longitudinal pattern of transition proneness and poorer psychosocial adjustment.

Another question still remains: Is the timing of first sexual intercourse simply part of a pattern of psychosocial development, or, consistent with the stage termination model, is having first sexual intercourse early detrimental to subsequent psychosocial adjustment? The following are analyses testing the second hypothesis.

Outcomes of First Sexual Intercourse

We tested assumptions of the stage termination model using a 3 (timing group) × 2 (gender) analysis of covariance (ANCOVAs). This design tested the association between the

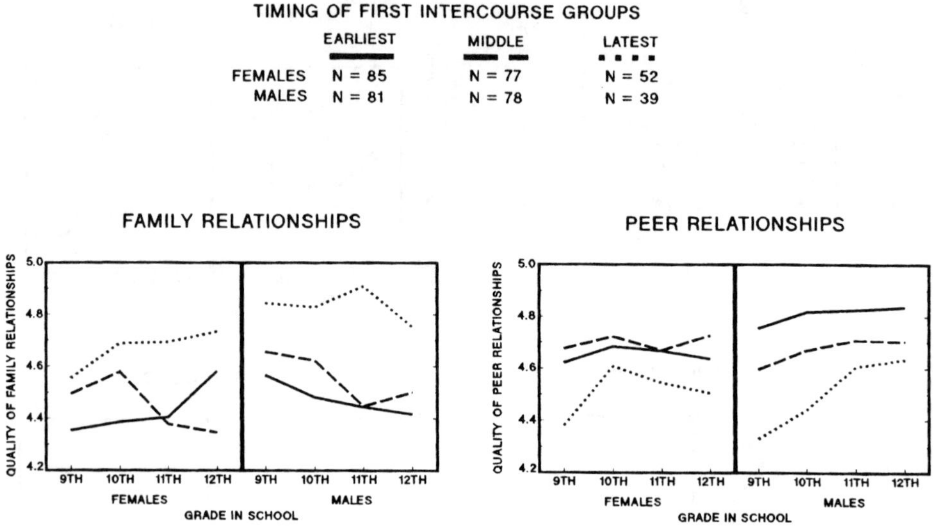

Figure 3. Quality of family and peer relationships from 9th to 12th grade by gender and timing group.

timing of first sexual intercourse and 12th-grade psychosocial adjustment when psychosocial adjustment before first intercourse was statistically controlled. This design was used to examine each of the 10 outcome measures. In each case, two covariates were used. The first was the indicator of prior adjustment, which was measured at the first survey when the participants were in 7th, 8th, and 9th grades. The time lag between the measurement of prior psychosocial adjustment and

Table 2
Associations Between Timing of First Sexual Intercourse and Longitudinal Patterns of Psychosocial Adjustment

	Between-subjects effect			Within-subjects effect			
Psychosocial outcome	Timing	Gender	Timing × Gender	Grade	Grade × Timing	Grade × Gender	Grade × Timing × Gender
Problem behaviors							
Multivariate *F*	30.00***	14.48***	3.25**	13.68***	2.09**	1.00	1.56
Deviance	36.60***	43.57***	4.08*	0.44	1.34	1.00	1.56
Drunkenness	90.87***	12.06***	7.09***	36.13***	4.20***	2.55	1.13
Drug use	36.34***	11.87***	5.67**	10.78***	0.44	0.76	0.61
Conventional behaviors							
Multivariate *F*	7.44***	6.26***	1.18	9.37***	0.82	2.34*	0.95
Church	20.17***	0.97	0.83	23.23***	1.20	1.33	0.81
Plans	6.15**	0.10	0.28	3.94**	0.87	2.18	0.62
Marks	7.55***	14.91***	1.03	2.30	0.47	3.39*	1.36
Quality of relationships							
Multivariate *F*	9.06***	1.19	1.08	3.32**	1.90*	3.11**	1.11
Family	5.92**	2.39	0.25	0.89	2.85**	3.15*	1.29
Peers	4.09*	0.41	1.06	5.17**	0.92	1.78	0.60
Psychological adjustment							
Multivariate *F*	0.50	10.48***	0.57	5.01***	0.61	3.30**	0.34
Self-esteem	0.35	15.42***	1.10	1.79	0.38	2.95*	0.24
Positive affect	0.01	20.89***	0.70	6.93***	0.61	2.10	0.28

*$p < .05$. **$p < .01$. ***$p < .001$.

the measurement of 12th-grade adjustment varied for participants from the three grade cohorts (6, 5, and 4 years, respectively). The second covariate, grade cohort, was added to the model to control for spurious effects created by these differences in time lag.

In order for analysis of covariance to provide adequate statistical control, it is necessary that the covariate be measured before the event being examined (Neter, Wasserman, & Kutner, 1985). In the present case, that event was first sexual intercourse. Forty-five participants (10 girls, 35 boys) reported that they were nonvirgins when they completed the first survey. For reasons of design integrity, these participants were excluded from the 10 ANCOVAs. Some additional participants were missing at least one of the covariates, resulting in slight fluctuations in the sample size for each of the ANCOVAs.

Results of the ANCOVAs are reported in Table 3. No negative psychosocial outcomes were associated with the timing of first sexual intercourse once prior psychosocial adjustment and grade cohort were statistically controlled. Although significant timing group differences were found for drunkenness, the adjusted means in Table 3 indicate that this effect resulted from the late timing group having a lower level of drunkenness in comparison with the other two timing groups. These results suggest that the timing of first sexual intercourse, per se, is not associated with negative psychosocial outcomes. This is not to say that other factors associated with early sexual intercourse (i.e., unwanted pregnancy, sexually transmitted diseases, or AIDS) do not result in negative psychosocial outcomes.

Gender as a Moderator

The third hypothesis posited that the effects of early first sexual intercourse would be more severe for girls than for boys. The moderating effect of gender was tested simultaneously with the other hypotheses by examining interactions between gender and timing of sexual intercourse in the D-MANOVAs and ANCOVAs discussed previously. In all, only three interactions of gender and timing group were observed. These interactions were found in the longitudinal association between timing and problem behavior from 9th and 12th grade, and resulted from greater timing group differences for boys than for girls (see Figure 1). Where minor deviance and drug use were concerned, differences between the early and middle timing groups were greater for boys than for girls. For drunkenness, differences among all three timing groups were greater for boys than for girls. Despite these differences in level of problem behavior, longitudinal timing group patterns were the same for both genders; that is, earlier timing was associated with more, and later timing with less, problem behavior at all four grades and for both genders. Although it can be concluded that gender was associated with the strength of the timing effects, it cannot be concluded that the effects of early intercourse are more severe for girls than for boys. Hence, the gender moderation hypothesis was not supported.

Discussion

The present research tested hypotheses drawn from problem behavior theory, the stage termination model, and the sexual double standard regarding the association between the timing of first sexual intercourse and psychosocial development. Results indicated the following: (a) Earlier first intercourse is associated with poorer psychosocial development, thus supporting problem behavior theory (Bingham et al., 1990; R. Jessor et al., 1983; S. L. Jessor & Jessor, 1977; Ketterlinus, Lamb, Nitz, & Elster, 1992); (b) contrary to hypotheses generated from the stage termination model, timing of first sexual intercourse does not result in detrimental psychosocial outcomes; and (c) contrary to hypotheses based on the sexual double standard, the effects of early intercourse are not more severe for girls than they are for boys.

Neither self-esteem nor level of affect were found to be longitudinally associated with the timing of first sexual intercourse. One of two processes may account for this lack of results. First, it may be that the timing of first intercourse is simply not related to self-esteem and level of affect. Second, perhaps other factors, such as socialization and beliefs regarding sex, act independent of timing to shape adolescents' emotional reactions to first intercourse, thus giving rise to a variety of emotional outcomes to having had intercourse that are not directly tied to its timing.

Other results from the present research demonstrated a consistent association between positive psychosocial development and the postponement of first sexual intercourse; however, the quality of peer relationships was an exception. Contrary to hypothesized expectations and other research (Hurrelmann, 1990), adolescents who initiated sexual intercourse the latest had the poorest, rather than the best, quality peer relationships. One explanation of this contradictory finding is that adolescents in the late timing group have difficulty identifying compatible peers (Billy et al., 1988). Adolescents in the late timing group reported the most positive family relationships, the most frequent church attendance, the greatest commitment to education, and the lowest involvement in problem behaviors of any of the three timing groups. Involvement in this constellation of behaviors undoubtedly distinguished these adolescents from their earlier initiating peers. It should be recalled that the present sample consisted of a majority of the adolescents attending a single high school within a single school district, and that the late timing group was the smallest of the three groups in the sample. Because of the small size of this group of adolescents, not to mention their behavioral and interpersonal features, they may have had difficulty finding compatible peers.

A second explanation of the association between timing and peer relationships is that having positive peer relationships may catalyze involvement in problem and sexual behaviors. Having more positive peer relationships may enable adolescents to obtain beer and other substances, help them to identify peers who are willing accomplices in problem behaviors or who are available sexual partners. Having poorer quality family relationships and being less committed to social institutions such as church and school may also disinhibit adolescents, allowing them more freedom to defy the expectations of conventional society (Hirschi, 1969). Thus, positive peer relationships, especially when combined with poor family relationships and low involvement in conventional behaviors, may facilitate adolescents' involvement in problem and sexual behaviors.

One of the most important findings from the present research was the consistency of timing group differences in patterns of

Table 3
Results of Analysis of Covariance: Unadjusted and Adjusted Means for Timing of First Intercourse

Variable/timing group	Observed *M*	*M* adjusted		
		Grade cohort	Prior adjustment	Adjustment & cohort
Minor deviance				
Early	1.79_a	1.82	**2.17**	1.89
Middle	1.67_b	1.67	**1.52**	1.56
Late	1.46_c	1.47	**1.37**	1.49
Drunkenness				
Early	2.70_a	2.79	**3.07**	**2.79**
Middle	2.43_b	2.41	**2.44**	**2.44**
Late	1.64_c	1.64	**1.35**	**1.44**
Drug use				
Early	1.71_a	1.80	1.66	1.72
Middle	1.30_b	1.28	1.38	1.32
Late	1.15_b	1.15	1.02	1.11
Church attendance				
Early	1.58_a	1.59	2.44	2.59
Middle	2.01_b	1.96	2.09	1.91
Late	3.00_c	2.99	2.05	2.04
Academic plans				
Early	3.76_a	3.78	3.84	3.66
Middle	4.02_a	4.01	4.23	3.97
Late	4.47_b	4.45	3.87	4.70
Marks in school				
Early	6.07_a	6.02	6.27	6.16
Middle	$6.24_{a,b}$	6.24	6.69	6.04
Late	6.52_b	6.48	5.47	6.72
Family relationships				
Early	$4.57_{a,b}$	4.55	5.17	5.17
Middle	4.44_a	4.43	4.26	3.86
Late	4.76_b	4.76	4.43	4.91
Peer relationships				
Early	4.65	4.68	**5.34**	5.34
Middle	4.72	4.71	**4.19**	4.19
Late	4.58	4.58	**4.48**	4.49
Self-esteem				
Early	3.19	3.21	**4.01**	3.50
Middle	3.24	3.24	**3.32**	3.15
Late	3.24	3.24	**2.49**	3.08
Positive affect				
Early	4.56	4.59	**5.62**	4.71
Middle	4.59	4.59	**4.56**	4.52
Late	4.58	4.59	**3.75**	4.48

Note. Group means with the same subscripts are not significantly different. Post hoc test results are provided only for effects of timing group that were significant at alpha $< .05$. Values in boldface indicate tests in which timing group effects remained significant after the control variable was covaried.

psychosocial development from 9th to 12th grade. Longitudinal patterns of development for the three timing groups were primarily nonintersecting between 9th and 12th grade (see Figures 1 through 3) and represent distinct developmental trajectories. Individuals who had first sexual intercourse early demonstrated the poorest psychosocial adjustment at 9th grade, and the same negative developmental trajectory persisted through 12th grade. In stark contrast, adolescents in the late timing group had the most positive 9th-grade adjustment and the most positive trajectory of development through 12th grade.

These patterns of development from 9th to 12th grade were not outcomes associated with the timing of first sexual intercourse, as results presented earlier attest. Instead, they were a continuation of enduring developmental trajectories that preceded 9th grade. Timing group differences in psychosocial development were apparent at the beginning of 9th grade, suggesting that individual trajectories of development were well established by that time (see Figures 1, 2, and 3). Other evidence suggests that individual differences in psychosocial development were a result of childhood variation in variables such as temperament and family context (Jansen, Fitzgerald, Ham, & Zucker, 1995; Lambert & Windmiller, 1977; Patterson, DeBaryshe, & Ramsey, 1989). These early individual differences are thought to set the stage for later developmental and behavioral patterns that continue into adulthood (Zucker, 1987), resulting in trajectories of development extending from childhood to adolescence, and on to adulthood.

The consistency of psychosocial development, coupled with the failure to identify any net negative outcomes connected with the timing of first sexual intercourse, implies that the association between poor psychosocial development and early sexual intercourse is not attributable to the timing of first intercourse, per se. Instead, these findings suggest that this association is a continuation of preexisting developmental patterns—patterns that predispose the individual to developmental risks such as unprotected intercourse, sexually transmitted disease, pregnancy, problem behaviors, and isolation from conventional social institutions such as family and school.

Results from the present research provide several implications for intervention into adolescent sexual behavior. First, the longitudinal consistency of timing group differences in psychosocial development suggests that interventions into the sexual behavior of adolescents should protect adolescents from other risks resulting from poor psychosocial development as well. Such risks include substance use and delinquency (R. Jessor et al., 1983; S. L. Jessor & Jessor, 1977), social alienation (Hirschi, 1969), and the continuation of negative patterns of development (R. Jessor et al., 1983).

Results from the present research also indicate that early intervention into poor psychosocial development might be an efficient means of simultaneously preventing numerous negative developmental outcomes. Enhancing positive psychosocial development during childhood may shift developmental trajectories and effectively prevent entire constellations of negative outcomes during adolescence, including problem behavior involvement and negative outcomes resulting from the failure of young, sexually active adolescents to use safe-sex practices.

The present research examined a sample of Euro-American adolescents attending high school in a rural area of the United States. Future research examining the association between psychosocial development and the timing of first sexual intercourse should focus on other racial and ethnic populations, as well as adolescents who have dropped out of school, or who are experiencing more severe negative adjustment generally. In addition, more research is needed to examine the formation of developmental trajectories and the continuity of these trajectories from childhood, through adolescence, and into adulthood.

In summary, the results of the present research suggest that boys and girls who initiate sexual intercourse early are involved in more problem behavior and less conventional behavior and have poorer quality family relationships. It would also appear that these patterns of negative psychosocial development are not a result of the timing of first sexual intercourse but are a continuation of long-term patterns of poor psychosocial development that were established before ninth grade. On the basis of these results, it is suggested that interventions that enhance childhood psychosocial development might effectively circumvent a host of negative developmental outcomes.

References

Alexander, C. S., Ensminger, M. E., Kim, Y. J., Smith, J., Johnson, K. E., & Dolan, L. J. (1989). Early sexual activity among adolescents in small towns and rural areas: Race and gender patterns. *Family Planning Perspectives, 21,* 261–266.

Baltes, P. B. (1968). Longitudinal and cross-sectional sequences in the study of age and generation effects. *Human Development, 11,* 145–171.

Billy, J. O. G., Landale, N. S., Grady, W. R., & Zimmerle, D. M. (1988). Effects of sexual activity on adolescent social and psychological development. *Social Psychology Quarterly, 51,* 190–212.

Bingham, C. R. (1989). AIDS and adolescents: Threat of infection and approaches for prevention. *Journal of Early Adolescence, 9,* 50–66.

Bingham, C. R., Miller, B. C., & Adams, G. R. (1990). Correlates of age at first sexual intercourse in a national sample of young women. *Journal of Adolescent Research, 5,* 18–33.

Chilman, C. S. (1980). *Adolescent sexuality in a changing American society* (Report No. 79-1426). Bethesda, MD: U.S. Department of Health, Education, and Welfare.

Clement, U. (1989). Profile analysis as a method of comparing intergenerational differences in sexual behavior. *Archives of Sexual Behavior, 18,* 229–237.

Crockett, L. J., Bingham, C. R., Chopak, J. S., & Vicary, J. R. (1996). Timing of first sexual intercourse: The role of social control, social learning, and problem behavior. *Journal of Youth and Adolescence, 25,* 89–111.

Cvetkovich, G., Grote, B., Lieberman, E. J., & Miller, W. (1978). Sex role development and teenage fertility-related behavior. *Adolescence, 13,* 231–236.

Day, R. D. (1992). The transition to first intercourse among racially and culturally diverse youth. *Journal of Marriage and the Family, 54,* 749–762.

D'Augelli, T. R., & Bingham, C. R. (1993). Interventions to prevent HIV infection among young adolescents. In R. M. Lerner (Ed.), *Early adolescence: Perspectives on research, policy, and intervention* (pp. 353–368). Hillsdale, NJ: Erlbaum.

Dorius, G. L., Heaton, T. B., & Steffen, P. (1993). Adolescent life events and their association with the onset of sexual intercourse. *Youth and Society, 25,* 3–23.

Erikson, E. H. (1968). *Youth, identity, and crisis.* New York: Norton.

Forrest, J. D., & Singh, S. (1990). The sexual and reproductive behavior of American Women, 1982–1988. *Family Planning Perspectives, 22,* 206–214.

Gagnon, J. (1977). *Human sexualities.* Chicago: Scott, Foresman.

Galambos, N. L., Almeida, D. M., & Petersen, A. C. (1990). Masculinity, femininity, and sex role attitudes in early adolescence: Exploring gender intensification. *Child Development, 61,* 1905–1914.

Hayes, C. D. (1987). *Risking the future: Adolescent sexuality, pregnancy, and childbearing.* Washington, DC: National Academy Press.

Hirschi, T. (1969). *Causes of delinquency.* Berkeley: University of California Press.

Hofferth, S. L. (1987). Influences on early sexual and fertility behavior. In C. D. Hayes (Ed.), *Risking the future: Adolescent sexuality, pregnancy, and childbearing: Vol. 2. Working papers* (pp. 7–35). Washington, DC: National Academy Press.

Hurrelmann, K. (1990). Parents, peers, teachers, and other significant partners in adolescence. *International Journal of Adolescence and Youth, 2,* 211–236.

Jansen, R. E., Fitzgerald, H. E., Ham, H. P., & Zucker, R. A. (1995). Difficult temperament and behavior problems in three- to five-year-old sons of alcoholics. *Alcoholism: Clinical and Experimental Research, 19,* 501–509.

Jessor, R., Costa, F., Jessor, L., & Donovan, J. E. (1983). Time of first intercourse: A prospective study. *Journal of Personality and Social Psychology, 44,* 608–626.

Jessor, S. L., & Jessor, R. (1977). Transition from virginity to nonvirginity among youth: A social psychological study over time. *Developmental Psychology, 4,* 473–484.

Jones, E. F., Forrest, J. D., Goldman, N., Henshaw, S., Lincoln, R., Rosoff, J. I., Westoff, C. F., & Wulf, D. (1986). *Teenage pregnancy in*

industrialized countries (pp. 21–36). New Haven, CT: Yale University Press.
Jöreskog, K. G., & Sörbom, D. (1989). *LISREL7: A guide to the program and applications* (2nd ed.). Chicago: SPSS, Inc.
Ketterlinus, R. D., Lamb, M. E., Nitz, K., & Elster, A. B. (1992). Adolescent nonsexual and sex-related problem behaviors. *Journal of Adolescent Research, 7,* 431–456.
Koch, P. B. (1988). The relationship of first intercourse to later sexual functioning concerns of adolescents. *Journal of Adolescent Research, 3,* 345–362.
Lambert, N. M., & Windmiller, M. (1977). An exploratory study of temperament traits in a population of children at risk. *The Journal of Special Education, 11,* 37–46.
Lief, H. I. (1986). Sex and depression [Special issue: The physician's guide to sexual counseling]. *Medical Aspects of Human Sexuality, 20,* 38–53.
Long, I. (1976). Human sexuality and aging. *Social Casework, 57,* 237–244.
Miller, B. C., & Fox, G. L. (1987). Theories of adolescent heterosexual behavior. *Journal of Adolescent Research, 2,* 269–282.
Miller, B. C., McCoy, K., Olson, T. D., & Wallace, C. M. (1986). Parental discipline and control attempts in relation to adolescent sexual attitudes and behavior. *Journal of Marriage and the Family, 48,* 503–512.
Mott, F. L., & Haurin, R. J. (1988). Linkages between sexual activity and alcohol and drug use among American adolescents. *Family Planning Perspectives, 20,* 128–136.
Neter, J., Wasserman, W., & Kutner, M. (1985). *Applied linear statistical models* (2nd ed.). Homewood, IL: Irwin.
Ohannesian, C., & Crockett, L. J. (1993). A longitudinal investigation of the relationship between educational investment and adolescent sexual activity. *Journal of Adolescent Research, 8,* 167–182.
Patterson, G. R., DeBaryshe, B. D., & Ramsey, E. (1989). A developmental perspective on antisocial behavior. *American Psychologist, 44,* 329–335.
Peskin, H. (1967). Pubertal onset and ego functioning. *Journal of Abnormal Psychology, 72,* 1–15.
Peskin, H. (1973). Influence of the developmental schedule of puberty on learning and ego functioning. *Journal of Youth and Adolescence, 2,* 273–290.
Petersen, A. C. (1987, February). *Data estimation.* Paper presented to the staff of the Developmental Research Methodology Center, Pennsylvania State University, University Park.
Petersen, A. C., Schulenberg, J. E., Abramowitz, R. M., Offer, D., & Jarcho, H. D. (1984). A Self-Image Questionnaire for Young Adolescents (SIQYA): Reliability and validity studies. *Journal of Youth and Adolescence, 13,* 93–111.
Reiss, I. L. (1960). *Premarital sexual standards in America.* New York: Free Press.
Rob, M., Reynolds, I., & Finlayson, P. F. (1990). Adolescent marijuana use: Risk factors and implications. *Australian & New Zealand Journal of Psychiatry, 24,* 47–56.
Rosenbaum, E., & Kandel, D. B. (1990). Early onset of adolescent sexual behavior and drug involvement. *Journal of Marriage and the Family, 52,* 783–798.
Rosenberg, M. (1965). *Society and the adolescent self-image.* Princeton, NJ: Princeton University Press.
Schaie, K. W. (1965). A general model for the study of developmental problems. *Psychological Bulletin, 64,* 92–102.
Swisher, J. D., Shute, R. E., & Bibeau, D. (1985). Assessing drug and alcohol abuse: An instrument for planning and evaluation. *Measurement and Evaluation in Counseling and Development, 17,* 91–97.
Verner, A. M., & Stewart, C. S. (1974). Adolescent sexual behavior in middle America revisited: 1970–1973. *Journal of Marriage and the Family, 36,* 728–735.
Vicary, J. R. (1985). *Psychological impact of pregnancy on rural adolescents* (Office of Adolescent Pregnancy Prevention, Grant No. APR 000933-01, Contract No. 282-90-0047). Unpublished grant proposal.
Wade, J. T. (1989). A longitudinal analysis of sex by race differences in predictors of adolescent self-esteem. *Personality and Individual Differences, 10,* 717–729.
Wagner, C. A. (1980). Sexuality of American adolescents. *Adolescence, 15,* 567–579.
Watson, F. I., & Kelly, M. J. (1989). Targeting the at-risk male: A strategy for adolescent pregnancy prevention. *Journal of the National Medical Association, 81,* 453–456.
Zelnik, M., & Kantner, J. F. (1980). Sexual activity, contraceptive use, and pregnancy among metropolitan area teenagers: 1971–1979. *Family Planning Perspectives, 12,* 230–237.
Zucker, R. A. (1987). The four alcoholisms: A developmental account of the etiologic process. In P. C. Rivers (Ed.), *Nebraska symposium on motivation, 1986: Vol. 34. Alcohol and addictive behaviors* (pp. 27–84). Lincoln: University of Nebraska Press.

Received March 30, 1994
Revision received December 8, 1994
Accepted February 26, 1995 ■

JOURNAL OF RESEARCH ON ADOLESCENCE, 6(4), 427–455

The Impact of Apprenticeship on Youth: A Prospective Analysis

Stephen F. Hamilton
Cornell University

Wolfgang Lempert
Max Planck Institute for Human Development and Education

European apprenticeship systems, especially Germany's, have inspired a series of demonstration projects in the United States and a major new initiative by the Clinton administration, which is embodied in the School-to-Work Opportunities Act of 1994. German research on apprenticeship provides some prospective insights into how participation in apprenticeship and apprentice-like experiences might affect adolescents in the United States. Four questions guide an examination of that literature: How are young people allocated to apprenticeships and thereby to occupations? What are the occupational prospects for workers who have completed apprenticeships? How does apprenticeship affect young people's political socialization? How does apprenticeship affect young people's personality development? Results are summarized in recommendations for the design of a U.S. system.

Providing apprenticeships for American youth is a key component of the Clinton administration's policy for economic development and education reform. The School-to-Work Opportunities Act of 1994 responds to a serious gap in the United States' education system: a gap between the completion of full-time schooling and entry into "adult" careers by young people who do not graduate from 4-year colleges and universities (Haggstrom, Blaschke, & Shavelson, 1991; Hamilton, 1990; Osterman, 1980; William T. Grant Foundation Commission, 1988a, 1988b). Youth apprenticeship is just

Requests for reprints should be sent to Stephen F. Hamilton, HDFS, MVR Hall, Cornell University, Ithaca, New York 14853–4401.

one form of work-based learning envisioned in the Act, but the German apprenticeship system exemplifies the Act's purposes and was a key inspiration for its content (Lerman & Pouncy, 1990).

Practices and institutional arrangements derived from Germany and other countries where apprenticeship flourishes (notably Austria, Switzerland, and Denmark) have a major advantage over most policy ideas: They have already been tried. Rather than relying solely on the claims of advocates, policy analysts attempting to weigh the likelihood and conditions for their success can examine apprenticeship and its effects in those countries. Rose (1991) called this future-oriented examination of another country's practices *prospective evaluation.* He pointed out that program evaluation typically occurs after a program has been mounted and is limited, as a result, to providing data on whether and how well it worked in the past. By examining a comparable effort that is already underway in another country, Rose argued, one can provide empirical grounds for predicting how well and under what conditions it might work in a different country in the future.

Prospective evaluation (or analysis) captures nicely the spirit of this article, which reviews a selection of the research literature on apprenticeship in Germany in order to yield predictions about how a comparable system in the United States might affect adolescent development and recommendations on the optimal design of a system from the perspective of adolescent development. Obviously, such an exercise can be suggestive at best; adaptation rather than replication is the goal of American reformers, and even a system that strongly resembled German apprenticeship would function differently and have different consequences in the United States.

Ideally, a prospective analysis of apprenticeship for youth would address the questions deemed most critical by policymakers, educators, and employers in the United States. Our analysis is necessarily constrained by the topics German researchers have explored. From the American perspective, the most surprising lacuna in the German research literature is in cost–benefit analyses. The net costs of apprenticeship are a lively issue in Germany because they figure in labor–management negotiations (Sachverständigenkommission Kosten und Finanzierung der Beruflichen Bildung, 1974). The most persuasive explanation of why German firms are willing to invest in training young people is that large firms reap future returns when apprentices become highly qualified loyal workers, and small firms gain immediately when apprentices do low-skill tasks for less than adult helpers would cost (Soskice, 1994; see also Harhoff & Kane, 1994). This explanation is quite plausible but impossible to prove empirically because employers do not reveal their training costs. If small employers admitted that apprentices actually made money for them, they would lose tax benefits and face public censure.

Now that German apprenticeship has become a popular model for school-to-work systems in the United States, economists have begun to analyze differences in the two countries' labor markets, including labor laws, that help to explain why investment in training youth is common in Germany but rare in the United States. We do not attempt to synthesize this nascent literature, but refer the interested reader to other sources (Bailey, 1993; Harhoff & Kane, 1994; Heckman, Roselius, & Smith, 1994; Streek, Hilbert, van Kevelaer, Maier, & Weber, 1987). Nor do we take up the critical question of how a German-inspired youth apprenticeship system might be implemented in this country.[1]

The focus of this prospective analysis is on apprenticeship's impact on adolescent development. The relevant topics that German sociologists and psychologists have explored most thoroughly are career development, political socialization, and personality development, and these are the topics addressed in this review. Another issue must first be addressed, namely, the allocation of young people to apprenticeships. Our review is organized around four questions.

1. How are young people allocated to apprenticeships and thereby to occupations?
2. What are the occupational prospects for workers who have completed apprenticeships?
3. How does apprenticeship affect young people's political socialization?
4. How does apprenticeship affect young people's personality development?

These questions highlight the authors' concerns with apprenticeship's function as an educational institution that can foster social and economic mobility but also reproduce inequality, an institution that inevitably socializes young people while it educates and trains them. The first author has taught in an American vocational high school, conducted extensive field research on German apprenticeship, and directed a research and develop-

[1]Vickers (1991) has usefully pointed out that we can learn more about implementation by looking to the United Kingdom and Australia, which have already had experience in trying to borrow from the German system, than by examining the system in Germany, which is already well established. See Keep (1991) for a cautionary tale of failed implementation in the United Kingdom.

ment project in the United States as a contribution toward the creation of an American-style apprenticeship system. The second author is a former apprentice, craftsman, and vocational school teacher who is well known in Germany as a sociologist studying apprenticeship and as an advocate of reform. The authors agree that the German system has significant weaknesses, but that these weaknesses can be alleviated and, furthermore, that the principles underlying current German reforms should be built into any American adaptation of apprenticeship.

German research on apprenticeship addresses the four questions listed previously, allowing us to examine some possible effects on adolescents of an American-style youth apprenticeship. It will come as no surprise that this literature is not as decisive as one might wish. In particular, there is a dearth of comparisons between apprentices and similar adolescents who are not apprentices. The dearth results from the usual challenges to conducting comparative social research, but also from the selection processes built into the system.

A brief sketch of the German system introduces our literature synthesis. We conclude with suggestions for creating an American system that would avoid some of the problems that exist in Germany. With appropriate adaptations, the same suggestions would also improve the German system.

A SKETCH OF GERMAN APPRENTICESHIP

Known as the dual system because of its two loci–the school and the workplace–apprenticeship is the largest form of upper-secondary education in Germany. It trains both males and females. Males predominate in the traditional manual trades, such as carpentry and machining. Females are over-represented in occupations such as sales clerk and hairdresser. Both males and females use apprenticeship to enter careers in technical occupations, such as dental technician and chemical laboratory technician, and middle-level white-collar occupations, such as bookkeeper, personnel officer, and purchasing agent.

Apprenticeships typically last for 3 years. Participants usually spend a day or a day-and-a-half each week attending a part-time vocational school *(Berufsschule)*, where they receive instruction in German and social studies; in math, science, and other academic knowledge related to their occupation; and in the essential skills of their occupation, such as drafting or accounting. During their working time apprentices perform productive tasks and are paid, but they also receive instruction and the opportunity to gain proficiency in a range of new skills, which are specified for each occupation, as are the experiences and training they receive at work. Employers absorb the costs of training apprentices at work; state (*Land*) governments pay for schooling. Joint committees, with membership drawn from employers, workers, and government, design and monitor the system. The committees are convened by "chambers," nonvoluntary but self-governing associations of employers in related fields. Apprentices who pass the qualifying examination administered by the chamber at the completion of their training are certified as skilled workers and are thereby entitled to the compensation established for their occupation by collective bargaining agreements. They are privileged by law in applying for positions related to their career area; because they have received the training specified for their occupation, they have priority even if other applicants have more years of schooling.

The dual system evolved from medieval craft apprenticeship but was transformed at least twice over the past century to meet changing economic and political conditions. (See Stratmann & Schlösser, 1990, for an account of recent changes.) East Germany retained its dual system after World War II. Unification is rapidly eliminating the distinctive features it acquired under a communist regime and in a relatively underdeveloped economy. Statistics continue to be reported separately for the two parts of Germany. All research and statistics reported here are for the former West Germany.

The proportion of youth between ages 16 and 18 who are enrolled as apprentices increased continuously during the last decade, reaching three fourths of that cohort by 1990, including two thirds of the females (Federal Ministry of Education and Science, 1992, pp. 54–55). However, the age cohort of 16 to 18 no longer corresponds precisely to the age of apprentices. The mean age has increased since 1970 and by 1984 was more than 18 years (Althoff, 1986). This increase is attributable primarily to young people enrolling in more years of full-time schooling before entering apprenticeships and in some cases to males performing military or alternative service before becoming apprentices.

The secular trend toward longer enrollment in full-time schooling has been accompanied by a trend toward the enrollment of a larger proportion of youth in apprenticeships, a combination that is only possible when many young people combine advanced schooling with apprenticeship rather than choosing between the two. The trend toward increasing enrollments in apprenticeship has reversed in the 1990s, owing to continued enrollment growth in the selective secondary schools that qualify young people for postsecondary education and in postsecondary education. Germany's recent prolonged recession has increased the overall unemployment rate dramatically and led several major employers to reduce, and in a few cases eliminate, their apprenticeship programs. Some young people who cannot find an apprenticeship in their chosen occupation remain enrolled in school full-time, further increasing the proportion enrolled and the age and educational qualifications of future applicants for apprenticeships.

The dual system gives employers, along with schools and parents, responsibility for the education, training, and socialization of youth. Workplaces serve as learning environments for youth, enabling some to learn material that they failed to learn in class and motivating them to try to learn in class material that they see adults using at work and will need to master to qualify for skilled employment.

THE ALLOCATION OF YOUNG PEOPLE TO APPRENTICESHIPS

As a system of education and employment that meets employers' needs, does apprenticeship respect young people's right to equal opportunity and cultivate their varying capabilities and aspirations? This question may only be answered in relation to the internal differentiation in the system.

German apprenticeships and the occupations for which they prepare young people differ in prestige and pay.[2] Competition is fierce for apprenticeships in such occupations as administration[3] and chemical laboratory technology, especially in large firms. Successful completion of such an apprenticeship yields excellent occupational qualifications. Completers are typically hired by their training firm and, if they choose to look elsewhere, are eagerly sought by other firms. Even those who move into occupations that are not directly related to their training are greatly preferred by employers over untrained applicants because they have demonstrated their capacity to learn and their possession of such qualities as punctuality, reliability, and discipline.[4] Young adults who have completed such appren-

[2]The prestige hierarchy in apprenticeships is demonstrated, among other ways, by the percentages of graduates of the three secondary school forms who enter apprenticeships in different occupations and categories of firms. These percentages are reported in the Statistisches Bundesamt (1993, pp. 75–84). The same data support the statements made in the following paragraphs regarding the association among apprenticeship status, parental educations, and firm size.

[3]The term *Kaufmann,* literally buyer or merchant, applies to a wide range of mid-level administrative occupations, which are subdivided by economic sector (e.g., manufacturing, retail trade, insurance, banking) rather than by function, which ranges from secretary to account executive. Apprenticeships as *Kaufleute* (the neuter plural form) in large firms are prized, especially in manufacturing, insurance, and banking. The heads of many large German firms began their careers as apprentice *Kaufleute.*

[4]Employers select applicants for apprenticeships according to these qualities, believe they foster them by their training, and promote employees according to the extent to which they demonstrate them. Empirical research has not been conducted for two decades to test how well apprenticeship actually fosters these qualities, and the older studies tended to concentrate on a single quality and often provided only indirect evidence. That apprentices acquire these qualities is simply assumed by most Germans; it is *selbstverständlich* (taken for granted).

ticeships may subsequently gain economic and social status either by learning on the job or by attending additional evening or full-time courses to become masters, technicians, engineers, managers, or self-employed shop owners. This, of course, is the side of the system that advocates wish to adapt to the United States.

Small firms are generally less prestigious as locations for apprenticeship. Far more apprentices are trained as bakers, barbers, and hairdressers than are hired for regular positions in those trades, revealing the apprentices' function as cheap labor. The best way for young people in such fields to avoid unemployment is to abandon their occupation once training is complete and become semiskilled or even unskilled workers. Apprentices at this end of the prestige hierarchy may find themselves marginally trained in trades they entered as a last resort and cannot practice. Most apprentices are found between these two extremes; they receive training sufficient to start them on a modest career either in their training occupation or in another respectable occupation for which their initial training qualifies them in some way.

Location along the prestige hierarchy for occupations is strongly related to young people's school performance. Students with the best school records obtain the most desirable apprenticeships. Grades count; so does the type of secondary school attended. Apprentices with the highest educational levels are found in the business occupations and in some industrial technologies. The majority of craft[5] apprentices, in contrast, still complete only the lowest-level secondary school *(Hauptschule).* Although the Hauptschule was traditionally the school from which nearly all apprentices came, in 1991 only 30% of apprentices came from this school level. A larger proportion came from the intermediate school *(Realschule)* or equivalent. About 17% came from the gymnasium or *Fachoberschule,* whose main purpose is to qualify students for higher education (Federal Ministry of Education and Science, 1992, p. 61).[6]

---

[5]In Germany, the craft *(Handwerk)* sector means small firms, as compared to industry and commerce *(Industrie und Handel),* which designates large firms.

[6]The *Hauptschule,* or main school, ends after Grade 9 or 10. Originally, this was the school of the majority and it remains open to all. The college-preparatory *Gymnasium,* in contrast, extends through Grade 13. Once enrolling only 4 or 5% of youth, nearly all male, it now enrolls about a quarter divided evenly between males and females. The intermediate-level *Realschule* ends after Grade 10 but is selective, unlike the *Hauptschule.* It too has seen a dramatic increase in enrollments. The *Fachoberschule* is a full-time postsecondary vocational school whose graduates are qualified to enter higher education. Unlike the United States, where many forms of postsecondary education are lumped together as "college," Germans draw a sharp distinction between universities and all other postsecondary institutions.

As in the United States, parents' education is correlated with young people's performance in school and with the types of secondary schools they attend. Because those factors influence the occupations young people can enter and the prestige of their training firms, apprenticeship is implicated in maintaining social stratification (Pätzold, 1977); the connection between parents' education and apprenticeship prospects hampers upward mobility. On the other hand, several American observers have argued that the lack of a connection between school performance and employment prospects in the United States gives young people no incentive to work hard in school if they expect to be employed full time immediately after high school graduation (Bishop, 1989; Rosenbaum, Kariya, Settersten, & Maier, 1990). Even if they are skeptical of the genuine value of what they learn in school, German youth realize that how well they do will strongly affect their chances for getting a good apprenticeship in a field of their choice.

To the extent that school performance is an independent indicator of academic talent, selection of apprentices based on school performance may be defended as meritocratic. To the extent that parents' education and income enhance the school performance of some youth and constrain it for others, this connection perpetuates inequality.

Differential access to apprenticeships based on gender is clearly an indefensible form of inequity in the German system. Of some 380 apprenticeable occupations, the 10 occupations with the largest numbers of male apprentices enroll more than 38% of all males. They include motor vehicle mechanic, electrician, machine repairer, cabinetmaker, and painter and varnisher. Nearly 55% of female apprentices are concentrated in the 10 occupations training the largest number of females, which include doctor's receptionist, retail sales clerk, hairdresser, office helper (clerk), and office worker in industrial firms (*Industriekauffrau; Basic and Structural Data,* 1992, pp. 58–59). Only the last of these occupations carries relatively high prestige and pay. Young women in Germany have fewer occupational choices than young men and their choices offer less prestige and pay.

In summary, German apprenticeship, like most education systems, perpetuates class and gender distinctions.[7] Some apprenticeships provide better opportunities than others, and, as noted, the allocation process favors males and youth who perform well in school. However, as the next section shows, it leads to reasonably stable and well-paid careers, maintaining the social status and well-being of the working class.

[7]Access to desirable apprenticeships by non-Germans (i.e., "guest workers" and their children) is another serious equity issue, but we do not attempt to address it here.

GERMAN APPRENTICESHIP AS THE FOUNDATION FOR CAREERS

Apprenticeship is designed to give new workers the competence they need to perform in broad occupational areas. Experience with apprenticeship on a large scale in Germany and on a much more restricted scale in the United States (primarily in the construction-related crafts and in manufacturing) leaves no doubt that it is effective at teaching occupational skills. The key question is not whether apprenticeship can teach advanced skills but whether it channels working-class youth into narrow or dead-end jobs, restricting mobility and contributing to the reproduction of social and economic inequality. Putting the question affirmatively: To what extent do German apprentices acquire a broad spectrum of flexible practical skills, related theoretical knowledge, and worker virtues that facilitate access to a broad range of occupational positions and careers as well as pathways to further training and education? (See Crusius, & Wilke, 1973; Lempert, 1983; Lempert & Ebel, 1965; Hamilton, 1987.)

Firm Size and Training Quality

As noted previously, large firms tend to be more prestigious and more selective than small ones. They also tend to offer higher-quality training. Hence, initial inequalities in the educational backgrounds of apprentices in different occupations are seldom reduced by the vocational training and education provided during apprenticeship; more often inequalities are perpetuated. Large firms typically have well-equipped training centers and employ full-time training personnel. Beginning in these centers, apprentices acquire no only the basic skills of their chosen occupation but also of related trades (e.g., all kinds of metal work). After this initial period, which may last more than a year, apprentices rotate through different departments of their firm in order to gain wide experience. They return to the training center periodically, where they also receive instruction beyond what is given in the public part-time vocational school *(Berufsschule).* Large firms have the financial resources to make long-term investments in training, providing a solid foundation upon which subsequent training will rest. Furthermore, with larger and more diversified work forces, large firms need people to fill a wider variety of specialties than small firms.

Training in small firms is typically less comprehensive, planful, and elaborate than training in large firms. Owner-operators of small firms, who are required to be masters of their trade, are legally responsible for training their apprentices and have regular contact with them even when journeyworkers provide day-to-day supervision. Small firms typically cannot afford to invest in training for the long term. They achieve more immediate payoffs by engaging apprentices quickly in production, intensively training them only during lulls in productive work. The best training facility is likely to be an "instructional corner" *(Lehrecke)*, an out-of-the-way place in an office or shop where an apprentice can work on skill-building activities during slow times.

Although apprenticeship quality varies with firm size and other factors, industry-wide standards place a floor under all apprenticeships. Specific knowledge and skills are enumerated in apprenticeship regulations and curricula and are enforced by the examinations that qualify successful apprentices as skilled workers. All firms must meet these standards, which assure that apprentices receive general as well as firm-specific training.

Moreover, the usual superiority of large firms is not universal. Small firms are more accessible in their totality to apprentices, who may gain firsthand knowledge of their training firm's entire operation, something inconceivable in large firms. Apprentices in small firms are more likely to form close personal relationships with adult workers and to benefit from their mentoring. Owners of some small firms make a strong commitment to training and develop widespread reputations as the very best locations for apprentices.

Apprentices in middle-size firms may find themselves caught between the personal craft model of apprenticeship and the well-financed industrial model. Owners of middle-size firms have neither the time to care personally for their apprentices, as in a small shop, nor, as in the larger firms, resources to employ training specialists. Consequently, in middle-size firms learning takes place primarily on the job and depends heavily on the character of the work done by the firm, on the tasks allotted to apprentices, the advice given and the help granted to the apprentices by adult employees or older apprentices, and on the initiative of the young persons themselves, who are seldom able to learn and work autonomously (Lempert, 1986).

The vocational school *(Berufsschule)* cannot entirely compensate for deficiencies in work-based learning. A serious limitation is the tenuous link between learning on the shop floor and in school. This difficulty is inherent in the composition of classes, which include apprentices from multiple small shops, who inevitably perform a range of different tasks and learn new ones in varying sequences. Nevertheless, the proportion of craft apprentices (i.e., trained in small shops) who pass the qualifying examinations is nearly as high as the average for all apprenticeable trades. In 1991, the pass rate for craft apprentices was 83%, whereas for all apprentices it reached 88% (Federal Ministry of Education and Science, 1992, p. 62). Passing the examination separates the qualified from the unqualified.

Getting a high examination grade identifies apprentices as especially desirable to employers.

Postapprenticeship Careers

Apprentices who complete their training and pass their examination can look forward to good career prospects. In 1991–92, 56% of all of those who had completed an apprenticeship for skilled work in Germany were still employed as skilled workers. Only 11% had been downgraded to the level of an unskilled or semiskilled worker. However, 15% had raised their occupational and social status on the basis of learning on the job, without any additional formal training or education. Seventeen percent had been upgraded after graduating from a *Fachhochschule* (equivalent to a technical college) or university. In sum, 56% remained in an occupational level appropriate to their apprenticeship training, 32% advanced beyond it, and only 11% lost status (R. Jansen, personal communication based on research conducted but not yet published by the German Federal Institute for Vocational Training—BiBB: Bundesinstitut für Berufsbildung). Most former apprentices who move to higher positions (e.g., as technicians, engineers, or managers) report that they use the knowledge and skills acquired during their apprenticeship in their present job at least partly (Hofbauer, 1981, p. 130). Journeyworkers who have been trained in craft trades and in small and middle-size firms showed higher rates of downward and lower rates of upward mobility than the average, but the differences were not so great as might be expected, given the tendency for their training to be of lower quality (Hofbauer, 1981, pp. 137–138).

Gender is associated with greater divergence in careers than size of training firm. German women remain a sort of industrial reserve force, waiting to be admitted to jobs in which they could be more productive (Winkel, 1989). Until recently, women attended courses and institutions of further vocational training and education much less than men and were less likely to advance in status (Hofbauer, 1981, p. 137). Other studies have yielded similar results (e.g., *Berufsbildungsbericht*, 1987, p. 78–84) and have revealed large differences between more and less prosperous regions, particularly with regard to the inequality of occupational opportunities for men and women. Although German occupations continue to be highly gender-related, females in recent years have increased their school enrollment more than males and have made significant gains in earnings and occupational status because many of the "female" jobs in the expanding service sector have been relatively well paid and high status (Blossfeld, 1987).

Using nationally representative longitudinal survey data from the Panel Study of Income Dynamics in the United States and the Socio-Economic Panel in (West) Germany, Buechtemann, Schupp, and Soloff (1993) contrasted school-to-work transition patterns in the two countries. They found much higher levels of participation in postsecondary education and training and lower unemployment in their German sample. Five years after leaving secondary school, 40% of German youth but only 10% of U.S. youth were still enrolled in education or training, and nearly two thirds of German youth had earned skill credentials. The authors inferred that these differences in education and training accounted for the fact that unemployment among the German sample 4 to 5 years after secondary school graduation was 2%, compared to 11% for the sample in the United States. However, unemployment rates are sensitive to various influences; differences at a single time cannot demonstrate persistent institutional advantages for one country over another. Recent increases in German unemployment make this clear.

Apprentices' tendency to remain with their training employer contributes to employment stability in Germany. Eighty percent of apprentices in the sample analyzed by Buechtemann et al. (1993) remained with their training firm if they entered employment upon completion rather than continuing their education. Despite this stability, former apprentices are rather mobile following their initial job, demonstrating the portability of their credentials. The authors pointed out, however, that inoculation against loss of status, which credentials provide, is accompanied by limited chances for dramatic upward mobility and that the gap between earnings of vocationally trained and academically educated Germans remains large.

In another recent study using data from the Socio-Economic Panel, Witte and Kalleberg (1992) found that Germans who had received formal vocational training, including both apprenticeship and school-based training, found better jobs and reported higher earnings and greater intrinsic rewards (e.g., variety, independence, decision making) than those who were untrained, holding other variables constant. However, former apprentices gained these advantages regardless of the match between their training and their employment, whereas those who acquired their vocational training by other (primarily school-based) means lost these advantages if they were employed in a different occupation. Women who had been apprentices gained more intrinsic rewards than men. The dual system, the authors concluded, yields general skills that transfer better from one field to another than vocational skills learned at school. (See also Witte & Kalleberg, 1994.)

In their exploratory longitudinal research, the second author and his colleagues found that the generally favorable long-term benefits of apprenticeship sometimes accrue slowly (Hoff, Lempert, & Lappe, 1991). Following 23 young skilled workers in the metal industry from 1980 to 1987, they found that many apprenticeship completers who eventually succeeded in their occupational careers first went through a very difficult period of temporary dequalification. These workers stayed within their occupations and many of them also within their firms, but other studies have found that about half of all former craft apprentices have, in the past, had to change their employer and often also to leave their trade and lose their status as skilled workers, usually by taking semiskilled production jobs in industry. A structural cause of this dequalification is that craft firms have trained about twice as many apprentices as they employed afterwards, whereas the proportion of apprentices to fully trained workers in large industrial firms is relatively low. Although there is, as a result of these proportions, some movement of skilled workers from craft to industry, craft-trained workers must often receive additional formal training before they are capable of performing many skilled industrial jobs.

In sum, the German dual system offers many career advantages but some disadvantages at the same time. On the one hand, it imparts to the majority of young people at least basic vocational education, encompassing not only technical skill and knowledge but also worker virtues—such as reliability, precision, and perseverance—and trains a considerable number of these young people well, facilitating their access to stable jobs, stimulating many of them to acquire advanced theoretical knowledge and often serving as a basis for subsequent upward mobility. On the other hand, it also trains large numbers of apprentices in occupations in which they cannot be employed afterwards. By systematically selecting some applicants for the most desirable occupations and the highest-quality apprenticeships, it maintains and even reinforces social inequality, enhancing the advantages of those whose educational background is above average and exacerbating the disadvantages of many of the rest. Most seriously, because it is least justifiable in terms of differences in applicants' qualifications, apprenticeship perpetuates the assignment of women to lower-status and lower-paid occupations. However, in fairness it must be acknowledged that apprenticeship does not create gender inequity by itself; the dual system accurately reflects inequity pervading the German labor market and society. Women's progress in recent years demonstrates that the system is capable of improvement.

Perhaps the most positive finding for the United States from German research on apprentices' careers is that a system that relies heavily on work-based learning teaches general skills that can be transported to other employers and used as a basis for further formal and informal learning. Hence, even though the German system is stratified, it encourages lateral mobility and allows upward mobility.

WORK EXPERIENCE AS POLITICAL SOCIALIZATION

Interest in apprenticeship for youth in the United States has been stimulated primarily by its perceived economic benefits. But when work organizations serve as training institutions, they influence the social conceptions, political attitudes, and personality structures of trainees as well as their occupational qualifications. In addition to producing goods and performing services when they are at work, people also act as authoritative or authoritarian supervisors and autonomous or obedient subordinates. They cooperate or compete with their peers. They strive for profits, privileges, and power. They win and lose. These experiences shape conceptions, attitudes, and patterns of behavior that concern the world of work, but that are also generalized and transferred to other areas of life, structuring the whole social character of the individual (Jahoda, 1981; Kohn & Schooler, 1983). These socialization effects may be regarded as equal in importance with skill acquisition, even though they are typically given much less formal attention.

During the 1980s, several substantial research projects were devoted to the impact of apprenticeship on adolescents' political socialization. They were motivated in part by fears among labor leaders and their political allies that employers used apprenticeship to indoctrinate young people to passive roles as subordinates in the industrial hierarchy. A volume edited by Kärtner, Leu, Otto, and Wahler (1983) contains reports from three large-scale longitudinal surveys. Though different in their details, they converged in several crucial points (Lempert, 1986). The results did not substantiate fears of systematic indoctrination; however, they also gave scant comfort to those hoping that most apprentices would come to value and participate readily in collective action, both in the workplace and in society. Although many apprentices demonstrated increased recognition of inequality and increased willingness to engage in political action to reduce inequality, this movement was only registered by a minority. Many participants showed no sign of changes in political attitudes and beliefs over the 3 years of their training.

Such stability reflects the fact that apprenticeship is only one among many influences on adolescents' political socialization. Previous and simultaneous influences from family, peers, school, and other sources interact with work experience. Hence, the allocation process described previously is a critical factor in apprentices' political socialization. As employers select applicants, they also sort them according to their family background and school achievement, which are correlated with political beliefs (Harbordt, 1994).

Just as the technical quality of apprenticeship training varies with firm size and occupational category, so do opportunities to work collectively.

Apprentices in larger firms can band together in relatively large numbers to reflect critically on their workplace and engage in collective action to improve it. Their likelihood of success at obtaining fair training opportunities and relative autonomy at work is further enhanced by the support they can often count on from their works councils, which provide a voice for employees in large firms.

Although some participants in even the best apprenticeships experience frustrations—particularly immediately after their passage from school to apprenticeship and from training to initial employment—a large proportion of the less privileged majority passes through far more daunting processes of hierarchical selection, unskilled employment, and authoritarian control during the period from the end of their full-time schooling until their early 20s. Working mostly in smaller firms that train only one or a few apprentices and have no works councils, they lack support from peers and labor representatives. As a result, they often internalize the standards that guide their selection and control and, thus, develop rather submissive and individualistic orientations, which result in a low level of democratic participation and a low sense of social responsibility beyond the world of work (Kühnlein, 1983).

Submission and withdrawal at work can lead to apathy, cynicism, depression, anomie, and alienation from society (Lempert, 1986). In general, blue-collar apprentices in craft shops experience the most repressive training and working conditions and demonstrate the most political passivity (Seidenspinner, 1974). However, blue-collar industrial apprentices tend to become more dissatisfied with their status and working conditions than either white-collar or craft apprentices (Mayer, Schumm, Flaake, Gerberding, & Reuling, 1981).

To the extent that the explicit lessons or the "hidden curriculum" of the workplace (Lempert, 1981) teach less privileged apprentices to submit passively to the orders of more powerful persons, to bureaucratic rules, and to technical and economic constraints, while encouraging more privileged apprentices to act assertively on behalf of their interests, German apprenticeship contributes to maintaining social inequality. Insofar as German apprentices are introduced to democratic forms of work organization and to collective action, they become more active citizens. As in the realm of technical qualification, the system's impact varies. However, there is no evidence that its impact is generally repressive.

PERSONALITY DEVELOPMENT DURING APPRENTICESHIP

Studies of the impact of apprenticeship on personality development stand at the confluence of two streams of research, one examining the conditions that foster optimal personality development in adult workers (epitomized by Kohn & Schooler, 1983), the other identifying the presumably natural stages through which children and adolescents advance toward adulthood (epitomized by Kohlberg, 1976). Studying the personality development of employed adolescents requires attention simultaneously to the working conditions that have been found to foster or inhibit adult development and to the unique characteristics of adolescents. Such studies have concentrated principally on control consciousness and moral judgment ability as critical aspects of personality.[8]

Control consciousness is defined as the pattern of ideas concerning causality in one's own behavior, action, and biography. ("Locus of control" is a related concept.) In the stage-sequential paradigm, control consciousness is seen as beginning with fatalistic beliefs in chance, good and bad luck, and mood. Next it moves to deterministic views emphasizing the influences of either external or internal forces. Next come additive conceptions, in which different combinations of these factors are seen as controlling different periods, areas or situations. Some people take a further step toward a conception of permanent reciprocal interactions between persons and their environment. (See Hoff, 1986, chaps. 3 and 4; Hoff & Hohner, 1986.) Apprentices' development toward internal conceptions of control, that is, confidence in their own abilities and energies, will be fostered if they have some latitude for self-direction. This appears to be more often the case in traditionally masculine technical occupations in large companies and when apprentices appreciate their training conditions (Häfeli et al., 1988).

Moral judgment ability is defined as competence to propose and legitimate resolutions of social conflicts that should be acceptable for all individuals and groups involved. It progresses from a rather egocentric or *preconventional* level in which a person's perspective is difficult to reconcile with the perspectives of other persons, to a more sociocentric or *conventional* level, which requires often painful sacrifices of the ego. Under favorable circumstances, it advances further to a more equilibrated *postconventional* form, which concedes equal rights to ego and alter, the individual and society (Kohlberg, 1976).

In general, moral development occurs when social relationships are communicative and cooperative rather than authoritarian. The transition from preconventional to conventional moral orientations will be facilitated

[8]See Hoff, 1990, for an account of relations between control consciousness and moral judgment ability. Häfeli, Kraft, and Schallberger (1988) have found that apprenticeship also stimulates alterations within other psychological realms such as intelligence, motivation, and emotion.

when masters, trainers, other experienced adults, or even other apprentices care empathically for the individual, grant him or her recognition as a person and as a member of the group, but also give feedback on the effects of (mis)behaviors and actions on others (Hoff et al., 1991). In a significant exception to the advantages cited previously for training in large firms, this is more likely to occur in very small firms.

Further transitions toward interactionist control consciousness and postconventional moral thinking, which occur at the end of adolescence and consequently after the completion of apprenticeship, may also be stimulated by social experiences within the workplace. The simultaneous experience of autonomy and dependency, which is characteristic of middle management positions, furthers managers' development toward interactionist conceptions. Confrontation with conflicting claims of clients, subordinates, the goals of entire institutions, and the common good demand and promote the formation of postconventional orientations. These may be encountered in some professional tasks and in management roles. (See also Kohlberg & Higgins, 1984.) Jobs that require strategic or even manipulative behavior against other persons and organizations—sales and litigation, for instance—inhibit rather than foster moral development.

Biographical continuity and environmental consistency are important determinants of the development of control consciousness and moral thinking and of their transfer between work and other spheres of life. Generally speaking, modest amounts of discontinuity and inconsistency are found in the lives of people who demonstrate progress in moral development, whereas extreme discontinuities result in stagnation or even in regression. An Austrian study of young women who were trained as apprentices in male-dominated technical occupations illustrates the maintenance at work of political and moral perspectives acquired elsewhere. When these women were employed as skilled workers, they were willing to use their qualifications to prove themselves at least as competent as their male colleagues, but they refused to compete with each other when competition jeopardized their interpersonal relationships, apparently obeying the imperatives of their earlier female socialization (Wagner, 1984).[9]

The impact of apprenticeship on personality development cannot, therefore, be viewed as either independent or unidirectional. It interacts with other influences and it may be positive or negative depending upon circumstances in the work setting. Under the best circumstances, apprentices are challenged to think about the consequences of their actions and take respon-

[9]German research has not yet incorporated Gilligan's (1982) feminist critique of Kohlberg's theory of moral development.

sibility for them, with the result that they move toward postconventional moral reasoning (Klaghofer, Oser, & Schläfli, 1985; Lind, 1983). Research on adult workers indicates that some circumstances contribute to low levels of personality development and even to regression (Giegel, Frank, & Billerbeck, 1988; Heine & Mautz, 1989; Volmerg, 1988).

The second author's long-term longitudinal study traced the interaction of 23 skilled workers' occupational biographies with their moral reasoning and control consciousness over 7 years after they had completed apprenticeships (Lempert, 1994). This exploratory research, along with an extensive review of literature (Lempert, 1988, 1993a, 1993b), identified seven conditions that foster personality development in workers, or, if they are absent, undermine it:

> 1. Involvement in manifest (instead of repressed or transferred) social problems and conflicts of interest.
> 2. Free (instead of standardized, one-way, or manipulative) communication.
> 3. Participation in cooperative decision making ... (instead of subordination, rivalry or mere talk).
> 4. Abiding empathy, love, care, and recognition (instead of indifference, hatred, rejection, depreciation, or contempt).
> 5. Information about the social impact of individual and collective behavior and action (instead of unfounded rules prescribing or proscribing certain actions).
> 6. Substantial involvement in contradictions between individual expectations, interpersonal rules, social norms, and cultural values that preclude one-sided solutions (instead of either enforced harmony or lack of common maxims).
> 7. Ascription of responsibility for one's own life and (subsequently) for others according to one's growing capabilities ... (instead of either distrustful strict control or uncontrolled laissez faire). (Lempert, 1994, pp. 453–454)

These are the conditions that should lead to desirable effects on apprentices' personality development. Opposite conditions would be expected to have less desirable or undesirable effects. For example, apprenticeship in firms with an authoritarian and competitive atmosphere may impede the personality development of apprentices (Lind, 1983). However, such effects must be assessed in comparison with the other settings where young people might spend their time instead of at work. The same negative conditions prevail in many schools. Furthermore, unskilled work and unemployment may lead to even worse psychological results than a suboptimal apprenticeship.

The importance of differences among workplaces to the impact of apprenticeship on adolescent development leads us back to the apprenticeship system in order to shed light on the issue of how and to what extent apprenticeships can be shaped to approximate the favorable conditions just specified. That issue is embedded in the conflicts of interest among the parties to the apprenticeship system. Conflicts are not inherently negative. They are inevitable; they must be dealt with. Moreover, constructive engagement in manifest conflict can, as indicated previously, promote the development of apprentices.

CONFLICTS OF INTEREST IN GERMAN APPRENTICESHIP

Collaboration among employers, employees, educators, and government is one of the most impressive aspects of German apprenticeship to American observers, but that collaboration is accompanied by conflict. Although all participants in principle have an interest in fostering high-quality apprenticeships, in practice they differ about many issues.

With regard to the allocation of youth to apprenticeships, applicants for positions as apprentices want open access to desirable jobs, but skilled employees wish to maintain high earnings by limiting the supply of competing workers in the labor market. In most occupations, employers limit the number of apprentices they train to the number of vacancies they anticipate. This avoids the training of excessive numbers of skilled workers in a given area, to the advantage of both incumbent and prospective workers. But it also prevents some young people from acquiring training in the field of their choice. (It is starkly different from U.S. practice, in which vocational training from high school through the Ph.D. is primarily driven by student demand and graduates are held responsible for finding related employment.)

A second conflict is between preferences for general versus specific training (Becker, 1964). A dynamic economy requires comprehensive, general qualifications, which make skilled workers more adaptable. The workers benefit from general skills because they are prepared to assume multiple responsibilities in many different firms. Some employers would prefer to train their apprentices very narrowly in order to employ (or exploit) them as soon as possible as cheap labor and to limit their value to competitors. This preference is constrained by national standards that define what apprentices in each occupation should learn and by national examinations that assess individual apprentices' performance in relation to those standards but also, by implication, the employers' competence at training. Firms that consistently turn out apprentices who perform badly on the qualifying examination can lose the privilege of training.

The interests of different participants in the apprenticeship system may diverge from each other regarding its socializing function at least as much as they do regarding its training function. Employers and managers strive not only for high and stable profits but also for control of their labor force; desire for control leads them to prefer compliant workers. Employees and organizations that represent them, in contrast, struggle for higher wages, job security, and solidarity among their members. Government institutions are expected to coordinate the interests of both employers and employees, but also have a self-interest in building their own autonomy from external forces (Offe, 1975). Finally, socializing young people to democracy fosters societal progress.

The German dual system took its current shape around the turn of the century, not only to meet economic needs associated with modern industry, but also to reduce the attractiveness of the Social Democratic Party to young males and to integrate them into the hierarchical social structure and authoritarian political order of the German empire. Apprenticeship was part of a disciplinary process that began in authoritarian families and was continued by military service (Greinert, 1975; Kerschensteiner, 1901). Partly as a result of advocacy by organized labor and educators, apprentices now have more legal rights at work and receive social studies instruction at school designed to teach them their rights as well as their responsibilities. But the nature of apprentices' socialization continues to be a source of conflict between employers and unions, with the government shifting from one side to another depending upon which party is in power.

One aspect of that conflict is the question of what sort of personality development to foster in young working people. Many employers and managers prefer employees who have developed a kind of split personality. In their dealings within the firm, such employees view themselves as externally controlled by representatives, rules, and goals of their firms and behave accordingly in a strict conventional manner (Edwards, 1979). But outside the firm, these same employees are expected to interact self-confidently and rather ruthlessly with suppliers, competitors, customers, and others. Such a split is inimical to consistent self-conceptions and advanced developmental stages among workers.

Economic and technological forces are converging with political forces to bring the interests of the "social partners" (i.e., employers, employees, and government) closer than they have been in the past. Effective use of new technology and competitiveness in a global economy require workers who are not only well-trained but also well-educated, who are not merely compliant but capable of self-management. Employers' expectations of their workers increasingly coincide with definitions of the well-educated citizen in a democracy—they are expected to be capable of teamwork, problem solving, self-control, communication, ecological responsibility, and lifelong learning. As changes are made in the German system to help apprentices meet these expectations, the system more closely approximates the ideal we have described, and it becomes much more appropriate as a model for the United States because it becomes more consistent with prevailing political ideals and labor market realities.

Briefly stated, current and proposed changes aim to consolidate related occupations and to link apprenticeship more closely to postsecondary education. Consolidation, which has already been implemented in the metalworking industry, results in broader training and increased employment options. Specifically, 42 metalworking occupations were combined into six larger categories (Schmid, 1992). Both formal policy changes and ad hoc choices of young people have increasingly combined apprenticeship with extended schooling at the secondary and postsecondary levels. (For more detail on these changes and their implications for the United States, see Hamilton & Hurrelmann, 1994.)

CONCLUSIONS AND RECOMMENDATIONS

Apprenticeship can be a positive force in personality development and political socialization as well as a source of occupational competence if it incorporates in its regulations and operation principles found in the highest-quality training now provided in German firms. The same principles may be applied to the United States and other countries (Hamilton, 1990). An ideal system of apprenticeship is neither, like many schools, a mere teen-sitting institution, nor does it serve, as many apprenticeships in the past, only to provide cheap labor and docile workers. Achieving a system approaching the ideal would help to overcome or at least to diminish the duality of labor markets, occupational career patterns, and life chances. The following recommendations for an American system respond to problems in the German system by building on best practices there. Their full implementation in Germany would also be welcome.

1. Breadth is a crucial principle in apprenticeship. Training should, from the beginning, be in diverse and challenging work tasks. Occupations in which simple, highly repetitive tasks predominate should not be apprenticeable. High-performance work practices, such as cross-training, job rotation, job enrichment, self-managed work teams, and the use of technology to perform routine tasks should be incorporated into apprentices' training.

Completers should be able to enter and succeed in a large number of different jobs.

2. Academic rigor is a necessary complement to occupational breadth. Apprentices should take trade-related theoretical courses (e.g., electronics, accounting) and academic courses (e.g., foreign languages, math) at levels equivalent to college preparatory courses. Differences among courses should be in pedagogical style rather than content level. Many young people currently defined as unable to learn "higher-order skills" can do so quite adequately when given appropriate instruction, support, and the motivation of work-based learning. Setting higher academic standards for all is consistent with current school reform and with the American ideal of making higher education accessible to everyone.

When apprenticeship achieves broad educational purposes that contribute to the welfare of society, it transcends training. Accordingly, institutions of higher education should accept apprentices' qualifications, whether acquired in school or at work. The key to achieving this goal is defining qualifications in terms of demonstrated mastery rather than credit hours, which too often mean nothing more than a number of hours spent in classes.

3. Poor and minority youth and females should have equal access to training in desirable training firms and occupations. Size of firm should not constrain the quality of training. Government financial support can help to overcome these sources of inequality. It might take the form of tax incentives, subsidies, or a levy-grant system whereby all firms are required to contribute to a fund from which eligible firms receive payments (Sachverständigenkommission Kosten und Finanzierung der Beruflichen Bildung, 1974).[10] Although employers properly take the lead in apprenticeship, government can fulfill the public educational role and spread its costs by supporting curriculum development, staff training, and the assessment of apprentices' learning (Streek et al., 1987).

Effective schooling is essential to equalizing access to desirable apprenticeships. Forms of instruction and school structures that enable all young people to achieve high standards prepare them all for demanding apprenticeships. While they are apprentices, young people need school-based instruction, especially in social studies, which enhances their capacity and readiness for democratic participation at the workplace and in the commu-

[10]However, it would be impossible to create a large-scale system based primarily on government subsidies. The German system functions as well as it does primarily because it meets employers' needs. Subsidies should be considered only as a means of shaping a system to meet public goals. Core support must come from employers and serve their self-interest. Recognition of this necessity (which is consistent with current fiscal and political constraints) is a strength of the School-to-Work Opportunities Act.

nity. To promote active citizenship more effectively, such instruction should engage apprentices in thinking and talking about real issues and dilemmas, rendering problematic what has been taken for granted—such as the production and distribution of energy, the sources and costs of pollution, and the distribution of tasks and of authority in firms. This will help young workers participate more fully and thoughtfully in management and, at the same time, constitute a form of general learning, preparing apprentices intellectually for higher education.[11]

4. Apprenticeship training should be restricted to firms that are competent to teach "all aspects of the industry,"[12] to provide caring supervision, and to provide pedagogically sound training. All training firms should be able to meet the criteria spelled out previously for workplaces that enhance human development. Small firms can meet these criteria, especially when they form consortia to share apprentices, allowing them to rotate through different firms. Small firms are absolutely essential to any viable apprenticeship system, but their standards of training should be as high as large firms' standards.

Although it may seem odd to limit employer participation when the most critical question in the United States is whether significant numbers of employers will choose to make the commitment to training youth, the German experience, like the experience of marginal cooperative education programs in the United States, demonstrates that the quality of work-based learning must be paramount. Creating a low-quality system would benefit no one. This limitation does not apply to less elaborate forms of work-based learning than apprenticeship (e.g., job shadowing, some forms of cooperative education), which might be sponsored effectively by firms that cannot meet the criteria for apprenticeship.

These recommendations are less utopian than they may appear at first glance, for they are in accord with current trends in the dual system in Germany, as well as those in Denmark and Switzerland. Shrinking youth cohorts have reduced the number of applicants for apprenticeships, facilitating the allocation of those applicants to the most promising trades and highest-quality training firms. Because German young people are choosing to remain in full-time schooling longer, they are more mature when they begin apprenticeship—enhancing their ability to learn autonomously dur-

---

[11] A book written for teachers by Simon, Dippo, and Schenke, 1991, contains a rationale and many examples for using work experience as a basis for disciplined social analysis.

[12] The phrase "all aspects of the industry" is prominent in both the School-to-Work Opportunities Act and the Carl D. Perkins Vocational and Applied Technology Act (1990; which funds conventional vocational education). It is a useful touchstone for breadth of learning.

ing their apprenticeship and qualifying them to enroll in institutions of further education afterwards.

German employers' need for flexible, multiskilled workers who can continue learning throughout their careers has already led to the revision of many training regulations in ways that are consistent with some of these recommendations, notably by enlarging the breadth of training. Other revisions will follow as employers abandon Taylorist strategies of overspecialization and increasingly challenge the whole range of their employees' capabilities. (See Baethge & Oberbeck, 1986; Commission on the Skills of the American Workforce, 1990; Kern & Schumann, 1984; Piore & Sabel, 1984; Finegold, 1991). Broader, more flexible training and work that is more interesting and challenging are also required to motivate a sufficient number of young people to complete apprenticeships and to remain in jobs as skilled workers in the future (Lutz, 1989). This progressive trend also meets the needs for more autonomy, meaning, and satisfactory interpersonal relationships at the workplace, expressed by an increasing segment of the young generation (Baethge et al., 1988; Yankelovich, 1974, 1981; Zoll, 1989).

Careful examination of Germany's apprenticeship system reveals limitations and inequalities along with a range of means to overcome them. Most critically, it demonstrates that the quality of an apprenticeship is paramount; simply moving young people out of classrooms into workplaces is not acceptable. Advocates of apprenticeship for youth in the United States must understand the weaknesses as well as the strengths of the German dual system, then try to replicate its strengths and those of other countries' systems, carefully devising adaptations and solutions appropriate to a different culture and economy. Happily, efforts to do just this are underway in many parts of the country. Soon they will begin to yield research results to join and build upon the findings of prospective analyses like this one.

ACKNOWLEDGMENTS

Stephen F. Hamilton, Cornell University; Wolfgang Lempert, Max Planck Institute for Education and Human Development.

This article originated with a presentation by Wolfgang Lempert to a symposium at Cornell University in June 1990. We appreciate the contributions of Urie Bronfenbrenner, Glen Elder, and Phyllis Moen to an early draft and the suggestions of several anonymous reviewers.

REFERENCES

Althoff, H. (1986). Das zunehmende Alter der Auszubildenden: Ursachen und Auswirkungen [The increasing age of apprentices: Causes and effects]. *Berufsbildung in Wissenschaft und Praxis, 15*, 119–123.

Baethge, M., & Oberbeck, H. (1986). *Zukunft der Angestellten: Neue Technologien und berufliche Perspektiven in Büro und Verwaltung* [The future of white-collar workers: New technologies and occupational perspectives in office and administration]. Frankfurt, Germany: Campus.

Baethge, M., Hantsche, B., Pellul, W., & Voskamp, U. (1988). *Jugend: Arbeit und Identität: Lebensperspektiven und Interessenorientierungen von Jugendlichen* [Youth: Work and identity: Life perspectives and interest orientations of young people]. Opladen, Germany: Leske & Budrich.

Bailey, T. S. (1993). Can youth apprenticeship thrive in the United States? *Educational Researcher, 22*(3), 4–10.

Becker, G. S. (1964). *Human capital: A theoretical and empirical analysis, with special reference to education*. New York: Columbia University Press.

Bishop, J. (1989). Why the apathy in American high schools? *Educational Researcher, 18*(1), 6–10.

Blossfeld, H -P. (1987). Labor-market entry and the sexual segregation of careers in the Federal Republic of Germany. *American Journal of Sociology, 93*, 89–118.

Buechtemann, C. F., Schupp, J., & Soloff, D. (1993). Roads to work: School-to-work transition patterns in Germany and the United States. *Industrial Relations Journal, 24*, 97–111.

Bundesministerium für Bildung und Wissenschaft. (1987). *Berufsbildungsbericht 1987* [Vocational education report 1987]. Bonn, Germany: Author.

Carl D. Perkins Vocational and Applied Technology Education Act, 20 U. S. C. § 2301 *et seq.* (1990).

Commission on the Skills of the American Workforce. (1990). *America's choice: High skills or low wages! The report of the Commission on the Skills of the American Workforce*. Rochester, NY: National Center for Education and the Economy.

Crusius, J., & Wilke, M. (1978). Möglichkeiten der Mitgestaltung und betriebspolitisches Verhalten der Lehrlinge (Possibilities of mutual influence and apprentices' political behavior in firms). In Daviter, J. (Ed.), *Der Lehrling im Betrieb* (The apprentice at work). Munich, Germany: Deutsches Jugendinstitut.

Edwards, R. C. (1979). *Contested terrain: The transformation of the workplace in the twentieth century*. New York: Basic Books.

Federal Ministry of Education and Science. (1992). *Basic and structural data: Education Statistics for the Federal Republic of Germany 1992/93*. Bonn, Germany: Author.

Finegold, D. (1991). Institutional incentives and skill creation: Preconditions for a high-skill equilibrium. In P. Ryan (Ed.), *International comparisons of vocational education and training for intermediate skills*. London: Falmer Press.

Giegel, J. -J., Frank, G., & Billerbeck, U. (1988). *Industriearbeit und Selbstbehauptung: Berufsbiographische Orientierungen und Gesundheitsverhalten in gefärdeten Lebensverhältnissen* [Industrial work and self-assertion: Orientations to occupational biographies and health behavior in endangered living relationships]. Opladen, Germany: Leske und Budrich.

Gilligan, C. (1982). *In a different voice: Psychological theory and women's development*. Cambridge, MA: Harvard University Press.

Greinert, w. -D. (1975). *Schule als Instrument sozialer Kontrolle und Objekt privater Interessen: Der Beitrag der Berufsschule zur politischen Erziehung der Unterschichten* [The school as an instrument of social control and as the object of private interests: The vocational school's contribution to the political education of the lower classes]. Hannover, Germany: Schroedel.

Häfeli, U., Kraft, U., & Schallberger, U. (1988). *Berufsausbildung und Persönlichkeitsentwicklung: Eine Längsschnittstudie* [Apprenticeship and personality development: A longitudinal study]. Bern, Switzerland: Huber.

Haggstrom, G. W., Blaschke, T. J., & Shavelson, R. J. (1991). *After high school, then what?: A look at the postsecondary sorting-out process for American youth* (R–4008–FMP). Santa Monica, CA: RAND.

Hamilton, S. F. (1987). Work and maturity: Occupational socialization of non-college youth in the U.S. and West Germany. In R. G. Corwin (Ed.), *Research in Sociology of Education and Socialization* (Vol. 7, pp. 243–312). Greenwich, CT: JAI.

Hamilton, S. F. (1990). *Apprenticeship for adulthood. Preparing youth for the future.* New York: Free Press.

Hamilton, S. F., & Hurrelmann, K. (1994). The school-to-career transition in Germany and the United States. *Teachers College Record, 96,* 329–344.

Harbordt, S. (1994). *Führung, Konflikt, und Demokratie* [Leadership, conflict, and democracy]. Unpublished manuscript, Technische Universität, Berlin.

Harhoff, D., & Kane, T. J. (1994). Financing apprenticeship training: Evidence from Germany. In *School-to-work: What does research say about it?* (pp. 33–56). Washington, DC: U.S. Department of Education, Office of Research.

Heckman, J. J., Roselius, R. L., & Smith, J. A. (1994). U.S. education and training policy: A re-evaluation of the underlying assumptions behind the "new consensus." In L. C. Solomon & A. R. Levenson (Eds.), *Labor markets, employment policy, and job creation* (pp. 83–121). Boulder, CO: Westview Press.

Heine, H., & Mautz, R. (1989). *Industriearbeiter contra Umweltschutz?* [Industrial workers against environmental protection?]. Frankfurt am Main, Germany: Campus.

Hofbauer, H. (1981). Berufswege von Erwerbstätigen mit Facharbeiterausbildung [Occupational paths of employees trained as skilled workers]. *Mitteilungen aus der Arbeitsmarkt-und Berufsforschung, 14,* 127–138.

Hoff, E. -H. (1986). *Arbeit, Freizeit und Persönlichkeit: Wissenschaftliche und alltägliche Vorstellungsmuster* [Work, free time and personality: Scientific and everyday images]. Bern, Switzerland: Huber.

Hoff, E. -H. (1990). Kontrolle und Moral: Problematische Arbeitsprodukte im Urteil von Arbeitern [Control and morale: Problematic consequences of work in the judgment of workers]. In F. Frei & I. Udris (Eds.), *Menschenbilder—Handlungsspielraum—Arbeits—und Lebenswelt: Festschrift für Eberhard Ulich zum 60 Geburtstag* [Profiles of people—Scope of action—The worlds of life and work: A commemorative volume for Eberhard Ulich on his 60th birthday] (pp. 91–106). Bern, Switzerland: Huber.

Hoff, E. -H., & Hohner, H. -U. (1986). Occupational careers, work, and control. In M. M. Baltes & P. B. Baltes (Eds.), *The psychology of control and aging* (pp. 345–371). Hillsdale, NJ: Lawrence Erlbaum Associates, Inc.

Hoff, E. -H., Lempert, W., & Lappe, L. (1991). *Persönlichkeitsentwicklung in Facharbeiterbiographien: Eine Längsschnittstudie* [Personality development in skilled worker biographies: A longitudinal study]. Bern, Switzerland: Huber.

Jahoda, M. (1981). Work, employment, and unemployment: Values, theories, and approaches in social research. *American Psychologist, 36,* 184–191.

Kärtner, G., Leu, H. R., Otto, E. -M., & Wahler, P. (Eds.) (1983). *Ausbildung und Arbeitsplatzrisiko Jugendlicher: Workshop-Bericht aus der empirischen Forschung zur beruflichen Sozialisation* [Risks for young people in finding training and workplaces: A workshop report from the empirical research on occupational socialization]. Munich, Germany: DJI Verlag.

Keep, E. (1991). The grass looked greener: Some thoughts on the influence of comparative vocational training research on the UK policy debate. In P. Ryan (Ed.), *International comparisons of vocational education and training for intermediate skills.* London: Falmer.

Kern, H., & Schumann, M. (1984). *Das Ende der Arbeitsteilung: Rationalisierung in der industriellen Produktion* [The end of the division of labor: Rationalization in industrial production]. Munich, Germany: Beck.

Kerschensteiner, G. (1901). *Staatsbürgerliche Erziehung der deutschen Jugend* [Educating German youth for citizenship]. Erfurt, Germany: Villaret.

Klaghofer, R., Oser, F., & Schläfli (1985). Eine Querschnitterhebung zur Sozial- und Moralkompetenz von Lehrlingen [A cross-sectional survey of the social and moral competence of apprentices]. *Zeitschrift für Berufs- und Wirtschaftspädagogik, 81,* 14–24.

Kohlberg, L. E., (1976). Moral stages and moralization. In T. Lickona, G. Geis, & L. E. Kohlberg (Eds.), *Moral development and behavior: Theory, research, and social issues* (pp. 31–53). New York: Holt, Rinehart & Winston.

Kohlberg, L. E., & Higgins, A. (1984). Continuities and discontinuities in childhood and adult development revisited again. In L. E. Kohlberg (Ed.), *Essays on moral development. Vol. 2: The psychology of moral development: The nature and validity of moral stages* (pp. 426–497). San Francisco: Harper & Row.

Kohn, M. L., & Schooler, C. (1983). *Work and personality: An inquiry into the impact of social stratification.* Norwood, NJ: Ablex.

Kühnlein, G. (1983). Betriebliche Ausbildung als Erfahrungsprozeß: Die Entwicklung von Berufsperspektiven auf dem Hintergrund sich verändernder betrieblicher Anforderungen [Apprenticeship as an experience process: The development of occupational perspectives against a background of changing industrial demands]. In Kruse, W., Kühnlein, G., & Müller, U. (Eds.), *Arbeitsmarkterfahrungen und Berufsorientierungen Jugendlicher* [Labor market experiences and occupational orientations of young people] (pp. 46–63). Munich, Germany: Deutsches Jugendinstitut.

Lempert, W. (1981). Moralische Sozialisation durch den "heimlichen Lehrplan" des Betriebs [Moral socialization through the "hidden curriculum" of the firm]. *Zeitschrift für Pädagogik, 27,* 723–738.

Lempert, W. (1983). Ausbildung zum Facharbeiter: Startbahn oder Parkplatz, Aufzug oder Abweg? Bildungsgänge unter Berufsverläufe gelernter Dreher, Maschinenschlosser und Werkzeugmacher im Spiegel einer repräsentativen Erhebung [Training to become a skilled worker: Runway or parking spot, the way up or the way astray? Educational paths in the occupational careers of trained lathe operators, millwrights, and tool-makers as reflected in a representative survey]. *Berufsbildung in Wissenschaft und Praxis, 12,* 77–83.

Lempert, W. (1986). Sozialisation in der betrieblichen Ausbildung: Der Beitrag der Lehre zur Entwicklung sozialer Orientierungen im Spiegel neuerer Längsschnittuntersuchungen [Socialization through in-firm training: The contribution of apprenticeship to the development of social orientations, as reflected in recent longitudinal studies]. In H. Thomas & G. Elstermann (Eds.), *Bildung und Beruf: Soziale und ökonomische Aspekte* [Education and occupation: Social and economic aspects] (pp. 105–144). Berlin: Springer.

Lempert, W. (1988). Individual morality and industrialized work: Some theoretical considerations. *Economic and Industrial Democracy, 9,* 475–496.

Lempert, W. (1993a). Moralische Sozialisation im Beruf: Bedingungsvarianten und konfigurationen, Prozeßstrukturen, Untersuchungsstrategien [Moral socialization at work: Conditional variations and configurations, process structures, strategies for research]. *Zeitschrift für Sozialisationsforschung und Erziehungssoziologie, 13,* 2–35.

Lempert, W. (1993b). Moralisches Denken, Handeln und Lernen in einfachen Berufen: Ergebnisse einer Auswertung sozialwissenschaftlicher Veröffentlichungen [Moral thinking, action, and learning in simple occupations: Results of an evaluation of social scientific publications]. *Zeitschrift für Berufs- und Wirtschaftspädagogik, 89,* 5–25.

Lempert, W. (1994). Moral development in the biographies of skilled industrial workers. *Journal of Moral Education, 23,* 451–468.

Lempert, W., & Ebel, H. (1965). *Lehrzeitdauer, Ausbildungssystem und Ausbildungserfolg: Grundlagen für die Bemessung des Zeitraums der Ausbildung bis zum Facharbeiterniveau* [Length of training, the apprenticeship system and success in apprenticeship: Bases for the allocation of time to apprenticeship up to the level of skilled worker]. Freiburg im Breisgan, Germany: Rombach.

Lerman, R., & Pouncy, H. (1990, Fall). The compelling case for youth apprenticeship. *The Public Interest, No. 101,* 62–77.

Lind, G. (1983). *Moralische Urteilskompetenz und berufliche Ausbildung* [Competence in moral judgment and apprenticeship]. Fribourg, Switzerland: Pädagogisches Institut der Universität Fribourg.

Lutz, B. (1989). Das Ende des Facharbeiters: Die soziale Entwicklung bis zum Jahr 2000 und ihre Bedeutung für qualifiziertes Baustellenpersonal [The end of the skilled worker: Social development up to the year 2000 and its significance for skilled construction workers]. In *Sonderforschungsbereich 33 der Universität München: Entwicklungsperspektiven der Arbeit, Mitteilungen 1,* 5–16.

Mayer, E., Schumm, W., Flaake, K, Gerberding, H., & Reuling, J. (1981). *Betriebliche Ausbildung und gesellschaftliches Bewußtsein* [Apprenticeship and societal consciousness]. Frankfurt, Germany: Campus.

Offe, C. (1975). *Berufsbildungsreform: Eine Fallstudie über Reformpolitik* [Vocational education reform: A case study of the politics of reform]. Frankfurt, Germany: Suhrkamp.

Osterman, P. (1980). *Getting started: The youth labor market.* Cambridge, MA: MIT Press.

Pätzold, G. (1977). *Auslese und Qualifikation: Institutionalisierte Berufsausbildung in westdeutschen Großbetrieben* [Selection and qualification: Institutionalized apprenticeship in large West German firms]. Hannover, Germany: Schroedel.

Piore, M. J., & Sabel, C. F. (1984). *The next industrial divide: Possibilities for prosperity.* New York: Basic Books.

Roditi, H. F. (1992, March 16). High schools for docile workers. *The Nation 254*(10), 340–343.

Rose, R. (1991). Prospective evaluation through comparative analysis: Youth training in a time–space perspective. In P. Ryan (Ed.), *International comparisons of vocational education and training for intermediate skills* (pp. 68–92) London: Falmer.

Rosenbaum, J. E., Kariya, T., Settersten, R., & Maier, T. (1990). Market and network theories of the transition from high school to work: Their application to industrialized societies. In *Annual Review of Sociology, 16,* 263–299.

Sachverständigenkommission Kosten und Finanzierung der beruflichen Bildung. (1974). *Kosten und finanzierung der beruflichen Bildung* (Abschlußbericht) [The costs and financing of apprenticeship (Final report of an investigative commission)]. Bielefeld, Germany: Bertelsmann.

Schmid, G. (1992). Flexible coordination: The future of the dual system from a labour market policy angle. *Vocational Training, 1,* 48–51 [A periodical publication of CEDEFOP, the European Centre for the Development of Vocational Training, Berlin].

School-to-Work Opportunities Act of 1994, Pub. L. No. 103–239, 108 Stat. 568 (1994).

Seidenspinner, G. (1974). *Lehrlinge im Konfliktfeld Betrieb* [Apprentices in the field of conflict of the firm]. Munich, Germany: Juventa.

Simon, R. I., Dippo, D., & Schenke, A. (1991). *Learning work: A critical pedagogy of work education.* Toronto: Ontario Institute for Studies in Education.

Soskice, D. (1994). Reconciling markets and institutions: The German apprenticeship system. In L. Lynch (Ed.), *Training and the private sector: International comparisons* (pp. 25-60). Chicago: University of Chicago Press.

Statistisches Bundesamt. (1993). *Bildung und Kultur, Fachserie 11, Reihe 3: Berufliche Bildung 1991* [Education and culture, Series 11, Number 3: Occupational education 1991]. Stuttgart, Germany: Metzeler-Pöschel.

Stratmann, K., & Schlösser, M. (1990). *Das duale System des Berufsausbildung: Eine historische Analyse seine Reformdebatten* [The dual system of vocational training: A historical analysis of the reform debates]. Frankfurt, Germany: Verlag der Gesellschaft für die Förderung arbeitsorientierter Forschung und Bildung.

Streek, W., Hilbert, J., van Kevelaer, K -H, Maier, F., & Weber, H. (1987). *The role of the social partners in vocational training and further education in the Federal Republic of Germany*. Berlin: European Centre for the Promotion of Vocational Training (CEDEFOP).

Vickers, M. (1991). *Building a national system for school-to-work transition: Lessons from Britain and Australia*. Somerville, MA: Jobs for the Future.

Volmerg, B. (1988). Ein sozialpsychologischer Ansatz zum Verständnis von Subjektivität und industrieller Arbeit [A social psychological beginning toward understanding subjectivity and industrial work]. In R. Schmiede (Ed.), *Arbeit und Subjektivität* [Work and subjectivity] (pp. 197–211). Bonn, Germany: Informationszentrum Sozialwissenschaften.

Wagner, I. (1984). Zwischen Erfolg und Selbstbeschränkung: Arbeitserfahrungen weiblicher Lehrlinge und junger Facharbeiterinnen in gewerblich-technischen Berufen aus der Perspektive der moralischen Urteilsfähigkeit [Between success and self-limitation: Work experiences of female apprentices and young female skilled workers in commercial/technical occupations from the perspective of the ability to make moral judgments]. *Soziale Welt, 35*, 214–235.

The William T. Grant Foundation Commission on Work, Family, and Citizenship. (1988a). *The forgotten half: Non-college youth in America*. Washington, DC: Author.

The William T. Grant Foundation Commission on Work, Family, and Citizenship. (1988b). *The forgotten half: Pathways to success for America's youth and young families*. Washington, DC: Author.

Winkel, R. (1989). *Berufsstart in Nordrhein-Westfalen: Absolventen einer betrieblichen Berufsausbildung beim Übergang in die Beschäftigung* [Starting an occupation in North Rhine-Westphalia: Apprenticeship completers at the point of transition into employment]. Düsseldorf, Germany: Der Minister für Arbeit, Gesundheit und Soziales des Landes Nordrhein-Westfalen.

Witte, J. C., & Kalleberg, A. L. (1992). *Vocational training and job quality: Career attainment in the German labor market* (Discussion paper No. 57). Berlin: Deutsches Institut für Wirtschaftsforschung.

Witte, J. C., & Kalleberg, A. L. (1994). Determinants and consequences of fit between vocational education and employment in Germany. In *School-to-work: What does research say about it?* (pp. 3–32). Washington, DC: U.S Department of Education, Office of Research.

Yankelovich, D. (1974). *The new morality. A profile of American youth in the 70's*. New York: McGraw-Hill.

Yankelovich, D. (1981). *New rules. Searching for self-fulfillment in a world turned upside down*. New York: Random House.

Zoll, R. (1989). *"Nicht so wie unsere Eltern!" Ein neues kulturelles Modell?* ["Not like our parents!" A new cultural model?]. Opladen, Germany: Westdeutscher Verlag.

Received September 23, 1994
Revision received May 1, 1995
Accepted June 14, 1995

Comprehensive Health Care for High-Risk Adolescents: An Evaluation Study

FELTON EARLS, MD, LEE N. ROBINS, PHD, ARLENE R. STIFFMAN, PHD, AND JACK POWELL, PHD

Abstract: This study was designed to evaluate the effectiveness of a large scale program to improve health care for high-risk adolescents. Seven clinics, funded to provide comprehensive primary care to adolescents, were compared to three non-funded clinics. The majority of the 2,788 adolescent patients sampled in these clinics were female (78 percent) and Black (71 percent). Each patient was initially interviewed at the time of a clinic visit and reinterviewed 12 months later; their medical records were systematically reviewed. As expected, the funded clinics detected and treated a wider range of medical and behavioral problems than the comparison clinics, a finding that was based on the self-reports of patients and confirmed by documentation in the medical records. However, improvements in life-style and in specific medical outcomes were not observed. To build on the limited success of this program, efforts are needed to encourage more males to receive care and to develop more specific interventions for patients in this age group. (*Am J Public Health* 1989; 79:999–1005).

Introduction

The problems adolescents take to doctors challenge conventional approaches to medical care. To promote a focused and intensive effort to improve the health care of young people, adolescent medicine[1–4] has been quick to identify the major causes of mortality and the most common morbidities characterizing this age group[5]; less certainty exists on knowing how effective interventions have been in improving the health of adolescents, however.[1–5] To a large extent this is because the approach to problems such as unprotected sexual intercourse, substance abuse, and violent behavior require behavioral and life-style changes that go beyond traditional medical practices.

Results of a broad-scale program to improve the health care of high-risk populations of adolescents are reported in this paper. The project, introduced as the Program to Consolidate Health Services for High-Risk Young People and sponsored by the Robert Wood Johnson Foundation, was started in 1981. Twenty medical schools were selected to receive funds to provide comprehensive services to youths at higher risk than the national average for the major problems characteristic of this age group, and by improving the training of physicians in adolescent medicine.[6]

The concept was based more on the capacity to provide comprehensive health services than on the organizational characteristics of the participating programs. For this reason the evaluation was guided by five objectives:

1) Do the funded clinics attract truly high-risk youths?
2) Do they detect their problems?
3) Are comprehensive services provided?
4) Are these services implemented?
5) Are health outcomes improved?

To address these questions, the clinics receiving grants from the Johnson Foundation were compared to a group of clinics that did not have a special focus on adolescents. Because of their location in inner-city areas, all of the clinics were in a position to serve high-risk youths.

Address reprint requests to Felton Earls, MD, Professor of Child Psychiatry, Department of Psychiatry, Washington University School of Medicine, 4940 Audubon Avenue, St. Louis, MO 63110. Dr. Robins is Professor of Sociology in Psychiatry; Dr. Stiffman is Assistant Professor, George Warren Brown School of Social Work; Dr. Powell is Statistical Data Analyst; all at Washington University. This paper, submitted to the Journal April 18, 1988, was revised and accepted for publication January 4, 1989.

Methods

Research Design

The research design was that of a two-wave survey in which youths attending primary health clinics were interviewed twice at a 12-month interval. Of the 20 funded clinics, seven were chosen to participate in this evaluation study because they had a relatively large volume of patients in the adolescent age range from which to sample. The 20 clinics linked medical school training programs in adolescent medicine to a range of services based in hospitals, neighborhoods, and schools. However, each program was given considerable leverage in choosing how to develop a consolidated program. Of the seven programs studied, five had clinics in multiple settings including three with school-based clinics; those that operated from a single locus had established ties with other services; all seven had multidisciplinary staffs that included social workers, psychologists, special education counselors, midwives, and recreational counselors as well as physicians and nurses.

The seven funded programs (all associated with academic medical centers in Boston, MA; New Haven, CT; Indianapolis, IN; Chicago, IL; Jackson, MS; Dallas, TX; and Los Angeles, CA) were compared to clinics that were part of three non-specialized services (located in Buffalo, NY; St. Louis, MO; and New Orleans, LA). The comparison clinics did not offer special services to teenagers, nor did they have training programs in adolescent medicine. They were typically staffed only with physicians and nurses and had few administrative ties to other community-based clinics; none operated school-based clinics. The funded and non-funded clinics were similar in that they were all located in major public medical centers in their respective cities and were accessible to indigent patients. A brief description of the 10 programs, highlighting some of their similarities and differences, is provided in Appendix A.

Sampling

Between 150 and 360 youths were sampled from each clinic between November 1984 and May 1985. The age range of patients was restricted to 13–18 year olds. The sample represented a series of consecutive and unduplicated teenage patients appearing on days when the clinics were operating. The variation in the number sampled reflected the volume of patients in this age range attending the clinics during this six-month period, and in that sense the patients are representative of a typical day in the operation of primary health clinics. Most were interviewed on the same day that they attended the clinics in an on-site space where confidentiality could be maintained and their medical care not compromised.

During the six-month field period of Wave 1, 3,102 patients became eligible to participate in the study, based on their age and presentation at one of the clinics. Of these, 2,788 were interviewed. Among the 314 patients who were identified but not interviewed, 115 refused; 199 were not interviewed either because they were over the age of 18, too ill, or could not be located during or following their visit. Eighty-seven percent of those interviewed during Wave 1 were reinterviewed 12 months later during Wave 2. Because of the time consumed in locating and reviewing medical records, only about 83 percent of youths completing both the Wave 1 and Wave 2 interviews had their records abstracted. Complete data are available for 72 percent of the original sample.

There were no substantial differences in the number of patients completing all aspects of the study in the three types of programs, as shown in Table 1.

Interviews and Record Reviews

Highly structured interview protocols covered the youths' reasons for attending the clinics, other health services used, their physical and mental health status, family background, school adjustment, peer relations, stressful events, social adjustment, social supports, health practices, and extracurricular activities. Sections of the interview dealing with depression, anxiety, alcohol/drug use and abuse, tobacco use, and physical symptoms were taken from the Diagnostic Interview Schedule (DIS).[7] A section on aggressive and antisocial behavior was taken from the Diagnostic Interview for Children and Adolescents (DICA).[8] The follow-up interview, completed 12 months after the initial interview, covered these same issues and assessed change in health status and satisfaction with services received. During this second wave, the medical records of the youths were reviewed and abstracted.

At the Wave 2 interview, (75 percent of which was done at home) particular treatment for problems that had been identified in the Wave 1 interview was also queried. These problems included the presenting problem for which the youth was seeking help as well as any others reported during the interview session, regardless of whether or not they were known to health personnel at the study clinic.

TABLE 1—Sample Sizes at Wave 1 and Wave 2

Type of Clinic	Total Number Interviewed at Wave 1	Of Those Completing Wave 1: Completed Wave 2 Interview		Of Those Completing Wave 1: Completed Wave 2 Interview and Had Medical Record Review	
	N*	f	%	f	%
Funded NH	1320	1087	(82)	925	(70)
Funded S	616	568	(92)	452	(73)
Comparison	852	760	(89)	625	(73)
Total	2788	2415	(87)	2002	(72)

*This number represents 86%, 97%, 92%, and 90% of all eligible cases in the Funded NH, Funded S, and Comparison clinics and the total sample, respectively.
NH - Neighborhood/hospital-based
S - School-based

A structured protocol, designed to complement the interview, was used to abstract information from the medical records. The interviewing and record reviews were done by professional interviewers (Survey Research Associates of Baltimore) who were trained prior to each wave of interviews. An effort was made to collect records from all services used by patients even if they were not affiliated with the study programs.

Results

Sample Description

Females made up over three-fourths of the sample and Blacks represented 71 percent. Black females constituted the largest sex-race group and were the most uniformly distributed across all the sites, while White males represented the smallest and least well distributed group. Of the three types of clinics, the school-based clinics had the largest proportion of males (43 percent), followed by the funded neighborhood/hospital-based clinics (21 percent), and the comparison neighborhood/hospital-based clinics (12 percent).

This patient sample is unrepresentative of the general population of youths who lived in the urban areas where the clinics were located. In some cases, youths originally residing outside these areas were attracted to these clinics because they wished to avoid stigma or sanctions that might have accompanied help-seeking in their own communities. Even among those living in the same areas as the clinics, self-selection operated to yield a group in which females predominated and males not in school were underrepresented. In the neighborhood and hospital-based clinics, 19 percent of the youths were not in school, a rate which varied from 4 percent for Black males to 42 percent for White females. Fifty-seven percent of the youths' families were headed by persons with blue collar jobs, and 7 percent of their breadwinners were unemployed. Nine percent of the youths lived in circumstances in which there was no parent or parent surrogate present.

Presenting Problems and Risk Factors

Table 2 shows the frequency of the presenting problems reported at the initial interview. Over three-fourths of the youths were attending for problems unrelated to illness (i.e., pregnancy, birth control, check-up, and preventive care), a percentage that varied from 61 percent in the funded neighborhood/hospital-based clinics to over 90 percent in the comparison clinics. Those attending the funded clinics had higher rates of utilization for acute medical problems, contraceptive needs, mental health problems, sexually transmitted diseases, and chronic illnesses than those in the comparison clinics; and lower rates for pregnancy. Not unexpectedly, the school-based clinics attracted the largest proportions of youths requesting check-ups and other forms of preventive care. These differences among the three types of clinics remained after controlling for age, race, and sex.

Table 3 shows the percentage of individuals attending the three types of clinics who had ever experienced a variety of life-style and behavioral problems. A cumulative index was derived by summing the presence of each problem over the life-span prior to Wave 1 and its occurrence (or recurrence) in the interval between Wave 1 and Wave 2 interviews. The definition of each risk factor is given in Appendix B. As a measure of highest risk, the proportion of youths with three or more of these risk factors is included in Table 3. These indicators represent some of the major risks for injury and social problems in adolescents and, quite apart from their

TABLE 2—Percentage Distribution of Presenting Problems of Adolescents at Three Types of Clinics

Presenting problem	Funded NH (N = 1087) %	Funded S (N = 568) %	Comparison (N = 760) %	Total (N = 2415) %
Pregnancy*	19	7	53	29
Check-Up/Preventive	20	49	17	26
Acute Medical Problem	26	19	11	20
Contraceptive Needs	23	5	17	17
Psychiatric	7	6	<1	5
Chronic Illness	7	3	2	4
Sexually Transmitted Disease	6	1	<1	3

*Females only (Funded NH, N = 878; Funded S, N = 326; Comparison, N = 674).
NOTE: Percentages total more than 100 because youths could present with more than one problem.

TABLE 3—Life-style and Behavioral Problems Ever Experienced by Youths at Three Types of Clinics as Reported at Initial Interview

Life-style and Behavioral Problems	Funded NH (N = 1087) %	Funded S (N = 568) %	Comparison NH (N = 760) %	Total (N = 2415) %
Physical Fights	67	71	62	66
Contraceptive Needs	60	58	69	62
Pregnancy	34	16	64	39
Regular Tobacco Use	37	16	33	31
Hopelessness	37	21	27	30
Heavy Alcohol/Drug Use	31	18	20	25
Runaway	24	13	20	20
School Drop-Out	19	4	27	18
Arrests	23	11	18	19
Use of Weapons	14	10	13	13
Suicidal Behavior	12	6	8	9
3+ Problems	60	41	64	57

presenting problems, should be of keen concern to health providers.

The school-based clinics had the lowest proportion of high-risk youths (41 percent) and these youths had lower rates on all but one (fighting) of the 11 individual risk factors compared to youths in the other types of clinics. Engaging in physical fights and unprotected sexual activity (shown by the proportion with contraceptive needs) were the most common problems. Suicidal behavior was the least common.

Pattern of Utilization and Care

To examine the impact of the funded programs, 11 problems were selected that included both traditional medical conditions, such as asthma and sexually transmitted diseases (STD), and behavioral and life-style problems, such as those listed in Table 3. The list, based on problems designated by the youths in the initial interviews regardless of whether or not such problems constituted the reason for seeking care, conforms to the types of problems targeted by the funding agency in its charge to improve services for high-risk youths.

Table 4 illustrates the extent to which this range of health problems was recognized and treated in the three types of clinics. The most important contrast is between the funded neighborhood/hospital-based and the comparison clinics, since they were located in similar settings. The funded school-based clinics provide data to contrast with the neighborhood/hospital-based clinics. The Table shows that youths in the funded clinics were more likely to inform providers about their behavioral and life-style problems than youths in the comparisons clinics. On the other hand, informing the clinics about more clear-cut medical problems (contraceptive needs, asthma, injury and STD) was done with greater consistency and at higher rates among all clinics than they were for behavioral and life-style problems.

Informing a clinic about a problem constitutes a first step toward getting help. Table 5 shows the proportion of youths who actually received help among those who had told a clinic about their problems. In most cases, help was obtained on-site. But because having the capacity to refer patients to other services when needed was a key element of the effort to consolidate services, it is also included in the Table. Youths with asthma and conduct or interpersonal problems in the funded clinics were more likely to be treated on-site than youths in the comparison clinics. What is most striking, however, is that the numbers of youths available to be treated in the comparison clinics were greatly reduced because fewer had informed the health care providers about their life-style and behavioral problems. Differences in the rate of referral among the clinics were not striking.

Medical Record Documentation

While the research interview was designed to comprehensively assess the health and psychosocial status of the youths, providers were faced with the need to specifically address the patient's presenting problem. Within the limited and often pressured time frame of most patient encounters, they also had to conduct a general examination of their patients and record their findings in the medical record.

We compared the youths' health and psychosocial profiles based on data from the interview to that abstracted from the medical records by counting the number of problems identified in each document using a common list such as that

TABLE 4—Percentages of Youths Who Returned to the Clinic between Waves 1 and 2 and Informed Providers about Their Health Problems in Funded Neighborhood/Hospital Clinics (N = 1087), Funded School Clinics (N = 568), and Comparison Clinics (N = 760)

Health-Related Problem		N with Problem	Percent with Problem Who Returned and Informed Clinic about Their Problem
Contraceptive Needs	FNH	606	72
	FS	272	50
	COM	485	66
Physical Symptoms	FNH	742	44
	FS	293	39
	COM	535	36
Depressive Symptoms	FNH	378	21
	FS	98	22
	COM	195	6
Conduct Problems	FNH	274	11
	FS	72	21
	COM	123	2
Asthma	FNH	115	55
	FS	55	44
	COM	69	58
Quitting Tobacco	FNH	258	24
	FS	46	11
	COM	168	12
Interpersonal Problems	FNH	525	10
	FS	211	11
	COM	350	3
Anxiety Symptoms	FNH	235	22
	FS	54	22
	COM	136	10
Injury	FNH	204	22
	FS	90	34
	COM	93	30
Alcohol/Drug Abuse	FNH	152	25
	FS	44	25
	COM	56	9
Sexually Transmitted Disease	FNH	61	57
	FS	14	43
	COM	22	54

FNH - Funded neighborhood/hospital-based clinics
FS - Funded school-based clinics
COM - Comparison clinics

shown in Table 4. The findings are shown in Figure 1. As expected, the interviews provided more information than the medical records. The largest discrepancy occurred in the comparison clinics. While youths in the funded neighborhood/hospital-based clinics and the comparison clinics had the same mean number of risk factors based on the interview data, the number of risk factors documented in the records was significantly higher in the funded clinics. This supports the self-reports of the youths and indicates that funded clinics were clearly superior to the comparison clinics in detecting a broad range of health problems in their patients.

Outcome Measures

Two approaches were taken to detect differences in outcomes between youths in the funded and comparison clinics. One approach was aimed at detecting changes in the number of behavioral and life-style problems in the 12-month period preceding the Wave 1 and Wave 2 interviews, and the other examined the degree of recurrence or persistence of specific medical or psychiatric problems. No evidence was found favoring the funded clinics in either case. The proportion of youths experiencing three or more risk factors in the year preceding the Wave 2 interview remained the same as it had been in the 12 months preceding the Wave 1 interview in both the funded and the comparison clinics. Even when age, race, sex, and the number of problems present at Wave 1 were controlled, the risk status of the youths at Wave 2 was not diminished in the funded programs. This was true not only when the proportion of youths with multiple problems was examined, but also for a reduction in the average number of behavioral and life-style problems reported in the year following the initial interview. In fact, there was a small increase in the proportion of youths with multiple problems suggesting that the interventions were not able to overcome the expectable increase in risk associated with the aging of an adolescent sample.

A number of specific outcomes were examined next. The frequency of sexually transmitted diseases in the interval between Waves 1 and 2 among youths with a previous history of such infections was not reduced in the funded clinics compared to the nonfunded clinics. This was also true for having a second (or third) pregnancy. In fact, for most of the problems examined, we failed to find evidence of a reduction in risk among youths attending the funded clinics. Although the proportion with unmet contraceptive needs remained uniformly high in all the clinics, we found, unexpectedly, that the proportion with persisting depressive symptoms and heavy alcohol/drug use at Wave 2 was actually higher in youths in the funded neighborhood/hospital clinics than in the comparison programs, as shown in Table 6.

Discussion

The answer to the first question of this evaluation study—"Do the funded clinics attract truly high-risk youths?"—is affirmative. Nearly two-thirds of the youths attending the neighborhood and hospital-based clinics had multiple behavioral and life-style problems that placed them at high risk for the social morbidities characteristic of adolescence and young adulthood and for early death. However, the proportion of such youths in the funded clinics was no greater than that in the comparison clinics. All the clinics turned out to be particularly appropriate places to reach high-risk females, a finding supported by another recently completed study of an adolescent clinic in a suburban setting.[9] While the school-based clinics had a lower proportion of high-risk youths, they attracted more males than did the neighborhood/hospital-based clinics. All of the clinics, however, failed to attract males who were not in school. This remains a challenge since these males represent the highest risk group for intentional and unintentional injury in the community. One approach to attracting a larger number of high-risk males is through liaison with juvenile detention facilities. This was pursued by one funded neighborhood/hospital-based clinic which, not surprisingly, had the highest proportion of males attending these types of clinics.

Clinicians in adolescent medicine are faced with detecting and treating a spectrum of problems for which traditional pediatric training may not have thoroughly prepared them. In addition to traditional medical problems, such as sexually transmitted diseases, and pregnancy, their experience must also alert them to the importance of behavioral and life-style problems such as depression, delinquency, substance abuse, unprotected sexual intercourse, and cigarette smoking.[10] For this reason we were especially interested in the answer to the second question of the evaluation regarding the detection of a broad range of health and social problems in adolescent patients. The superiority of the funded clinics in recognizing

TABLE 5—Percentages of Youths Treated, Referred, or Receiving No Care among Those Who Informed Providers about Their Problems in Funded Neighborhood/Hospital Clinics (N = 1087), Funded School Clinics (N = 568), and Comparison Clinics (N = 760)

Health-Related Problem		Of Those Who Informed Providers N	Percent Treated On-Site	Percent Referred	Percent with No Care
Contraceptive Needs	FNH	437	94	0	6
	FS	135	89	2	9
	COM	319	89	7	4
Physical Symptoms	FNH	328	72	3	25
	FS	113	76	8	16
	COM	195	69	3	28
Depressive Symptoms	FNH	80	76	15	21
	FS	22	95	18	4
	COM	12	75	17	25
Conduct Problems	FNH	73	63	10	36
	FS	46	83	2	17
	COM	10	20	10	80
Asthma	FNH	63	59	10	40
	FS	24	42	8	54
	COM	40	27	0	73
Quitting Tobacco	FNH	61	46	—	54
	FS	5	60	—	40
	COM	20	45	—	55
Interpersonal Problems	FNH	55	80	0	20
	FS	24	79	0	21
	COM	10	50	0	50
Anxiety Symptoms	FNH	52	58	0	42
	FS	12	92	0	8
	COM	13	46	8	46
Injury	FNH	45	62	9	29
	FS	31	77	7	16
	COM	27	70	11	19
Alcohol/Drug Abuse	FNH	38	47	0	53
	FS	11	73	0	27
	COM	5	40	0	60
Sexually Transmitted Disease	FNH	35	97	0	3
	FS	6	100	0	0
	COM	12	75	25	0

FNH - Consolidated neighborhood/hospital-based clinics
FS - Consolidated school-based clinics
COM - Comparison clinics

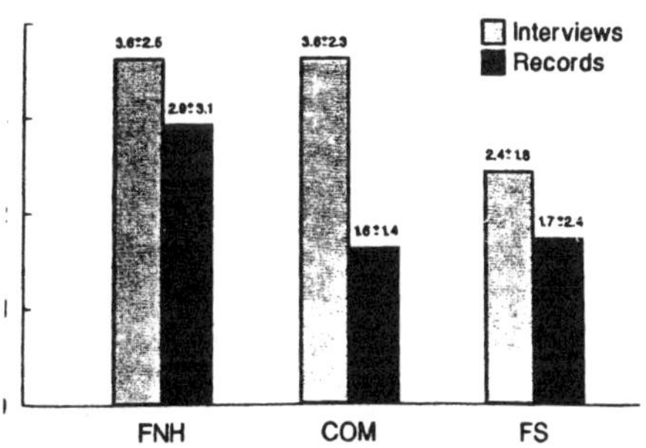

FIGURE 1—Comparison of the Mean Number of Adolescent Health Problems Reported on Interviews and Found in Medical Records
FNH = Funded Neighborhood/Hospital-Based Clinic
COM = Comparison Clinic
FS = Funded School-Based Clinic

behavioral and lifestyle problems was clearly shown by the higher proportion of youths reporting such problems to them and by their more extensive demonstration of such problems in their medical records.

No doubt the greater recognition of problems in the funded clinics was a function of their more diverse and specially trained staffs. Their success in this regard resulted in more youths receiving treatment and interventions being provided for a broader range of problems than in the comparison clinics. This answers the third question of the evaluation regarding the availability and implementation of comprehensive services.

It is worth emphasizing that, although the quality of care was not directly assessed, a higher quality of care in the funded clinics can be inferred from their more extensive documentation of problems.[11,12] Nevertheless, the funded

TABLE 6—Percentages of Youths with Persistent Problems from Wave 1 to Wave 2* in the Three Types of Clinics

Type of Clinic	Persistent Depressive Symptoms %	Unmet Contraceptive Needs %	Heavy Alcohol or Drug Use %
FNH (N = 1087)	23[a]	36	31[b]
FS (N = 568)	12	29	15
COM (N = 760)	14	33	21

*Persistence is defined as the presence of the problems in the 12 months prior to the Wave 1 interview and again in the 12-month interval between the Wave 1 and Wave 2 interview.
a) FNH - COM = 9% (95% CI = 5.5, 12.5)
b) FNH - COM = 10% (95% CI = 6.0, 14.0)

clinics were not able to alter the propensity of their patients to continue their adverse life-styles and to accumulate additional problems.

There are at least three reasons to explain why we failed to detect outcome differences:

- The follow-up period of one-year was a short interval over which to find differences in problems many of which have their bases in lifestyle orientations.
- More time may be needed to judge the impact of specialized primary health care for adolescents since pediatricians have only recently begun to develop skills in these areas. One goal of the Robert Wood Johnson Foundation was to inspire efforts to develop training programs and to promote the concept of interdisciplinary, consolidated health care for this age group. While the Foundation's initiative was clearly successful in supporting many new programs throughout the country, the long-term success of this field will depend on the extent to which stable support is found to maintain its focused agenda.
- A more sobering reason why we may not have detected outcome differences relates to the inherent nature of many of the problems characteristics of high-risk youths. Perhaps their difficulties are so deeply embedded in the economic and social contexts from which they come that improvements in their health status require more than medical clinics can provide. If this is the case, then the goals of treatment should relate more to the stabilization of risk conditions, than to their actual reduction.[13]

There are two limitations of the present study that deserve special mention. As in many evaluation studies, the research design for this one was developed after the programs had already been funded. This resulted in less comparability among the clinics in their organizational patterns and in the character and intensity of the interventions they provided. The other limitation relates to the possibility that biased reporting of health-related information occurred in the interviews. Efforts were made to minimize this problem by using highly structured and carefully validated interview methods, systematic training, and monitoring of interviewers, and by comparing information derived from the interviews with that included in medical records.

Overall, the evaluation demonstrates that the Johnson Foundation's objectives met with limited success. Continued progress in the identification of the behavioral and life-style problems possessed by these youths must be followed by finding ways to attract more males as patients and by devising interventions that, at a minimum, have the capacity to slow down the progression of life-style and behavioral problems that are typically occurring at their peak rates during the later adolescent years.

APPENDIX A

Ten Participating Clinics Included Seven with Adolescent Services (Funded Clinics) and Three with Non-specialized Services (Comparison Clinics)

Funded Clinics

1. A hospital-based adolescent clinic, a neighborhood-based adolescent clinic, and a school-based clinic were included in this program in New Haven, Connecticut. The multidisciplinary staff included an adolescent medicine specialist, fellows in adolescent medicine, a nurse-midwife, a social worker, and a psychologist.

2. A hospital-based adolescent clinic, a neighborhood-based clinic, and a school-based clinic were components of the program in Chicago, Illinois. The staff consisted of an adolescent medicine specialist, fellows in adolescent medicine, a nurse practitioner, a school nurse, a social worker, a guidance counselor, and a special education counselor.

3. Two high-school-based clinics, with neighborhood and hospital-based clinics serving as part of a consolidated network, composed the program in Jackson, Mississippi. The staff included an adolescent medicine specialist, fellows in adolescent medicine, a nurse, a social worker, and an educational counselor.

4. A hospital-based clinic and a neighborhood-based adolescent clinic made up this program in Boston, Massachusetts. The staff was composed of adolescent medicine specialists, fellows in adolescent medicine, a nurse, a psychologist, and a recreational counselor; the program also sponsors a school-based violence prevention program.

5. This program in Dallas, Texas consisted of a hospital-based adolescent clinic that placed emphasis on screening and diagnostic evaluation. It tied to an extensive referral network of neighborhood-based clinics throughout the city. The multidisciplinary staff included an adolescent medicine specialist, fellows in adolescent medicine, a nurse, a nurse practitioner, a social worker, and a consulting psychiatrist.

6. A neighborhood-based adolescent clinic and a closely associated hospital-based adolescent clinic constituted the two components of this program in Los Angeles, California. The staff consisted of a specialist in adolescent medicine, fellows in adolescent medicine, a nurse, a social worker, and an educational counselor.

7. The program in Indianapolis, Indiana was composed of several neighborhood-based adolescent clinics which were coordinated through a hospital-based adolescent medicine program. The multidisciplinary staff included an adolescent medicine specialist, fellows in adolescent medicine, nurses, and social workers.

Comparison Clinics

1. The clinics in New Orleans, Louisiana were all located in the largest public general hospital in the city. The hospital was part of a large academic medical center with no special clinics for adolescents. Patients were sampled through a walk-in clinic for all non-emergency cases, and through an obstetrical clinic. The staff included staff physicians, residents, and nurses only.

2. Publicly supported neighborhood health clinics with no special services for adolescents made up this service in St. Louis, Missouri. Adolescents were sampled through pediatric, dental, and obstetrical clinics. The staff included only staff physicians and nurses.

3. This site in Buffalo, New York was composed of general outpatient, emergency, and obstetrical clinics of a Children's Hospital and a hospital-based family practice center. The staff included physicians, nurses, and residents in pediatrics, obstetrics-gynecology, and family practice.

APPENDIX B

Risk Factors	Definitions
Pregnancy	Pregnant one or more times.
Use of Weapon	Threatened anyone with a knife or gun or any kind of weapon such as a pick, soda bottle, or something else.
Physical Fights	• Been in physical fights, *or* • Hurt someone badly in a fight, *or* • Taken things from other people by purse-snatching, holding them up, or threatening them.
Legal Problems	Been in trouble with the police or a juvenile officer.
Runaway	Run away overnight or longer from the place where living.
Contraceptive Needs	If had sex *and*: • respondent and partner do not use birth control most of the time, *or* • withdrawal is one type of birth control used.
Regular Tobacco Use	Smoked cigarettes, cigars, or pipes; chewed tobacco; or used snuff every day for a month or more.
Heavy Alcohol/Drug Use	• Drank four or more glasses/drinks of beer/wine/liquor at one time, *or* • Averaged drinking more than once a week or for short concentrated periods over the last year, *or* • Used a drug more than once a week or for short concentrated periods over the last year.

continued

APPENDIX B continued

Risk Factors	Definitions
Suicidal Behavior	Attempted suicide.
Hopelessness	• During a period of feeling blue or depressed (defined as: 1) two weeks or more during which respondent felt sad, blue, depressed, and lost interest and pleasure in things he/she cared about and enjoyed; *or* 2) two years or more when respondent felt sad or depressed almost all the time), work at school, at home, or on the job suffered, *or* • A period of two weeks or more when life felt hopeless or pointless.
School Drop Out	Not in school; highest grade completed was less than 12th.

ACKNOWLEDGMENTS

This research was supported by the Robert Wood Johnson Foundation Grant No. 6743. Field work was conducted by Survey Research Associates, Baltimore, Maryland. A preliminary version of this paper was presented at the annual meeting of the Society of Adolescent Medicine, Seattle, Washington, February 1987.

REFERENCES

1. Cohen MI: Importance, implementation, and impact of the adolescent medicine components of the report of the task force on pediatric education. J Adolesc Health Care 1980:1:1–8.
2. Silber TJ: Adolescent medicine: the development of a new specialty. Adolescence 1980;15:496–499.
3. Gallagher JR: The origins, development and goals of adolescent medicine. J Adolesc Health Care 1982;3:57–63.
4. Irwin CE: Why adolescent medicine? J Adolesc Health Care 1986;7:2–25.
5. Blum R: Contemporary threats to adolescent health in the US. JAMA 1987;257:3390–3395.
6. Lear JG, Foster HW, Wylie WG: Development of community-based health services for adolescents at risk for sociomedical problems. J Med Educ 1985;60:777–785.
7. Robins LN, Helzer JE, Croughan J, *et al*: The NIMH Diagnostic Interview Schedule: Its history, characteristics and validity. Arch Gen Psychiatry 1981;38:381–389.
8. Welner Z, Reich W, Herjanic B, *et al*: Reliability, validity and parent-child agreement studies of the Diagnostic Interview for Children and Adolescents (DICA). J Am Acad Child Adolesc Psychiatry 1987;26:649–653.
9. Fisher M, Marks A, Trieller K: Meeting the health care needs of suburban youth: Review of a clinical service. Pediatrics 1988;81:8–13.
10. Stiffman, AR, Earls F, Robins LN, Jung KG: Problems and help seeking in high-risk adolescent patients of health clinics. J Adolesc Health Care 1988;9:305–309.
11. Lyons TF, Payne BC: The relationship of physicians' medical recording performance to their medical care performance. Med Care 1974;12:463–469.
12. Zuckerman AE, Starfield B, Hochreiter C, Kovasznay B: Validating the content of pediatric outpatient medical records by means of tape-recording doctor-patient encounters. Pediatrics 1975;56:407–411.
13. Earls F: Delivering health services to older adolescents. *In*: Lerner RM, Petersen AC, Brooks-Gunn J (eds): Encyclopedia of Adolescence. New York: Garland Publishing Co, (In press).

Amer. J. Orthopsychiat. 42(4), July 1972

DELIVERY OF SERVICES

PEER COUNSELING IN THE SECONDARY SCHOOLS: A Community Mental Health Project for Youth

Beatrix A. Hamburg, M.D., and Barbara B. Varenhorst, Ph.D.

The Peer Counseling Program trains high school and junior high school students to help other students with personal problems or situational stress. Training is carried out in small groups in weekly sessions, and it includes behavioral principles, issues of relevance to adolescents, and supervised practical experience. Criteria are suggested for judging the suitability and effectiveness of students in the counseling role.

Youth problems, particularly alienation, drug abuse, and violence, are a source of major social concern at present. It is generally agreed that the roots of these problems are to be found in the full spectrum of effects that derive from the complex technological society of today.[1, 5] The schools find themselves at the center of these problems although, of course, they are not the prime cause. In response to this, schools have been accorded increasing responsibilities in recent years for the non-academic education of young people, so that schools are now becoming a powerful influence in the socialization of the child. In many instances, parents have explicitly extended the sphere of influence of the schools. For example, they often expect the schools to set and enforce standards of dress and social behavior. They have expected the schools to assume major responsibility for drug abuse programs. There is still controversy, but there are strong feelings in some quarters that sex education should be a function of the schools. In other instances, the schools have felt the impact of the heightened

Submitted to the JOURNAL *in 1972.*

DR. HAMBURG *is Clinical Associate Professor of Psychiatry at Stanford University, School of Medicine, Palo Alto, Calif.;* DR. VARENHORST *is Consulting Psychologist, Palo Alto Unified School District.*

emotional needs of their students but not identified the specific problems nor had any solutions.[3] The modern American nuclear family, with its smallness, mobility, and relative isolation from other kinship ties,[2] has need of a network of non-familial supports. The schools have become the social institution that would appear to have the necessary ingredients for playing a major role in the meeting of these needs. The role of teachers and counselors as parent surrogates can be clearly seen. The role of students as surrogates, models, bridging persons, and sources of useful information for each other has been somewhat overlooked.

Some prior work has shown the value of using peers in tutorial and/or counseling roles with other students.[6, 8, 9, 11] However, the bulk of such efforts have been at the college level.[4, 16] We wished to see the principle extended to the secondary schools. Therefore, we undertook to devise a program of peer counseling that would utilize students in grades 7–12 (ages 12 through 18 years). Other studies have further shown that, in addition to the considerable help that can be rendered by students to each other, there is a highly significant gain to the helping person. Therefore, in assigning a student to help another student, the intervention is of mutual benefit. For some students who are lonely and tending toward alienation, it may be uniquely pertinent and therapeutic to become involved in a helping role. There is an almost universal quest among young people today for "relevance," and there is commitment to "human" rather than materialistic goals. These motivations are salient in recruiting a large and varied group of students to helping roles.

Present counseling and guidance services are inadequate both in terms of manpower effectiveness and also in terms of acceptability to a significant percentage of students. Furthermore, it seems important to reach out also to less troubled students with preventive approaches. This latter student is almost never seen by a busy conselor.

In the spring of 1970, students at Cubberly High School in Palo Alto, California, were asked to respond to a survey questionnaire regarding counseling and guidance services in their school. Among the questions asked was one concerning the kinds of counseling services they would like to have, that they were not receiving. A large majority of them said they would like peer counselors. They did not want to replace their present adult counselors, but felt a need for help from other students in areas where this help would be unique because of the age and experience similarity.

In view of the above considerations, it was felt that a comprehensive program of peer counselors would fill an important mental health need. We felt that students could be involved in a wide range of counseling roles. Peer counselors were not conceived of merely as academic tutors but viewed as assistants in solving personal problems; teaching social skills; giving information about jobs, volunteer opportunities, and mental health resources in the community; acting as models; developing friendships; acting as a bridge to the adult world for disaffected students; and finally, over a period of time, serving as agents of change where the school atmosphere is characterized by coldness and indifference.

We felt that it would be advantageous to have a comprehensive program of peer counselors with widespread involvement of the entire school district. In their training, we wished to expose the students to a range of points of view deriving from their different school experiences, from their different developmental ages and stages, and from their different ethnic and racial backgrounds. This has proved to be a valuable aspect of the program.

We also felt that the inclusion of target populations of "normal" adolescents who are undergoing situational stresses was useful in further consolidating an image of peer counseling that was positive in the minds of the student body and not solely linked to pathology. We felt that, if the image were negative, many students who could benefit from such an association would not do so in order to avoid being automatically labeled as deviant or disturbed.

The Peer Counseling Project is the initial stage of a comprehensive school mental health plan. The long-range objective is to develop a totally self-sustaining peer counseling program that can function effectively within a school system with a minimum necessity for involvement of outside mental health professionals. In addition to our detailed curriculum for the training of peer counselors, we also wish to set up a training program for teachers and counselors to enable them to select effectively and train and supervise students as peer counselors. This training will have the additional benefit of improving the skills of the teachers and counselors in the performance of their regular duties. We hope to define the personality and motivational criteria for selecting the appropriate school personnel to act as trainers in this program. This training will be based in part on the existing experience in training selected individuals as mental health counselors.[12, 13] Finally, we wish to outline the minimal requirements for an administrative person within the school who can assume responsibility for the coordination and continued implementation of a comprehensive peer counseling program.

A pilot phase to assess the feasibility, community acceptance, and potential value of the project was carried out in the 1970–71 school year in Palo Alto in close collaboration with mental health professionals. The mental health professionals refer to a team of four psychiatrists and a clinical social worker from the Stanford University Department of Psychiatry. These resource people contributed expertise on group process, adolescent psychiatry, community consultation and principles of psychotherapy. In addition, each of these persons acted as a supervisor of a training group. Under the leadership of the authors, this group met regularly with school personnel who were also acting as supervisors. A very useful complementarity of knowledge, skills, and experience emerged at the supervisors' meetings.

In addition to the substantive contribution of the psychiatric consultant to the design and implementation of the program, her interest and endorsement of the program in its early planning stages was significant in gaining school and community acceptance for the peer counseling program.

In going from concept to implementation there was a crucial preliminary period of preparing the ground so as to ensure acceptance by the community and the school hierarchy. Any program that is innovative and that significantly affects the traditional structure of an established institution is viewed with suspicion. This was particularly a concern to us in a project that utilized minors in relatively responsible roles.

The initial step was the formation of a Planning Committee composed of students, parents, teachers, counselors, the Central Office staff, and the co-developers of the project. This group was useful in generating practical suggestions and gave strong encouragement to the idea of a peer counseling project. Before any contacts were made with students, the Superintendent of Schools was consulted. The background, objectives, and procedures of the project were discussed with him, and his approval was obtained. The entire guidance staff, including all of the psychologists in the School District, was informed and consulted. The Director of Guidance and the Director of Guidance Research were both significantly involved from the beginning and continue to have an integral role in the project. All of the PTA groups in the School District were individually consulted, and some valuable suggestions were elicited. The principals of all elementary schools in the District were contacted; they unanimously endorsed the plan to have all of the graduating sixth grade students assigned to peer counselors for help in making the transition to junior high school. Finally, the approval of the School Board was obtained. These informational efforts were a major activity in the fall of 1970, and very time-consuming, but they have proved to be a vital aspect of the procedures. In addition to all of these personal contacts, articles explaining the program were written for the PTA newsletters, the School District's News Bulletin, and the newspaper of each secondary school.

RECRUITMENT OF STUDENTS

With general approval and support from all of these groups, we proceeded to the next step—recruiting students who might be interested in the program. It had been agreed that all of the six secondary schools in the Palo Alto Unified School District, three junior high and three senior high schools, would be involved. The Planning Committee had determined that methods used to contact students should be tailored for each student body. In general, small group approaches were more successful than speaking to assemblies, sending letters, or putting articles in the student newspapers. It should be noted that, in addition to these methods, students interested in the program recruited a significant number of other students. This was perhaps the most effective of all the methods employed.

An orientation meeting was held in March 1971, at a centrally located high school. Students from all six schools managed to come to a 3:30 meeting with their own transportation, many coming quite a distance to attend. Approximately 225 students attended this meeting. The six schools have a total student population of approximately 7,000 students.

The purposes of this meeting were to give an overview of the program, to outline the nature of the training, and to describe eventual assignments. The range of potential counseling roles with individuals and in groups was described. It was indicated that we would try and match student preferences and skills with the needs of other students, for example, such preferences as working with the handicapped, disadvantaged, or students new to the District. Students with tutoring skills in sports, academic, or hobby areas were assured that they would be used appropriately. Heavy emphasis was given to the importance of their commitment. Those who were still interested were asked to fill out a formal registration form. Approximately 175 completed these registration forms.

For the eventual purpose of the program to succeed, students were needed who had positive personal characteristics, a strong sense of responsibility, high dedication to their work, and a feeling of involvement. Therefore, the training program was set up in such a way that initially, and at various points during the course of training, hurdles and obstacles were designed to weed out students of lesser commitment. Students had to initiate action to get in, find their own transportation to the training meetings, attend meetings on their own time, check a designated mailbox for important notices, call if they could not attend a meeting, and make up missed sessions. Requirements of this kind provided behavioral evidence of a degree of responsibility and commitment that was necessary if students were to continue in the program.

Finally, the program was based on the theory of self-selection and volunteer participation. No student was denied admittance if it was requested. No pre-training screening took place. However, before counseling assignments are made, students are evaluated in terms of demonstrated skill. At the present time, it is our preference not to drop anyone out of training. Differential assignments will be made, based on evaluations, with the provision that before some students are given any assignment, they may be asked to repeat the training program. It may be necessary eventually to drop individuals who may be evaluated as detrimental to the work or to others. When this is done, it will be based on observed evidence related to task performance rather than on pre-training subjective evaluations. So far this has not been necessary.

In view of the mental health benefits of the training program to the participants, we feel that it is a very useful service to help an adolescent work through his personal problems with the eventual goal of being able to help others, rather than rejecting him. So far, this approach has appeared to be quite practical. The stringent requirements of the training program and the emphasis on a high degree of responsibility have apparently acted to weed out the highly disturbed or psychopathic students who might otherwise be a potential problem.

TRAINING CURRICULUM FOR PEER COUNSELORS

1. ORGANIZATIONAL FRAMEWORK

The major structure of the training program was the small group organization, with a Supervisor assigned to each group. In this pilot group only professional persons with prior group experience were used as supervisors. The groups were 8–10 in number and met either at 3:30 in the afternoon (after school) or 7:30 at night for one-and-a-half hours. Afternoon groups met each day of the week and evening groups on Monday and Wednesday. The range of meetings was to accommodate the varied schedules of students. However, once a student was assigned to a particular afternoon or evening group, he was expected to continue on a regular basis with that group. If there was a need to miss a meeting, he could make it up by attending another group that week. This was possible because of the coordination of the curriculum through the Supervisors' meetings. A high degree of group cohesiveness quickly developed despite the calculated disparities in the group composition. As previously mentioned, each group had representation from each of the schools and each grade level.

At the midpoint of the training, all students were reassigned to a new group, to provide an additional experience in meeting new students and in working with a different Supervisor.

Supervisor Trainers. In addition to the authors, four psychiatrists from the Stanford Medical School and six District staff members volunteered to serve as Supervisors for the small group training. An additional District person served in a substitute capacity for the others. The school people included the head of Guidance of the School District, three psychologists, one counselor, and one secondary English teacher. These people received no remuneration for their services.

These twelve staff members met on a regular basis to review stages of the curriculum, to coordinate their sessions, to evaluate progress, and to recommend future steps. Each Supervisor was asked to evaluate the progress of students in his or her group at the conclusion of the training and to summarize techniques and activities that had proven to be successful throughout the process of the group.

2. LIFE CAREER GAME

An introductory phase of the training sessions involved large group exposure to the Life Career Game, a decision-making simulation.[14, 15] The Game, because of its varied activity, provided Supervisors with an opportunity to scan the overall student-training population. It gave some preliminary indication of the extent of interest and aptitude shown by the participants.

The Game was an "ice-breaker" in meeting fellow trainees. Its random coupling of students to play as a team meant that students were talking and working with those they had not known before. Here was an immediate experience in getting acquainted and relating to another who may have been different in age, sex, or race. This proved to be one of the meaningful experiences of this activity.

The Life Career Game is a technique that introduces students to counseling problems. The Game deals with a hypothetical person whose life they are asked to plan. Usually the Profile Student has certain specific problem areas that must be attended to, in order to plan that person's life.

At the same time, the Game presents a quantity of accurate information about current high school requirements, options open to students in life planning, and actions necessary, including required study time, to achieve desired goals. In reflecting on the Game experience, many students acknowledged the value of the specific information they had learned by playing the Game.

Finally, the Game provided all students with a common experience from which to begin their small group work the following week. During the first small group discussion, reactions were given as to what had been learned, liked, and disliked about it. In spite of initial disappointment in being confronted with a person in a simulated way, it was apparent that students continued to use the Game as a resource. References were frequently made to it throughout the remaining sessions.

3. SMALL GROUP TRAINING

Following the Life Career Game activity, 162 students indicated an interest in continuing in training. This was our Core Group of trainees. In assigning these students to small groups, a conscious effort was made to maximize exposure to a wide range of points of view within each group. Each group was composed of a mixture of students from the six schools. This meant that every group had both junior and senior high school students as members, and, as far as possible, an equal distribution of boys and girls. There was also an effort to maximize exposure to different ethnic and racial groups.

Some students indicated on their registration forms that they had had prior experience in a helping role. It was previously planned that each group would have both student leaders and student observers. The selection of these people was based on this stated prior experience. To provide additional experience, these positions were shifted from time to time, with most students having a turn in these roles. This meant that most students would have a chance to be leaders, observers, and participants at various times throughout their training.

4. CURRICULUM CONTENT

Three content tasks formed the structure of the curriculum in a basic sequence of four weeks, four weeks, and two weeks. These tasks were:

I. Understanding people (Interpersonal Relations)
II. Relevant topics in Peer Counseling
III. Particulars of the Peer Counseling Role (Strategies in Counseling and a Practicum Experience)

The content of the curriculum and the methods used for implementation are briefly outlined in what follows. Since groups and Supervisors differed, the mode of teaching varied somewhat from group to group, despite the fact that all groups covered the same content. The activities suggested represent some of the techniques that proved to be most successful in various groups.

In the following discussion, the term *Supervisor* refers to the professionally trained adult who was responsible for the group. The term *Leader* refers to the student assigned the responsibility of conducting the particular group session.

I. UNDERSTANDING PEOPLE (MEETINGS 1–4)

A. Defining the Task of the Training Group and Clarifying Roles (To be Done by the Supervisor)

1. GROUP PURPOSE AND TASK

The training group is task oriented and time oriented. The work of this group is to learn skills and principles that will assist members to more effectively help other students. The group is time oriented in that there is a definite number of meetings that have been designated to accomplish this task. This is not a sensitivity or encounter group. Its prime purpose is to prepare members to perform certain roles with respect to fellow students.

2. SETTING UP THE GROUP

a. Role of Student Leaders. Students selected to act as group leaders will attempt to keep students working and talking on the topic of the session. They will monitor the discussions in terms of both content and quality of participation, and they will bring to the attention of group members their observations as the group proceeds.

b. Role of Observer or Discussant. The observer withdraws from verbal participation during most of the session. He will listen and observe in an attempt to evaluate objectively what is taking place in the group. The last twenty minutes of each session will be devoted to hearing from the observer. His comments will be directed to such items as: 1) Did the group keep to the task? 2) To what extent was the student leader helpful and understanding? 3) What was the mode of participation among members? 4) What was contributed by member participation? Group members react to these comments in a final discussion period. Issues arising out of these discussions may form the basis for the next group meeting.

c. Role of the Participants. Participants are encouraged to speak freely on the topics being discussed. As they will be learning from one another, the more active they are in participating, the more experience they will gain in interpersonal relations. The particular aspect of honesty is worthy of discussion in terms of the impact honest feedback may have on other members of the group. The difference between honesty and hostility might be important to discuss. Honesty should not be used as a license for harsh attack. Since the matter of the silent member might be an issue at some point in group sessions, reasons for silence might be discussed. Participation may be affected by differing motivations for being in the program, age differences, and different interests among group members.

d. Responsibility of the Supervisor. The Supervisor will act as a model in structuring the group, launching the discussions and setting patterns for participation. At times, the Supervisor will present materials or situations containing principles of counseling and will summarize the accomplishments of the sessions at the end of each meeting. The Supervisor may take a more active leadership role from time to time, depending on the skill and mode of the student leader and the level of group participation.

B. Turning the Group Meeting Over to the Leader

a. The Leader asks members to introduce themselves and to offer their reasons for entering the Peer Counseling program.

b. The Leader then may ask for reactions about their feelings of insecurity in this new role, starting with the Leader's own feelings about his role as leader. Feelings of younger students (junior high school students) in working with "older people" (senior high school students) can be explored, as well as the feelings of strangeness and awkwardness due to being with people not previously known.

c. Reactions to the Life Career Game should be elicited. What was their idea of why they were asked to do this? What did they think was the point of the Game? What did they like about it? Dislike about it? What did they think was the main problem faced by the Profile student? What did they learn about themselves in playing the Game? These kinds of questions invariably evoked a lot of discussion and substantial group cohesiveness was noted by the end of the first session.

MEETING 2: COMMUNICATION

The factors influencing distortions or failures in interpersonal communication were reviewed for the group members. These principles were learned by the students through observation and practice in one-to-one and small group interview and role-playing situations. The following are the significant factors discussed in detail in the group:

1. Distortions from the sender (lack of clarity of message, discrepancy between the verbal and non-verbal message, non-verbal habits relating to eye contact, smiles, frowns, sneers, etc., role expectations having to do with age or status of sender, etc.).
2. Factors related to the listener (the effectiveness of the feedback that the listener gives the sender, listener distortion due to strong wish to hear a message in a particular way, distorting effect of a high anxiety or arousal, impairments due to drugs, etc.).
3. Personal characteristics of both sender and listener (effect of stereotypes, the "hippie," the "square," the "adult").
4. Choice of vocabulary and its use in effective communication.
5. Pace of communication (is it too fast or too slow for effective communication?).

Throughout these discussions the students across groups exhibited a surprising awareness and sophistication in these areas. They were on a par with many of the medical students in these insights.

MEETING 3: ONE-TO-ONE RELATING

The development of skills in relating to new persons was discussed and practiced. Exercises consisted of role-playing, in which one student takes the role of a peer counselor and another student acts the role of the troubled student in the initial session. Pair off the group and give ten minutes for them to get to know each other. Choose pairs of students who are actually strangers to each other. Group discussion then centers on the following points:

1. Kinds of openers used in starting conversations.
2. Experiencing of interest and encouragement on the part of others.
3. Recognition of blocks to talking.
4. Things that happened or were done to make the other person feel at ease.
5. Evidence or signs of lack of ease.

MEETING 4: RELATING TO A GROUP

Although the entire training course was an experience in group dynamics and group counseling, the goal of this particular unit was to teach some specifics to prepare students for particular group assignments during and after training. Such assignments would include meeting sixth graders and ninth graders preparing to enter junior high and senior high school respectively. Anticipation of these assignments in a few weeks time gave this session great salience. Some of the groups chose to spend the fourth meeting continuing work on the one-to-one relating task. When this was done, the topic of group dynamics was taken up in one of the sessions on counseling strategies. Both places in the sequence are appropriate.

II. RELEVANT COUNSELING TOPICS (MEETINGS 5–8)

Four broad areas of student concern were delineated and a different one presented at each of these four sessions: 1) academic motivation and relevancy of school; 2) deviations from the norm; 3) family relationships and problems; and 4) future planning and goal setting. The content of these four sessions was largely drawn from the personal experiences, knowledge, and feelings of the group members. The Supervisor summarized and gave needed perspective.

The approach used was to state the topic for a particular session and then open the content discussion with the question "What sort of problems might a fellow student bring to you about . . . ?" The question was completed with the topic for the day. Guidelines for the discussion which followed were these:

1. Defining the facts of the problem to the degree they are known.
2. What alternatives are available for changing the situation or solving the problem?
3. What personal resources are available to solve the problem?
4. When is it appropriate to turn a problem over to a professionally trained person or other responsible adult?

MEETING 5: ACADEMIC MOTIVATION

The persistent themes raised by students can be summarized as follows:

1. Climate of individual schools: Friendly? Cold? Isolated? Rejecting? Competitive?
   a. What personal experience have students had in coming to the school? In making friends? In getting into organizations?
   b. Is the morale of the school cohesive? Fragmented? Cooperative?
   c. What activities go on in school that help students, attract students, involve students?
   d. What can peer counselors do to improve the climate of a school?
   e. What can be done for the new student, the lonely student, the isolated student?
   f. What school-wide changes or avenues are open to improve the climate of the school?
2. Academic relevancy and motivational factors:
   a. School regulations and requirements.
   b. Academic competition and its effect on motivation and achievement.
   c. Interest on the part of teachers, counselors and administrators in individual students.
   d. Suggested curriculum and scheduling alternatives.
   e. Factors affecting individual motivation and future goal setting.
   f. Relationship of school achievement to "establishment" patterns and entrance requirements to colleges or specialized training programs.
   g. Society's values and behaviors.

MEETING 6: DEVIATION FROM THE NORM

This topic covers a wide scope of adolescent problems. The main areas include: drug usage; emotional and psychological disturbances; physical handicaps; such other handicaps as mental retardation, hearing loss, blindness; unwanted pregnancy; and ethnic and racial differences. The discussions here were very enlightening to the adults. We found this to be a rare opportunity to sample the opinions of a representative group of young persons on topics that are of deep concern. In this, as in other respects, the involvement with these groups was an important educational experience for the adults.

1. What are the problems faced by students so identified?
2. Emphasis on the limited scope of student responsibility in dealing with complex issues.
3. What resources are available for students with these problems? (Adults at school, agencies in the community.)
4. Assessment cues as to identification of problems.

5. Areas where peers can help and point at which problem should be referred.
6. Causes related to onset of problem.
7. Stereotypes associated with these problems.
8. Factual information-giving regarding problems.
9. Effective methods for treating and helping students with these problems.
10. Suggested preventive programs.

MEETING 7: FAMILY PROBLEMS

Persistent Themes:

1. Effect of divorce on children in the family.
2. Family restrictions, norms and sub-cultures.
3. Sibling rivalry.
4. Family pressures and expectations.
5. Isolation within the family.
6. Major adjustments within the family, caused by such things as death, economic change, illness and living adjustments related to relatives or others sharing home.
7. Emotional changes and stages related to growth and development.
8. Self identity, sense of security, praise and punishment as experienced, practiced and learned in the family.

MEETING 8: PLANS AND GOALS

This was an area of great searching and confusion for many students. There is a tremendous interest in alternatives to the traditional career choices, desire to interrupt the schooling sequence after high school for a while, even when college is planned, and a desire to explore a range of life style possibilities.

1. Projected sources of satisfaction and goal attainments.
2. Adolescent values and future values.
3. Sources of values.
4. Opportunities available.
5. Information needed.
6. Present or suggested programs, methods, or experiences that would aid students in planning for their futures.

More will be said later about the emotional and cognitive differences between the high school and junior high school students. The discussions and activities in this section of the curriculum brought these differences most sharply into focus. It became clear that the introspection and abstract abilities of the junior high school students was surprisingly poor and that they needed to handle the material on a more concrete basis.

Personal anecdotes and experiences of close friends supplied by the students proved to be the most effective source of material for dealing with all of these topics. Students commented that they learned more from this type of personal sharing than from the hypothetical cases and other materials introduced. These additional activities were of some use, however, sometimes as a springboard for discussion, and will be mentioned.

Prepared case studies and profiles of adolescents who were experiencing a particular problem were distributed. Some of the groups talked through the issues raised. Other students role-played the situation raised by the case study.

Role-playing was also used to enact situations derived from personal experiences contributed by group members. Frequently, one student would take the role of a peer counselor attempting to help the individual with the problem. There was noticeable improvement and progress observed in the ability of students to handle these roles.

Specific information was distributed to the groups listing referral resources related to most of the relevant topics. The use of these community resources in such areas as family therapy, drug abuse clinics, abortion advice, vocational and volunteer job opportunities, etc., was discussed. The role of the peer counselor was seen as information-giving, but they urged not to make these contacts on behalf of their counselees. Adult support in referrals and use of community resources was stressed. It has become clear, subsequently, that our concern that peer counselors might be rash and take on too much responsibility in this area has not been borne out. The students uniformly err on the side of caution and look to and need adult guidance in times of critical decisions. In general, it was evident that specific, reliable facts and information needs to be put into the hands of all students. Their level of ignorance was surprising.

III. TRAINING PRACTICUM EXPERIENCE (MEETINGS 9–10)

These sessions followed the assignment of peer counselors to the task of visiting the elementary schools and meeting with the sixth-grade students. This part of the course came in late May and early June when the challenge of entering junior high school was very salient for these sixth graders. The peer counselors met with them in small groups. Peer counselors were expected to meet with their groups without adult supervision. They could choose to do so with or without a student co-leader. The task of the group was to discuss feelings about the transition to junior high school and to inform the sixth graders of the fact that peer counselors would be available to them on arrival at their junior high school in the fall.

The training group was used to discuss the events and experiences of the peer counselors in this initial practical experience in the helping role.

SUMMARY

The training was planned to prepare students for eventual school-wide service assignments. Students started their training by practicing counseling on one another in the group.

A shift in groups was made as a second phase of training whereby students would branch out to a new group, practicing skills learned in the first group. The second group focused on preparation to reach out to school-wide groups and clientele.

The final phase of the training involved a model, though pertinent, experience in meeting with a client group and using this practical example to recapitulate and consolidate the prior learning in the training course.

Strategies of counseling had been taught and used throughout the training course. These were reviewed and summarized in the final meeting of the training.

Ethical responsibilities were reviewed. Accepting a role of Peer Counselor carries certain responsibilities that necessitate the setting aside of personal opinions and attitudes, when in the role of counselor. It also requires the exercise of maintaining information shared in a confidential manner, and use of sound judgment regarding any disclosure. This means that Peer Counselors, when in this role, must maintain the general stance of supporting the established cultural norms, the positions of parents, the regulations of the school, and the school system itself.

Difference between counseling and advice-giving was discussed. This was the most difficult strategy to understand and learn of all that were covered in the training. In most of the practice exercises, role plays, and group discussions, a common reaction was to give advice to the troubled student. Supervisors demonstrated and then reviewed the process of counseling as an exploration of alternatives, leaving the final decision for action with the counselee. Peer Counselors found it hard to accept the emotional ambiguity of a counseling interaction that might end in the counselee rejecting positive alternatives, acting on negative alternatives, or deciding not to take any action. Recognizing that everyone has a right to choose to fail was difficult for them to accept. It was also hard for them to accept that not all counselees can be reached. This will be given further attention in the Supervised Practicum that will take place as the next phase of the program as they are functioning on assignments.

EVALUATION

Despite a minimal recruitment effort, 162 students entered the training program and 155 completed the program. A few students dropped out at the time the shift in groups was made. A few others were forced to drop because of heavy schedules of spring activities. Students represented a wide range of age groups, racial and ethnic groups, personality types, and personal problems. Some students entered the program seeking personal help and a sense of worth. Others entered to find relevant service activity and meaningful relationships with others. The impact of the program, both on their lives and on programs throughout the school, was varied.

It has been abundantly clear that the training program has represented a significant experience in personal growth for the student participants. We have come to feel that this type of program may well represent a major vehicle for improving the mental health of adolescents. We feel that those students who entered the program seeking personal help and who received it are legitimate users of our services. We would by no means evaluate the success of the project solely in terms of the numbers of peer counselors who are placed on assignments.

It was useful to learn that the adult supervisors, although members of the school and professional mental health establishments, were well received and respected by students. They were not rejected because of their positions in society ("establishment"). Any differences seen in relationships between the student and a Supervisor was usually due to personal attributes of the Supervisor. Those who evidenced an open, honest manner, respected students, did not talk down or intimidate them in any way were highly successful in reaching and teaching their groups.

EVALUATIONS BY SUPERVISORS

Supervisors were positive, enthusiastic, and supportive of the program. They all indicated great respect for the level of sophistication evidenced by the students in their groups, both in terms of knowledge and in depth of personal problems and experiences. Although professionally trained, individuals said they had learned much about adolescents in the process of working with their trainees. In obtaining their evaluations of students, no effort was made to check-list attributes or in any other way structure the reports. We are using these varied statements to generate a meaningful standard evaluation form. Specific other evaluations made by Supervisors are:

The pace of the training was broken by the shift in groups. It was difficult for Supervisors to give up their first group and to carry on the sequence of the curriculum following the shift.

A need was expressed for Co-Supervisors for each group. This would eliminate the interruptions that occurred when a Supervisor had to miss a meeting and would provide for greater coordination and communication. They suggested that the Co-Supervisor should be a person from the school, such as a counselor or teacher.

It was felt that specific criteria guidelines should be prepared for evaluating the progress of students. The use of video taping was suggested, to be used in the ongoing process of the training.

A catalog of students with information about individual specialties, training, and hobbies should be prepared. This would be used in making peer counseling assignments.

A more uniform use of the curriculum was needed, with additional suggestions for implementation.

"Office hours" for Supervisors should be scheduled at the schools. This would enable Peer Counselors to drop in for consultation over and beyond their group sessions.

EVALUATIONS BY STUDENTS

The attendance record in the program, retention level, and personal recruitment of other students indicates a positive evaluation on the part of students. Specific student evaluations were these:

Group sessions should be longer (possibly two hours) and there should be more of them.

Shifting of groups was generally disliked. Students felt they had just been integrated into their group when the shift was made. Some handled this by attending two sessions per week—their old group and their new group. (In light of this feedback, the plan for the coming year has been changed accordingly—see below.)

Students wanted the practical experience to come earlier in the training program.

They requested some specific information. One suggestion was a session on the dynamics of the school itself. This would include descriptions of the roles and functions of vice-principals, mechanics of running a school, relationships of a building to the central office, etc.

Students wanted a session devoted to methods of intervening with teachers and learning to talk with adults.

Transportation to the training meetings was difficult. Students would like training sessions either held in their own school buildings, or car pools organized to facilitate transportation.

Small training groups were requested of about five to eight in number rather than the 10–15 sized groups they had been in.

It was felt that a more detailed preparation for the Life Career Game would make this experience more meaningful.

SIGNIFICANT EFFECTS ON STUDENTS

The peer counseling program proved to have many unanticipated benefits. A number of examples reveal part of the impact of the program:

A counselor revealed that a student she would never have recommended for the program because he had been in trouble at school had proven to be one of the most effective in working with the sixth graders. He had improved in his school work and behavior and had volunteered to help another student with problems similar to his own.

A group of Peer Counselors at one high school decided to organize a program to make their school more friendly. They identified students who appeared to be lonely. In a natural way, individuals would approach these students with a friendly greeting and follow that up another day with further conversation. They were impressed with the positive response their efforts received. This same group helped one another in their ability to approach others. One student who found it hard to do this would be backed up by a friend. When an approach would be made, the friend would compliment the effort and encourage the next approach.

A high school student began working with a junior high girl in her peer counseling group who had revealed a need for help. This was done on her own time and made a significant difference to the fellow trainee.

A high school girl verging on alienation reported that the training group was the one thing she looked forward to in her school week.

A boy involved in school politics entered the program. During the group sessions, in receiving feedback from students, he learned about himself. He found that many of his approaches to others were received negatively. He learned what changes he would need to make if he were truly to become more effective in relating to others.

A mother reported that her daughter had lost interest in school and in future educational work. Since entering the program, she was becoming involved again and was making plans for the future.

A mother reported that her son learned to understand his father through the course of his training program. His attitude and manner, and consequently the atmosphere of the home, had improved greatly.

Other parents, learning that their children were in the program, called Dr. Varenhorst at the school regarding problems they faced with their children. This has opened communication between parents and children and initiated more specific counseling help.

OVERALL EVALUATION

This pilot phase showed that the Peer Counseling Program does fill a perceived mental health need in the schools. It also demonstrated that the hurdle of community and school hierarchy acceptance can be surmounted. There has been gratifying enthusiasm on the part of the students, parents, and school personnel—including administrators—for the continuation and expansion of the program.

Supervisors and students were both involved in evaluations of the program. These initial evaluations are viewed as heuristic rather than definitive. They serve as the basis for the detailed evaluations of every aspect of the program, which is to be a major effort in the next stage of the project.

Extensive evaluation procedures are now underway. Criteria and rating measures are being devised for judging the suitability and effectiveness of the student in his continued performance in the role of Peer Counselor. We plan to utilize social indicators to judge the overall impact of the program, such indices as level of school achievement in relation to potential, truancy, drop-out rates, disciplinary school actions, incidence of drug abuse, incidence of violence or vandalism in the schools, and teacher turnover rates. The personal growth of the Peer Counselors is best measured by self-esteem scales.

As the program has become known, contacts have been made requesting the services of Peer Counselors. At the present time, 90 students are on assignments. The Coordinator of the Special Education Program and the Educationally Handicapped has asked for help. Parents of students in the mentally retarded classes requested a meeting regarding possible help. Elementary teachers have asked for specific services. District personnel have indicated a desire to explore possibilities of Peer Counselors helping students with attendance problems and aiding in vocational guidance. School counselors are beginning to use Peer Counselors for research activities and other services. All of this would indicate a positive acceptance and anticipation of future growth for the program.

REFERENCES

1. ARIES, P. 1962. Centuries of Childhood. Knopf, New York.

2. BOTT, E. 1957. Family and Social Network: Roles Norms, and External Relationships in Ordinary Urban Families. Tavistock, London.
3. BOWER, E. 1961. Primary prevention in a school setting. *In* Prevention of Mental Disorders in Children, G. Caplan, ed. Basic Books, New York.
4. BRENMAN, E. 1966. College students and mental health programs for children. Paper presented at annual meeting of American Public Health Association, Community Mental Health Section.
5. EISENBERG, L. 1970. Student unrest: sources and consequences. Science 167: 1688–1692.
6. GOODMAN, G. 1969. Companionship as therapy: the use of nonprofessional talent. *In* New Directions in Client-Centered Psychotherapy, J. Hart and T. Tomlinson, eds.
7. HILGARD, J. AND MOORE, U. 1969. Affiliative therapy with young adolescents. J. Acad. Child Psychiat. 8:577–603.
8. LIPPITT, P. AND EISEMAN, J. 1969. Cross-age helping program. Center for Research in Utilization of Scientific Knowledge. University of Michigan, Ann Arbor.
9. MATTSON, J. 1970. e. Peer Counseling, CAPS Capsule 3:1–9, Counseling and Information Center, University of Michigan, Ann Arbor.
10. REINHERZ, H. 1964. The therapeutic use of student volunteers. Children 11:137–142.
11. RIOCH, M. ET AL. 1963. NIMH pilot study in training mental health counselors. Amer. J. Orthopsychiat. 33:678–689.
12. RIOCH, M. 1971. Pilot project in training mental health counselors (follow-up). Public Health Service Pub. No. 1254, U.S., Printing Office, Washington, D.C.
13. RYAN, T. 1967. Effectiveness of counseling in college residence halls on student's study behavior. Final Report. Educational Research Center, University of Michigan, Ann Arbor.
14. VARENHORST, B. 1969. Learning the consequences of life's decisions. *In* Behavioral Counseling: Cases and Techniques. J. Krumboltz and C. Thoresen, eds. Holt, Rinehart and Winston, New York.
15. VARENHORST, B. 1968. Palo Alto Unified School District's Life Career Game Kit, Palo Alto, Calif.
16. VRIEND, T. 1969. High-performing inner city adolescents assist low-performing peers in counseling groups. Pers. Guid. J. 48: 897–904.

For reprints: Dr. Beatrix A. Hamburg, Department of Psychiatry, Stanford University Medical Center, Stanford, Calif. 94305

JOURNAL OF RESEARCH ON ADOLESCENCE, 4(1), 71–97

Life Events and Adjustment in Adolescents: The Significance of Event Independence, Desirability, and Chronicity

Ann S. Masten
University of Minnesota

Jennifer Neemann
University of Maryland, Baltimore County

Signe Andenas
University of Minnesota

In this study, we examined the significance of three objectively defined characteristics of life events for understanding the relation between stressful life experiences and adolescent adjustment. Using a questionnaire method, a normative sample of 176 adolescents and their mothers provided information on multiple aspects of adolescent adjustment as well as life events. Judges classified events on their independence, desirability, and chronicity. Events independent of the adolescent's behavior were expected to have lower correlations with adjustment scores than events that could be influenced by the adolescent or that were overlapping in content with adjustment. Results supported this hypothesis, suggesting that a substantial portion of the covariance between life events and adjustment is due to item overlap and adolescent behavior. Results also supported the validity of distinguishing positive from negative events and discrete from chronic events. Implications for the interpretation of existing data and design of future studies are discussed.

Requests for reprints should be sent to Ann S. Masten, Institute of Child Development, University of Minnesota, 51 East River Road, Minneapolis, MN 55455–0345.

One of the most important questions in developmental psychopathology is how stressful life experiences and adjustment are related in development (Masten, Best, & Garmezy, 1990). Over the past 20 years, this question has been the focus of numerous studies. More recently, it has become a salient topic in studies of adolescents, ranging from studies of normative stressors like the transition to junior high school (e.g., Simmons & Blyth, 1987) and common stressors like divorce (e.g., Hetherington & Anderson, 1988), to trauma associated with war (Realmuto et al., 1992). A popular but controversial approach to this question has been the study of heterogeneous life events by questionnaire method, prominent since Coddington (1972a, 1972b) first adopted the Holmes and Rahe (1967) scale for use with children.

The purpose of this study was to examine the significance of three objectively defined characteristics of life events for understanding how life experiences and adjustment in adolescence might be linked. These three objective characteristics were: (a) the independence of events from adolescent behavior, (b) the desirability of events, and (c) the chronic versus discrete nature of the events.

EVENT INDEPENDENCE

Event independence is at the heart of the controversy about interpreting data from studies of life events, which centers on whether and how measures of life events and adjustment are confounded. Correlations of life events and adjustment measures could be confounded in three interrelated ways. First, there are life events that could also be viewed as adjustment indicators. Item overlap would serve to inflate the correlations of life event and adjustment scores. The items most likely to appear on both types of measures are those that depend in some part on adolescent behavior, such as "failed a grade in school." Second, some events could be the result of adolescent adjustment problems, rather than the cause of adjustment difficulties. For example, poor school work, attention problems, or antisocial behavior (often assessed on adjustment measures) could contribute to life events like failing a grade or being arrested (often included on life event measures). Third, adolescent behaviors, including the symptoms of mental disorders, could produce both life events and adjustment problems.[1] Impulsivity or aggression, for example, could con-

[1]It is because of this third possibility that we chose the term *independence* over the term *controllability* in describing events. The term controllable implies that events are under one's voluntary control, which may not be the case for events precipitated by symptomatic behaviors. Moreover, few events are totally under the control of the adolescent; adolescent behaviors or symptoms can lead teachers, peers, parents, or police to precipitate adolescent life events.

tribute to failing a grade, being arrested, and peer problems. Each of these three types of confounding involve life events that could depend on the subject's behavior; that is, events that are "nonindependent."

The issue of confounded measures has been hotly contested in the adult literature (Brown & Harris, 1978; Cohen, 1988; Dohrenwend & Dohrenwend, 1974; Dohrenwend, Dohrenwend, Dodson, & Shrout, 1984; Dohrenwend & Shrout, 1985; Hudgens, 1974; Lazarus, 1990; Lazarus, DeLongis, Folkman, & Gruen, 1985; Lazarus & Folkman, 1984; Thoits, 1983; Zimmerman, 1983). In one of the few empirical studies of this issue, Dohrenwend et al. (1984) demonstrated that a substantial proportion of the items frequently appearing on adult life event questionnaires could also be viewed as symptoms of disorder, inflating correlations between measures of life events and symptoms. Concerns about confounded measures also have been raised in reviews of the child and adolescent life event literature, although few investigators have addressed this issue empirically (Compas, 1987; Garmezy & Rutter, 1985; Johnson, 1986).

The issue of confounded measures has particular importance for scholars of adolescent development. First, as independence and autonomy of action develop, adolescents have increasing influence over their own experiences. One of the most important ways in which adolescents shape their own environments (Scarr & McCartney, 1983) may be related to their own role in their exposure to stressful life experiences (Cohen, Burt, & Bjorck, 1987). Second, the proliferation of studies using the life event method with adolescents demands greater attention to such critical methodological issues.

The question of confounded measurement has not been adequately addressed in studies of children or adolescents. In one study of adolescents, the authors analyzed the covariance of independent and nonindependent event scores with various adjustment indicators in adolescents (Rowlison & Felner, 1988). The independent events score appeared to have lower correlations than the nonindependent score with some adjustment variables (e.g., grade point average) but not with others (e.g., physical symptoms). However, differences between the correlations with adjustment for the two kinds of life events scores were not directly tested. Moreover, the scoring strategy for life events was not optimal for evaluating the issue of confounded measures. Scores were based on adolescents' subjective judgments of "bad" versus "good" events. Thus, events included in this score varied from adolescent to adolescent, depending on whether the adolescent viewed the event as "bad." In addition, the classification of independence or nonindependence of events was based solely on the rational judgments of the authors of the instrument used in the study (Johnson & McCutcheon, 1980).

Other investigators have addressed the confounding issue by computing scores based only on events independent of the child's functioning. Results from such studies have yielded inconsistent findings (Cohen, 1988). On the one hand, significant associations have been found between major life events and adjustment in studies of adolescents (Dubois, Felner, Brand, Adan, & Evans, 1992; Newcomb, Huba, & Bentler, 1986) as well as in studies of young elementary school-age children (Cowen, Weissberg, & Guare, 1984; Sandler & Block, 1979; Sterling, Cowen, Weissberg, Lotyczewski, & Boike, 1985). A large prospective study of 4-to-16-year-old children in the Netherlands found the number of major life events was related to increases in behavioral and emotional problems reported by parents over a 2-year interval (Berden, Althaus, & Verhulst, 1990). In another prospective study, the frequency of independent major life events reported by young adolescents predicted increases in psychological distress and decreases in grade point average (GPA) 2 years later (Dubois et al., 1992). In addition, Goodyer and colleagues (Goodyer, Kolvin, & Gatzanis, 1985; Goodyer, Wright, & Altham, 1990) have found a greater number of recent, moderately to severely threatening life events among child and adolescent psychiatric cases than among case controls. On the other hand, independent events occurring during the past 5 years had little relation to current adjustment problems in a large study of 11-to-23-year-olds (Gersten, Langner, Eisenberg, & Simcha-Fagan, 1977). Moreover, in a prospective study of elementary-age children with a 2-year follow-up, major life events also failed to predict changes in adjustment (Dubow, Tisak, Causey, Hryshko, & Reid, 1991).

Two prospective studies of adolescents have compared the predictive significance of independent versus nonindependent events (Cohen et al., 1987; Swearingen & Cohen, 1985). Independent ("uncontrollable") events did not predict changes in adolescent distress, whereas nonindependent ("controllable") events were related to increases in distress over a 5-month interval (Cohen et al., 1987). In both studies, emotional distress at Time 1 (T1) was the best predictor of both types of events. Investigators concluded that psychological functioning might contribute to "controllable" events rather than vice versa. Different causal processes were implicated by the results for independent events because, by definition, these events were not influenced by the subject's psychological functioning. One possibility is that underlying processes like parental conflict or dysfunction might produce both greater distress in the child and a greater number of stressful life events independent of the child's behavior.

EVENT DESIRABILITY AND CHRONICITY

Adolescent life events also can be objectively classified with respect to *desirability*. Events usually viewed as "positive" or "negative" consistently have shown different relations to outcome measures (Johnson, 1986; Zimmerman, 1983). Negative events have shown a stronger link than positive events to adjustment indicators in children and adolescents (Cohen et al., 1987; Johnson, 1986). However, most studies have focused on negative outcome indicators, so that the relative linkage of negative and positive events to positive aspects of adjustment is unknown.

The third characteristic was event *chronicity*, referring to whether events index an ongoing situation or an event that occurs on a specific date. Many of the stressors experienced by adolescents are controlled or influenced by family situations that are chronic in nature, such as interparental conflict. Ongoing stressful family situations, moreover, could produce more discrete life events, such as separation or divorce (Garmezy & Masten, 1994).

In addition to the role parents play in producing or maintaining chronic and discrete family stressors, parents may directly affect child behavior through their caregiving, modeling, and discipline (Belsky & Vondra, 1989; Emery, 1982; Patterson, 1982). Parents with mental health problems or troubled relationships are more likely to be ineffective with their children. In such families, child adjustment might appear to be causally related to discrete life events when in fact there are underlying causal processes that are more chronic and more pervasive. For example, in the studies by Sandler and Block (1979), Sterling et al. (1985), and Cowen et al. (1984) discussed earlier, problematic family functioning or parenting may have been responsible for both the life events and maladjustment in the children, rather than exposure to life events causing maladjustment in the children.

The role of chronic family-related stressors in relation to discrete events may be important for understanding how stressful experiences are related to development. As yet, however, there have been few systematic attempts to contrast chronic stressful family situations with discrete onset stressors in relation to child or adolescent adjustment.

HYPOTHESES

The primary hypothesis examined in this study was that nonindependent events would have substantially higher correlations than independent events with current adjustment in adolescents because of the three types of possible confounding just discussed. We also hypothesized that negative events would be more strongly related to negative adjustment indicators (more symptoms, less competence) than positive events. Positive events were expected to relate to positive adjustment indicators, particularly when the items were potentially confounded (nonindependent). Finally, we hypothesized that chronic experiences would be related to adjustment, both directly and indirectly. We expected a direct relation between chronic independent events and adjustment because these events often reflect a family milieu that is stressful and unsupportive. We expected chronic stressors also to have indirect effects because such family environments are likely to produce more discrete events. Thus, chronic events were expected to account, at least in part, for the relation of discrete events to adjustment.

To test these hypotheses, life events were classified on three dimensions: independence, desirability, and chronicity. Judges categorized the events on a life event questionnaire developed for adolescents participating in a longitudinal study of adaptation. Both adolescents and mothers reported on adolescent life events and adjustment. Adjustment measures were then related to life event scores that varied on the three dimensions of interest.

METHOD

Sample

The participants in this study were part of a normative, community cohort recruited 7 years earlier (T1) from third- through sixth-grade classrooms in two elementary schools. These schools served urban neighborhoods diverse in socioeconomic status and ethnicity. The original cohort's socioeconomic status ranged from 7.0 to 92.3 on the 100-point Duncan Socioeconomic Index (Hauser & Featherman, 1977), with the average score equaling 43, representing lower middle-class skilled labor and clerical jobs. Thirty-five percent of the cohort lived in single-parent homes. Of the 205 original participants, 92% were located, and 86% (n = 176) of the adolescents agreed to participate in a follow-up study of competence and resilience. Eighty-eight percent of the parents or guardians of the original sample also participated; all but a few were mothers. The follow-up sample consisted of 97 female subjects and 79 male subjects, ranging in age from 14 to 19 years. Twenty-five percent were minorities. No significant differences were found between the follow-up sample and nonparticipants from the original cohort on earlier measures of social or academic competence.

Measures

Life events. In this study, life events during the last year were measured with a newly developed Life Event Questionnaire for Adolescents (LEQ–A), which was a revision of a questionnaire developed for the T1 assessment (Garmezy & Tellegen, 1984; Masten et al., 1988). The T1 questionnaire was a 50-item modification of Coddington's (1972a, 1972b) Social Readjustment Rating Scale for Children (Garmezy & Tellegen, 1984; Linder, 1985). It was revised for the follow-up study to add age-appropriate items and to improve its psychometric properties. First, based on recommendations from a systematic content analysis (Herzog, 1984), 12 items that were low in severity or unclear in meaning were deleted, and others were rewritten to reduce ambiguity. Second, a list of potential new items was compiled from three sources: (a) life event questionnaires for children and adolescents published before 1984, (b) stressors and predisposing factors noted in the Diagnostic and Statistical Manual of the American Psychiatric Association (1980), and (c) "write-in" events from the T1 questionnaire. The items were then organized by content, and redundant items were deleted; the goal was to create a concise but comprehensive sampling of life experiences widely viewed as significant for adolescents. The resulting 67 items were grouped by content area on the questionnaire to facilitate recall and to reduce inconsistent responding. Parallel versions were created for parents and adolescents.

To develop meaningful life event scores, each item was classified by 20 clinical and child psychology graduate students on the three dimensions of interest: (a) Discreteness of onset—discrete, chronic, or ambiguous; (b) Desirability—positive, negative, or ambiguous; and (c) Independence—out of the child's control, child had some control, or control depends on the context of the event (*control* refers to the possible influence of an adolescent's behavior on the event). Items classified by 60% or more of the raters as context-dependent on the independence dimension were excluded from scores because a clear objective distinction between nonindependent and independent items was essential to this study. The remainder of the items were then grouped according to their classification on all three dimensions. The criterion for including items in a group was at least 60% agreement by judges on all three dimensions of classification. Thus, for example, the item "a parent died" was grouped with other discrete–negative–independent items because it was classified by 95% of judges as discrete, 100% as negative, and 100% as independent of the adolescent's behavior. Exceptions were made to include items for which the agreement was 50% to 59% on one of the three dimensions, and 60% or more on the other two dimensions.

Theoretically, 12 different groups were possible. However, classification by these criteria resulted in 6 groups. Some groups had no items (e.g., there were no chronic or discrete–positive–independent items). Three items (19, 33, and 34) with mixed or ambiguous desirability ratings were added to the discrete–negative–nonindependent group because there were too few discrete–ambiguous–nonindependent items to form a separate score, and because these items are often studied as negative events for adolescents. This process yielded the following mutually exclusive groups: (a) discrete–negative–independent, (b) chronic–negative–independent, (c) discrete–ambiguous–independent, (d) discrete–negative–nonindependent, (e) chronic–negative–nonindependent, and (f) discrete–positive–nonindependent.

Events endorsed *yes* were summed across items in a given group for each score. Items included in each score are listed in Table 1.

Symptoms. Current symptoms were assessed with the Child Behavior Checklist (CBCL; Achenbach & Edelbrock, 1983) completed by mothers and the corresponding Youth Self-Report (YSR; Achenbach & Edelbrock, 1987) completed by adolescents. Both are widely used and highly regarded as reliable and valid indicators of behavioral and emotional problems in adolescents (Boyle & Jones, 1985; Sattler, 1990). Results are reported for standardized Internalizing and Externalizing problem scores, using the most recent norms (Achenbach, 1991).

Self-worth. Psychological well-being was indexed with a new measure of perceived competence (Neemann & Masten, 1988), modeled after the Self-Perception Profile for Children (Harter, 1982, 1985) and the preliminary version of the Self-Perception Profile for Adolescents (Harter, 1986). Adolescents rated themselves on 5-item scales tapping 10 domains of perceived competence and global self-worth. Mothers rated their adolescents on the same domains. Only the self-worth score was included in this study as a global indicator of internal adjustment. This scale has an alpha reliability coefficient of .86 for mothers' reports and .78 for adolescents' reports (Neemann & Masten, 1988).

Competence. Adolescents and their mothers completed parallel versions of a Status Questionnaire (SQ) designed to obtain biographical information regarding demographic status, school and work

TABLE 1
Scoring Classification and Endorsement Reported by Mothers and Adolescents for Items From the Life Events Questionnaire for Adolescents

Item	Percent Endorsement[a]	
	Mothers	Adolescents
Discrete Onset–Negative–Independent		
5. My brother or sister became seriously ill or was injured during this past year.	6.3	5.7
6. During this past year, at least one parent became seriously ill or was injured.	10.8	13.6
10. I was a victim of violence (mugging, sexual assault, robbery) during this past year.	5.7	7.4
11. A member of my family was a victim of violence (mugging, sexual assault, robbery) during this past year.	10.8	8.0
12. During this past year, one of my parents died.	0.0	0.0
13. A brother or sister died during this past year.	0.6	0.6
14. A grandparent died during this past year.	18.2	19.9
15. One of my close friends died during this past year.	8.5	10.2
20. A member of my family ran away from home during this past year.	4.5	6.3
21. My parents separated during this past year.	6.3	5.7
22. My parents divorced during this past year.	4.5	2.3
37. One parent lost his or her job during this past year.	13.6	12.5
44. The family had funds cut off by some government agency during this past year (e.g., welfare, food stamps, AFDC, disability, etc.).	13.1	9.7
45. My family was evicted from a house or apartment during this past year.	1.7	3.4
54. During this past year, a member of my family attempted suicide.	4.5	1.7
61. A brother or sister was arrested or went to jail during this past year.	6.3	9.7
62. A parent was arrested or went to jail during this past year.	5.7	4.5
Chronic–Negative–Independent		
36. During this past year, one of my parents had problems at work (demotion, trouble with boss or co-workers, change in working hours, etc.).	22.7	26.1
42. The family financial situation was difficult during this past year.	54.0	35.8
49. There were many arguments between adults living in the house during this past year.	18.2	20.5
50. There were many arguments between a parent and a former or separated spouse during this past year.	9.7	6.8
55. A member of my family developed severe emotional problems during this past year.	17.0	15.3
57. A brother or sister became involved with drugs or alcohol during this past year.	9.7	13.1
58. During this past year, a parent had trouble with alcohol or drugs.	9.7	13.1

(continued)

TABLE 1 *(continued)*

Item	Percent Endorsement[a]	
	Mothers	Adolescents
Discrete Onset–Ambiguous–Independent		
1. I have a new brother or sister who was born during this past year.	4.0	5.7
2. Our family moved to a new home or apartment during this past year.	18.2	17.6
16. Another adult has come to live with my family during this past year.	19.9	15.9
23. One of my parents remarried during this past year.	8.0	4.5
35. An unmarried family member became pregnant during this past year.	10.2	11.9
38. My mother began to work some time during this past year.	11.9	16.5
Discrete Onset–Negative–Nonindependent		
19. During this past year, I ran away from home.	9.7	9.1
29. I did not get into a group or activity that I wanted to get into (music group, sports team, theater, etc.).	15.9	23.3
30. I failed or was "held back" during this past year.	15.3	15.9
31. During this past year, I did much worse than I expected in an important exam or course.	24.4	41.5
32. I was threatened with suspension or was suspended from school at least once during this past year.	22.7	28.4
33. During this past year I became pregnant (for female subjects).	6.3	6.3
34. I got someone pregnant during this past year (for male subjects).	1.7	1.7
59. During this past year, I got in trouble with the law.	13.6	17.6
60. I went to jail during this past year.	6.8	5.7
66. I broke up with a girlfriend or boyfriend during this past year.	36.4	61.4
Chronic–Negative–Nonindependent		
46. During this past year I had many arguments with brother(s) and/or sister(s).	36.4	43.2
47. I had many arguments with my parent(s) during this past year.	35.8	46.0
48. During this past year, my parent(s) and I had many arguments over my choice of friends and/or social activities, such as use of the car or hours to stay out.	30.7	39.8
52. I was not accepted by other people my age during this past year.	5.1	8.0
53. During this past year, I had suicidal thoughts.	10.2	16.5
56. I became involved with drugs or alcohol during this past year.	19.3	19.9
Discrete–Positive–Nonindependent		
24. I had at least one outstanding personal achievement this past year.	53.4	66.5
25. I was voted or appointed to a leadership position in this past year (for example, class office, team captain, etc.).	19.3	22.7

(continued)

TABLE 1 *(continued)*

Item	*Percent Endorsement*[a] *Mothers*	*Adolescents*
Discrete-Positive-Nonindependent *(continued)*		
26. I received a special award (ribbon, trophy, plaque, certificate, etc.) for something *done at school* during this past year.	36.4	33.0
27. I received a special award for some activity *outside of school* during this past year (ribbon, trophy, plaque, certificate, etc.).	19.9	22.7
28. I received special recognition for athletic competition during this past year.	19.3	14.8
Items Excluded from Scores		
3. I changed schools during this past year.	34.1	27.3
4. I became seriously ill or was injured during this past year.	8.5	7.4
7. I was involved in a serious accident during this past year.	1.7	5.1
8. During this past year, I was left with a visible physical handicap due to an accident, injury, or illness.	1.1	1.1
9. During this past year, I had an important change in physical appearance which upset me (acne, braces, glasses, physical development, etc.).	11.4	14.8
17. During this past year, I left home to live under the care of another parent, relative, or others.	11.4	14.8
18. During this past year, I left home to live on my own.	5.1	6.3
39. There has been a change in a parent's job during this past year so that my parent is away from home more often.	19.3	18.2
40. During this past year, I had little contact with one parent.	31.8	36.4
41. During this past year, I tried to get a job and failed.	25.0	18.8
43. During this past year, there was some damage or loss of family property (such as apartment, house, car, or bike).	31.8	21.6
51. There were many family arguments with inlaws or relatives during this past year.	5.1	12.5
63. I began to date during this past year.	38.6	47.7
64. I began "going steady," despite my parents disapproval, during this past year.	11.4	17.6
65. I got married during this past year, despite my parents disapproval.	0.6	1.1
67. I lost a close friend this past year.	14.8	34.7

[a]Percent of 176 mothers and adolescents who answered *yes*.

achievement, relationships with peers and parents, health and mental illness, and trouble with the law. Two clinical judges blindly and independently rated each mother-reported and self-reported questionnaire on nine scales of current functioning (Andenas & Morison, 1988; Morison & Masten, 1991). Three global ratings of adjustment were selected for this study: global adaptation (interrater reliability r = .88 and .86, respectively, for mother and adolescent data), trouble with the law (r = .91 and .91), and mental health problems (r = .80 and .89). Judges' ratings were then averaged within informant for final scores.

Academic achievement. Both adolescents and their mothers gave specific permission to obtain academic records from schools attended by these subjects. GPAs were computed for the 152 adolescents for whom school records could be obtained and who were in school any time during the current academic year. In all but a few cases, life events were reported for 1984 and GPA was calculated for the 1984/1985 school year. Grades were averaged using only the academic subjects of English, social studies, math, science, foreign language, and comparable classes. Those who dropped out prior to the current academic year were excluded for this variable. For the 10 students who went to alternative schools with no grades, a grade of D was recorded for each academic credit earned. In all 10 cases, the students had D or F averages in their previous schools and attended schools with minimal standards for credit and no penalties for incomplete courses. Exclusion of these subjects would have biased further the subsample available for this variable, which already excluded long-term dropouts. The GPA scores ranged from 0 to 4.0, with 0 equivalent to an F average and 4.0 equivalent to an A average. The sample average was 2.07, the equivalent of a C.

Procedure

Mothers were contacted by mail. They were asked to complete the LEQ–A, and permission was obtained to contact their adolescents. Five months later, the three adaptation questionnaires were mailed to mothers who had returned a completed LEQ–A. In the interim, recruitment letters were sent to adolescents for whom mothers had given permission to contact. At that time, they were asked to complete the LEQ–A and the perceived competence measure. Two months later, the YSR and SQ were mailed to the adolescents. Because mothers and adolescents did not receive the LEQ–A at the same time, they were instructed to report events for the same previous calendar year. The amount of time between completion of the LEQ–A by mothers and adolescents averaged 3 months, corresponding to the mailing interval. At all phases, telephone calls were made to nonresponders to maximize participation.

RESULTS

Descriptive Data on the LEQ–A

Adolescent–mother agreement. High agreement between mothers and adolescents was not expected. Some events may be concealed from mothers or vice versa, and some mothers have much less contact with their adolescents than do others. Agreement was calculated for only those 159 mother–adolescent pairs who responded within 6 months of each other. The average agreement for all events was 85%. Average agreement was highest for items classified as discrete–negative–independent (92%) and lowest for positive event items (77%). A stricter test of agreement was obtained by considering only *yes* responses. Sixty percent of all events endorsed by mothers were also reported by adolescents, and 52% of events reported by adolescents were also endorsed by mothers. However, of all events reported by either mothers or adolescents, only 37% were reported by both.

Because of the variable base rates of items, both "kappa" (Cohen, 1960) and Yule's "Y" statistics (Spitznagel & Helzer, 1985) were computed to correct for chance agreement. Kappa ranged from –.03 to .87, with a median value of .36. (Items 12 and 13 with base rate 0 were excluded.) In the majority of cases, kappa was significantly greater than the chance value of 0, but quite modest. Kappa has rarely been reported for life events scores, but the results obtained here are similar to the values reported for agreement on life events between adult patients with significant others (Zimmerman, 1983). Because base rates for items were frequently low and kappa is highly sensitive to base rates, values for Y were typically higher, with a median of .47.

Intercorrelations of scores. Intercorrelations of mother-report and adolescent-report LEQ–A scores are shown in Table 2. Correlations for the same score across reporter were moderate, ranging from .38 to .67, and intercorrelations of scores within reporter were also moderate, except that positive scores had little or no relation to negative scores.

Means for scores. Means and standard deviations for mother and adolescent LEQ–A scores are also shown in Table 2. The average number of combined independent negative events reported by mothers and

TABLE 2

Intercorrelations and Means of Nonoverlapping Life Events Scores as Reported by Mothers and Adolescents

	LEQ–A Scores						Means (SD)			
LEQ–A Scores	DNI	CNI	DAI	DNN	CNN	DPN	Mother		Adolescent	
Discrete–Negative–Independent (DNI)	.38***	.52***	.25***	.25***	.16*	−.02	1.21[a]	(1.22)	1.21[a]	(1.36)
Chronic–Negative–Independent (CNI)	.37***	.56***	.26***	.30***	.38***	.01	1.41[a]	(1.32)	1.31[a]	(1.34)
Discrete–Ambiguous–Independent (DAI)	.32***	.27***	.55***	.25***	.21**	−.07	.72[a]	(.89)	.72[a]	(.88)
Discrete–Negative–Nonindependent (DNN)	.31***	.38***	.30***	.60***	.39***	−.09	1.53[b]	(1.47)	2.11[b]	(1.51)
Chronic–Negative–Nonindependent (CNN)	.19**	.46***	.16*	.45***	.48***	−.02	1.38[b]	(1.44)	1.73[b]	(1.52)
Discrete–Positive–Nonindependent (DPN)	−.16*	−.08	−.11	−.12	−.13*	.67***	1.48[a]	(1.56)	1.60[a]	(1.40)

Note. Correlations above the diagonal are for adolescents, below are for mothers ($N = 176$). Underlined correlations on the diagonal represent the correlations between mother scores and adolescent scores ($N = 159$).

[a]Means for mother and adolescent scores do not differ significantly. [b]Means for mother and adolescent scores are significantly different.

$^{*}p < .05$. $^{**}p < .01$. $^{***}p < .001$.

adolescents as a group did not differ ($M = 3.24$ and 3.34, $SD = 2.74$ and 2.57, respectively). However, for negative scores based on nonindependent events, adolescents reported significantly more events: For the negative–nonindependent composite score, $M = 3.84$ for adolescents and 2.90 for mothers, t ($df = 175$) = 5.31, $p < .001$.

Relations of Life Events to Adjustment

Data provided by adolescents and mothers were analyzed separately. In other studies, adolescents and parents usually agree only moderately about life events (Cohen et al., 1987) and adolescent adjustment (Achenbach, McConaughy, & Howell, 1987). We assumed that each perspective was valid, and separate analyses provided better tests of the hypotheses as well as interesting comparison data. One adjustment criterion, GPA for adolescents currently in school at the time of the assessment, provided an independent source of data.

The correlations of life event scores with adjustment outcomes are presented in Tables 3 and 4, for adolescent- and mother-reported data, respectively. The pattern of correlations differed in direction for positive in contrast to negative life event scores and in magnitude for nonindependent in contrast to independent life event scores. The significance of the difference in parallel scores that differ only on the independence dimension were tested using a t-test comparison of nonindependent correlations (Hotelling, 1931), as recommended by McNemar (1969), and results are also indicated in each table. In 19 of 28 cases, the nonindependent scores had significantly higher correlations with a given adjustment criterion than the corresponding independent score. The potentially most confounded scores based on nonindependent events often accounted for more than twice the variance in adjustment measures than did scores based on independent events. The difference was particularly marked for discrete life event scores. To check whether an intrareporter response set was responsible for the correlations of life event scores to adjustment, correlations across reporter were also examined. When mother-reported life event scores were correlated with adolescent-reported adjustment measures and vice versa, the magnitude and pattern of correlations were very similar, suggesting that a response set was not responsible for the covariance within reporter. Correlations were also similar for mother and adolescent life event scores with GPA, the only adjustment criterion independent of both reporters.

Item overlap. The issue of item overlap was examined more closely by inspecting each item in the LEQ–A composite scores for

TABLE 3

Correlations of Life Events Scores With Adjustment as Reported by Adolescents

	Life Event Scores					
	Independent			*Nonindependent*		
Adjustment Measure	*Discrete-Negative*	*Chronic-Negative*	*Discrete-Ambiguous*	*Discrete-Negative*	*Chronic-Negative*	*Discrete-Positive*
Youth Self-Report						
Externalizing	.15[a]	.24[b]**	.02	.39[a]***	.42[b]***	−.12
Internalizing	.06	.13[c]	.03	.14	.38[c]***	−.11
Perceived competence						
Self-worth	−.09	−.18[d]*	−.17*	−.25***	−.36[d]***	.34***
Status Questionnaire						
Trouble with the law	.17[e]*	.18*	.16*	.52[e]***	.23**	−.14
Mental health problems	.14[f]	.22**	.22**	.38[f]***	.31***	−.14
Global adaptation	−.27***	−.23**	−.24***	−.38***	−.33***	.44***
Grade point average	−.20[g]**	−.18*	−.15	−.51[g]***	−.24**	.19*

Note. n = 176 except for YSR where n = 174 and grade point average where n = 152. Pairs of correlations that were tested and found to differ significantly ($p < .05$) from each other have the same superscript.

*$p < .05$. **$p < .01$. ***$p < .001$ (two-tailed tests).

TABLE 4

Correlations of Life Event Scores With Adjustment as Reported by Mothers

	Life Event Scores					
	Independent			*Nonindependent*		
Adjustment Measure	*Discrete-Negative*	*Chronic-Negative*	*Discrete-Ambiguous*	*Discrete-Negative*	*Chronic-Negative*	*Discrete-Positive*
Child Behavior Checklist						
Externalizing	.10[a]	.24[b]**	.08	.48[a]***	.42[b]***	−.14
Internalizing	.10	.15[c]*	.00	.25***	.34[c]***	−.26***
Competence ratings						
Self-worth	−.09[d]	−.13[e]	−.04	−.41[d]***	−.34[e]***	.25***
Status questionnaire						
Trouble with the law	.19[f]**	.16*	.15	.50[f]***	.28***	−.20**
Mental health problems	.15[g]*	.17[h]*	.24***	.41[g]***	.36[h]***	−.29***
Global adaptation	−.20[i]**	−.18[j]*	−.21**	−.52[i]***	−.38[j]***	.54***
Grade point average	−.17[k]*	−.19[l]*	−.08	−.43[k]***	−.36[l]**	.29***

Note. n = 176 except for CBCL where n = 174 and grade point average where n = 152. Pairs of correlations that were tested and found to differ significantly ($p < .05$) from each other have the same superscript.

*$p < .05$. **$p < .01$. ***$p < .001$ (two-tailed tests).

possible overlap with the adjustment measures. Examples are provided in Table 5. Item overlap is indicated for the discrete–negative–nonindependent score and two of its component items. These two items were selected for illustration because they differed in overlap pattern but had similar base rates of endorsement. Item 59 had almost the exact wording of the global adjustment rating scale, "trouble with the law," but did not explicitly overlap with GPA. Item 30, "failed a grade in school", did not overlap directly with "trouble with the law," but overlapped with the content of GPA. Both items overlapped partially in content with the data judges used to rate global adaptation, but neither overlapped with the self-worth measure. Also shown in Table 5 are the respective correlations of this score and these individual items with the adjustment scores. The correlations in Table 5 suggest that item overlap plays some role in the covariance of the nonindependent scores. To examine the effects of removing the item overlap, correlations were recomputed for four of the adjustment measures (excluding global adjustment, which had almost all overlapping items). The new correlations were .34 for mental health problems, .25 for externalizing symptoms, –.41 for GPA, and .37 for trouble with the law ($p < .001$ in all cases). In all but one case (externalizing), these nonoverlapping correlations were still significantly higher than the corresponding correlations of the discrete–negative–independent score with the same adjustment measures. The presence of significant correlations for nonoverlapping scores suggests sources of covariance other than item overlap.

TABLE 5
Correlations of Life Events and Adjustment Showing Item Overlap (Adolescent Report)

Adjustment Score	*Discrete–Negative–Nonindependent LEQ–A Score*		*Item 30 "Failed a Grade"*		*Item 59 "Got in Trouble With the Law"*	
YSR internalizing	.14	(0)	.13	(0)	.06	(0)
Self-worth	–.25**	(0)	–.16*	(0)	–.16*	(0)
Mental health problems	.38***	(2)	.32***	(0)	.38***	(1)
Global adaptation	–.38***	(8)	–.32***	(1)	–.36***	(1)
YSR externalizing	.39***	(3)	.19*	(0)	.33***	(1)
Grade point average	–.51***	(2)	–.39***	(1)	–.23**	(0)
Trouble with the law	.52***	(2)	.30***	(0)	.57***	(1)

Note. $n = 176$ except for YSR scores where $n = 174$ and GPA where $n = 152$. The number of items overlapping with each adjustment measure is shown in parentheses.
*$p < .05$. **$p < .01$. ***$p < .001$.

Chronic versus discrete events. It was hypothesized that the chronic–negative–independent score would have both direct effects on adjustment indicators and indirect effects through its relation to discrete negative events. This model was tested by means of path analysis.

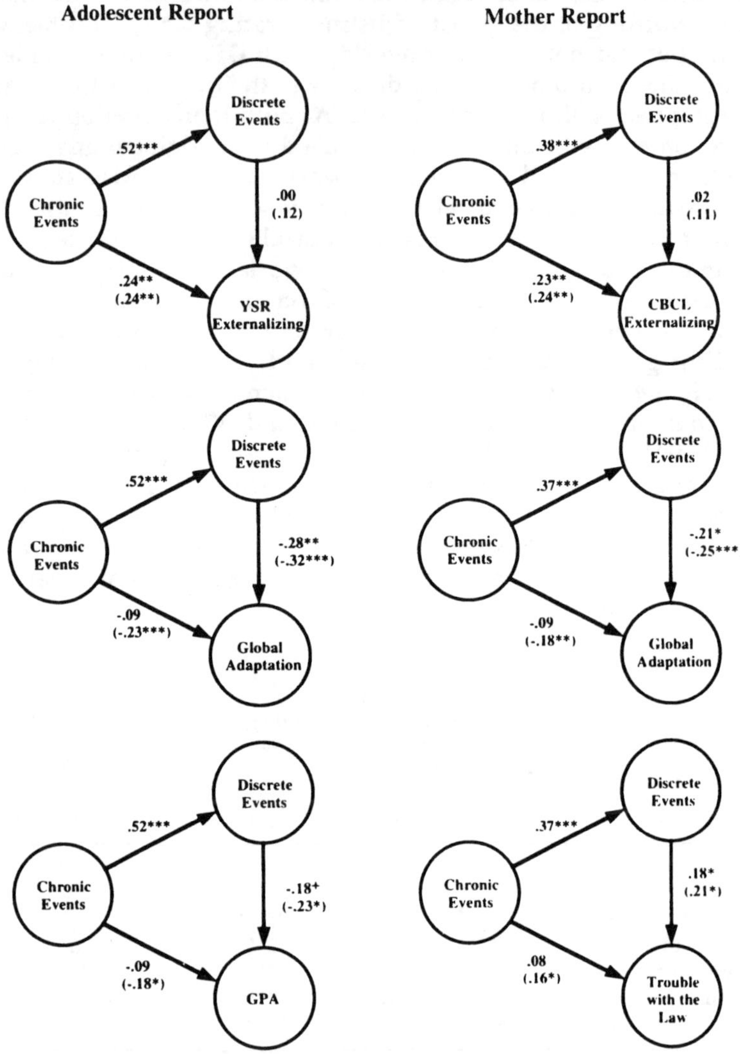

FIGURE 1 Results for path analysis showing significant direct and indirect paths linking chronic independent events to adolescent adjustment. Beta values and significance level are shown next to the path. Simple correlations are shown in parentheses. *$p < .05$. **$p < .01$. ***$p < .001$. $^{+}p = .0539$.

The composite of all discrete–negative and ambiguous–independent events was used for these analyses because it was more comprehensive and had greater variance than the discrete–negative score alone. First, the discrete composite score was regressed on the chronic score. Then each adjustment indicator was regressed on the discrete composite and the chronic score simultaneously. Analyses with significant direct or indirect paths are illustrated in Figure 1. For externalizing symptoms, chronic events had only direct effects, whether reported by adolescents or mothers. For global adaptation, for both mother and adolescent report, chronic events were found to have only indirect effects, through their relation with discrete events, suggesting that discrete events mediated the effect of chronic–negative life experiences on the broadest indicator of adjustment. Two other analyses suggested indirect effects: mother reports of trouble with the law and adolescent reports of life events in relation to GPA. In all other cases, the effects of chronic events were either nonsignificant to begin with or partially indirect but nonsignificant for both direct and indirect paths.

DISCUSSION

Event Independence

The main hypothesis of this study was supported: Life event scores based on objectively defined independent events were found to have substantially lower correlations with adjustment measures than did scores based on nonindependent events. Moreover, judges classified a sizable proportion of events commonly included in life event questionnaires for adolescents as not independent of the adolescent's behavior.

Results were consistent with three different sources of covariance between measures of nonindependent life events scores and adjustment. In some cases, item or content overlap appeared to play a role. In other cases, where there was no explicit overlap, adolescent behavior related to the adjustment problem could have contributed in some way to the event. Alternatively, ongoing disorder or symptoms in the adolescent could have led to both the events and the adjustment problems.

A fourth possibility is that a negative response-set accounted for the covariance of events and maladjustment. This does not seem likely because the magnitude of correlations with adjustment differed substantially for the two kinds of negative life event scores (independent vs. nonindependent) and because correlations across reporter (e.g., mothers' report of events with adolescents' report of adjustment) were also significant.

Other studies have found nonindependent negative events to be strongly related to self-reported distress in adolescents. For example, in two prospective studies, earlier distress was found to be the best predictor of later distress, and it also was a predictor of "controllable" negative life events (Cohen et al., 1987; Swearingen & Cohen, 1985). Findings from these studies suggest that there may be complex bidirectional processes linking nonindependent events and distress across time.

Two important processes that may underlie possible bidirectional linkages have received little attention in the adolescent literature. One concerns the relation of chronic mental disorder to life events. Depue and Monroe (1986) have discussed the implications of chronic disturbance for the study of life events in adults. They suggest that life events, rather than initiating disturbance, may serve to maintain disorder in some vulnerable individuals. Chronic disturbance is likely to produce behavior that leads to more life events. Thus, the behavior of adolescents may contribute to the incidence and nature of nonindependent events, but these events may still be distressing. Moreover, distressed adolescents may be unable or disinclined to avoid such events. Chronic distress or disorder may in part be maintained by stressful events precipitated by the child's own disorder-related behavior in a self-defeating cycle.

It has also been suggested in the adult literature that a personality trait, negative affectivity, may underlie the relations among self-reported stress, physical symptoms, and distress (Watson, 1988). Negative affectivity refers to an enduring tendency to experience negative mood states and to have a negative self-concept (Tellegen, 1985; Watson & Clark, 1984; Watson & Tellegen, 1985). Persons high in negative affectivity tend to be stress-reactive and to report more negative experiences. Watson and his colleagues have found strong relations between perceived stress and negative affectivity in several studies (Watson, 1988; Watson & Pennebaker, 1989; Watson, Pennebaker, & Folger, 1987). As yet, little work has focused on the measurement or possible significance of a predisposition to negative affect in adolescents.

The role of chronic mental disturbance or personality traits that yield vulnerability to distress and life-event-producing behavior needs to be examined carefully in relation to nonindependent events. If there are stress-vulnerable adolescents who induce or do not avoid such events, interventions might be developed to help such adolescents reduce their stressful experiences or to manipulate environmental conditions with a similar goal.

Desirability

Results for the objectively classified desirability of life events support previous findings that negative events are related to maladjustment, whereas positive scores are related to better adjustment. The ambiguous score in this study, consisting of discrete, independent events like the remarriage of a parent, was related to adjustment in much the same way as the negative independent scores, suggesting that in many cases, for this sample, these events were more negative than positive.

Results for nonindependent scores were clearly confounded with several adjustment measures. The discrete–negative–nonindependent events score, for example, which included events like failing a grade and suspension from school, was strongly related to a poor GPA. Similarly, the positive events score, which consisted of discrete achievements, was strongly related to a global adaptation rating that was based in part on achievements. Depending on the adjustment criteria included in a particular study, results could be interpreted to mean that negative life events have more impact on adjustment than do positive events, when the negative score was simply more confounded with the chosen criterion.

In this study there was only one positive events score, consisting of nonindependent achievement events clearly confounded with adjustment. However, the domain of positive events was not systematically sampled, as was attempted for the Adolescent Perceived Events Scale (Compas, Davis, Forsythe, & Wagner, 1987). Future studies could examine the processes associated with positive events more effectively by contrasting nonindependent and independent events.

Chronic Versus Discrete Stressors

Results partially support the hypothesis that chronic independent events would have both direct and indirect effects on adjustment (mediated by discrete events). The effects of chronic experiences on global adaptation, the broadest assessment of adjustment, were entirely indirect and mediated by discrete events. Similar indirect effects were found for academic achievement (adolescent report) and trouble with the law (mother report). The shared variance between discrete and chronic independent events may be due to the same underlying processes in the family. Discrete events, such as "parent lost a job" or "family member attempted suicide" or "parents divorced," could be particular manifestations of or causally related to chronic conditions like a "difficult family financial situation" or "parent had trouble with alcohol/drugs" or "there were many arguments among household adults." It is possible that one mechanism by which chronic adversity, such as family problems, contributes to current adolescent adjustment problems is through the added discrete stressors adolescents in these situations must face.

Externalizing symptoms, on the other hand, showed only direct effects for chronic stressors and no effects for discrete independent events once chronic stressors were controlled. Externalizing symptoms may have a more chronic history and be related to long-standing family problems or dysfunction in parents.

Conclusions

Results of this study demonstrate the importance of distinguishing life events with respect to the dimensions of independence, desirability, and chronicity, and underscore the complexity of studying the relation of life events to adjustment in adolescents. The conceptual and operational separation of independent from nonindependent events is particularly important for more decisive analyses of the complex processes that may underlie the linkages of life events and adjustment. For independent events, the role of parental functioning needs to be examined further in relation to life events and adolescent functioning. For nonindependent events, methodological issues, such as overlapping items, need to be dealt with first, and then the role of personality and other possible vulnerability factors needs to be considered in relation to how adolescents contribute to their own stressful experiences. Future studies also could begin to delineate additional ways in which independent and dependent events may differ and how these differences contribute to adolescent development.

Differences across studies in the specific life experiences included on questionnaires and in the scoring strategies may account in part for the inconsistent findings in this literature. Differentiating scores on the basis of the three characteristics addressed in this study is important. In addition, other aspects of item content may play a role. For example, a number of life events were excluded from all of our scores because they did not meet the classification criteria. These items often appear in other questionnaires. Thus, our substantive results may differ from other studies partly because these items were excluded. On the other hand, including such events would present difficulties for interpretation because of their ambiguity on key event dimensions. Careful analysis of item content and scoring strategies is essential for advancing research in this area.

This study had two major limitations. Because the assessment of life events was limited to the questionnaire method, the context of specific events could not be determined. Contextual details would allow individual events to be classified more accurately on independence. Events excluded from scores because they were ambiguous in this study might be clearly classified as independent in a specific case (cf. Brown & Harris, 1978; Goodyer et al., 1985, 1990). This more comprehensive score would probably have greater validity. In addition, contextual details would allow for better specification of item or content overlap, facilitating more precise examinations of this aspect of confounded measurement. Second, this study was limited by its cross-sectional design. It was not possible to control for preexisting adjustment problems to assess changes in adjustment in relation to discrete onset negative life experiences. Longitudinal studies generally would provide a stronger test of the direction of causal effects linking life events and adolescent behavior, particularly if careful distinctions were made on the independence, chronicity, and desirability of the events.

Prospective studies are essential for the formidable task of sorting out the complex mechanisms intimated by this and other studies. However, longitudinal designs will not solve the problems of confounded measures or constructs. Progress in understanding how life events and adjustment are related over the course of development requires greater attention to conceptual and methodological issues as well as longitudinal studies of the processes linking life experiences to adjustment.

ACKNOWLEDGMENTS

This study was supported by grants from the National Institute of Mental Health (MH33222) and the William T. Grant Foundation to Norman Garmezy, Ann Masten, and Auke Tellegen and a McKnight–Land Grant Professorship to Ann Masten.

This study required the collaboration of colleagues on the Project Competence research team, for which we are deeply grateful. In particular, we acknowledge the roles of Paul Marshall and Sherry Machen in revising the life event measure and Kevin Larkin in data analysis. We also thank W. Andrew Collins, Stephen Cole, Norman Garmezy, Scott Gest, Patricia Morison, Auke Tellegen, and anonymous reviewers for their helpful comments on this article.

REFERENCES

Achenbach, T. M. (1991). *Manual for the Child Behavior Checklist/4–18 and 1991 Profile.* Burlington: University of Vermont, Department of Psychiatry.

Achenbach, T. M., & Edelbrock, C. (1983). *Manual for the Child Behavior Checklist and Revised Child Behavior Profile.* Burlington: University of Vermont, Department of Psychiatry.

Achenbach, T. M., & Edelbrock, C. (1987). *Manual for the Youth Self-Report and Profile.* Burlington: University of Vermont, Department of Psychiatry.

Achenbach, T. M., McConaughy, S. J., & Howell, C. T. (1987). Child/adolescent behavioral and emotional problems: Implications of cross-informant correlations for situational specificity. *Psychological Bulletin, 101,* 213–232.

American Psychiatric Association. (1980). *Diagnostic and statistical manual of mental disorders* (3rd ed.). Washington, DC: Author.

Andenas, S. H., & Morison, P. (1988, March). *Assessing adaptation in adolescence: Clinical ratings of a biographical questionnaire obtained from adolescents and their mothers.* Paper presented at the meetings of the Society for Research in Adolescence, Alexandria, VA.

Belsky, J., & Vondra, J. (1989). Lessons from child abuse: The determinants of parenting. In D. Cicchetti & V. Carlson (Eds.), *Child maltreatment: Theory and research on the causes and consequences of child abuse and neglect* (pp. 153–202). New York: Cambridge University Press.

Berden, G. F. M. G., Althaus, M., & Verhulst, F. C. (1990). Major life events and changes in the behavioural functioning of children. *Journal of Child Psychology and Psychiatry, 31,* 949–959.

Boyle, M. H., & Jones, S. C. (1985). Selecting measures of emotional and behavioral disorders of childhood for use in general population. *Journal of Child Psychology and Psychiatry, 26,* 137–159.

Brown, G. W., & Harris, T. (1978). *Social origins of depression: A study of psychiatric disorder in women.* New York: Free Press.

Coddington, R. D. (1972a). The significance of life events as etiologic factors in the diseases of children: I. A survey of professional workers. *Journal of Psychosomatic Research, 16,* 7–18.

Coddington, R. D. (1972b). The significance of life events as etiologic factors in the diseases of children: II. A study of a normal population. *Journal of Psychosomatic Research, 16,* 205–213.

Cohen, J. (1960). A coefficient of agreement for nominal scales. *Educational and Psychological Measurement, 20,* 37–46.

Cohen L. H. (1988). Measurement of life events. In L. H. Cohen (Ed.), *Llfe events and psychological functioning: Theoretical and methodological issues* (pp. 11–30). Beverly Hills, CA: Sage.

Cohen, L. H., Burt, C. E., & Bjorck, J. P. (1987). Life stress and adjustment: Effects of life events experienced by young adolescents and their parents. *Developmental Psychology, 23,* 583–592.

Compas, B. E. (1987). Stress and life events during childhood and adolescence. *Clinical Psychology Review, 7,* 275–302.

Compas, B. E., Davis, G. E., Forsythe, C. J., & Wagner, B. M. (1987). Assessment of major and daily stressful events during adolescence: The adolescent perceived events scale. *Journal of Consulting and Clinical Psychology, 55,* 534–541.

Cowen, E. L., Weissberg, R. P., & Guare, J. (1984). Differentiating attributes of children referred to a school mental health program. *Journal of Abnormal Child Psychology, 12,* 397–410.

Depue, R. A., & Monroe, S. M. (1986). Conceptualization and measurement of human disorder in life stress research: The problem of chronic disturbance. *Psychological Bulletin, 99,* 36–51.

Dohrenwend, B. S., & Dohrenwend, B. P. (1974). *Stressful life events: Their nature and effects.* New York: Wiley.

Dohrenwend, B. S., Dohrenwend, B. P., Dodson, M., & Shrout, P. E. (1984). Symptoms, hassles, social supports, and life events: Problem of confounded measures. *Journal of Abnormal Psychology, 93,* 222–230.

Dohrenwend, B. S., & Shrout, P. E. (1985). "Hassles" in the conceptualization and measurement of life stress variables. *American Psychologist, 40,* 780–785.

Dubois, D. L., Felner, R. D., Brand, S., Adan, A. M., & Evans, E. G. (1992). A prospective study of life stress, social support, and adaptation in early adolescence. *Child Development, 63,* 542–557.

Dubow, E. F., Tisak, J., Causey, D., Hryshko, A., & Reid, G. (1991). A two-year longitudinal study of stressful life events, social support, and social problem-solving skills: Contributions to children's behavioral and academic adjustment. *Child Development, 62,* 583–599.

Emery, R. E. (1982). Interparental conflict and the children of discord and divorce. *Psychological Bulletin, 92,* 310–330.

Garmezy, N., & Masten, A. S. (1994). Chronic adversities. In M. Rutter, L. Herzov, & E. Taylor (Eds.), *Child and adolescent psychiatry* (3rd ed.; pp. 191–208). Oxford, England: Blackwell.

Garmezy, N., & Rutter, M. (1985). Acute reactions to stress. In M. Rutter & L. Hersov (Eds.), *Child psychiatry: Modern approaches* (2nd ed.; pp. 152–176). Oxford, England: Blackwell.

Garmezy, N., & Tellegen, A. (1984). Studies of stress-resistant children: Methods, variables, and preliminary findings. In F. Morrison, C. Lord, & D. Keating (Eds.), *Advances in applied developmental psychology* (Vol. 1, pp. 231–287). New York: Academic.

Gersten, J. C., Langner, T. S., Eisenberg, J. G., & Simcha-Fagan, O. (1977). An evaluation of the etiologic role of stressful life-change events in psychological disorders. *Journal of Health and Social Behavior, 18,* 228–244.

Goodyer, I., Kolvin, I., & Gatzanis, S. (1985). Recent undesirable life events and psychiatric disorder in childhood and adolescence. *British Journal of Psychiatry, 147,* 517–523.

Goodyer, I., Wright, C., & Altham, P. (1990). The friendships and recent life events of anxious and depressed school-age children. *British Journal of Psychiatry, 156,* 689–698.

Harter, S. (1982). The perceived competence scale for children. *Child Development, 53,* 87–97.

Harter, S. (1985). *Manual: Self-perception profile for children.* Unpublished manuscript, University of Denver, CO.

Harter, S. (1986). *Manual: Self-perception profile for adolescents.* Unpublished manuscript, University of Denver, CO.

Hauser, R. M., & Featherman, D. L. (1977). *The process of stratification: Trends and analysis.* New York: Academic.

Herzog, J. G. (1984). Life events as indices of family stress: Relationships with children's current levels of competence (Doctoral dissertation, University of Minnesota, 1984). *Dissertation Abstracts International, 45,* 1017B.

Hetherington, E. M., & Anderson, E. R. (1988). The effects of divorce and remarriage on early adolescents and their families. In M. D. Levine & E. R. McAnarney (Eds.), *Early adolescent transitions* (pp. 49–67). Lexington, MA: Heath.

Holmes, T. H., & Rahe, R. H. (1967). The social readjustment rating scale. *Journal of Psychosomatic Research, 11,* 213–218.

Hotelling, H. (1931). The generalization of Student's Ratio. *Annals of Mathematical Statistics, 2,* 360–368.

Hudgens, R. W. (1974). Personal catastrophe and depression: A consideration of the subject with respect to medically ill adolescents, and a requiem for retrospective life-events studies. In B. S. Dohrenwend & B. P. Dohrenwend (Eds.), *Stressful life events: Their nature and effects* (pp. 119–134). New York: Wiley.

Johnson. J. H. (1986). *Life events as stressors in childhood and adolescence.* Beverly Hills, CA: Sage.

Johnson, J. H., & McCutcheon, S. (1980). Assessing life stress in older children and adolescents: Preliminary finding with the Life Events Checklist. In I. G. Sarason & C. D. Spielberger (Eds.), *Stress and anxiety* (Vol. 7, pp. 111–125). Washington, DC: Hemisphere.

Lazarus, R. S. (1990). Theory-based stress measurement. *Psychological Inquiry, 1,* 3–13.

Lazarus, R. S., DeLongis, A., Folkman, S., & Gruen, R. (1985). Stress and adaptational outcomes: The problem of confounded measures. *American Psychologist, 40,* 770–779.

Lazarus, R. S., & Folkman, S. (1984). *Stress, appraisal, and coping.* New York: Springer.

Linder, H. D. (1985). *A contextual life events interview as a measure of stress: A comparison of questionnaire-based versus interview-based stress indices.* Unpublished doctoral dissertation, University of Minnesota, Minneapolis.

Masten, A. S., Best, K. M., & Garmezy, N. (1990). Resilience and development: Contributions from the study of children who overcome adversity. *Development and Psychopathology, 2,* 425–444.

Masten, A. S., Garmezy, N., Tellegen, A., Pellegrini, D. S., Larkin, K., & Larsen, A. (1988). Competence and stress in school children: The moderating effects of individual and family qualities. *Journal of Child Psychology and Psychiatry, 29,* 745–764.

McNemar, Q. (1969). *Psychological statistics* (4th ed.). New York: Wiley.

Morison, P., & Masten, A. S. (1991). Peer reputation in middle childhood as a predictor of adaptation in adolescence: A 7-year followup. *Child Development, 62,* 991–1007.

Neemann, J. D., & Masten, A. S. (1988, March). *The nature of perceived competence in adolescence.* Poster presented at the meeting of the Society for Research in Adolescence, Alexandria, VA.

Newcomb, M. D., Huba, G. J., & Bentler, P. M. (1986). Life change events among adolescents: An empirical consideration of some methodological issues. *The Journal of Nervous and Mental Disease, 174,* 280–289.

Patterson, G. R. (1982). *Coercive family process.* Eugene, OR: Castalia.

Realmuto, G. M., Masten, A., Carole, L. F., Hubbard, J., Groteslúschen, A., & Chun, B. (1992). Adolescent survivors of massive childhood trauma in Cambodia: Life events and current symptoms. *Journal of Traumatic Stress, 5,* 589–599.

Rowlison, R. T., & Felner, R. D. (1988). Major life events, hassles, and adaptation in adolescence: Confounding in the conceptualization and measurement of life stress and adjustment revisited. *Journal of Personality and Social Psychology, 55,* 432–444.

Sandler, I. N., & Block, M. (1979). Life stress and maladaptation of children. *American Journal of Community Psychology, 7,* 425–439.

Sattler, J. M. (1990). *Assessment of children* (3rd ed.). San Diego, CA: Jerome M. Sattler.

Scarr, S., & McCartney, K. (1983). How people make their own environments: A theory of genotype–environment effects. *Child Development, 54,* 424–435.

Simmons, R. G., & Blyth, D. A. (1987). *Moving into adolescence: The impact of pubertal change and school context.* Hawthorne, NY: Aldine de Gruyter.

Spitznagel, E. L., & Helzer, J. E. (1985). A proposed solution to the base rate problem in the kappa statistic. *Archives of General Psychiatry, 42,* 725–728.

Sterling, S., Cowen, E. L., Weissberg, R. P., Lotyczewski, B. S., & Boike, M. (1985). Recent stressful life events and young children's school adjustment. *American Journal of Community Psychology, 13,* 87–98.

Swearingen, E. M., & Cohen L. H. (1985). Life events and psychological distress: A prospective study of young adolescents. *Developmental Psychology, 21,* 1045–1054.

Tellegen, A. (1985). Structures of mood and personality and their relevance to assessing anxiety, with an emphasis on self-report. In A. H. Tuma & J. D. Maser (Eds.), *Anxiety and the anxiety disorders* (pp. 681–716). Hillsdale, NJ: Lawrence Erlbaum Associates, Inc.

Thoits, P. A. (1983). Dimensions of life events that influence psychological distress: An evaluation and synthesis of the literature. In H. G. Kaplan (Ed.), *Psychosocial stress: Trends in theory and research* (pp. 33–103). New York: Academic.

Watson, D. (1988). Intraindividual and interindividual analyses of positive and negative affect: Their relation to health complaints, perceived stress, and daily activities. *Journal of Personality and Social Psychology, 54,* 1020–1030.

Watson, D., & Clark, L. A. (1984). Negative affectivity: The disposition to experience aversive emotional states. *Psychological Bulletin, 96,* 465–490.

Watson, D., & Pennebaker, J. W. (1989). Health complaints, stress, and distress: Exploring the central role of negative affectivity. *Psychological Review, 96,* 234–254.

Watson, D., Pennebaker, J. W., & Folger, R. (1987). Beyond negative affectivity: Measuring stress and satisfaction in the workplace. *Journal of Organizational Behavior Management, 8,* 141–157.

Watson, D., & Tellegen, A. (1985). Toward a consensual structure of mood. *Psychological Bulletin, 98,* 219–235.

Zimmerman, M. (1983). Methodological issues in the assessment of life events: A review of issues and research. *Clinical Psychology Review, 3,* 339–370.

Received September 12, 1991
Revision received June 12, 1992
Accepted April 30, 1993

JOURNAL OF RESEARCH ON ADOLESCENCE, 6(4), 379–396

Great Transitions: Preparing American Youth for the 21st Century—The Role of Research

David A. Hamburg
Carnegie Corporation of New York

Ruby Takanishi
Carnegie Council on Adolescent Development

This article summarizes the findings of the Carnegie Council on Adolescent Development's concluding report, *Great Transitions: Preparing Adolescents for a New Century* (Carnegie Council on Adolescent Development, 1995). Research indicates that adolescents face increasingly poor odds for success in today's rapidly changing societies. The natural inclination to experiment with risky behavior is occurring at an earlier age, and the potential for disability, even death, is thus greater. *Great Transitions* recommends a generic approach to preventive interventions for adolescents that includes: reengaging families with their adolescents, designing developmentally appropriate schools, promoting the health of adolescents, strengthening communities with youth, and promoting the constructive potential of media. Research opportunities suggested by the report include: biological aspects of adolescence, economic factors in adolescent development, time use studies on families and adolescents, and evaluation of preventive interventions.

Great Transitions: Preparing Adolescents for a New Century, the concluding report of the Carnegie Council on Adolescent Development, represents a decade-long commitment by Carnegie Corporation of New York to raise the critical adolescent years higher on our nation's agenda (Carnegie Council on Adolescent Development, 1995). The central message of this report is that adults in society's pivotal institutions, those that profoundly affect the life chances of adolescents—families, schools, health care agencies, community organizations, and the media—must redress the neglect of this age group and cooperate to adopt broad-based solutions to the interrelated threats facing adolescents today. If the nation continues to neglect this age group, *Great Transitions* warns, millions of adolescents will continue to be lifelong casualties of drug and alcohol abuse, premature parenthood, AIDS, suicide, violence, and inadequate education.

The report puts the spotlight on a crucial period for preventive interventions with young people between the ages of 10 and 14, the period of early adolescence when adolescents naturally experiment with risky activities but before damaging behavior patterns have become firmly established. In 1993, approximately 7.3% (19 million) of the U.S. population were young adolescents, ages 10 through 14. Of these, approximately 20% (4 million) were living below the federal poverty line, which in 1993, was $14,763 for a family of four (Day, 1993). By the year 2000, more than one third of all adolescents will be members of racial or ethnic minorities (O'Hare, 1992). To compete successfully in the transnational economy of the 21st century, America will need every one of these youths to be healthy, well educated, and committed to a civil society.

However, as *Great Transitions* documents, today's young adolescents are already exhibiting many of the very risky behaviors that were once associated with middle and late adolescence (see Table 1).

No segment of the adolescent population is immune from the problems confronting young people. The risks facing adolescents affect those in families of all income levels and are present in urban, suburban, and rural

TABLE 1
Young Adolescents Face Serious Risks

In 1993, approximately 7.3% (19 million) of the U.S. population were young adolescents, ages 10 to 14 (U.S. Department of Commerce, 1994). Of these, approximately 20% were living below the federal poverty line, which in 1993 was $14,763 for a family of four. Minority adolescents were disproportionately poor: 43% of African American adolescents and 38% of Hispanic–Latino adolescents lived in poverty, compared with 15% of European American adolescents. By the year 2000, one third of all young adolescents will be members of racial or ethnic minorities: African Americans (16%), American Indian, Eskimo, and Aleut (1%), Asian Pacific Americans (5%), and Hispanic–Latino (14%; Day, 1993). To compete in the global economy of the 21st century, America will need all of these young people to be healthy and well educated.

Health Risks

- Injuries are the leading cause of death for young adolescents. The largest single cause of death among these adolescents is injuries from motor vehicle crashes (U.S. Department of Education, National Center for Health Statistics, 1994).
- The firearm homicide rate for 10- to 14-year-olds more than doubled between 1985 and 1992 (from 0.8 to 1.9 per 100,000). For male African Americans, the rate increased from 3.0 to 8.4 per 100,000 during the same period (U.S. Department of Education, National Center for Health Statistics, 1994).

TABLE 1 *(Continued)*

- The highest overall victimization rate of any age group is found among 12- to 15-year-old girls and boys. From 1972 to 1992, the rate of reported rape has increased for girls of this age from 1.3 per 1,000 to 1.9 per 1,000 (U.S. Department of Justice, 1994).
- In a national representative sample of adolescents 10 to 16 years old, one fourth of respondents reported having experienced an assault or abuse in the previous year (Finkelhor & Dziuba-Leatherman, 1994). Approximately 20% of the documented child abuse and neglect cases in 1992 involved young adolescents between the ages of 10 and 13 years old (U.S. Department of Commerce, 1994).
- Use of alcohol and cigarettes remains more widespread than use of illegal drugs.
- Although it is illegal to sell alcohol to individuals under 21 years of age, two thirds of eighth graders report that they have already tried alcohol and a quarter say that they are current drinkers. Twenty-eight percent of eighth graders claim that they have been drunk at least once (Johnson, O'Malley, & Bachman, 1994).
- Eight percent of eighth graders report smoking cigarettes daily, with many smoking a half-pack or more (Johnson et al., 1994).
- Marijuana use among eighth graders more than doubled between 1991 and 1994, from 6.2% to 13.0% (Johnson et al., 1994).
- Over the last three decades, the age of first intercourse has declined. Higher proportions of adolescent women and men reported being sexually experienced at each age between the ages of 15 and 20 in 1988 than in the early 1970s. In 1988, 27% of girls and 33% of boys had intercourse by their 15th birthday (The Alan Guttmacher Institute, 1994).
- While the number of births to those ages 15 and younger is not large, this group is experiencing the greatest rate of increased births. Pregnancy rates for all girls less than 15 years old rose 4.1% in the United States during the period between 1980 and 1988—higher than any other teenage group (U.S. General Accounting Office, 1995).
- Current evidence indicates that increases in depressive disorders and moods are greater for girls than for boys during adolescence. By age 14 to 15, girls are twice as likely as boys to suffer from depression, a gender difference that persists into adulthood.
- From 1980 to 1982, the rate of suicide among young adolescents increased 120% and increased most dramatically among young African American males (300%) and young European American females (233%). Suicide rates for 10- to 14-year-old American Indians are four times higher than those for 10- to 14-year-olds of all races ("Suicide among," 1995; U.S. Congress, Office of Technology Assessment, 1990).

Educational Risks

- The average proficiency in science, mathematics, and writing among 13-year-olds was slightly higher in 1992 than it was in the 1970s. However, these achievements have not improved enough to keep pace with the higher level of skills required in a global economy (U.S. Department of Education, 1995).
- Only 28% of eighth graders scored at or above the proficiency level in reading in 1994, and 2% read at or above an advanced level (U.S. Department of Education, 1995).
- In 1990, 7% of the eighth-grade class of 1988 (most of whom were then 15 and 16 years old) were dropouts, that is, they were not enrolled in school and had not finished high school. By their senior year (1992), 12% of this class were dropouts. Dropout rates vary by students' race and ethnicity—European American (9.4%), African American (14.5%), Hispanic (18.3%), Asian and Pacific Islanders (7.0%), and American Indian (25.4%; U.S. Department of Education, National Center for Education Statistics, 1994).

areas. Nonetheless, those who grow up in areas of concentrated poverty are typically more vulnerable than those who live in safer, more affluent neighborhoods.

Massive social, economic, and cultural transformations have contributed to the current state of affairs. More parents of adolescents are in the workplace, largely due to economic restructuring and declining wages for many workers. Both adolescents and their parents report that life is more difficult and neighborhoods more dangerous than in the past (Princeton Survey Research Associates, 1993). About 27% of eighth graders spend 2 or more hours at home alone after school (U.S. Department of Education, 1990). Adolescents left on their own or only with peers during the out-of-school hours stand a significantly greater chance of being involved in substance abuse, juvenile crime, activity leading to unintended pregnancy and sexually transmitted diseases, and doing poorly in school (Zill, Nord, & Loomis, 1995).

One in every two adolescents will live with only one parent at some point in their lives, through parental divorce and separation or having never married (Hernandez, 1993). These disruptions in family and close relations can be distressful to children at all ages. Today's adolescents are bombarded with more media influences than ever before in human history. By midadolescence, they have watched about 15,000 hours of television—more time than they have spent with teachers in school (Huston et al., 1992). Radio and music take increasing amounts of time during adolescence (Christenson & Roberts, 1990). The advent of personal computers, interactive video games, and the Internet is so recent that little is yet understood about their potential influences.

Despite these social and economic upheavals of the last half century, all adolescents have enduring human needs that must be met if they are to grow up to be productive adults. Adolescents need close, dependable, and durable relationships with a few adults, and they must have the perception of meaningful opportunities in mainstream society, including being a valued member of a constructive group (Baumeister & Leary, 1995).

Great Transitions offers concrete guidance about how pivotal institutions can foster healthy development during adolescence and describes promising broad-based, developmentally appropriate strategies. Its recommendations are closely tied to a rich body of research in the biological, behavioral, and social sciences and to evaluations of preventive interventions. Thus, researchers can take well-deserved pride in having contributed to identifying ways in which communities and the nation can better support adolescents as they make the crucial transition from childhood into productive adulthood. Researchers' continuing inquiries into the second decade of life are vital for understanding the nature of adolescence itself and, by linking their findings with policy and practice, for improving the education, health, and well-being of all the nation's young people.

KEY RECOMMENDATIONS

Many adolescents negotiate their way through the critical transition between childhood and adulthood with relative success. With caring families, good schools, and supportive community institutions, they grow up reasonably well educated, committed to families and friends, and prepared for the workplace and the responsibilities of citizenship. Even under less-than-optimal conditions for growth—including the absence of supportive adults, poverty, inadequate schools, and resource-depleted neighborhoods—adolescents can become contributing members of their society. Some achieve this status despite facing threats to their well-being, such as AIDS and easy access to lethal weapons and drugs, that were all but unknown to their parents and grandparents.

The Carnegie Council on Adolescent Development urges the pivotal institutions that have the greatest influence on young adolescents to adapt to current conditions in ways that meet the essential requirements that adolescents have always had for their healthy development. These institutions have fallen behind in their vital functions and must now be strengthened in their respective roles and linked into a mutually reinforcing system of human and institutional support for adolescents.

A Generic Approach

The framing of this comprehensive approach is firmly rooted in research findings, particularly with respect to interventions that routinely target single problem behavior, such as substance abuse. Although such targeted approaches can be useful, they often do not take adequate account of two critical findings from research: Serious problems tend to cluster in the same individual and reinforce each other (e.g., Donovan & Jessor, 1985; Elliott, 1993; Jessor & Jessor, 1977; Lerner, 1995), and such behaviors often have common antecedents in childhood experience and educational failure (Dryfoos, 1990).

On the other hand, those who engage in healthy lifestyles are more likely to do well in school and to come from supportive family and community structures that reward their efforts and promote self-respect and decent human relationships (Haggerty, Sherrod, Garmezy, & Rutter, 1994; Werner & Smith, 1992). These findings suggest the families, schools, and other social institutions have a special opportunity, and indeed an obligation, to foster healthy lifestyles in childhood and adolescence, taking into consideration the underlying factors that promote either positive or negative outcomes.

Thus, the Carnegie Council's recommendations focus on generic approaches that deal with the factors that predispose adolescents to engage in high-risk or problem behaviors. They are different from targeted approaches that focus on single problems. Generic approaches are oriented to the positive possibilities in the adolescent transition, for educating and motivating young adolescents to pursue healthy lifestyles, to foster social and decision-making skills to help them choose alternatives to very risky behavior, and providing them with motivation and skills to build constructive lives.

Such generic approaches that can be adopted by pivotal institutions include not only strengthening family relationships and providing excellent basic education, but also cross-cutting approaches such as social support networks, adult mentoring, health promotion programs involving human biology, peer-mediated strategies, and social and life-skills education to help young people address problems and conflicts in their everyday lives. If these approaches are sustained over a period of years, they can offset the negative effects of low self-respect, underdeveloped social and decision-making skills, indifference to learning, lack of information about health-enhancing practices, low perception of opportunities, and limited incentives for delaying immediate gratification and investing in their long-term futures.

The following summary of recommendations from *Great Transitions* identifies ways in which pivotal institutions in society can adapt to a world-in-transformation and enhance the life chances of adolescents so essential for their future well-being.

Reengaging Families With Their Adolescent Children

Adolescents may be growing, but they are far from grown up. Contrary to many parents' mistaken belief that they should get out of the way during adolescence, young people continue to seek their support and guidance. Indeed, surveys indicate that adolescents report that the increased involvement of their parents is their greatest need. These surveys and research on family relationships during adolescence (e.g., Who's Who Among American High School Students, 1995; Louis Harris and Associates, 1989; Steinberg, 1990) coalesced to result in strong Council recommendations regarding the reengagement of parents and families with their adolescent children.

Great Transitions recommends that parents be actively engaged in their adolescents' education and lives. Schools, for their part, should welcome and work with parents as allies and cultivate parents' support for their adolescents' education. Schools, health care agencies, and other community institutions, including religious organizations, can help parents deal with the adolescent transition by providing information on developmental changes and characteristics and ways to renegotiate their relationships with children who have growing cognitive, emotional, and social competencies. They can create parent support and education groups, especially during the transitional years from childhood into adolescence.

Employers, both public and private, can pursue more family-friendly policies for parents with young adolescents, including flexible work hours and other measures that allow parents to spend more time with adolescents or volunteer in school or youth organizations. Under certain circumstances, child care tax credits could be extended to parents of young adolescents so they may participate in high-quality after-school programs supervised by responsible, caring adults. Evidence that such after-school experiences contribute to positive rather than undesired outcomes is now substantial (Zill et al., 1995).

Designing Developmentally Appropriate Schools

A volatile mismatch exists between the organization and curriculum of many middle grade schools and the intellectual and social needs of young adolescents (Carnegie Task Force on Education of Young Adolescents, 1989). Middle schools were largely ignored in the education reforms of the 1980s, but their potential for change is now beginning to be realized in schools in at least 15 states throughout the nation. Several foundations, including Carnegie Corporation of New York, the Edna McConnell Clark Foundation, and the Lilly Endowment, have stimulated middle grade reforms in recent years.

Based on the Carnegie Council's 1989 report, *Turning Points: Preparing American Youth for the Twenty-First Century* (Carnegie Task Force on Education of Young Adolescents, 1989), middle schools can be organized to meet the developmental needs of young adolescents. States and school districts should give teachers and principals the authority and resources to change middle schools into developmentally appropriate and health promoting environments—settings that are small scale and safe, that promote stable relationships between students and their teachers and peers, that are intellectually stimulating, that employ cooperative learning strategies and deemphasize tracking, that provide health education and life skills training, and that offer primary health care services either in or near the schools. These schools should provide a core curriculum and instructional methods that excite students' curiosity and build on their natural desire to explore, strengthen their analytic and problem-solving abilities, and provide an understanding of human biology and their place in the world.

Preliminary results from a statewide evaluation of *Turning Points* schools indicate that when the recommendations are adopted in whole, measurable changes in the expected direction for student achievement, teacher satisfaction, and student behavior occur (Felner et al., in press). The *Turning Points* effort illustrates how research can both inform the design of educational reform and policies and how it can subsequently investigate the effects of such reforms on students and teachers.

Promoting the Health of Adolescents

Since 1960, the burden of adolescent illness has shifted from the traditional causes of disease to the more behavior-related problems, such as sexually transmitted diseases, teenage pregnancy, motor vehicle accidents, gun-related homicides and suicides, depression, and the abuse of drugs, including alcohol and tobacco.

Helping adolescents to acquire the knowledge, skills, and motivation that foster physical and mental health will require substantial changes in the ways health professionals work and how they connect with families, schools, and community organizations. It will also require filling serious gaps in health services for adolescents as well as improving the life sciences education experienced by young adolescents in middle grade schools. Such a curriculum is aimed at improving their knowledge of human biology as a basis for understanding the influence of health-damaging and health-enhancing practices on their own bodies.

The Council made three major recommendations regarding the promotion of health among adolescents. First, the training of health providers (nurses, social workers, physicians, psychologists) with deep and sensitive understanding of the needs of adolescents should be a high priority. Second, health insurance coverage of adolescents, including their preventive and mental health needs, is necessary. Third, school-based and linked adolescent-health facilities should be expanded to meet the health needs of those who have no or little access to health care services. These measures combined could significantly improve the health outcomes for adolescents, both in the near and long term.

Strengthening Communities with Youth

In December 1992, the Carnegie Council released *A Matter of Time: Risk and Opportunity in the Nonschool Hours,* which focused public attention on the large amounts of out-of-school time available to young adolescents. Based on what was then a small number of suggestive studies, the report pointed to the potential risks of unsupervised after-school time on adolescents and to the positive outcomes of participating in well-supervised, positive activity settings (Carnegie Council on Adolescent Development, 1992).

A Matter of Time recommended that communities should provide more attractive, safe, growth-promoting settings during the high-risk, after-school time when parents are often not able to supervise their children and adolescents. The report called on a wide array of youth and community organizations—religious groups, adult service clubs, libraries, museums and science centers, and parks and recreation centers—to expand their reach to young adolescents and to engage them in community service and other positive activities. Coinciding with widespread concern about the prevention of youth violence, the report provided the case for safe haven and other after-school programs in communities throughout the nation.

Partially stimulated by the release of *A Matter of Time,* the U.S. Department of Health and Human Services commissioned a study using several national databases to examine the connection between the constructive use of after-school time and adolescent outcomes. That study documented that there is a positive relation for adolescents between well-supervised, skill-building programs and the reduction of poor outcomes (Zill et al., 1995). Since the release of *A Matter of Time,* independent evaluations of youth organizations indicate that the adult mentoring, combined with a comprehensive, long-term commitment, can have powerful effects on adolescents from very disadvantaged circumstances (Hahn, 1995).

Promoting Media's Constructive Potential

An ever-expanding array of media bombard adolescents with messages that can powerfully shape their attitudes and behavior (Strasburger, 1995). Growing, serious criticism has been directed toward television, films, music media, and video games for their preoccupation with violence and sexuality. The portrayal of youth on news programs is almost uniformly negative, focusing on acts of violence, crime, disaffection, and apathy (Wallack, Winett, Dorfman, & Woodruff, 1994).

The undeniable power of the media could be used far more constructively in the lives of young adolescents than is now the case. Families, schools, and youth organizations can help young people become more "media literate" (one communications critic coined the term "crap detectors") so that they can interpret media messages more critically. The active involvement of youth themselves in print and electronic media production can also contribute to their media literacy. Families, schools, and youth organizations can work with media organizations and industry to develop health-promoting programming and media campaigns to encourage healthy practices. And they can work with businesses to support actions that discourage the media from glamorizing violence and sex as well as drinking, smoking, and other drug use.

The negative portrayal of young people in news and other media should be remedied. Young people justifiably feel that they are not well represented for their service and other constructive contributions to their communities.

The arrival of new media technologies is so recent that research has not kept up with their potential impact, immediate or long-term, on children and adolescents. Cross-national, longitudinal studies, similar to those conducted by Huesmann and Eron (1986) on an earlier generation of youth of the television generation, would be highly desirable in this new multimedia age. The effects of prolonged exposure to interactive video games and the Worldwide Web should move beyond speculation to careful studies of the impact of ways such exposure to technology may affect how young people process information, as well their effects on attitudes toward violence and human relationships during adolescence and beyond.

INVESTING IN OUR FUTURE: CHALLENGES FOR RESEARCHERS

In all major reports of the Carnegie Council on Adolescent Development, we drew heavily from the rich findings generated by researchers. *Great Transitions* represents an effort to integrate fundamental research on the second decade of life with the design of approaches to foster the optimal development of all adolescents. The report reflects the Carnegie Council's founding aspiration to synthesize available knowledge about adolescents (Feldman & Elliott, 1990; Millstein, Petersen, & Nightingale, 1993) and to use that knowledge to inform the formation of policies and programs that shape the life chances of every young person.

But the Council went beyond its synthesis function to identifying research opportunities in adolescent development and health and even further in actively disseminating these opportunities to public and private funding sources. Thus, the Council contributed to creating new knowledge about adolescent development by convening a regular series of research symposia for funders and offering cogent syntheses that aided in the development of agendas of federal research support agencies.

The collaborative study undertaken by the Carnegie Council on Adolescent Development and the former U.S. Congress Office of Technology

Assessment (OTA) on adolescent health is also worth noting (U.S. Congress OTA, 1991a, 1991b, 1991c). As part of that study, the OTA documented the relatively low level of federal research support on the development and health of adolescents, which led to joint National Institutes of Health research initiatives on the promotion of adolescent health. Partially as a result of all of the Council's science policy activities and the wide ranging OTA study, a 5-year, nationally representative, and comprehensive study of American adolescents (ADD Health) is now in progress. This potentially landmark study, as well as other public and private efforts, are bound to yield new insights about a fascinating and complex period in the lifespan.

As we worked on *Great Transitions,* we came across several significant gaps in knowledge about the development of adolescents that could have strengthened the Council's concluding report. These gaps include understanding the biological bases of adolescence, economic factors in adolescent educational and health status, time use studies, and a continuing lack of rigorous evaluation studies of preventive interventions for adolescents.

Biological Aspects of Adolescence

Given the advances in the behavioral aspects of the study of adolescent development, a major frontier lies ahead in connecting knowledge about behavioral development (especially cognitive, social, and emotional) with biological development during the second decade of life. As one example, although the primary attribution for adolescent behavior is their "raging hormones," the scientific basis for this belief remains underexplored. Researchers have begun to examine the interactions of biological, psychosocial, and environmental factors contributing to pubertal development (Paikoff & Brooks-Gunn, 1990), but more research is clearly needed to understand the transactions among hormonal, behavioral, and contextual factors.

The onset of puberty, including possible variations in different ethnic groups and their influences on social and emotional development of adolescents, requires attention. Although puberty is occurring earlier than a century ago, more current data on the factors that contribute to earlier or to later puberty among boys and girls are essential. The findings would clearly challenge current notions that adolescence begins at 13 and may enable researchers to address the question of why several adolescent problems are occurring at earlier ages than in the past.

An exciting area for future investigation is brain development during adolescence, which clearly lags behind understanding such development during the earliest years of life (Chugani, 1993). There is noteworthy "pruning" of the neuronal structures of the brain during early adolescence, but almost nothing is known about the factors and processes involved (J. Gied, personal communication, 1995) and their relation to crucial cognitive outcomes, such as increased competence in abstract reasoning, problem-solving, and decision making that emerges during adolescence. The brain–behavior nexus during the adolescent period could be one of the new frontiers of research in the developmental neurosciences (Fischer & Rose, 1994).

Economic Factors in Adolescent Development

Although samples of adolescents are more varied than in the past, major gaps persist. African American, Latino, American Indian, Pacific Islanders, and some ethnic groups of Asian Americans are disproportionately living in poverty compared to European American adolescents. Yet, current reporting of national statistics does not permit the separation of economic from racial and ethnic factors in looking at health and educational indicators among adolescents. Would, for example, comparable economic resources lead to similar outcomes regardless of racial and ethnic backgrounds of adolescents? There is evidence to suggest that when socioeconomic background is controlled, Latino adolescents are no more likely to drop out of schools than European American students (Rumberger, 1995). Information along these lines could have powerful implications for social policies. One effort to address this gap is the "oversampling" strategy of the ADD Health study to include African American adolescents from middle class families in this nationally representative study of American adolescents.

The growing income disparity among American workers presents new issues in examining the contribution of the economic resources of families to adolescent outcomes. Although the educational attainment of parents has been strongly associated with economic status of families, such a relation may not continue to hold in certain subgroups. At the minimum, national education and health statistics should report indicators based on economic circumstances and on racial and ethnic group membership of adolescents (U.S. Congress OTA, 1991a, 1991b, 1991c).

Time Use Studies on Families and Adolescents

How American adolescents spend their time is important to understanding how their experiences have changed. Yet the available data are outdated, having been collected in the late 1970s and early 1980s (Timmer, Eccles, & O'Brian, 1985).

It is generally assumed, if not accepted, that American parents are spending less time with their children and even less with their adolescents than they have in the past (Goldstein, 1993). Common sense would tell us that when both parents are working outside the home, when 25% more Americans are working more than one job than in 1985, and when single-parent homes have increased, that American young people have less contact with their parents than in the past.

However, our current understanding is complicated by several factors. American families are smaller than in the past, and presumably parents can spend more time with individual children than in the past when families were larger. Apparently the total time per child may have changed only slightly in European American, two-parent families over the past 50 years (Bryant & Zick, in press). American family structure is itself increasingly diverse, and most of our knowledge is based on European American, middle-class, two-parent families. Information about African American, Latino, Asian Pacific, and American Indian adolescents and their family life, as well as about single-parent households, remains limited.

Given the important roles that families can play in the lives of adolescents, we need better information on how well-documented changes in the structure of American families (Hernandez, 1993) are affecting the amount of time that adolescents in these different family forms are spending with parents, how they are spending this time, and what factors serve to mediate the amount of time that parents spend with their adolescents.

Evaluation of Preventive Interventions

Many good programs for adolescents now exist, but relatively little is known about how and why they work, and documentation of their effects is sparse. At the same time, programs that are ineffective or possibly harmful are allowed to continue. It is virtually a mantra among those involved with preventive interventions that programs rarely receive the systematic evaluation they deserve (Cook, Anson, & Walchi, 1993). Despite the large number of programs aimed at the prevention of adolescent pregnancy, for example, very few of them have been well evaluated and even fewer have been found to be enduring in their preventive effects (Brown & Eisenberg, 1995).

The issue is no longer the technology of evaluation, but why more programs that are well designed and implemented are not evaluated. One solution is for the involvement of outreach universities and colleges, working with program people in communities, around issues of needs assessments, program design, and evaluation (Lerner & Simon, in press). Independent researchers and evaluators from higher education, working collaboratively with community leaders and program staff, should play a more prominent role in generating better information about the effectiveness of programs and how they can be improved and adapted to local conditions and groups. As a result, more innovative and effective programs—informed by research and more responsive to the needs of adolescents—are likely to emerge.

We have touched on some of the areas of research that our work on *Great Transitions* suggested. A broader agenda can be found in the Council's publications (see appendix B of *Great Transitions: Preparing Adolescents for a New Century;* Carnegie Council on Adolescent Development, 1995) and in the field itself.

CONCLUSIONS

The Carnegie Council on Adolescent Development is part of Carnegie Corporation of New York's integrated, birth-through-adolescence strategy to increase every child's chance for a productive adult life. A 1994 Corporation report, *Starting Points: Meeting the Needs of Our Youngest Children* (Carnegie Task Force on Meeting the Needs of Young Children, 1994) focused on the prenatal period through age 3; the Council's work has concentrated on early adolescence, from about 10 through 14 years of age. In 1996, the Corporation's Task Force on the Primary Grades will bridge the gap between ages 3 and 10 with its recommendations for education and healthy development during the early and middle childhood years.

A common thread woven through these and the Carnegie Council's activities is that the developmental needs of children and adolescents can only be met through strong collaboration among pivotal societal institutions such as families, schools, health agencies, community organizations, and the various media. In its decade-long study of adolescent development, the Council concluded that careful examination of the facts, nonpartisan analyses, broad dissemination of information, involvement of leaders in key sectors of the society, and commitment that can be sustained over a number of years are critical ingredients in improving the life chances of young adolescents.

In the past 15 years, scientific inquiry into the biological and psychosocial development of adolescents and the environmental factors affecting them has expanded dramatically. The result has been new ways of understanding the second decade of life and the transition from the childhood years into adolescence. New findings hold great promise for preventing adolescent casualties and for promoting healthy development during adolescence and beyond. However, funds for research on adolescence have been relatively small in comparison to those allocated to other stages in the life span.

As the Council ends its work, it will be the responsibility of researchers in "science-rich" institutions such as higher education and the scientific and professional organizations to sustain what were initial efforts on the part of the Carnegie Council on Adolescent Development to stimulate needed research on adolescents and to encourage the connections among research, program development, and policies.

Researchers must and will continue to do good science, and at the very least they must be more supportive of efforts that take their findings into the realms of practice, policy, and social action than they now are. At the very best, they can be actively engaged through their universities, scientific societies, and in their communities in exploring the implications of their research for the healthy development of adolescents. The growing work of outreach universities (Lerner & Simon, in press) is a prime example of what can be achieved. We firmly believe that such engagement will rebound to the benefit of the sciences relevant to adolescence, young people themselves, and the nation.

ACKNOWLEDGMENTS

Our thanks to Elliott Milhollin for his research assistance and preparation of the reference section of this article.

REFERENCES

The Alan Guttmacher Institute. (1994). *Sex and America's Teenagers*. New York: Author.

Baumeister, R. F., & Leary, M. R. (1995). The need to belong: Desire for interpersonal attachments as a fundamental human motivation. *Psychological Bulletin, 117*, 497–529.

Brown, S., & Eisenberg, L. (Eds.). (1995). *The best intentions: Unintended pregnancy and the well-being of children and families*. Washington, DC: National Academy Press.

Bryant, W. K., & Zick, C. D. (in press). An examination of parent–child shared time. *Journal of Marriage and the Family*.

Carnegie Council on Adolescent Development. (1992). *A matter of time: Risk and opportunity in the nonschool hours*. Washington, DC: Author.

Carnegie Council on Adolescent Development. (1995). *Great transitions: Preparing adolescents for a new century*. Washington, DC: Author.

Carnegie Task Force on Education of Young Adolescents. (1989). *Turning points: Preparing American youth for the twenty-first century*. Washington, DC: Carnegie Council on Adolescent Development.

Carnegie Task Force on Meeting the Needs of Young Children. (1994). *Starting points: Meeting the needs of our youngest children*. New York: Carnegie Corporation of New York.

Christenson, P. G., & Roberts, D. F. (1990). *Popular music in early adolescence*. Washington, DC: Carnegie Council on Adolescent Development.

Chugani, H. (1993). Positron emission tomography scanning in newborns. *Clinics in Perinatology, 20*, 398.

Cook, T. D., Anson, A. R., & Walchi, S. (1993). From causal description to causal explanation: Improving three already good evaluations of adolescent health programs. In S. G. Millstein, A. C. Petersen, & E. O. Nightingale (Eds.), *Promoting the health of adolescents: New directions for the twenty-first century* (pp. 339–374). New York: Oxford University Press.

Day, J. C. (1993). *Population Projections of the United States by Age, Sex, Race, and Hispanic Origin: 1993–2050* (U.S. Bureau of the Census, Current Population Report, pp. 25–1104). Washington, DC: U.S. Government Printing Office.

Donovan, J., & Jessor, S. L. (1985). Structure of problem behavior in adolescence and young adulthood. *Journal of Consulting and Clinical Psychology, 53*, 890–940.

Dryfoos, J. G. (1990). *Adolescents at risk: Prevalence and prevention*. New York: Oxford University Press.

Elliott, D. S. (1993). Health-enhancing and health-compromising lifestyles. In S. G. Millstein, A. C. Petersen, & E. O. Nightingale (Eds.), *Promoting the health of adolescents: New directions for the twenty-first century* (pp. 119–145). New York: Oxford University Press.

Feldman, S. S., & Elliott, G. R. (Eds.). (1990). *At the threshold: The developing adolescent*. Cambridge, MA: Harvard University Press.

Felner, R., Jackson, A., Kasak, D., Mulhall, P., Brand, S., & Flowers, N. (in press). The impact of school reform for the middle years: A longitudinal study of a network engaged in Turning Points-based comprehensive school transformation. In R. Takanishi & D. Hamburg (Eds.), *Preparing adolescents for the 21st century: Challenges facing Europe and the United States*. New York: Cambridge University Press.

Finkelhor, D., & Dziuba-Leatherman, J. (1994). Children as victims of violence: A national survey. *Pediatrics, 94*, 413–420.

Fischer, K. W., & Rose, S. P. (1994). Dynamic development of coordination of components in brain and behavior: A framework for theory and research. In G. Dawson & K. W. Fischer (Eds.), *Human behavior and the developing brain* (pp. 3–66). New York: Guilford.

Goldstein, N. (1993, January). *Are changes in work and family harming children?* Background paper prepared for the Task Force on Meeting the Needs of Young Children, Carnegie Corporation of New York.

Haggerty, R. J., Sherrod, L. R., Garmezy, N., & Rutter, M. (1994). *Stress, risk, and resilience in children and adolescents: Process, mechanisms, and interventions*. New York: Cambridge University Press.

Hahn, A. B. (1995). *Quantum Opportunities Program: A brief on the QOP pilot program*. Waltham, MA: Brandeis University, Heller Graduate School, Center for Human Resources.

Hernandez, D. (1993). *America's children: Resources from family, government, and the economy*. New York: Russell Sage Foundation.

Huesmann, L. R., & Eron, L. D. (Eds.). (1986). *Television and the aggressive child: A cross-national comparison*. Hillsdale, NJ: Lawrence Erlbaum Associates, Inc.

Huston, A. C., Donnerstein, E., Fairchild, H., Feshbach, N. D., Katz, P. A., Murray, J. P., Rubinstein, E. A., Wilcox, B. L., & Zuckerman, D. (1992). *Big world, small screen: The role of television in American society*. Lincoln: University of Nebraska Press.

Jessor, R., & Jessor, S. L. (1977). *Problem behavior and psychosocial development: A longitudinal study of youth*. New York: Academic.

Johnson, L. D., O'Malley, P. M., & Bachman, J. G. (1994). *National survey results on drug use from the Monitoring the Future study, 1975–1993.* Rockville, MD: National Institute on Drug Abuse.

Lerner, R. M. (1995). *America's youth in crisis: Challenges and options for programs and policies.* Thousand Oaks, CA: Sage.

Lerner, R. M., & Simon, L. A. K. (Eds.). (in press). *Creating outreach universities for America's youth and families: Building university–community collaboration for the twenty-first century.* New York: Garland.

Louis Harris and Associates, Inc. (1989). *Girl Scouts survey on the beliefs and moral values of America's children.* New York: Girl Scouts of the United States of America.

Millstein, S. G., Petersen, A. C., & Nightingale, E. O. (Eds.). (1993). *Promoting the health of adolescents: New directions for the twenty-first century.* New York: Oxford University Press.

O'Hare, W. P. (1992). America's minorities: The demographics of diversity. *Population Bulletin, 47*(4).

Paikoff, R. L., & Brooks-Gunn, J. (1990). Physiological processes: What role do they play during the transition to adolescence? In R. Montemayor, G. R. Adams, & T. P. Gullotta (Eds.), *From childhood to adolescence: A transitional period?* (pp. 63–81). Newbury Park, CA: Sage.

Princeton Survey Research Associates. (1993). *Newsweek–Children's Defense Fund Poll.* Conducted October 18–November 7, 1993.

Rumberger, R. W. (1995, Fall). Dropping out of middle school: A multilevel analysis of students and schools. *American Educational Research Journal, 32,* 583–625.

Steinberg, L. (1990). Autonomy, conflict, and harmony in the family relationship. In S. S. Feldman & G. R. Elliott (Eds.), *At the threshold: The developing adolescent* (pp. 255–276). Cambridge, MA: Harvard University Press.

Strasburger, V. C. (1995). *Adolescents and the media: Medical and psychological impact.* Newbury Park, CA: Sage.

Suicide among children, adolescents, and young adults—United States, 1980–1992. (1995, April 21). *Morbidity and Mortality Weekly Report, 44*(15).

Timmer, S. G., Eccles, J., & O'Brian, I. (1985). How children use time. In F. T. Juster & F. B. Stafford (Eds.), *Time, goods and well-being.* Ann Arbor: University of Michigan, Institute for Social Research.

U.S. Congress Office of Technology Assessment. (1990). *Indian adolescent mental health.* Washington, DC: U.S. Government Printing Office.

U.S. Congress Office of Technology Assessment. (1991a). *Adolescent health: Vol. 1: Summary and policy options.* Washington, DC: U.S. Government Printing Office.

U.S. Congress Office of Technology Assessment. (1991b). *Adolescent health: Vol. 2: Background and the effectiveness of selected prevention and treatment services.* Washington, DC: U.S. Government Printing Office.

U.S. Congress Office of Technology Assessment. (1991c). *Adolescent health: Vol. 3: Crosscutting issues in the delivery of related services.* Washington, DC: U.S. Government Printing Office.

U.S. Department of Commerce, Bureau of the Census. (1994). *Statistical abstract of the United States: 1994.* Washington, DC: U.S. Government Printing Office.

U.S. Department of Education, Office of Educational Research and Improvement, National Center for Education Statistics. (1990). *A profile of the American eighth grader: NELS: 88 student descriptive summary.* Washington, DC: U.S. Government Printing Office.

U.S. Department of Education, Office of Educational Research and Improvement, National Center for Education Statistics. (1994). *The condition of education, 1994* (NCES 94–149). Washington, DC: U.S. Government Printing Office.

U.S. Department of Education, Office of Educational Research and Improvement, National Center for Education Statistics. (1995, April). *1994 NAEP reading: A first look.* Washington, DC: U.S. Government Printing Office.
U.S. Department of Justice, Bureau of Justice Statistics. (1994). *Criminal victimization in the United States, 1992* (NCJ—145125). Washington, DC: U.S. Government Printing Office.
U.S. General Accounting Office. (1995). *Welfare dependency: Coordinated community efforts can better serve young at-risk teen girls* (GAO/HEHS/RCED–95–108). Washington, DC: Author.
Wallack, L., Winett, L., Dorfman, L., & Woodruff, K. (1994, August). *An analysis of three strikes in California newspapers: September 1993–March 1994.* Paper presented at Media Matters: The Institute on News and Social Problems sponsored by the Benton Foundation at Brandeis University, Waltham, MA.
Werner, E. E., & Smith, R. S. (1992). *Overcoming the odds: High-risk children from birth to adulthood.* Ithaca, NY: Cornell University Press.
Who's Who Among American High School Students. (1995). *A Portrait of a generation: 25 years of teen behavior and attitudes.* Lake Forest, IL: Educational Communications, Inc.
Zill, N., Nord, C. W., & Loomis, L. S. (1995). *Adolescent time use, risky behavior, and outcomes: An analysis of national data.* Rockville, MD: Westat, Inc.

Received January 19, 1996
Accepted March 4, 1996

Journal of Adolescence 1990, **13**, 231–250

Health promotion for adolescents: preventive and corrective strategies against problem behavior

KLAUS HURRELMANN*

This paper, in its first part, gives an overview of research on "problem behavior" in adolescence. Adolescence is considered to be a stage in life characterized by more experimentation, exploration, risk-taking, and rebellion than any other stages. Many health-damaging behaviors (drug consumption, precocious sexual activity, riskful driving, aggressive behavior, etc.) have important psychosocial functions in adolescents' developments. Some of these behaviors can be signals of "stress", defined as a bio-psycho-social state of tension resulting from a variety of stressors which confront adolescents daily in modern industrial societies.

In the second part of the paper, the implications of this research for strategies of intervention are discussed. The systematic analysis distinguishes between different stages in the process by which problem behavior emerges and separates "preventive" from "corrective" forms of intervention. Additionally, the analysis differentiates between the dimensions targeted by the measures: interventions addressed toward individual behavior ("personal resources") on the one hand, and living conditions ("social resources") on the other hand. The resulting types of intervention approaches are illustrated with examples and discussed in view of how appropriate they are for health promotion in adolescence. Implications for "social policy for adolescents" are discussed.

INTRODUCTION

In adolescence, many personal behaviors contribute to morbidity and mortality: smoking, heavy drinking, using illegal drugs, precocious and unprotected sexual activity, no regular participation in sports and exercise, riskful driving, aggressive and other forms of behavior that Richard Jessor (1984) has called "problem behavior". Adolescence, obviously, is a stage in the life span characterized by more experimentation and exploration, risk-taking and rebellion than is the case in other stages. Although experimentation with health risks is normal in adolescence, parents, teachers, and youth

* Reprint requests should be addressed to Klaus Hurrelmann, Research Center "Prevention and Intervention in Childhood and Adolescence", University of Bielefeld, POB 8640, D-4800 Bielefeld, FRG.

0140–1971/90/030231 + 20 $03.00/0

workers are challenged to safeguard such experimentation from irretrievable consequences that can alter the direction and compromise the quality of adolescents' lives.

As Richard Jessor (1989) in his plenary address to the World Health Organisation, in May 1989, has pointed out, adolescence is a key lifestage for the shaping of health in adulthood and in later life. At the same time, adolescence is in itself a stage of high risk for morbidity and mortality. Poverty, ubanization, rapid social change, and the decline of traditional social supports and controls have exacerbated such health risks in several subgroups of the adolescent population of various countries, both industrialized and non-industrialized. Consequently, to change personal behaviors from health-damaging to health-promoting ones is a main target of intervention strategies. Traditionally, this has been done by providing information, education and counseling programs. However, the limits of this approach are clearly to be seen: they do not take into account the social and psychological motivations and functions of health-damaging behavior, because they neglect the social context of the behavior. Therefore, we have to rethink the concept of "health education" and include it into the more comprehensive approach of "health promotion" for adolescents.

HEALTH BEHAVIOR IN ADOLESCENCE

In recent interdisciplinary research, health is used as a comprehensive term, defining a physical and mental state in which an individual is capable of processing inner and outer reality in a productive and satisfying manner. This concept follows modern theoretical approaches to human development that are based on the assumption that social (environmental), psychological (personal) and biological (somatic) factors jointly affect the formation of personality. Socialization is understood as the process of the emergence, formation, and development of the human personality in dependence on and in interaction with the human organism on the one hand, and the social and material environment on the other (Featherman and Lerner, 1985).

The notion of the "healthy personality"

According to this concept, a healthy personality does not form independently from society in any of its functions or dimensions but is continually shaped in a concrete, historically conveyed lifeworld throughout the entire length of the life span. The lifelong interplay between biological, psychological, and cultural/societal potentials and constraints determines the individual's state of health. In contrast to the viewpoint in medicine, the comprehensive definition of health proclaimed here emphasizes the integration of well-being into all of the dimensions of daily life. Self-responsible behavior and self-regulation are regarded as essential factors in the development of a healthy personality. Thus, health-conscious and health-promoting lifestyles can only be expected when the prerequisites for such factors are available. Health, therefore, is both a personal and a collective variable:

> *"Health describes the objective and subjective state of well-being that is present when the physical, psychological, and social development of a person is in harmony with his/her own possibilities, goals, and prevailing living conditions. Health is impaired when demands that arise in one or more of these areas cannot be coped with by the person in his/her respective stage of life. The impairment may be manifest in symptoms of social deviance, psychological disorder, or physical-physiological disease" (Hurrelmann, 1989, p. 5).*

Thus, health is composed of physical, psychological, and social aspects which influence each other reciprocally. Health is closely connected to individual and collective value systems and behavior patterns which are manifest in personal lifestyles. It is a state of equilibrium which must be continuously maintained during the life course. It is not a state of well-being that is passively experienced, as suggested by the purely physical definition within classical medicine: instead, it is the result of actively pursuing the establishment and maintenance of a social, psychological, and physical capacity for action. Social, economic, ecological, and cultural living conditions thereby form the framework with which the potential for health can develop.

According to this concept, *the state of health reflects the subjective processing of and coping with physiological, psychological, and social conditions*. Health is only possible when a person is able to establish constructive social relationships, is socially integrated, able to adapt his/her individual lifestyle to the changing aspects of the environment and thereby secure personal self-regulation, and act in accordance with the prevailing biogenetic, physiological and physical capacities. The modern theoretical approaches in social medicine, social psychology, social pediatrics, social pedagogy, social epidemiology, and medical psychology stress the interdependency of human development on the one hand, and the development of the social and physical environment on the other. The criterion of a "healthy" development is seen in the acquisition of social, psychological, and physical competencies which enable individuals to act adequately and develop an identity of their own, at the same time taking into account their needs and personality structures. The theoretical foundations of these approaches have been developed, among others, by Engel (1962), Levi (1971), Bronfenbrenner (1979), and Matarazzo, Weiss, Herd, Miller and Weiss (1984).

Psychosocial functions of health behavior

Modern youth research is increasingly making use of these theoretical models (Hurrelmann, 1989, p. 35). Health-enhancing as well as health-damaging behaviors in adolescence are seen as part of the process of solving developmental tasks. Thus, risk behavior is a behavior that has to be understood as being functional: that is, it is instrumental, purposeful and goal-directed (Jessor, 1984). "Problem behaviors" such as cigarette smoking, getting drunk, engaging in unprotected intercourse, unhealthy eating habits, risk-taking activities, and illicit drug use can fulfil important functions for a young person, even though they are likely to compromise that young person's health:

> *"In this way, behavioral risk factors are different from other kinds of risk factors—they can have positive as well as negative consequences. Health-compromising behaviors such as cigarette smoking, although placing the adolescent at risk for lung and heart disease, may simultaneously enable that adolescent to attain important positive satisfactions such as being accepted by the peer group, or just feeling more grown up. Other functions that adolescent health-risk behaviors may serve have emerged from a great deal of research: engaging in risk behaviors, e.g. using illicit drugs, can be a means of expressing opposition to adult authority and conventional society; heavy alcohol use can be a coping mechanism for dealing with frustration and anxiety; risky driving or drinking and driving can affirm an important personal identity such as being "macho" or cool; and risk behaviors can be a way of attaining independence from parental authority and taking personal control of one's own life, e.g., by initiating sexual intercourse or by early childbearing" (Jessor, 1989, p. 3).*

Those patterns of behavior that can be considered as "problem behavior" are chosen because, in a specific social and personal situation, they provide a way of defining a public image and achieving social status. In many cases, they have their social context in the peer group, which is one of the most important reference groups in adolescence:

> *"According to problem behavior theory, vulnerability to peer pressure and the risk of substance abuse would be greater for adolescents who have fewer effective coping strategies in their repertoire, fewer skills for handling social situations, and greater anxiety about social stituations. For these adolescents, the range of options for achieving personal goals would be restricted at the same time that discomfort in interpersonal situations was high, motivating them to take whatever actions they thought might be reasonable coping responses" (Botvin and Dusenbury, 1989, p. 8).*

In other words: *problem behaviors, in this respect, are signals of "stress", of a bio-psycho-social state of tension resulting from a variety of stressful "developmental tasks"* (Coleman, 1989), which confront adolescents daily in peer group, family, school, and work. Problem behavior emerges as soon as the personal as well as social resources are insufficiently developed in an adolescent's life setting in terms of structure and profile. If the preconditions and foundations needed for self-efficacious and self-regulated behavior are lacking, the probability increases that physiologically, psychologically, and socially problematic forms of behavior will develop (Garmezy and Rutter, 1983; Peterson and Ebata, 1989).

Whether or not specific constellations or stressful situations, events, and life situations (e.g., strain at school, difficulties in establishing peer-group relations, problematic school-to-work transition) lead to problem behavior depends first and foremost on the adolescent's *specific skills and abilities to cope with stressors*. For example, if a discrepancy is perceived between action competencies and actions to be performed, the adolescent has to mobilize strategies to overcome the former. These strategies can be developed if and when there is the ability and readiness on the part of the adolescent to realistically perceive and assess his or her own action competencies and to identify as precisely as possible in which areas a discrepancy exists in relation to the competencies required. Following this diagnosis, in order to eliminate the discrepancy, strategies that are adequate to the situation then have to be implemented to correct and control individual action competencies on the one hand, and the situational demands for action on the other.

The possibilities and patterns of constructing strategies for coping behavior are influenced, directly and indirectly, by the *social and material living conditions*. Social resources are important moderating factors that determine whether or not stress leads to problem behavior. These social resources can be defined in terms of the potential material, financial, informational, instrumental, emotional, cultural, and social stimuli, as well as support by the environment to the individual in a specific life situation (Thoits, 1983).

This theoretical interpretation is supported by the results of the *Bielefeld Study on Adolescence*, which demonstrates that the main risk factors for drug, alcohol, and tobacco consumption and aggressive behavior, for example, are to be seen in (a) parents' unfulfilled expectations of the adolescent's school performance, (b) strong subjective strain due to scholastic demands, (c) experiences of failure in school, (d) difficulties in achieving recognition and integration into the peer group, and (e) relative material disadvantage in comparison with friends and peers. The occurrence of one or more of these risk factors correlates with a high probability that problem behaviors of the type mentioned will emerge (Engel, Nordlohne, Hurrelmann and Holler, 1987; Hurrelmann, Engel, Holler and Nordlohne, 1988; Hurrelmann and Engel, 1989*a*).

In our study, aggressive delinquent behavior and drug consumption are strongly associated with difficulties in the process of integration into peer groups. If adolescents are not successful in achieving an appropriate degree of acceptance from the peer group, and in establishing an undisputed social position within this group, and if they suffer from lack of popularity and recognition among their peers, a considerable insecurity in their social orientation and self-esteem results. Appearing to be at a disadvantage and to not be able to keep up with the peer group's material (financial) standards serves as a decisive factor in the establishment of these types of problem behaviors. The strain and demands on adolescents in this respect are particularly high when emotional tensions with parents conflict with the peer group's lifestyle. Those adolescents who report having conflicts with their parents in various areas of life are also those who have the highest risk of manifesting aggressive behavior and drug use (Engel and Hurrelmann, 1989).

Results of this type are supported by several *other research groups* (Jessor and Jessor, 1977; Bachman, O'Malley and Johnston, 1982; Siddique and D'Arcy, 1984; Butler and Corner, 1984; Elliot, Huizinga and Ageton, 1985; Irwin and Millstein, 1986; Mechanic and Hansell, 1988). They show the importance of applying a comprehensive theoretical approach to explain problem behavior in adolescence. Many research results show agreement that problem behaviors have to be conceptualized as a syndrome (Botvin and Dusenbury, 1989), because there are consistently strong intercorrelations between different types of substance use (e.g., smoking, drinking, and drug use) and between different types of health compromising behaviors (e.g, substance use and precocious sexual behavior). These behaviors also correlate with indices of psychosocial risk, including environmental and personality variables such as: more friends' models for deviant behavior, greater attitudinal tolerance for problem behavior, and independence being valued more highly than academic recognition; again this suggests a common underlying cause (Jessor, 1984). These results point to the fact that substance users differ from non-users on several behavioral dimensions, suggesting an underlying difference in values and ambition. For instance, individuals who use psychoactive substances are more likely than non-users to have poorer academic performance and engage in antisocial behavior, and are less likely to participate in organized extracurricular activities (e.g., sports or clubs).

> *"These studies suggest that diverse health behaviors are influenced more by general styles of adaption that underlie daily routines and are socially and culturally rewarding than by specific motivations to be healthy. Much of the behavior associated with good health is integrated into complex behavioral repertoires that are sustained by interlocking networks of reinforcements. Smoking, alcohol use, exercise, and many other health-related behaviors are components of pervasive cultural patterns associated with religious and moral*

orientations, educational levels, and the values and expectations of particular subgroups in the population" (Hansell and Mechanic, 1990, p. 78).

Thus, we face a complex set of factors which turn adolescence into a specific high-risk stage of life for health. In adolescence, the balance between health-compromising and health-enhancing activities is at stake. As Jessor has pointed out, the risk to health of engaging in health-compromising behaviors should probably be seen as a variable; at the same time its magnitude will often depend on the extent, the variety, and the intensity of the health-enhancing behavior engaged in by the adolescent:

> *"Health risk in adolescence can refer to risk that is immediately consequential within adolescence (e.g., the risk from driving after consuming alcoholic beverages); to risk that has consequences for the post-adolescent period—that is, for adulthood and later life (e.g., the risk from obesity, or from a diet high in saturated fats); or to risks that include both present and remote consequences (e.g, the risk from becoming pregnant). It can refer to risk deriving from behavior (e.g., from cigarette smoking or from not using seat belts); to risk deriving from personality characteristics (e.g., risk from the sense of powerlessness or from having a strong need for independence and rebelliousness); to risk related to aspects of the environment (e.g, the risk from contracting a sexually transmitted disease or from having adolescent hypertension); or to variable risks that depend for their consequences on the presence of certain situational factors (e.g., the risk from using marijuana just before driving), on gender (the risk from heavy drinking when pregnant), or on age (e.g, the risk from insufficient hours of sleep in early adolescence)" (Jessor, 1984).*

GENERAL IMPLICATIONS FOR STRATEGIES OF INTERVENTION

Measures carried out by public or private institutions, organizations, and associations are generally subsumed under the term "intervention". As the discussion of research results in the previous section has shown, it is very important to distinguish between different stages in the emergence and development of symptoms of problem behavior which demand different intervention approaches. Therefore, in the following, I will roughly distinguish between two stages of intervention: intervention that attempts to prevent potential disorders in the (health) development of personality ("preventive or prophylactic intervention"), and the intervention that aims to reduce and if possible remove disorders already manifest ("postventive or corrective intervention").

The term *preventive intervention* is used to describe measures which are implemented before any symptoms of problem behavior are manifest. The aim is to avoid the personal and social conditions which are known to lead to behavioral problems in adolescence. In this sense, they are anticipatory or "preventive" in the strictest sense of the word.

In contrast, the term *corrective intervention* is used to describe measures which are employed after symptoms of stress are already manifest. In an attempt to strictly discriminate these measures from those of preventive intervention, the term "postventive intervention" could also be used. Corrective intervention, being directed toward problem behavior which is already manifest, uses appropriate measures in an attempt to check and reverse this behavior. Corrective intervention includes those measures which concentrate on preventing a consolidation and increase in problem behavior. Primarily, the aim is to reduce the consequences of problem behavior and its damaging side-effects in other areas of activity, as these can result in a "vicious circle" and in the establishment of a "social career" of deviance.

The terminology chosen here is given preference over the terms "primary, secondary, and tertiary prevention" used in medicine (Caplan and Grunebaum, 1967), because it avoids an inappropriate inflationary use of the term "prevention". However, distinct connections to medical terminology are apparent which are indicative of a common concept, inasmuch as measures are classified and defined according to their point of application in the process whereby problem behavior is manifest.

Besides this differentiation between the stages in the process by which disorders and deviance emerge and develop, we can also differentiate between the effective dimensions targeted by the measures. This "target of intervention" can be divided into personal and social resources.

The intervention is addressed toward the *personal resources* when the individual is the target of the activities, and where, for example, attitudes, behavior, action competence, and habits are to be influenced and modified. The intervention is directed toward *social resources* when ecological, material, and environmental factors are to be influenced. In this case too, the aim is to have a repercussive effect on the behavior of the individual (Hurrelmann, 1987; 1988).

The acknowledgement given to interventions directed toward social resources has been completely unsatisfying in recent years. Most intervention activities have been focused directly on the individual behavior of adolescents, thereby neglecting the psychosocial functions of this behavior and its contextual relations. What we need, however, is a coordinated application of all the above-mentioned types of intervention if they are to be effective against health-impairing problem behavior. Interventions have to encourage and strengthen individual *and* social resources. In respect to individual resources, the emphasis is on *promoting competence;* in respect to social resources, the emphasis is on the *promotion of networks*. Intervention measures must be directed toward both poles of this relationship; they cannot be restricted to changing individual factors alone. Having arisen in a social context—that of a concrete social and ecological environment—the individual's capacity for action and coping can only be influenced and modified within this context. Such a context must be made the object of health-promotion policies for adolescents if these are to have a lasting effect (Heller and Swindle, 1983).

If intervention concentrates only on the adolescent's individual attempts to cope with developmental tasks and thereby avoids contact with the social basis of these attempts, it must remain ineffective or, at best, result in symptom displacement: the adolescent who drinks alcohol or smokes to relieve stress recognizes that such behavior results in impairments to health; as a consequence, he/she may possibly shift the conflict mechanism, become aggressive or depressive, acquire unhealthy eating habits, or seek refuge in other such behaviors that lead to long-term health impairments (Silbereisen, Eyferth and Rudiger, 1986).

Promotion of individual competency and social resources must be viewed together, because as has been shown health depends on biological, psychological, socioeconomic, and natural living conditions, and on genetic disposition. Promoting personal and social resources entails endowing all adolescents with a greater degree of autonomy in organizing their living conditions, thereby enabling them to contribute toward their own health. In order to achieve a comprehensive sense of physical, mental, and social well-being, it is necessary for adolescents to be able to satisfy their needs, to recognize and achieve their hopes and dreams, and to deal with and modify their environment in a productive manner (Hurrelmann and Engel, 1989*b*).

PROMOTING COMPETENCE AND PROMOTING NETWORKS IN ADOLESCENCE

It is the aim of the following discussion to assess the limits and potentials of the different measures, to evaluate their advantages and disadvantages, and to give each measure its appropriate place in the overall ensemble of possible intervention strategies.

By referring to the categorical discussion above, we can differentiate four *"ideal types" of measures of intervention* (see Figure 1).

We now look at these four types of measures in detail.

A-type measures: training individual competency

Education, and particularly *health education*, being widely available, is a predominant mode of strengthening personal resources. Within industrial societies, the most important institutions for offering education are families, preschool facilities, schools, vocational training schemes, and institutions of higher education and training. The term "health education" denotes the consciously planned, directive influence on individual personality development by means of another individual who is usually more knowledgeable and competent. In conveying knowledge, attitudes and skills by systematically initiating learning steps, health education aims at positively influencing the personality development of the recipient, strengthening his/her behavioral competency in various dimensions, and encouraging an autonomous process of acquisition by which an individual can have access to and adopt this competency.

To give an example: the most widely used approach to *drug abuse prevention* over the years has been one which relies on the dissemination of factual information stressing the adverse consequences of substance use. Some approaches have attempted to emphasize and even to dramatize the risk associated with tobacco, alcohol, and drug use. The underlying assumption is that evoking fear should be more effective than an objective presentation of factual information. Other programs attack the problem of drug use from a moral perspective (Botvin, 1986).

All approaches of these types only have a limited success, because they only

	Target dimension	
Stages	Personal resources (individual behavior)	Social resources (living conditions)
Preventive	*A-type measures:* Training individual competency — Health education — Personal and social skills training — Scholastic competence training — Counseling	*C-type measures:* Improving social living conditions — Improving the opportunity structure — Creating possibilities for participation
Corrective	*B-type measures:* Systematic behavior modification — Treatment — Therapy	*D-type measures:* Constructing support networks — (Re-)Construction of social networks

Figure 1. Examples for health-promoting intervention strategies in adolescence.

affect adolescents with a specific attitudinal structure and in other adolescents may even arouse curiosity. Therefore, recently, programs focusing on resistance skills and/or on personal and social life skills have been developed that pay primary attention to the psychosocial factors promoting substance use initiation:

> *"The primary distinguishing feature of these approaches is that they typically include two or more of the following components: (1) general problem-solving and decision-making skills (e.g., brainstorming, systematic decision-making techniques); (2) general cognitive skills for resisting interpersonal or media influences (e.g., identifying persuasive advertising appeals, formulating counterarguments); (3) skills for increasing self-control and self-esteem (e.g., self-instruction, self-reinforcement, goal-setting, principles of self-change); (4) adaptive coping strategies for relieving stress and anxiety through the use of cognitive coping skills or behavioral relaxation techniques; (5) general interpersonal skills (e.g., initiating social interactions, complimenting, conversational skills); and (6) general assertive skills (e.g, making requests, saying "no", expressing feeling and opinions). These skills are generally taught by using a combination of instruction, demonstration, feedback, reinforcement, behavioral rehearsal (practice during class), and extended behavioral homework assignments" (Botvin and Dusenbury, 1989, p. 26).*

These programs take into account that drug use is woven into a fabric of daily coping strategies. Accordingly, these measures are aimed directly at the psychosocial function that drugs have for adolescents. The aim is to offer direct help in establishing appropriate capabilities for coping with complicated and stressful life events and day-to-day situations. In order to be ultimately effective, however, it is imperative that functionally equivalent activities can be introduced; that is, behavior that is just as attractive and that receives as much attention as drug use, and which adolescents can accept as a consciously sought alternative with which to avoid drugs and their consequences and side-effects for health (Perry and Jessor, 1985). In this respect, these programs have to be complemented with measures of type C.

Other measures of type A will only be described briefly:

(a) The results of the studies mentioned above have shown that many symptoms of health impairment are closely related to scholastic performance. Improving student performance in school through appropriate *scholastic training* can result in greater achievement and thereby neutralize an important cause of problem behavior. For this reason, advancement of social, intellectual, emotional, cultural, and psychomotoric competency within scholastic instruction is one of the most important intervention measures which can be applied within the context of school (Engel and Hurrelmann, 1989).

(b) In addition to conveying scholastic knowledge and health skills through instruction, *counseling* plays a key role in promoting competency. In theory, this type of intervention is based on the principle of respecting and strengthening adolescents' autonomous behavior and self-esteem. The recipients are regarded as active subjects who possess the potential for goal-oriented, constructive actions. They are viewed as self-responsible people, who, in principle, possess the capability and the will to make rational decisions. Counseling offers temporary help in unravelling and coping with stressful situations in cases where adolescents are in difficulty as a result of lacking the full capacity to deal with their problems. The counselor must possess enough professional competence to give "help for self-help"; that is, to enable the individual to rediscover and redevelop capabilities which have been retarded or weakened (Ingersoll and Orr, 1988).

B-type measures: systematic behavior modification

Various *therapeutic methods* using different psychological, psychiatric or medical treatments, can be included within the area of corrective intervention aiming at personal behavior. The central aim of therapy is to instigate and structure a process by which habitual and long-lasting problem behaviors are recognized as being inadequate coping strategies which are to be reduced or made superfluous. Within therapy a treatment situation is required in which verbal and other symbolic exchanges governed by rules are utilized and, as a consequence, the usual behavior patterns of daily life are suspended.

In order to modify and "correct" the behavior of adolescents, the therapist has to view the client as an independent and self-responsible partner to whom support can be given in his/her attempts to better achieve his/her goals. Insight is encouraged in the client, by which more understanding can be gained within a process of increasing self-knowledge and self-control. Such insight must augment existing coping potentials within subjective theories of day-to-day living. Accordingly, in a mutual effort to reach agreement in assessing potential solutions, therapist and client have to undertake a combined search for the most suitable solutions to particular problems.

Systematic behavior modification is a means of precise and systematic corrective influence, mainly with respect to aggressive and delinquent behavior. By giving instant feedback, an attempt is made to divert students from undesirable behavior which is classified as deviant and to reward them for desirable behavior which conforms to the rules maintained in school, neighborhood and work. It is imperative that intensive training and further education be offered to teachers and professional personnel with knowledge of behavior modification techniques for dealing with aggression and violence. The stronger the concepts of therapy are connected with school instruction and social norms of behavior, the more effective they are. That is why such measures have been successful which constitute a direct control and reward of improved behavior during instruction (Felner, Jason, Mortisugu and Farber, 1983; Jason, Durlak and Holton-Walker, 1984).

B-type measures are widespread in the field of adolescent intervention strategies. Usually, they are based on solid scientific and practical knowledge and expertise. However, with the growing expansion of severe forms of problem behavior, the *social* and, above all, the *financial limits of this type of intervention* become obvious. Therefore, we have to strengthen preventive strategies which promise to effectively reduce the number of adolescents with severe manifestations of problem behavior.

C-type measures: improving social living conditions

As we have seen, adolescents find it difficult to adopt healthy behaviors because their physical and social environments contain many obstacles to engaging in health-promoting activities. Therefore, we have to recognize the important roles that physical and social environments play in shaping both personal behavior and the health status. Some environmental factors even encourage health-damaging behaviors (for example advertisements for cigarettes). In addition to targeting the individual's behavior, intervention programs have to address the immediate environment that reinforces health-related behaviors. Thus, they may help adolescents to create an environment that enables them to engage in health-promoting actions.

Preventive measures which are oriented toward the social and ecological environment act on the knowledge that adolescents must be offered a variety of opportunities for development in order to refrain from problem behavior. The basis for such measures lies in the areas of schooling and vocation: adolescents must be given *appropriate opportunity structures* to express and present themselves as individuals, to put thoughts and ideas into practice, and to have a chance to earn their living. The most important step is to create possibilities for adolescent employment and to tackle the high levels of unemployment. Even in our so-called "leisure society", self-concept and prestige are essentially determined by one's occupation. Society places adolescents in enormous difficulties by not being able to guarantee training or employment on completion of school. It thereby destroys the necessary amount of confidence in the future, which adolescents are dependent on during this phase of life (Baethge, 1989). Intervention measures of this preventive type, therefore, have very clear overall political implications and are themselves of a *political* nature. They touch upon the entire social make-up of life opportunities in adolescence.

Specific approaches which are oriented toward *school* include such factors as the quality of instruction, the social relationships between teachers and students, and means of regulating social conflicts. Here we are referring to (a) the quality of the curriculum and its suitability for the students' scholastic standing and motivation, and (b) appropriate performance demands and standards of assessment which are transparent and understandable. Such measures can only be implemented when there is agreement among the teaching staff in respect of pedagogical and social-educative principles within the curricular and extra-curricular activities. The prerequisite for such unity is a systematically organized school structure with clear decision-making processes based on democratic principles.

The establishment and continual improvement of distinct rules of assessing students' scholastic potential and scholastic performance is of fundamental importance. These measures of assessment must contain clear rules regarding punishment and reward within areas of scholastic achievement which are objective, fair, and predictable, and which offer each student, including those with unusual performance and behavior, a chance to gain recognition and acceptance. The school must offer a clear opportunity structure for individual development and ensure that teachers make allowances for the individual wishes and interests of the students—to the extent that this is possible with scholastic means.

The school must do everything to ensure that it is viewed by the students as a "just community". By doing so, it can serve as an exemplary model for future areas of experience in occupation and in adulthood. In school, students experience the elementary rules of society in respect to achievement and the evaluation of their behavior according to particular standards. If such assessments and their consequences are regarded by the students as being consistent and transparent, they can be an important factor in stifling the emergence of problem behaviors at the source (McPartland and McDill, 1977).

Additionally, a broad *participation* of adolescents in organizing and carrying out events proves to be a possibility for increasing identification with the cultural institutions important for adolescents and of reducing feelings of estrangement toward them. Such measures prove particularly effective when the situation within the institutions (schools, working places, youth centers, etc) is open to political influence, whereby the possibility of a personal relationship with the structures of day-to-day life can be established. For measures of this preventive type to be effective, it is important that the entire social environment be incorporated in such a way that the measures are introduced within the context of the adolescent's or adult's familial, scholastic/occupation, and other social relationships. Educational, occupational, and community policy for adolescents must find answers to the question of how the desires for independence, intensive experiences, companionship, self-knowledge, accomplishment, and self-confidence can be satisfied. Adolescents seek possibilities for participation which extend beyond the boundaries set by the official institutions of socialization. Health-promoting measures must attempt to allow for social structures which support adolescents in their efforts to find an individual lifestyle (Donovan and Jessor, 1985). The aim is to provide adolescents with *interesting, stimulating and satisfying real-life experiences* that are more appealing than problem behaviors; thus, involvement in these activities (entertainment, sports, experiential learning, etc) could actually take the place of the involvement with the problem behavior.

D-type measures: constructing support networks

In a corrective perspective, too, we have to be aware of the great importance of the social context and structure of social relationships in coping with problem behavior. In recent years the promotion of social networks within the family, neighborhood, school, and employment situations, and their relationship to formal and informal health care, has increasingly become a subject of discussion. Viewed in terms of socioepidemiology and social hygiene, the goal of corrective intervention is to *eliminate environmental risk factors*, and to strengthen factors which are conducive to competent behavior and good health. The more an adolescent is bound into a favorable social network of relationships, the more he/she is able to deal with unfavorable living conditions, critical life events, and long-term stressors, and the less prone he/she is to resort to problem behavior. The social network can be seen to function as an aid in coping with problems (Kessler, Price and Wortman, 1985; Garbarino, Schellenbach and Sebes, 1986).

The rationale of these measures can be formulated as follows: if adolescents have already been drawn into the vicious circle of peer-group dynamic processes leading to problem behavior, an attempt must be made to "lever" them out of this circle by *making new offers of social relationships and of membership in groups*. The goals thereby are as follows (Gottlieb, 1981):

1. To strengthen the already existing support systems within the social environment and to incorporate the respective reference persons as "natural counselors" into the helping process;
2. To construct alternative networks in cases where it is not possible or expedient to work with the natural networks;
3. To establish institutions of youth counseling which serve as a meeting point and contact address within the relationship network of adolescents with problems; and

4. To carry out the counseling process within the adolescent's natural surroundings.

In *school*, for example, efforts must be aimed at gradually reducing contacts to delinquent subgroups and at replacing them with stable and satisfying contacts to other peers, thereby availing the adolescents of new possibilities of social development. In this context, tutor programs could be utilized, inasmuch as establishing contact to older adolescents provides for positive reference people. In this area, the school and the teachers must be given substantial support by trained personnel recruited from counseling centers and youth work.

In the area of adolescent *leisure activities*, situations must be created which offer adolescents experiences and encounters which distract them from the temptations of consumerism and which dissuade them from participating in deviant group behavior. Adolescents today have access to many social and material possibilities but, at the same time, they lack real challenges and means of satisfying their interests and needs due to the superficial satisfaction offered by present-day mass media and a consumer-oriented society. Such fulfilment often entails a false sense of adventure and experience; there exists a lack of real challenges and personal experiences which enable a young person to utilize his/her physical prowess and mental and social competence.

Situations are lacking in which non-commercial, unorganized, unsupervised, and "non-pedagogical" activities can take place which enable adolescents to test their potential and limitations, and in which they are free to "experiment" with the limits set by laws and conventions without fear of inappropriate sanctions. Our highly organized and structured environment leaves little room for such "free space". Herein lies a great challenge to youth work and youth support; an attempt must be made to "artificially" recreate such free spaces. In other words, social resources must be created which stimulate and support a healthy development of personality, and which have ceased to exist as a result of the organization of daily life that is typical of industrial societies.

CONCLUSION

Adolescence, as a stage in the life course characterized by specific forms of problem behavior, needs appropriate answers in terms of intervention measures. As has been shown, it is important to distinguish between different stages and targets of intervention in order not to overtax the effectiveness of the various measures. It is necessary to shift the emphasis from the highly elaborated, traditional, person-oriented measures to the underdeveloped measures concentrating on social structures as resources for coping with problem behavior.

As Ingersoll and Orr (1988) have properly stated, usually there is no single cause and no well-defined pattern of adolescent problem behavior, and consequently, neither is there a single intervention strategy appropriate to all who display problem behaviors. Nevertheless, our understanding of adolescent development can guide us in designing appropriate interventions:

> *"One must identify, to the extent possible, the underlying basis for the at-risk behavior and determine whether it represents a normative process, a psychopathology, or misguided attempts to meet psychosocial needs. Given the assessment, the appropriate intervention might be education with help in resisting peer pressure, psychological evaluation and therapy, or providing a substitute behavior. The linked nature of many risk behaviors suggests that categorical interventions limited to only one component of a series of problem behaviors and ignoring the others will be unsuccessful . . . Whatever the format, intervention must be matched to the adolescent's developmental needs. Mismatching the intervention environment and developmental traits will result in treatment failure and further diminish the already low feelings of personal adequacy in the at-risk adolescent" (Ingersoll and Orr, 1988, p. 6).*

For interventions to be effective it is important to encourage individual responsibility, to activate adolescents' involvement in the planning and impementation of the program, to encourage peer support and to recruit an adult staff whose approach to adolescents is open, supportive, and non-judgmental. Health promotion is clearly an interdisciplinary concept for intervention strategies that include the fields of medicine, biology, epidemiology, psychology, psychiatry, sociology, and education. As yet, no integrated system of health promotion exists that incorporates health education, "social hygiene", health counseling, therapy, and networking. Instead, these fields of practical work are divided into numerous areas. It is an urgent future task that the various activities be brought together. As a first step, community-based health counseling institutions, health bureaus, and medical doctors could cooperate with, for example, family counseling services, teachers and social workers in schools, adolescent counselors, psychiatric clinics, drug counseling services, and crisis centers (Coates, Peterson and Perry, 1982).

In all areas of intervention, we have to look for the *promotive and empowering potentials* of measures and activities in order to overcome their *controlling and interdicting components*.

Promotive components underline individual and social action as a source of well-being and health and enable the individual adolescent to take his/her active part in influencing and shaping the social and political environment. Promotive aspects are gaining ground in all fields of welfare policy for children and adolescents, thereby dislodging the traditional notion of "protection" which—at least in the European tradition— has always had several patriarchal components, even within preventive approaches. As has been shown, the (health) promotive approach makes allowance for the adolescent's autonomy in respect to decision-making, risk-taking, coping with risks, and shaping the environment (Jessor, 1982).

Because of the uneven effects of social and economic change and the accumulation of disadvantages (unemployment, poverty) in several ethnic and social subgroups of the adolescent population, we have to direct specific financial resources to these subgroups in order to compensate for such hardships. To avoid the risk of patronizing, we have to include promotive strategies in order to achieve empowerment and strengthen self-help activities. The result is a pluralistic strategy of interventions using a diversity of sources: these include the state, the private sector, the voluntary sector, local groups, self-help groups, and the individual adolescents themselves as active agents in the organization of health provision (Albee, 1987).

Today, no one can give a clear answer to the question of which intervention strategy best fits the needs of which at-risk adolescent (Hurrelmann, 1987). Theory and research have not yet progressed adequately to offer a satisfying answer. But it does appear reasonable to assume that all of the strategies discussed in this paper are valuable devices which can empower the personal and social competences and resources of adolescents.

REFERENCES

Albee, G. W. (1987). Powerlessness, politics, and prevention. In *Social intervention: Potential and constraints*, Hurrelmann, K., Kaufmann, F. X. and Lösel, F. (Eds), pp. 37–52. Berlin: De Gruyter.

Bachman, J. G., O'Malley, P. M. and Johnston, L. D. (1982). *Youth in transition*, Vol. 7. Ann Arbour: University of Michigan Press.

Baethge, M. (1989). Individualization as hope and as disaster. In *The social world of adolescents. International perspectives*, Hurrelman, K. and Engel, U. (Eds), pp. 37–42. Berlin/New York: De Gruyter.

Botvin, G. J. (1986). Substance abuse prevention research: Recent developments and future directions. *Journal of School Health*, **56**, 369–386.

Botvin, G. J. and Dusenbury, L. (1989). Preventing tobacco, alcohol and drug abuse. Paper presented at the 5th International Symposium on Prevention and Intervention, Bielefeld.

Bronfenbrenner, U. (1979). *The ecology of human development*. Cambridge: Harvard University Press.

Butler, N. R. and Corner, B. B. (Eds). (1984). *Stress and disability in childhood*. Bristol: Wright.

Caplan, G. and Grunebaum, H. (1967). Perspectives on primary prevention. A review. *Archives in Genetic Psychiatry*, **17**, 331–346.

Coates, T. J., Pearson, A. C. and Perry, C. (Eds). (1982). *Promoting adolescent health*. New York: Academic Press.

Coleman, J. C. (1989). The focal theory of adolescence: A psychological perspective. In *The social world of adolescents. International perspectives*, Hurrelman, K. and Engel, U. (Eds), pp. 43–56. Berlin: De Gruyter.
Donovan, J. E. and Jessor, R. (1985). Structure of problem behavior in adolescence and young adulthood. *Journal of Consulting and Clinical Psychology*, **53**, 890–904.
Elliot, D. S., Huizinga, D. and Ageton, S. S. (1985). *Explaining delinquency and drug use*. Beverly Hills: Sage.
Engel, G. L. (1962). *Psychological development in health and disease*. Philadelphia: Saunders.
Engel, U., Nordlohne, E., Hurrelmann, K. and Holler, B. (1987). Educational career and substance use in adolescence. *European Journal of Psychology of Education*, **11**, 365–374.
Engel, U. and Hurrelmann, K. (1989). Delinquent behavior in adolescence: Potential and constraints of preventive strategies. In *Legal and ethical perspectives of social intervention*, Albrecht, P. A. and Backes, O. (Eds). Berlin/New York: De Gruyter.
Featherman, D. L. and Lerner, R. M. (1985). Ontogenesis and sociogenesis: Problematics for theory and research about development and socialization across the life span. *American Sociological Review*, **50**, 659–676.
Felner, R. D., Jason, L. A., Mortisugu, J. and Farber, S. S. (Eds). (1983). *Preventive psychology: Theory, research, and practice*. New York: Pergamon.
Garbarino, J., Schellenbach, C. J. and Sebes, J. M. (1986). *Troubled youth, troubled families*. New York: Aldine de Gruyter.
Garmezy, N. and Rutter, M. (Eds). (1983). *Stress, coping, and development in children*. New York: Aldine de Gruyter.
Gottlieb, B. H. (1981). *Social networks and social support*. Beverly Hills/London: Sage.
Hansell, S. and Mechanic, D. (1990). Parent and peer effects on adolescent health behavior. In *Health hazards in adolescence*, Hurrelmann, K. and Lösel, F. (Eds). Berlin/New York: De Gruyter.
Heller, K. and Swindle, R. W. (1983). Social networks, perceived social support, and coping with stress. In *Preventive psychology: Theory, research, and practice*, Felner, R. D., Jason, L. A., Mortisugu, J. and Farber, S. S. (Eds). New York: Pergamon.
Hurrelmann, K. (1987). The limits and potential of social intervention in adolescence. In *Social intervention: potential and constraints*. Hurrelmann, K., Kaufmann, F. X. and Lösel, F. (Eds), pp. 219–238. Berlin/New York: De Gruyter.
Hurrelmann, K. (1988). *Social structure and personality development*. New York: Cambridge University Press.
Hurrelmann, K. (1989). *Human development and health*. New York: Springer.
Hurrelmann, K. and Engel, U. (1989*a*). Delinquency as a symptom of adolescents' status- and success-orientation. Research paper. University of Bielefeld.
Hurrelmann, K. and Engel, U. (Eds). (1989*b*). *The social world of adolescents. International perspectives*. Berlin/New York: De Gruyter.
Hurrelmann, K., Engel, U., Holler, B. and Nordlohne, E. (1988). Status insecurity and psychosomatic disorders in adolescence. *Journal of Adolescence*, **10**, 112–124.
Ingersoll, G. and Orr, D. P. (1988). Adolescents at risk. *Counseling and Human Development*, **20**, 1–7.
Irwin, C. E. and Millstein, S. G. (1986). Biopsychosocial correlates of risk-taking behaviors during adolescence. *Journal of Adolescent Health Care*, **7**, 825–956.
Jason, L. A., Durlak, J. A. and Holton-Walker, E. (1984). Prevention of child problems in the schools. In *Prevention of problems in childhood*, Roberts, M. C. and Peterson, L. (Eds), pp. 311–341. New York: Wiley.

Jessor, R. (1982). Critical issues in research on adolescent health promotion. In *Promoting adolescent health: A dialogue on research and practice*, Petersen, A. C. and Perry, C. L. (Eds), pp. 447–465. New York: Academic Press.

Jessor, R. (1984). Adolescent development and behavioral health. In *Behavioral health. A handbook of health enhancement and disease prevention*, Matarazzo, J. D., Weiss, S. M., Herd, J. A., Miller, N. E. and Weiss, S. M. (Eds), pp. 69–90. New York: Wiley.

Jessor, R. (1989). *The health of youth*. Plenary address. WHO Conference, May 1989, Geneve.

Jessor, S. J. and Jessor, R. (1977). *Problem behavior and psychosocial development: A longitudinal study of youth*. New York: Academic Press.

Kessler, R. C., Price, R. H. and Wortman, C. B. (1985). Social factors in psychopathology: Stress, social support and coping processes. *Annual Review of Psychology*, 531–572.

Levi, L. (Ed.). (1971). Society, stress, and disease. In *The psychosocial environment and psychosomatic diseases*. London: Oxford University Press.

Matarazzo, J. D., Weiss, S. M., Herd, J. A., Miller, N. E. and Weiss, S. M. (Eds). (1984) *Behavioral health: A handbook of health enhancement and disease prevention*. New York: Wiley.

McPartland, J. M. and McDill, E. L. (1977). *Violence in school*. Lexington: Lexington Books.

Mechanic, D. and Hansell, S. (1988). Adolescence competence, psychological well-being, and self-assessed physical health. *Journal of Health and Social Behavior*, **28**, 364–374.

Perry, C. L. and Jessor, R. (1985). The concept of health promotion and the prevention of adolescent drug abuse. *Health Education Quarterly*, **12**, 169–184.

Petersen A. C. and Ebata, A. (1987). Developmental transitions and adolescent problem behavior. In *Social intervention: Chances and constraints*, Hurrelmann, K., Kaufmann, F. X. and Lösel, F. (Eds), pp. 167–184. Berlin: De Gruyter.

Siddique, C. M. and D'Arcy, C. (1984). Adolescence, stress, and psychological well-being. *Journal of Youth and Adolescence*, **13**, 459–473.

Silbereisen, R. K., Eyferth, K. and Rudinger, G. (Eds). (1986). *Development as action in context*. Berlin: Springer.

Thoits, P. A. (1983). Dimensions of life events that influence psychological distress: An evaluation and synthesis of the literature. In *Psychosocial stress: trends in theory and research*. Kaplan, H. B. (Ed.), pp. 33–103. New York: Academic Press.

Features and Principles of Effective Youth Programs: Promoting Positive Youth Development Through the Integrative Vision of Family and Consumer Sciences

Richard M. Lerner

This article is based in part on material from Richard M. Lerner's book, ***America's Youth in Crisis: Challenges and Options for Programs and Policies***, sponsored by the National 4-H Council and published by Sage Publications, Thousand Oaks, California, in 1995.

Richard M. Lerner is director, Institute for Children, Youth and Families, Michigan State University, East Lansing.

A vision of multidimensional integration is inherent in the field of family and consumer sciences (Lerner & Miller, 1993; Lerner, Miller, & Ostrom, 1995; Miller & Lerner, 1994). To understand the lives of individuals and families, as they develop across the life span within their ecologically valid contexts, family and consumer sciences integrates multiple disciplines and multiple professions. Together, these two dimensions of integration result in a third dimension: The field involves a synthesis of (both basic and applied) science with service. Moreover, this synthesis of science and service is pursued in a unique, and again in an integrative, manner within family and consumer sciences: The knowledge generation and application activities of family and consumer scientists are used to address community-based issues in a community-collaborative manner.

Through such collaboration, the multidisciplinary and multiprofessional knowledge and skills of family and consumer sciences professionals are synthesized with the "voice" of the community. Accordingly, to-be-addressed issues of individual and family life are specified in the context of a scholar-community relationship; the "products" of this collaboration — knowledge about these community-based issues and/or about programs and policies pertinent to the issues — represent "outreach scholarship," i.e., scholarship addressing community-defined issues and needs (Lerner, 1995; Lerner, et al., 1994; Miller & Lerner, 1994; Votruba, 1992). Moreover, such scholarship underscores the substantive significance of diversity — involving variation in disciplines, in professions, and in communities, and hence in people and cultures — within the theoretical and empirical vision of family and consumer sciences.

Over the course of its history (e.g., see Lerner, et al., 1994; Miller & Lerner, 1994), family and consumer sciences has provided exemplars of the productive generation of such diversity-sensitive, integrative scholarship. Today, in America, there is an historically unprecedented need for family and consumer scientists to continue to provide leadership for the production of this outreach scholarship. This critical need arises because of a national crisis confronting America's youth.

America's Youth in Crisis

Across the communities of our nation, children and adolescents are dying—from violence; from drug and alcohol use and abuse; and from unsafe sex (Dryfoos, 1990; Hamburg, 1992; Huston, 1991; Lerner, 1993b, 1995; Schorr, 1988). And, if our children are not dying, their life chances are being squandered—by school failure, underachievement, and dropout; crime; teenage pregnancy and parenting; lack of job preparedness; prolonged welfare dependency; challenges to their health (e.g., lack of immunizations, inadequate screening for disabilities, insufficient prenatal care, poor nutrition, and lack of sufficient infant and childhood medical services); and the feelings of despair and hopelessness that pervade the lives of children whose parents live in poverty and who see themselves as having little opportunity to have a life marked by societal respect, achievement, and opportunity (Dryfoos, 1990; Huston, 1991; Huston, McLoyd, & Coll, 1994).

There are numerous manifestations of the severity and breadth of the problems besetting our nation's youth, families, and communities (Lerner, 1995). To illustrate, consider the four major categories of risk behaviors in late childhood and adolescence:

1. Drug and alcohol use and abuse;
2. Unsafe sex, teenage pregnancy, and teenage parenting;
3. School underachievement, failure, and dropout; and
4. Delinquency, crime, and violence (Dryfoos, 1990).

Participation in any one of these behaviors would diminish a youth's life chances. Engagement in some of them would eliminate the young person's chances of even having a life. Today, in America, there are approximately 28 million children and adolescents between the ages of 10 and 17 years. About 50% of these youth engage in two or more of these four categories of risk behaviors, and 10% engage in all four (Dryfoos, 1990).

Accordingly, America is hanging over a precipice. Unless dramatic and innovative action is taken soon, millions of our nation's children and adolescents—the human capital upon which America must build its future—will fall into an abyss of risk, despair, and hopelessness. Moreover, even if one believes that his or her own children are not engaged directly in high risk behaviors, and even if one's own family is not poor, few people consider themselves or their children immune from such dangers as random violence; few believe that their communities or businesses can continue to prosper if the economic competitiveness of the American economy rests on cohorts of youth wherein drug and alcohol use and abuse, school failure and dropout, delinquency and crime, and teenage pregnancy and parenting are increasingly prototypic. As such, it is not just some youth who are at risk, or just some communities that face the problems of losing much of their next generation. It is all of America's children, all our children, who are at risk.

The loss of so much of our young generations is needless. Knowledge exists about how to prevent the actualization of the numerous behavioral risks besetting our nation's youth and many of the sequelae of persistent and pervasive poverty. Scholars and child advocates such as Joy Dryfoos (1990), David Hamburg (1992), Rick Little (1993), Karen Pittman (1995), Lisbeth Schorr (1988), and Marian Wright Edelman (1992) remind us that considerable information is available, both in America and internationally, about how to design and deliver programs that will prevent the development of problem behaviors among youth and/or promote positive youth development.

Both the features of successful youth programs and the principles underlying these endeavors reflect the multidisciplinary, multiprofessional, and community-collaborative syntheses stressed in the integrative vision inherent in family and consumer sciences. As such, the features and principles of effective youth programs underscore the importance of the emphasis on diversity that is integral in this vision. Moreover, the congruence between the vision and the features and principles of effective youth programming point to the special leadership role (and responsibilities) placed on family and consumer sciences professionals.

Features of Successful Programs

A primary feature of successful programs is *intensive and individualized attention to the participants in the program.* Thus, consistent with the stress inherent in family and consumer sciences, an emphasis on the diversity of the people in the program is essential. This diversity includes race, ethnicity, culture, physical ability status, and—as Hamburg (1992) emphasizes—the developmental level of the people in the program. Similarly, Little (1993), in formulating the 17 criteria used by the International Youth Foundation (IYF) to identify successful youth programs, also stresses that good programs are developmentally appropriate. Moreover, rather than focusing on either remediation or treatment, successful programs seek to meet youth needs by promoting positive development, for example, in regard to one or more of the attributes that Little (1993) believes are key developmental requirements of young people: competence, connection, character, and confidence.

In turn, and with a similar emphasis on instances of diversity, Schorr (1988) stresses that successful programs are designed to be ***responsive to the individual needs of the people most at risk.*** In addition, both she and Hamburg (1992) note that programs sensitive to these significant problems of the individual establish a nonbureaucratic program culture, one that is "user friendly," flexible, and evolves to be increasingly responsive to individual needs.

Furthermore, Dryfoos (1990), Schorr (1988), and Hamburg (1992) emphasize that the focus on the individual must occur within a program structure that *integrates* key features of the context within which the individual is embedded. For example, Dryfoos (1990) indicates that successful prevention programs for adolescents involve the four social institutions essential to development during this period: the family, the peer group, the work place, and the school.

Dryfoos (1990) notes as well that contextually-sensitive programs should involve communitywide, multiagency collaborative—and integrated—approaches, that is approaches wherein agency or program turf is ceded for the benefit of providing a comprehensive and integrated focus on the totality of the individual and his or her context—and not on artificially segmented portions of his or her individual and/or social functioning. Similarly, Schorr (1988) indicates that successful programs involve integration—of children within the family and, as well, families within their communities. Accordingly, programs (and policies) should take an integrated, case management approach to services.

Where may such integrated and comprehensive services be located? Dryfoos (1994) suggests schools. In contemporary American society, the school is the institution wherein the largest number of our nation's children and adolescents can be reached at one time, both in terms of the number of hours per day that youth are in school and in terms of the number of years in which they remain in school. Dryfoos (1990) finds that when school-based programs are successful they are administered by nonschool agencies. That is, the school gives up some of its turf to other community agencies and programs who, in turn, integrate their delivery of services within schools. When this collaboration occurs between the school and the youth- and family-serving agencies and programs within the community in which the school is embedded, an integrated and comprehensive communitywide system is established. Dryfoos (1994) terms this entity a "full-service school." Moreover, in addition to being embedded within communitywide, multiagency integrated structures, such as full-service schools, successful programs have several other distinctive features.

America is hanging over a precipice. Unless dramatic and innovative action is taken soon, millions of our nation's children and adolescents — the human capital upon which America must build its future — will fall into an abyss of risk, despair, and hopelessness.

The Importance of Training

Dryfoos (1990), Schorr (1988), and Little (1993) stress that training in the components of the program and in social skills are among the most important of these features. Often, the personnel delivering a program are not experienced in the substance of the program, are not familiar with the principles of human development that pertain to the participating youth and families, or may not possess the particular social skills requisite for interacting effectively with these program participants.

Successful programs include, then, arrangements for training in the substance of the program, for education about the developmental and cultural characteristics of the program participants, and for building culturally competent social skills (Dryfoos, 1990; Schorr, 1988); ones wherein the content, strategy, and leadership of the program are appropriate to the culture of the community (Little, 1993). Such programs thereby support the establishment of trusting and meaningful relationships among program personnel and participants (Schorr, 1988).

Finally, in order to be successful in continuing a program over time, personnel must have, or be trained to possess, the ability to develop a feasible plan to become self-sustaining in financial support; facilities and materials; leadership; organizational planning, monitoring, evaluation, and feedback; and continuing to address identified needs (Little,

1993). Furthermore, successful programs are those that, to the greatest extent possible, include the youth participants not only in these organizational activities but, as well, in the implementation of, and dissemination about, the program (Hamburg, 1992; Little, 1993).

Building a Caring Community

Effective programs, while they may be primarily located in schools, need to also be situated in the community more pervasively. That is, children and adolescents are not always in schools: They spend time on the streets of their neighborhoods, in other youth-serving institutions (e.g., 4-H clubs), "hanging out" at malls or at friends' homes, or just being by themselves (Carnegie Corporation of New York, 1992). These contexts must not become "cracks" through which our youth fall. Communities must provide continuity of programming efforts that extend to all portions of neighborhoods and community members must ensure that all youth in need of a program have access to it (Hamburg, 1992). In short, the community must ensure that, no matter where a child or adolescent goes in the community, he or she is supported and protected.

Simply, programs and community resources and efforts must be integrated: All features of the ecology of human development must be synthesized to best ensure that positive youth development will be promoted.

Key Principles Involved in Successful Prevention Programs

A corollary to the idea—that the basis for building successful youth programs lies in an integration of the multiple features of the context of human development—is the view that the problems of contemporary American children and youth were not produced by a single event or derived from a single cause. Neither poor parenting; poverty; inappropriate media influences; inadequate health care; problems of local, state, and the federal economies; a failed educational system; racism; territoriality among social service and other youth- and family-serving agencies; nor inadequate state and federal policies alone produced the problems faced by America's children. However, all these phenomena are a part of the developmental system within which America's children are embedded (Ford & Lerner, 1992), and it is this system that is implicated in the production of the problems of our nation's youth.

However, as stressed above, given that development in the context of this system provides the bases of these problems, this same system has to be engaged in any comprehensive solution to these problems. As such, and as Dryfoos (1990) points out, *there is no one solution to a problem of childhood or adolescence*. The developmental system may be—and, for comprehensive and integrated solutions, must be—engaged at any of the levels of organization (e.g., the individual, the family, or social policy) comprising the developmental context of youth (Lerner, 1993a, 1993b, 1995).

A second reason why recognition of the potential for multiple solutions to a problem is important is that *high-risk behaviors are interrelated*. For instance, as noted earlier, about 50% of America's 10 to 17 year-olds engage in multiple high-risk behaviors (Dryfoos, 1990). Similarly, Schorr (1988) notes that poverty is associated with several rotten behavioral outcomes; for example, school failure and dropout, unemployability, prolonged welfare dependency, and delinquency and crime.

The interrelation, and systemic bases, of high-risk behaviors means, then, that no one type of program is likely to be of sufficient scope to adequately address all the interconnected facets of a problem. Instead, as Dryfoos (1990) notes, *a package of services is needed within each community*. However, because of the systemic interconnections of the problems this package is to address, program comprehensiveness, in and of itself, will not be adequate. Rather, *an integration of services is required*. Moreover, because of the systemic nature of the problems of children and youth, the integrated services that are provided to address these problems should be directed to this system, and not solely at the individuals within it. In other words, since relations—among individuals, institutions, and levels of the context—provide both the bases of, and potential sources of change in, the problems of children and youth, *interventions should be aimed at changing the developmental system, within which people are embedded, rather than at changing individuals* (Dryfoos, 1990).

Diversity and integration are key concepts involved in the features and principles of effective youth programs. These concepts reflect ideas core to the family and consumer sciences vision of outreach scolarship pertinent to the enhancement of youth development.

Furthermore, because of the systemic nature of youth problems and of their potential solutions, *the timing of interventions is critical* (Dryfoos, 1990; Lerner, 1984). That is, across life the developmental system not only becomes more organized, but this organization involves, in a sense, over-organization; in other words, redundant, as well as alternative, portions of the system function to support developmental functioning (Hebb, 1949; Schneirla, 1957). It is also the case that the developmental system remains open to intervention across the life span of individuals; that is, there is relative "plasticity" in human behavior and development across life (Lerner, 1984). Nevertheless, problems of behavior and development, once embedded in this redundantly organized system, are more difficult to alter than is the case if the same problems were embedded in the system at an earlier portion of its development (Clarke & Clarke, 1976; Ford & Lerner, 1992; Lerner, 1984). As such, interventions occurring later in life require greater expenditures of effort, and require involvement of greater portions of the system, than is the case in earlier portions of the life span (Baltes & Baltes, 1980; Lerner, 1984).

Of course, a system that remains open to changes for the better also remains open to changes for the worse. Thus, the interventive means through which human behavior and development change is *not* akin to inoculation to disease. Accordingly, "one shot" interventions into human behavior and development are unlikely to effect enduring changes. Instead, interventions must be designed to be longitudinal in scope (Lerner & Ryff, 1978) or, as both Dryfoos (1990) and Hamburg (1992) note, *continuity of programming must be maintained across development*. Programs, conceived of as life-span "convoys of social support" (Kahn & Antonucci, 1980), should be implemented in order to protect and enhance the positive effects of preventive interventions.

Clearly, such continuity of effort is expensive. However, a commitment to life-span programming must be coupled with a commitment to *discontinue programs that have proven to be ineffective* (Dryfoos, 1990). Accountability, the requirement to deliver a high quality program, is a necessary feature of professionally responsible, ethical, and humane programs (cf. Hamburg, 1992). Moreover, if only those programs that have been shown to be effective are continued, then resources devoted to poor programs may be saved. Of course, making such decisions requires that appropriate evaluation information exists.

Little (1993) observes that, all too often, evaluation is not central, or is under-funded, or is not a part of program development. He indicates that, to be appropriate (e.g., culturally competent) and useful (i.e., promotive of positive youth development), evaluations should include the perspectives of the stakeholders of a program; this information should be used to guide, enhance, and inform the evaluation process (Little, 1993). For example, the Development-in-Context Evaluation (DICE) model (Lerner, Ostrom, & Freel, 1995, in press; Ostrom, Lerner, & Freel, 1995) promotes positive individual and social development and change through the incorporation of participatory evaluation into program design and implementation (cf. Weiss & Greene, 1992). Ultimately, collaboration in such evaluations builds the capacity of community partners to themselves envision, enact, and sustain programs that promote the development of their youth in valued, positive directions.

Such evaluation approaches are predicated on the idea that *program- and community-specific evaluation is a requisite for all effective programming* (Dryfoos, 1990). Moreover, such evaluations are predicated on attention to the diversity that exists within a specific community; to the specific goals, values, and meaning systems that are present in the community and that shape the program. Recognition of the importance of such diversity appears critical in the design of effective prevention programs. As noted by Dryfoos (1990), *programs that pay attention to cultural and lifestyle diversity, as well as to individual diversity, are more likely to succeed.*

In short, then, diversity and integration are key concepts involved in the features and principles of effective youth programs. These concepts reflect ideas core to the family and consumer sciences vision of outreach scholarship pertinent to the enhancement of youth development.

Conclusions

Ultimately, to address the historically unprecedented crises confronting the youth of America, all scholars of human development and, indeed, all citizens, must educate themselves about the best means available to promote enhanced life chances among *all* of our youth, but especially those whose potential for positive contributions to our nation are most in danger of being wasted (Lerner, 1993a). The integrative and diversity-sensitive approach to outreach scholarship inherent within the field of family and consumer sciences represents a unique resource to America for leadership in such scholarship, especially because it is pursued in partnership with (and, in fact, promotes) strong, empowered communities.

Colleagues in the field of family and consumer sciences must, then, mount a proactive and visible campaign to promote this scholarly model, and the leadership strength it represents. This period in our nation's history requires the unique, integrative, and capacity-building approach to individuals, families, and communities found in the family and consumer sciences field. Colleagues must, then, "seize the high ground" and undertake the leadership duties that the corpus of work in the field deserves and that our nation so critically needs.

There is no time to lose in the initiation of such an agenda of outreach scholarship. American youth and, in fact, our nation itself, as we know it—and, even more, as we believe it can be—will be lost unless we act now. All the strengths and assets of family and consumer sciences professionals, and indeed of all of America's institutions and people, must be marshalled for this effort.

References

Baltes, P. B., & Baltes, M. M. (1980). Plasticity and variability in psychological aging: Methodological and theoretical issues. In G. E. Gurski (Ed.), *Determining the effects of aging on the central nervous system* (pp. 41-66). Berlin: Schering.

Carnegie Corporation of New York. (1992). *A matter of time: Risk and opportunity in the nonschool hours.* (Available from Carnegie Council on Adolescent Development, P.O. Box 753, Waldorf, MD 20604.)

Clarke, A.M., & Clarke, A.D.B. (Eds.). (1976). *Early experience: Myth and evidence.* New York: Free Press.

Dryfoos, J.G. (1990). *Adolescents at risk: Prevalence and prevention.* New York: Oxford University.

Dryfoos, J. G. (1994). *Full service schools: A revolution in health and social services of children, youth and families.* San Francisco: Jossey-Bass.

Edelman, M. W. (1992). *The measure of our success: A letter to my children and yours.* Boston: Beacon Press.

Ford, D. L., & Lerner, R. M. (1992). *Developmental systems theory: An integrative approach.* Newbury Park, CA: Sage.

Hamburg, D.A. (1992). *Today's children: Creating a future for a generation in crisis.* New York: Time Books.

Hebb, D.O. (1949). *The organization of behavior.* New York: Wiley.

Huston, A.C. (1991). Children in poverty: Developmental and policy issues. In A. C. Huston (Ed.), *Children in poverty: Child development and public policy* (pp. 1-22). Cambridge: Cambridge University Press.

Huston, A.C., McLoyd, V C., & Garcia Coll, C.T. (1994). Children and poverty: Issues in contemporary research. *Child Development, 65,* 275-282.

Kahn, R.L., & Antonucci, T C. (1980). Convoys over the life course: Attachment, roles, and social support. In P.B. Baltes & O.G. Brim (Eds.), *Life-span development and behavior, 3* (pp. 253-286). Hillsdale, NJ: Erlbaum.

Lerner, R.M. (1984). *On the nature of human plasticity.* New York: Cambridge University.

Lerner, R.M. (1993a). Early adolescence: Toward an agenda for the integration of research, policy, and intervention. In R. M. Lerner (Ed.), *Early adolescence: Perspectives on research, policy, and intervention* (pp. 1-13). Hillsdale, NJ: Erlbaum.

Lerner, R.M. (1993b). Investment in youth: The role of home economics in enhancing the life chances of America's children. *AHEA Monograph Series, 1,* 5-34.

Lerner, R.M. (1995). *America's youth in crisis: Challenges and options for programs and policies.* Thousand Oaks, CA: Sage.

Lerner, R.M., & Miller, J.R. (1993). Integrating human development research and intervention for America's children: The Michigan State University model. *Journal of Applied Developmental Psychology, 14,* 347-364.

Lerner, R.M., Miller, J.R., Knott, J.H., Corey, K.E., Bynum, T.S., Hoopfer, L.C., McKinney, M.H., Abrams, L.A., Hula, R.C., & Terry, P.A. (1994). Integrating scholarship and outreach in human development research, policy, and service: A developmental contextual perspective. In D. L. Featherman, R. M. Lerner, & M. Perlmutter (Eds.), *Life-span development and behavior, 12* (pp. 249-273). Hillsdale, NJ: Erlbaum.

Lerner, R.M., Miller, J.R., & Ostrom, C.W. (1995, Spring). Integrative knowledge, accountability, access, and the American university of the twenty-first century: A family and consumer sciences vision of the future of higher education. *Kappa Omicron Nu FORUM, 8*(1), 11-27.

Lerner, R.M., Ostrom, C.W., & Freel, M.A. (1995). Promoting positive youth and community development through outreach scholarship: Comments on Zeldin and Peterson. *Journal of Adolescent Research, 10,* 486-502.

Lerner, R.M., Ostrom, C. W., & Freel, M. A. (In press). Preventing health compromising behaviors among youth and promoting their positive development: A developmental-contextual perspective. In J. Schulenberg, J. L. Maggs, & K. Hurrelmann (Eds.), *Health risks and developmental transitions during adolescence.* New York: Cambridge University Press.

Lerner, R.M., & Ryff, C.D. (1978). Implementation of the life-span view of human development: The sample case of attachment. In P.B. Baltes (Ed.), *Life-span development and behavior, 1* (pp. 1-44). New York: Academic.

Little, R.R. (1993, March). *What's working for today's youth: The issues, the programs, and the learnings.* Paper presented at an ICYF Fellows Colloquium, Michigan State University, East Lansing.

Miller, J.R., & Lerner, R.M. (1994). Integrating research and outreach: Developmental contextualism and the human ecological perspective. *Home Economics Forum, 7,* 21-28.

Ostrom, C.W., Lerner, R.M., & Freel, M A. (1995). Building the capacity of youth and families through university-community collaborations: The development-in-context evaluation (DICE) model. *Journal of Adolescent Research, 10,* 427-448.

Pittman, K. (1995, July/August). Maybe it is rocket science. *Youth Today, 4*(4), 46.

Schneirla, T. C. (1957). The concept of development in comparative psychology. In D. B. Harris (Ed.), *The concept of development* (pp. 78-108). Minneapolis: University of Minnesota.

Schorr, L. B. (1988). *Within our reach: Breaking the cycle of disadvantage.* New York: Doubleday.

Votruba, J. C. (1992). Promoting the extension of knowledge in service to society. *Metropolitan Universities, 3*(3), 72-80.

Weiss, H. B., & Greene, J. C. (1992). An empowerment partnership for family support and education programs and evaluations. *Family Science Review, 5,* 131-148.

Journal of Consulting and Clinical Psychology
1991, Vol. 59, No. 6, 830–841

0022-006X/91/$3.00

Promoting Competent Young People in Competence-Enhancing Environments: A Systems-Based Perspective on Primary Prevention

Roger P. Weissberg, Marlene Caplan, and Robin L. Harwood
Yale University

Recent studies indicate that 15–22% of American children and adolescents suffer from diagnosable mental disorders. Researchers estimate that 25–50% engage in risk behaviors for negative health and behavior outcomes, such as drug abuse, unwanted pregnancy, AIDS, delinquency, and school dropout. The prevalence of problem behaviors, as well as current social trends, demands that effective primary prevention programs be developed and disseminated. This article reviews successful family-, school-, and community-based prevention efforts aimed at reducing the incidence and severity of children's psychosocial problems. High-quality, comprehensive, competence-promotion programs that focus on both children and their socializing environments represent the state of the art in prevention. Establishing enduring, effective preventive interventions requires increased attention to program design, implementation, and institutionalization.

During the late 1940s, the field of clinical psychology had the opportunity to decide how it could best contribute to what was defined as a staggering mental health service delivery crisis (Raimy, 1950). Large numbers of World War II veterans returned home with mental health problems, and there were not enough services available for those who needed them. Sarason's (1981) sociohistorical analysis describes how clinical adult psychology responded to this challenge by allying itself with what was then the prevailing ethos in American medicine and psychiatry. He questions the justification of psychology's chosen emphasis on individual treatment at the expense of a preventive orientation and wonders whether today's psychology could be more responsive to societal needs if it had made a primary commitment instead to collaborating with families, schools, and communities in establishing mental health promotion strategies for young people.

For better or worse, clinical child psychology has generally replicated the structure and function of clinical adult psychology (Walker & Roberts, 1983). Professionals direct their efforts primarily to the assessment, diagnosis, and treatment of disturbed children, rather than to the implementation and evaluation of systems-based approaches for promoting competence and preventing psychological dysfunction. This Special Section shares significant recent advances in research and practice geared toward improving the quality of life for many troubled children and their families. Despite these important gains, however, it remains clear that traditional mental health resources are insufficient to address the needs of all children who experience emotional and behavioral problems.

This article discusses the value of working proactively with families, the educational system, and communities to enhance the psychological, social, and physical health of children. We argue that a dual focus on promoting competent young people and creating competence-enhancing environments is essential both to prevent behavior problems in children and to improve the functioning of those who already suffer from such difficulties. We address the following key issues: (a) What are the nature and extent of behavior problems presently experienced by young people? (b) What implications do research findings regarding the prevalence and common predictors of behavior problems have for conducting preventive interventions in the context of families, schools, and communities? (c) Is there empirical evidence to indicate that such programs can be beneficial? (d) What key elements enable successful prevention programs to produce long-term positive effects? (e) What are important next steps in prevention research and practice, and what role should mental health professionals play in these developments?

Extent of Childhood Problem Behaviors and the Need for Primary Prevention

Recent epidemiological data suggest that 15–22% of the nation's 63 million children and adolescents have mental health problems severe enough to warrant treatment (Costello, 1990; National Advisory Mental Health Council, 1990; Tuma, 1989; Zill & Schoenborn, 1990). Given the links between maladjustment in childhood and a variety of negative psychosocial outcomes in adulthood, one feels concern both for the current suffering of this afflicted group and for the future generation of adults that our society is producing. Unfortunately, it has been

We gratefully acknowledge the support provided by the William T. Grant Foundation and the New Haven Public School System. We also appreciate the enormous intellectual contributions to this article made by Alice S. Jackson and the members of the William T. Grant Foundation Consortium on School-Based Social-Competence Promotion: Kenneth A. Dodge, Maurice J. Elias, J. David Hawkins, Leonard A. Jason, Philip C. Kendall, Cheryl A. Perry, Mary Jane Rotheram-Borus, and Joseph E. Zins.

Marlene Caplan is now at the Thomas Coram Research Unit at the University of London in England. Robin L. Harwood is now at the National Institute of Child Health and Human Development in Washington, DC.

Correspondence concerning this article should be addressed to Roger P. Weissberg, Department of Psychology, Post Office Box 11A Yale Station, Yale University, New Haven, Connecticut 06520-7447.

estimated that fewer than 20% of the young people with mental health problems currently receive appropriate services (Tuma, 1989).

In addition to concerns about the high prevalence of mental health disorders, educators, health professionals, and the business community have expressed alarm about the growing number of young people who engage in behaviors that put them at high risk for negative psychosocial health and behavior outcomes such as drug abuse, teen pregnancy, AIDS, delinquency, and school dropout (e.g., Committee for Economic Development, 1987; Gans, Blyth, Elster, & Gaveras, 1990). Recent estimates indicate that 25% of the 28 million 10- to 17-year-olds in America are extremely vulnerable, and an additional 25% are moderately vulnerable, to the negative consequences of engaging in multiple high-risk social and health behaviors (Dryfoos, 1990; Report of the Task Force on Education of Young Adolescents, 1989). Although the remaining 50% are at low risk for engaging in such behaviors, they may nonetheless need strong and consistent support to avoid such involvement.

Recently, the National Association of State Boards of Education and the American Medical Association jointly issued *Code Blue: Uniting for Healthier Youth* (National Commission on the Role of the School and the Community in Improving Adolescent Health, 1990), which expressed grave concern about the current unprecedented adolescent health crisis in our nation. *Code Blue*, a phrase used in hospitals to signal a life-threatening emergency, calls on diverse personnel to rush to a patient's bedside and collaborate to save the patient's life. By analogy, the Commission indicated that the country's state of adolescent health constitutes a national emergency that poses serious economic and social ramifications. For the first time, young people are less healthy and less prepared to assume responsible places in our society than were their parents. This is especially worrisome inasmuch as society is more complex and competitive than ever before.

The widespread health and behavior problems of America's young people are due, in large part, to significant changes that have occurred during the past few decades in families, schools, neighborhoods, and the media. Major social, environmental, and economic changes include increased poverty rates among children, dramatic alterations in family composition and stability, the breakdown of traditional neighborhoods and extended families, reduced amounts of meaningful and supportive personal contact between young people and positive adult role models, changing demographics resulting in large numbers of economically and educationally disadvantaged young people entering school, the proliferation of health-damaging media messages, inadequate housing, unsafe neighborhood environments, and societal attitudes and behaviors that hurt ethnic minorities (Cherlin, 1988).

Given such difficult societal conditions, we are faced with critical questions concerning the most realistic, cost-effective ways to meet the psychological, social, and health needs of our young people. In particular, it appears that traditional treatment approaches can address the needs of only a small proportion of children in need. First, there is an enormous discrepancy between the number of available service providers and children who require help (Tuma, 1989). Second, although many mental health professionals make use of effective screening and early identification methods coupled with timely intervention, the mental health system continues to be dominated by a passive-receptive stance toward treatment (Cowen, Gesten, & Weissberg, 1980). That is, treatment typically begins after an individual seeks or is encouraged to get help for serious dysfunctional behavior that has developed over several years. At that point, appropriate services are very expensive, usually requiring a great deal of expertise and sustained involvement. Ironically, because the prognosis for successful outcomes in such instances is unfavorable, one could argue that a major portion of our scarce mental health resources is being devoted too late and in a cost-ineffective manner toward a small segment of people who may show few benefits. Finally, mental health interventions are often overly child-centered and thus pay inadequate attention to the settings (e.g., family, school, and community) that create and perpetuate a child's difficulties.

Recognition of these concerns has prompted calls for widespread primary prevention programming to promote childhood competence and thus reduce the incidence of young people who develop mental health problems (e.g., Report of the Task Panel on Prevention, 1978). Primary prevention strategies differ from traditional treatment approaches with respect to the targeting and timing of their intervention practices. In particular, they are (a) systems- and group-oriented rather than targeted to individuals; (b) directed primarily toward essentially healthy people who are not currently suffering any disability due to the condition being prevented, although targets may appropriately include those who are epidemiologically at risk for negative behavioral outcomes; and (c) concerned with promoting health, building competencies, and establishing supportive systems and settings as a protection against dysfunction (Cowen, 1986; Elias & Branden, 1988).

Debate Regarding the Role of Primary Prevention

There is considerable debate regarding the specific achievements of primary prevention in the field of mental health, as well as the role that mental health professionals should play in these efforts (Marlowe & Weinberg, 1985). Some scholars focus on the growing number of studies demonstrating the positive effects that prevention programs can have on children's social and health behavior (e.g., Dryfoos, 1990; Price, Cowen, Lorion, & Ramos-McKay, 1988; Schorr, 1988). However, in spite of these findings, others emphasize that evaluations of these programs fail to demonstrate that major functional mental illnesses, or even less severe diagnosable mental disorders, have been prevented (Lamb & Zusman, 1982; Shaffer, 1989).

Disagreements between advocates and critics of primary prevention are due, in large part, to differences at the level of basic assumptions about what constitutes mental disorder and the appropriate scope of activity for mental health professionals (Ford, 1985). For instance, critics of primary prevention often distinguish sharply between normative problems of living and diagnosable mental illness, in terms of both causation and implications for treatment. They give priority to reducing the prevalence of serious mental disorders and suggest that this can be achieved by identifying and treating underlying biological causes (Lamb & Zusman, 1982; Shaffer, 1989). Furthermore, they point out that there are already more children than we can serve who are in need of direct treatment and that limited resources cannot be diverted from treatment to prevention programs. Thus, they contend that children with mental disorders would be best served if mental health professionals functioned within their traditional boundaries of training and expertise (e.g., the assessment, diagnosis, and treatment of patients suffering from mental disorders).

In contrast, primary prevention advocates tend to emphasize greater continuity between the causes of and the appropriate responses to psychosocial health and behavior problems. On the basis of the belief that psychological and environmental factors interact powerfully with biological predispositions to affect behavioral competence or disorders, they contend that the prevention of dysfunction requires attention to multiple contributors to the child's growth and that intervening early in multiple child contexts is of equal or greater importance than treating the child (Rutter, 1982; Sameroff, 1991). Thus, nontraditional approaches to mental health enhancement—such as family support, school-based competence promotion, and social policy reform—are deemed an important part of mental health practice (Albee, 1983). Recognizing that diverse intervention strategies (educational, legal, media, etc.) can be used in varied contexts to enhance the adaptive growth and development of children, primary prevention advocates also highlight the importance of multidisciplinary collaboration to promote positive mental health (Jason, Hess, Felner, & Moritsugu, 1987).

Reasons for Targeting Multiple Problem Behaviors and Focusing on Key Socializing Contexts

Recent research in behavioral epidemiology indicates that mental health problems often co-occur with social problems like school failure or delinquency, as well as with health problems such as substance abuse (Donovan, Jessor, & Costa, 1988; Elliott, Huizinga, & Menard, 1989). In addition, there are common personality, behavioral, and environmental factors that are associated with an increased probability of these negative outcomes. Examples of such psychosocial risk factors are residence in a neighborhood that is deprived and disorganized, poor and inconsistent family management practices and communication, school failure and low expectations for achievement, poor peer relations, and early age of initiation of problem behaviors (Dryfoos, 1990). In contrast, protective mechanisms include a neighborhood with informal resources and supports, a cohesive family, ongoing contact with a caring adult, peer models for conventional behavior, self-esteem and a positive social orientation, good school performance, and adaptive coping skills (Cowen & Work, 1988; Garmezy, 1985; Rutter, 1987).

These findings challenge mental health professionals to broaden the outcomes they are trying to affect, as well as the intervention approaches used to achieve them. Dryfoos (1990) argued that the emergence of common predictors of multiple problem behaviors lends force to the perspective that interventions should focus more on the predictors of the behaviors, which are amenable to intervention, than on the behaviors themselves. She suggested, for example, that enhancement of early schooling and the prevention of school failure should be given high priority not only by those who want to lower the dropout rate, but also by those interested in preventing substance abuse, unwanted pregnancy, and conduct problems.

According to Perry and Jessor (1985), effective family-, school-, and community-based preventive interventions have potential to affect four different but interrelated domains of health: psychological health (subjective sense of well-being); social health (role fulfillment and social effectiveness); personal health (realization of individual potential); and physical health (physical–physiological functioning). Similarly, Zigler and Berman (1983) cautioned that it is a mistake to evaluate the effectiveness of early interventions with one construct such as IQ or a single diagnosable mental disorder. They argued instead for multidimensional assessments of children's social competence because such programs have potential to improve physical health, cognitive ability, academic achievement, social interaction skills, and various indicators of motivation and emotional functioning. In addition, they highlighted the value of evaluating molar educational outcomes (e.g., being in mainstream rather than in special-education classrooms; completing high school) and behavioral outcomes (e.g., incidence of delinquency or unwanted teen pregnancy, being self-supporting rather than on welfare). Although researchers must clarify relations among these variables and various mental disorders, these variables clearly constitute important criteria by which to assess the effects of mental-health treatment or prevention efforts with young people.

With regard to intervention, Ford (1985) noted that adopting a *competence perspective* might serve to maximize areas of common ground between critics and advocates of primary prevention. Competence refers to the behavioral effectiveness of one's transactions with the environment, as well as to one's sense of personal well-being in diverse aspects of life. Competence deficits, on the other hand, are reflected not only in diagnosable mental disorders, but also in difficulties with certain aspects of functioning such as social relationship problems, failure to achieve in school, involvement in health-damaging risk behaviors, and low self-esteem. The competence perspective asserts that mental health interventions—whether restorative or preventive—should be, and in fact are, primarily concerned with building behavioral competence and feelings of efficacy in diverse aspects of life.

In closing, the identification of common predictors of multiple problem behaviors and findings about the multifactorial causation of psychological, social, and health problems support the view that effective prevention or treatment approaches require attention to the key socializing contexts in which children grow—specifically, the family and the school (Dryfoos, 1990; Rutter, 1982). Children are most likely to function effectively and feel competent when (a) they have opportunities to be actively involved with and to contribute meaningfully to their family and school; (b) they have the skills, motivation, and information to succeed in these settings; and (c) their social systems and socializing agents (e.g., parents, teachers, peers) consistently reinforce their positive, adaptive behavioral performance (Hawkins & Weis, 1985). Following this framework, we propose that family-, school-, and community-based prevention programs will be most effective when they attempt both (a) to enhance children's capacities to coordinate skills, prosocial values, and information in order to cope adaptively with society's social tasks, challenges, and stresses and (b) to create environmental settings and resources that support the development of young people's positive personal, social, and health behavior (Weissberg, Caplan, & Sivo, 1989). It is also important to recognize that both the family and the school are situated within broader community, national, and cultural contexts (Bronfenbrenner, 1979). Because of this, interventions aimed at the family and the school must be both culturally sensitive and coordinated with larger community and national reform efforts. Only by coordinating with these broader contexts can prevention efforts produce positive, lasting changes in young people and their socializing contexts.

Research Evidence Regarding the Efficacy of Primary Prevention

During the last decade, literature focusing on the evaluation of prevention programs for children and adolescents has expanded dramatically (e.g., Bond & Compas, 1989; Dryfoos, 1990; Kazdin 1991; Lorion, 1989; Mueller & Higgins, 1988; Price et al., 1988; Schorr, 1988; Zins & Forman, 1988). Although there are many promising demonstrations of beneficial prevention efforts, it is also true that many attempts at primary prevention fail to produce lasting behavior change (e.g., Bangert-Drowns, 1988). This outcome may be due to the fact that many of these so-called prevention programs are unrealistically short, are poorly implemented, or fail to intervene simultaneously with the child and his or her socializing contexts. Establishing effective prevention programs involves a complex set of tasks, and it is counterproductive to overpromise what prevention can achieve or to oversimplify the difficulties involved in developing and implementing such efforts (Price & Lorion, 1989; Weissberg et al., 1989). At this time, the field will advance from research that clarifies why certain programs accomplish or fail to accomplish their goals.

This section selectively reviews illustrative prevention programs that have had positive behavioral effects for young people and then describes elements that appear critical for their success. We have selected carefully evaluated models that have realistic length, substance, and scope. Most focus explicitly on enhancing the competence of both children and their socializing environments. In addition, these models are well-designed, and there is considerable advocacy for their broader dissemination. For children under the age of 5 years, high-quality family support and early childhood education programs have produced long-term benefits (Price et al., 1988). For older children, the most promising strategies involve multiyear, school-based, social-competence and health-education programs with peer, parent, school-support, and community components (Perry, Klepp, & Sillers, 1989; Weissberg, 1991).

Family Support Programs

In family support programs, specially trained community members or professionals provide ongoing support to families during pregnancy, infancy, and early childhood. The major goals of family support are to promote nurturing and attentive parenting, parents' personal development and psychological well-being, and ultimately, healthy child development. In contrast to social service delivery systems that are oriented toward ameliorating crises, family support programs attempt to empower parents to help themselves and their children (Zigler & Black, 1989). We describe two exemplars of family support programs, the Yale Child Welfare Research Project (Provence & Naylor, 1983) and the Houston Parent Child Development Center (Johnson, 1988), to illustrate this program model and its potential effects.

The Yale Child Welfare Research Project provided four interrelated services to 17 impoverished pregnant women expecting a firstborn child through 30 months postpartum. These included (a) 28 supportive home visits by a psychologist, social worker, or nurse that focused on solving practical problems such as obtaining more adequate food and housing or making decisions about future educational, career, and family goals; (b) 13–17 well-baby exams by a pediatrician; (c) an average of 13 months of center-based day care; and (d) 7–9 regularly scheduled developmental examinations. A 10-year follow-up study revealed that intervention mothers, relative to control mothers, obtained more education, were more likely to be employed, chose to bear fewer children, and were more active in seeking information about their child from classroom teachers. Although the two groups of children were comparable on IQ and achievement test performance, control boys were absent more often, rated by teachers as having more serious acting-out problems, and required an average of $1,120 more per year in special school services than did program children (Seitz, Rosenbaum, & Apfel, 1985). Although these findings suggest that family support combined with quality day care has considerable potential as a general model for preventive intervention, results from this study should be replicated with a larger sample, and greater attention must be paid to identifying the intervention components or mechanisms that contribute to improved maternal and child functioning.

The Houston Parent–Child Development Center offered a two-stage, 2-year program for Mexican Americans that required 550 hr of family involvement beginning when a child was 1 and ending at age 3 (Johnson, 1988). During the first year, mothers were visited in the home by a paraprofessional for twenty-five 90-min sessions focusing on information about child development, parenting skills, and using the home as a learning environment. During Year 2, mothers came to the Center four mornings per week for classes on child management and family communication skills while their children attended nursery school. In a 5- to 8-year follow-up study involving 139 second- through fifth-graders, program children performed better on a standardized achievement test and were rated by teachers as less aggressive and hostile and more considerate (Johnson & Walker, 1987). The Houston project has the methodological strengths of using a very large sample size and random assignment to groups. A high subject attrition rate, both during the intervention and at follow-up (primarily as a result of families moving out of the area), limits the generalizability of these positive findings to less mobile families.

Several other longitudinal studies demonstrate the long-term positive effects of family support on impoverished children and families (e.g., Infant Health and Development Program, 1990; Olds, 1988). In addition, Pierson (1988) reported that family support and early childhood programming positively affected the school performance and behavior of children of varying socioeconomic levels. The present research challenge is to identify more clearly the mechanisms by which such benefits are produced. This is a complicated task inasmuch as it appears that successful support services must be comprehensive, multifaceted, and flexible in order to be effective (Schorr, 1988). Seitz (1991) cautioned that family contacts per se do not guarantee parent involvement or improved child development. The timing of family contacts, the characteristics of the service provider, and the content of intervention activities are key variables to assess in future studies.

Early Childhood Education

Early childhood education may be broadly defined as any group program for children under age 5 that provides them with knowledge and social competence required for normal development or success in school (Haskins, 1989). This broad description includes a range of programs in terms of location (e.g., home day care, community center, or school) and educational approach (e.g., child-initiated learning, teacher-directed instruction). Research findings from the High/Scope Perry Preschool Study (Schweinhart & Weikart, 1988) and the Consortium for Longitudinal Studies (Lazar, Darlington, Murray, Royce, & Snipper, 1982) demonstrate that *high-quality* preschool programs can produce positive, enduring changes in children's social and behavioral functioning. On the basis of these positive research findings, there is growing national support for the widespread dissemination of early childhood education programs (e.g., Committee for Economic Development, 1987). In particular, the U.S. Department of Health and Human Services, Public Health Service (1990) recommended by the year 2000 that the country "achieve for all disadvantaged children and children with disabilities access to high quality and developmentally appropriate preschool programs that help prepare children for school, thereby improving their prospects with regard to school performance, problem behaviors, and physical health" (p. 254). Furthermore, Public Law 99-457, focusing on provision of early interventions for young handicapped and high-risk children, is providing a major impetus for early childhood services.

However, it should be emphasized that lasting benefits of early childhood education have been achieved only by high-quality programs characterized by a developmentally appropriate curriculum, based on child-initiated activities; teaching teams that are knowledgeable in early childhood development and receive ongoing training and supervision; class size limited to fewer than twenty 3- to 5-year-olds with at least two teachers; administrative leadership that includes support of the program; systematic efforts to involve parents as partners in their child's education, as well as sensitivity to the noneducational needs of the child and family; and evaluation procedures that are developmentally appropriate (Schweinhart & Weikart, 1988). These characteristics of program design and implementation appear to be central ingredients of most successful prevention efforts (Weissberg et al., 1989). In contrast, there is ample evidence to suggest that early childhood education programs of lesser quality do not result in such positive effects (Haskins, 1989).

Between 1962 and 1967, the High/Scope Perry Preschool Project served low-income Black 3- and 4-year-old children with IQ scores between 70 and 90 (Schweinhart & Weikart, 1988, 1989). Program evaluators randomly assigned 58 children to a preschool group and 65 children to a control group. The classroom program involved five 90-min classes a week for 7 months per year over a 2-year period. Classroom groups had 25 children and four well-trained teachers who implemented the High/Scope Early Childhood Curriculum, an educational approach that promotes intellectual, social, and physical development through child-initiated learning activities. In addition, teachers made weekly 90-min home visits to involve parents as partners in their child's education. Longitudinal follow-up data on children up to age 28 indicate that program children, relative to control subjects, showed stronger commitment to schooling, higher academic achievement, lower rates of grade retention, fewer placements in special education (16% vs. 28%), lower rates of classification of mental impairment (15% vs. 35%), better high school graduation rates (67% vs. 49%), fewer arrests (31% vs. 51%), higher employment (50% vs. 32%), and lower use of welfare assistance (19% vs. 41%).

Other high-quality programs have also promoted multiple competencies and prevented problem behaviors in children. Most notably, the Consortium for Longitudinal Studies evaluated the long-term effects of 11 preschool programs (including the Perry Preschool Project) on 2,008 experimental and control children between ages 9 and 19. Program children were less likely to be retained or to require special education. In addition, they were more achievement-oriented, and their parents had higher educational and occupational aspirations than did the parents of control children. Although for some programs the results were stronger than for others, findings also suggested that these programs have potential to affect rates of delinquency and crime, teen pregnancy, welfare use, and employment (Royce, Darlington, & Murray, 1983). One limitation of early childhood education research to date involves the paucity of longitudinal studies that compare the differential long-term effects of various educational approaches. The importance of this research question has been highlighted by Schweinhart and Weikart (1988), who reported suggestive findings that programs that emphasize child-initiated learning activities may have more positive long-term behavioral affects than those that emphasize teacher-directed instruction.

In summary, although early intervention projects were initially conceptualized as programs to help children at risk for school failure, these results clearly have implications for primary prevention in mental health. Many school-related variables (e.g., poor achievement motivation, low aspirations and expectations for educational accomplishment, poor school performance, and school dropout) are risk factors for a variety of later problem behaviors, including substance abuse, unwanted teen pregnancy, conduct problems, depression, and suicide (Elliott et al., 1989). Early school failure and placement in special education are two critical markers that constitute major turning points in the lives of many children, with long-term implications for future adjustment (Dryfoos, 1990; Hawkins, Doueck, & Lishner, 1988; Maughan, 1988). Thus, early childhood education could be viewed as an innovative mental health strategy that affects many risk and protective factors for diverse problem behaviors. The strongest effects are in the domain of behavioral conduct, although it will be instructive for investigators to broaden their future assessments to include measures of depression and anxiety.

There is considerable debate about why these early interventions produced long-term effects. One causal model suggests that preschool education promotes cognitive and social skills that result in greater school readiness and a smoother transition to kindergarten. Subsequently, this preparation leads to positive responses by kindergarten teachers, which foster more improved student attitudes about schooling and better school performance in later grades; and school success, in turn, serves as a protective factor to prevent behavioral maladjustment and delinquency (Schweinhart & Weikart, 1988). An alternative set of explanations emphasizes the importance of changing parents' behaviors or restructuring their social expectations as primary mechanisms to positively affect the adjustment of children (Sameroff, 1991). For example, it is possible that extensive home visitations in high-quality preschool programs enhance parental competence and involvement, leading parents to become more adept socializers and to have more realistic expectations regarding their children's performance as well as the teachers and schools that serve them. These changes, in turn, provide firmer foundations for improved family functioning and child behavior. Overall, programs that focus on both children and their socializing environments appear to produce the most long-lasting gains (Seitz, 1991). However, future research must clarify the differential benefits that are achieved when parents participate actively or are less meaningfully involved in their child's early education.

Although high-quality, comprehensive early interventions appear to promote long-term competencies, researchers have noted that relying too heavily on any one time period or any one context for preventive interventions is a mistake (Zigler & Berman, 1983). Furthermore, although these early interventions produced significant gains in program relative to control students, the number of children experiencing school and social difficulties is still considerably higher than acceptable. For these reasons, as children and adolescents face the complex challenges inherent in growing up, it is necessary to create ongoing educational experiences and supports that promote their continued positive social and behavioral development.

Comprehensive School-Based Social-Competence and Health Education

The educational system offers the most efficient and systematic means available to promote the psychological, social, and physical health of school-age children and adolescents. Schools are compulsory institutions that have significant and sustained contact with most children during formative years of personality development (Rutter, Maughan, Mortimore, & Ouston, 1979). They have the potential to be especially well-suited sites to teach life skills and to prevent social maladaptation and health-damaging behavior. Under the right circumstances, learning activities may be introduced and environments can be created to support the development of health-protective skills, attitudes, values, and behaviors. Many psychological disorders and problem behaviors either have their roots in or may be exacerbated by a child's school experiences (Maughan, 1988; Rutter, 1982). School-based interventions are needed both to prevent the development of dysfunction and to improve the functioning of all children (i.e., those with and without health and behavior problems).

Currently, school administrators and teachers are both receptive to and ambivalent about providing prevention programming. On the one hand, public pressure to raise achievement test scores and to increase academic competitiveness raises concern whenever limited curriculum time is devoted to activities that are not directly related to traditional academic content areas. On the other hand, educators recognize that enhancing children's mental and physical health will improve their ability to learn and achieve academically as well as their capacity to become responsible citizens and productive workers. Recently, there has been considerable advocacy for school-based programming to promote children's psychological and physical health, especially as a result of public health concerns about substance abuse, AIDS, and antisocial behavior (DeFriese, Crossland, Pearson, & Sullivan, 1990; Zins & Forman, 1988). Given this advocacy, there is a splendid opportunity for prevention program developers and researchers to introduce programming of sufficient scope and length to produce long-term positive behavioral outcomes. This section briefly reviews research that supports establishing ecologically valid, kindergarten to high school social-competence and health education programs that include peer, parent, school support, and community components.

A case for multiyear, multicomponent prevention programs that address multiple problem behaviors. Classroom-based social-competence promotion programs to enhance students' psychological and physical health represent the most commonly implemented and evaluated school-based prevention approach (Bond & Compas, 1989; Dryfoos, 1990; Zins & Forman, 1988).[1] Programs that produce short-term benefits have been established for children in preschool and kindergarten (Shure & Spi-

[1] Due to space limitations, we are not able to review other promising prevention programs that have been developed, such as individually oriented counseling services, mentoring programs, and health clinics (Dryfoos, 1990; Zabin, 1990); coping-skills and support programs for high-risk populations, such as children of alcoholic parents or divorcing parents (Emshoff, 1989; Pedro-Caroll & Cowen, 1985); training teachers to use proactive classroom management, interactive teaching, and cooperative learning methods to promote academic achievement, positive classroom behavior, and bonding to school (Hawkins et al., 1988; Slavin, 1983); and reorganizing school settings into smaller units (e.g., homerooms, grade clusters, and schools within schools) to provide increased student support, especially during times of transition from one school to another (Felner & Adan, 1988). Recently, investigators have combined the most effective of these programming elements to establish multicomponent individual and environmental school-based interventions that (a) promote students' academic and social competence (Gottfredson, 1986; Slavin, Madden, Karweit, Livermon, & Dolan, 1990) and (b) involve parents, teachers, mental health staff, and administrators in collaborative decision making about setting academic and social goals for students (Comer, 1988). Ultimately, a multifaceted array of school-based prevention strategies will be needed to address the diverse needs of today's young people. Educators, policymakers, and researchers will have to work together to determine the most effective ways to coordinate these varied efforts.

vack, 1988), elementary school (Elias et al., 1986; Rotheram-Borus, 1988; Weissberg et al., 1981), middle school (Botvin & Tortu, 1988; Weissberg & Caplan, 1991), and high school (Eisen, Zellman, & McAlister, 1990). Most of these efforts have been brief (i.e., less than 1 year), single-method, single-level intervention strategies. Unfortunately, there is little evidence to suggest that such programs promote behavioral improvements that will last for several years postintervention (Dryfoos, 1990). Currently, there is growing recognition that more sustained comprehensive interventions may be required to produce lasting behavioral gains in school-age children and adolescents (Mueller & Higgins, 1988; Schorr, 1988; Zigler & Berman, 1983). Creating multiyear, classroom-based skills training approaches at the core of larger multilevel-systems efforts to promote social competence and health is a particularly promising direction for prevention research.

A variety of classroom-based health promotion strategies have been evaluated, including programs that provide information about the consequences of engaging in certain high-risk behaviors, as well as programs that emphasize generic personal and social skills training. Research suggests that knowledge-only programs have minimal effects on children's behaviors (Botvin & Tortu, 1988; Tobler, 1986). In contrast, programs that teach generic, broadly applicable personal and social competencies—such as self-control, stress management, problem solving, decision making, communication, peer resistance, and assertiveness—have yielded significant benefits at least 1-year postintervention in broad areas of personal competence, such as social adjustment, assertive behavior, aggressive behavior, peer sociability, and coping with stressors (Elias et al., 1986; Gesten et al., 1982; Rotheram-Borus, 1988; Shure & Spivack, 1988).

In spite of these positive effects, generic skills training programs do not consistently produce positive outcomes in more problem-specific domains, such as substance use or high-risk sexual behavior (Caplan & Weissberg, 1989; Durlak, 1983). Combining general personal and social skills training—for example, in problem solving and decision making—with attempts to affect student knowledge, attitudes, and behavioral competence in specific domains appears to be a very promising approach for preventing specific problem behaviors (Botvin & Tortu, 1988; Caplan et al., in press). However, because research findings suggest children have limited capacities to transfer and generalize skills, attitudes, and information for handling stressors in one domain to address problems in another (Dodge, Pettit, McClaskey, & Brown, 1986), a major task for future research involves developing skills–attitudes–information training models that target multiple problem areas in the context of the same intervention.

Recent research suggests that multiple years of classroom-based social-competence-promotion training may be required to produce long-term improvements in students' behavior (e.g., Botvin, Baker, Dusenbury, Tortu, & Botvin, 1990; Connell & Turner, 1985; Perry et al., 1989; Weissberg, 1989). For example, Weissberg and Caplan (1991) trained middle-school teachers to implement a curriculum focusing on impulse control, stress management, a six-step social information processing model for resolving problems, and behavioral social skills training. Evaluation results with 421 early adolescents indicated that program students, relative to control subjects, improved in problem-solving skills, prosocial attitudes toward conflict resolution, teacher-rated impulse control and peer sociability, and self-reported delinquent behavior. During the following year, teachers conducted booster training with a sample of seventh-grade students who participated in the initial intervention. Weissberg (1989) assessed the long-term impact of 2 years (i.e., in sixth and seventh grade) versus 1 year (i.e., in sixth or seventh grade) versus no training on students' problem-solving skills and adjustment during the fall of eighth grade. Students with 2 years of training, but not those with 1, showed significant gains relative to the no-treatment control group.

Although brief classroom-based programs may produce short-term behavioral gains, it appears unrealistic to expect such efforts to have lasting effects. Furthermore, it is unclear precisely how many hours of instruction are needed to promote robust improvements in children's health-related knowledge, attitudes, and behavior. Although relatively few hours of instruction can produce large effects for knowledge acquisition, 40–50 hr may be necessary to establish stable effects for all three domains (Connell, Turner, & Mason, 1985). These findings suggest that researchers need to design and evaluate more substantial (e.g., 40–50 hr) multiyear interventions in order to test adequately the extent to which classroom-based social-competence-promotion programs can produce long-term preventive effects.

School-based programs that focus independently on the child or environment are not as effective as those that simultaneously educate the child and instill positive changes in the environment. Consequently, a word must be said regarding *person-centered* versus *ecologically oriented* skills training programs. Training programs may appropriately be considered person-centered when skills are taught in the absence of creating environmental supports for continued skill application in daily interactions. In contrast, ecologically oriented programs emphasize not only the teaching of skills, but also the creation of meaningful real-life opportunities to use skills and the establishment of structures to provide reinforcement for effective skill application. From this perspective, the success of skills training programs may depend largely on their attention to changing socialization patterns and supports in the intervention setting (Elias & Weissberg, 1989). For example, ecologically oriented problem-solving programs try to introduce a common social information processing framework that children and teachers can use to communicate more effectively about problem situations (Shure & Spivack, 1988; Weissberg & Caplan, 1991). In other words, they try to change not only the child's behavior, but also the teacher's behavior, the relationship between the teacher and child, and classroom and school-level resources and procedures to support adaptive problem-solving efforts (Weissberg et al., 1989).

In line with the ecological perspective, Pentz et al. (1989) contended that many school-based prevention programs may not produce significant and sustained behavioral changes because of a lack of integration between school-based training with community-based interventions, the mass media, and other environmental influences outside of school that conflict with the concepts taught in school. They proposed that multilevel, multicomponent prevention efforts that coordinate the efforts of multiple socializing influences—including parents, peers, community leaders, local school and government administrators, and mass media programmers—may be needed to produce long-term social, psychological, and health benefits. Specifically, Pentz et al. (1989) developed a substance abuse prevention program that combined 10 sessions of classroom-based peer-resistance skills training, 10 homework sessions interviewing parents and family members about issues related to drug abuse prevention, mass media programming, and community organization. Outcome analyses with 22,500 sixth- and seventh-grade students indicated significantly lower prevalence rates for alcohol, cigarette, and marijuana use for the program participants compared with control subjects. Positive effects were sustained 3 years following the classroom intervention with low-risk and high-risk subjects showing significant reductions in tobacco and marijuana use (Johnson et al., 1990).

Perry et al. (1989) evaluated effects from a 5-year school-based behavioral education program, for students moving from 6th through 10th grade, conducted in the context of a communitywide intervention to promote cardiovascular health. The primary program goals involved social skills training to enhance students' ability to resist pressures to engage in health-compromising behaviors as well as to generate health-enhancing alternatives, changing peer group norms, and providing alternative healthy role models. All programs used peer leaders, who were elected by their classmates and trained by community staff, as key trainers of new skills and information within the classroom setting. Reported findings, which focused on the intervention's impact on smoking, indicated that 13.1% of program students compared with 22.7% of control children were current smokers.

Perry et al. (1989) and Pentz et al. (1989) have demonstrated the potential efficacy of multiyear, multicomponent school-based interventions—that involve parents, peers, and the surrounding community—to prevent substance abuse. A crucial next step in research is to determine whether these models can be used to prevent multiple social and psychological problem behaviors in the context of the same intervention. There is growing support for planned, sequential, comprehensive health education in kindergarten through Grade 12 that (a) emphasizes personal and social skills training; (b) promotes positive social values and health attitudes; and (c) provides honest, relevant information about health issues such as substance abuse, sex, AIDS, violence, family life, and mental health (DeFreise et al., 1990; National Commission on the Role of the School and the Community in Improving Adolescent Health, 1990; Report of the National Mental Health Association's Commission on the Prevention of Mental-Emotional Disabilities, 1986). Most notably, the U.S. Department of Health and Human Services, Public Health Service (1990) proposed by the Year 2000 that at least 75% of the nation's schools provide high-quality comprehensive health education.

Weissberg (1991) suggested that effectively implementing carefully evaluated comprehensive social-competence and health education (C-SCAHE) that targets the prevention of multiple problem areas is an urgently needed educational reform for the 1990s. Although this approach has potential to benefit many young people, there are potential barriers that could undercut the efficacy of such programming. Most notably, health education historically has emphasized conveying science information and facts at the expense of focusing on skills training to effect changes in health practices. Secondly, such programs have traditionally focused on issues related to physical health more than social or psychological health. C-SCAHE, in highlighting the dual importance of both *social competence* and *health*, calls for a better instructional balance between these areas.

Researchers and practitioners must attend more to issues of program design, implementation, and institutionalization. Attention to multiple aspects of program development—design, implementation, and institutionalization—is also of critical importance in establishing beneficial, enduring, school-based primary prevention programs (Weissberg et al., 1989). In terms of design, effective programming must focus simultaneously on (a) enhancing children's personal and social skills, attitudes and values, and domain-specific knowledge and (b) creating socializing systems at multiple levels to promote positive youth development. Programs must promote a sense of shared values, culture, and support among students, school staff, parents, and the larger community. This integration underscores the importance of coordinating classroom-, school-, and community-level programming efforts.

Regardless of a program's quality, its potential for positive effects is diminished when program implementers are poorly trained, have inadequate organizational support for program delivery, or lack the necessary skills to provide effective training. Well-designed programs that are implemented with low integrity may appear ineffective, when in fact they are quite beneficial (see Botvin et al., 1990; Connell et al., 1985). School systems must provide time and resources for proficient staff training, ongoing supervision, on-site coaching, and program monitoring in order to ensure implementation integrity (Hall & Hord, 1987).

It must also be noted that many initially successful interventions fail to sustain their impact in future years (Berman & McLaughlin, 1978). Thus, researchers must identify organizational practices and system-level policies or structures that enable successful programs to endure with continued positive effects (McLaughlin, 1990). Institutionalizing successful school-based programs requires that they be adapted to the ecology of the school and community in which they occur (Price & Lorion, 1989). For C-SCAHE programming to endure, it is critical to design a clearly articulated kindergarten through 12th-grade curriculum scope and sequence; determine where such training fits in the overall instructional program at the building level; ensure that the training approaches and content comply with state and federal guidelines and policies; and develop a solid infrastructure of school system supports for effective program implementation, monitoring, and improvement. Ultimately, a comprehensive program that targets multiple problem behaviors has greater potential to endure in school settings than have discrete, ad hoc, short-term categorical interventions that target the prevention of single problem behaviors (DeFriese et al., 1990).

The need to coordinate C-SCAHE with clinical treatment services. Multiyear, multicomponent, competence-promotion programs—involving the child, classroom, school organization, and larger community setting—are most promising as primary prevention strategies because they have excellent potential to influence children's skills, attitudes, and social and health behaviors. At the same time, it is important to recognize that these programs are not panaceas. Although some high-risk children may benefit from program participation, there are many who will still require additional treatment to reduce psychological maladjustment and enhance their behavioral functioning. An important part of C-SCAHE will involve training program implementers to recognize when high-risk children have additional needs for treatment and to refer those individuals for the appropriate services they need. Following the perspective that school-based intervention strategies should be reinforced by parents, the peer group, and the community, we deem it equally important to coordinate intervention strategies used in prevention programs and clinical treatment to produce more powerful intervention packages for high-risk children. Illustratively, cognitive–behavioral and social-skills treatment approaches that promote children's self-control and problem solving appear to be very compatible with the competencies taught in classroom-based programs (e.g., Kendall & Braswell, 1985). It seems important to compare the effects of classroom training versus clinical treatment versus a combined package to determine their differential effects on children already experiencing behavior problems.

Conclusion

This article describes several prevention efforts that attempt to promote competent young children and competence-enhancing environments. There is substantial evidence to indicate that these programs, when implemented effectively, can produce lasting behavioral benefits for young people; however, it may take considerable time before research convincingly resolves whether such improvements will actually reduce the incidence of mental disorders. If these prevention programs improve the social functioning, academic performance, and health behavior of large numbers of children, then the investment of resources seems well spent—especially inasmuch as young people with diagnosable disorders can participate and benefit from them.

Mental health professionals must decide what roles they will play in the prevention field. Examples of constructive participation may involve taking the lead or collaborating to establish innovative, multidisciplinary, multicomponent prevention programs or coordinating one's treatment efforts more closely with family-, school-, and community-based prevention efforts. In contrast, refraining from any participation until prevention research definitively demonstrates that these programs lower the incidence of diagnosable mental disorders could seriously limit the meaningful contributions that a professional might offer in addressing the needs of many children and adolescents at risk for psychosocial health and behavior problems.

In 1930, the White House Conference on Children and Youth expressed concern about the potential unintended negative consequences of professional specialization:

> To the doctor, the child is a typhoid patient; to the playground supervisor, a first baseman; to the teacher, a learner of arithmetic. At different times, he may be different things to each of these specialists, but rarely is he a whole child to any of them. (cited in U.S. Department of Health, Education, and Welfare, 1967, p. 9)

Each mental health professional will have to decide whether to characterize and treat children only within the context of mental–emotional disorders or to expand their perceptions to incorporate the multiple aspects of children's functioning and environmental circumstances. This article supports Sarason's (1981) notion that mental health professionals should forge a stronger collaboration with families, schools, and communities in order to provide high-quality, comprehensive prevention programming to more children and youth. The critical question to address is not whether prevention programs work, but how they can be conducted most effectively.

References

Albee, G. W. (1983). Psychopathology, prevention, and the just society. *Journal of Primary Prevention, 4,* 5–40.

Bangert-Drowns, R. L. (1988). The effects of school-based substance abuse education: A meta-analysis. *Journal of Drug Education, 18,* 243–264.

Berman, P., & McLaughlin, M. W. (1978). *Federal programs supporting educational change: Vol. 8. Implementing and sustaining innovations.* Santa Monica, CA: Rand Corporation.

Bond, L. A., & Compas, B. E. (Eds.). (1989). *Primary prevention and promotion in the schools.* Newbury Park, CA: Sage.

Botvin, G. J., Baker, E., Dusenbury, L., Tortu, S., & Botvin, E. M. (1990). Preventing adolescent drug abuse through a multimodal cognitive–behavioral approach: Results of a 3-year study. *Journal of Consulting and Clinical Psychology, 58,* 437–446.

Botvin, G. J., & Tortu, S. (1988). Preventing adolescent substance abuse through life skills training. In R. H. Price, E. L. Cowen, R. P. Lorion, & J. Ramos-McKay (Eds.), *14 ounces of prevention: A casebook for practitioners* (pp. 98–110). Washington, DC: American Psychological Association.

Bronfenbrenner, U. (1979). *The ecology of human development: Experiments by nature and design.* Cambridge, MA: Harvard University Press.

Caplan, M., & Weissberg, R. P. (1989). Promoting social competence in early adolescence: Developmental considerations. In B. H. Schneider, G. Attili, J. Nadel, & R. P. Weissberg (Eds.), *Social competence in developmental perspective* (pp. 371–385). Boston: Kluwer.

Caplan, M., Weissberg, R. P., Grober, J. H., Sivo, P. J., Grady, K., & Jacoby, C. (in press). Social-competence promotion with inner-city and suburban young adolescents: Effects on social adjustment and alcohol use. *Journal of Consulting and Clinical Psychology.*

Cherlin, A. J. (1988). *The changing American family and public policy.* Washington, DC: Urban Institute Press.

Comer, J. P. (1988). Educating poor minority children. *Scientific American, 259,* 42–48.

Committee for Economic Development. (1987). *Children in need: Investment strategies for the educationally disadvantaged.* New York: Author.

Connell, D. B., & Turner, R. R. (1985). The impact of instructional experience and the effects of cumulative instruction. *Journal of School Health, 55,* 324–331.

Connell, D. B., Turner, R. R., & Mason, E. F. (1985). Summary of the findings of the School Health Education Evaluation: Health promotion effectiveness, implementation, and costs. *Journal of School Health, 55,* 316–323.

Costello, E. J. (1990). Child psychiatric epidemiology: Implications for clinical research and practice. In B. B. Lahey & A. E. Kazdin (Eds.),

Advances in clinical child psychology (Vol. 13, pp. 53–90). New York: Plenum Press.

Cowen, E. L. (1986). Primary prevention in mental health: Ten years of retrospect and ten years of prospect. In M. Kessler & S. E. Goldston (Eds.), *A decade of progress in primary prevention* (pp. 3–45). Hanover, NH: University Press of New England.

Cowen, E. L., Gesten, E. L., & Weissberg, R. P. (1980). An interrelated network of preventively oriented school-based mental health approaches. In R. H. Price & P. Politzer (Eds.), *Evaluation and action in the community context* (pp. 173–210). New York: Academic Press.

Cowen, E. L., & Work, W. C. (1988). Resilient children, psychological wellness, and primary prevention. *American Journal of Community Psychology, 16,* 591–607.

DeFriese, G. H., Crossland, C. L., Pearson, C. E., & Sullivan, C. J. (1990). Comprehensive school health programs: Current status and future prospects. *Journal of School Health, 60*(4).

Dodge, K. A., Pettit, G. S., McClaskey, C. L., & Brown, M. M. (1986). Social competence in children. *Monographs of the Society for Research in Child Development, 51*(2, Serial No. 213).

Donovan, J. E., Jessor, R., & Costa, F. (1988). The syndrome of problem behavior in adolescence: A replication. *Journal of Consulting and Clinical Psychology, 56,* 762–765.

Dryfoos, J. G. (1990). *Adolescents at risk: Prevalence and prevention.* New York: Oxford University Press.

Durlak, J. A. (1983). Social problem-solving as a primary prevention strategy. In R. D. Felner, L. A. Jason, J. N. Moritsugu, & S. S. Farber (Eds.), *Preventive psychology: Theory, research, and practice* (pp. 31–48). New York: Pergamon Press.

Eisen, M., Zellman, G. L., & McAlister, A. L. (1990). Evaluating the impact of a theory-based sexuality and contraceptive education program. *Family Planning Perspectives, 22,* 261–271.

Elias, M. J., & Branden, L. R. (1988). Primary prevention of behavioral and emotional problems in school-aged populations. *School Psychology Review, 17,* 581–592.

Elias, M. J., Gara, M., Ubriaco, M., Rothbaum, P. A., Clabby, J. F., & Schuyler, T. (1986). Impact of a preventive social problem-solving intervention on children's coping with middle-school stressors. *American Journal of Community Psychology, 14,* 259–275.

Elias, M. J., & Weissberg, R. P. (1989). School-based social-competence promotion as a primary prevention strategy: A tale of two projects. *Prevention in Human Services, 7,* 177–200.

Elliott, D. S., Huizinga, D., & Menard, S. (1989). *Multiple problem youth: Delinquency, substance use, and mental health problems.* New York: Springer-Verlag.

Emshoff, J. G. (1989). A preventive intervention with children of alcoholics. *Prevention in Human Services, 7,* 225–254.

Felner, R. D., & Adan, A. M. (1988). The School Transition Environment Project: An ecological intervention and evaluation. In R. H. Price, E. L. Cowen, R. P. Lorion, & J. Ramos-McKay (Eds.), *14 ounces of prevention: A casebook for practitioners* (pp. 111–122). Washington, DC: American Psychological Association.

Ford, M. E. (1985). Primary prevention: Key issues and a competence perspective. *Journal of Primary Prevention, 5,* 264–266.

Gans, J. E., Blyth, D. A., Elster, A. B., & Gaveras, L. L. (1990). *America's adolescents: How healthy are they?* Chicago: American Medical Association.

Garmezy, N. (1985). Stress-resistant children: The search for protective factors. In J. E. Stevenson (Ed.), *Recent research in developmental psychopathology* (pp. 213–233). Oxford, England: Pergamon Press.

Gesten, E. L., Rains, M., Rapkin, B. D., Weissberg, R. P., Flores de Apodaca, R., Cowen, E. L., & Bowen, R. (1982). Training children in social problem-solving skills: A competence building approach, first and second look. *American Journal of Community Psychology, 10,* 95–115.

Gottfredson, D. C. (1986). An empirical test of school-based environmental and individual interventions to reduce the risk of delinquent behavior. *Criminology, 24,* 705–731.

Hall, G. E., & Hord, S. M. (1987). *Change in schools: Facilitating the process.* Albany, NY: State University of New York Press.

Haskins, R. (1989). Beyond metaphor: The efficacy of early childhood education. *American Psychologist, 44,* 274–283.

Hawkins, J. D., Doueck, H. J., & Lishner, D. M. (1988). Changing teaching practices in mainstream classrooms to improve bonding and behavior of low achievers. *American Educational Research Journal, 25,* 31–50.

Hawkins, J. D., & Weis, J. G. (1985). The social development model: An integrated approach to delinquency prevention. *Journal of Primary Prevention, 6,* 73–97.

Infant Health and Development Program. (1990). Enhancing the outcomes of low-birth-weight, premature infants: A multisite randomized trial. *Journal of the American Medical Association, 263,* 3035–3042.

Jason, L. A., Hess, R. E., Felner, R. D., & Moritsugu, J. (Eds.). (1987). Prevention: Toward a multidisciplinary approach. *Prevention in Human Services, 5*(2), 1–309.

Johnson, C. A., Pentz, M. A., Weber, M. D., Dwyer, J. H., Baer, N., MacKinnon, D. P., Hansen, W. B., & Flay, B. R. (1990). Relative effectiveness of comprehensive community programming for drug abuse prevention with high-risk and low-risk adolescents. *Journal of Consulting and Clinical Psychology, 58,* 447–456.

Johnson, D. L. (1988). Primary prevention of behavior problems in young children: The Houston Parent-Child Development Center. In R. H. Price, E. L. Cowen, R. P. Lorion, & J. Ramos-McKay (Eds.), *14 ounces of prevention: A casebook for practitioners* (pp. 44–52). Washington, DC: American Psychological Association.

Johnson, D. L., & Walker, T. (1987). Primary prevention of behavior problems in Mexican-American children. *American Journal of Community Psychology, 15,* 375–385.

Kazdin, A. E. (1991). *Prevention of conduct disorder* (Preliminary report of the National Conference on Prevention Research). Bethesda, MD: National Institute of Mental Health.

Kendall, P. C., & Braswell, L. (1985). *Cognitive-behavioral therapy for impulsive children.* New York: Guilford Press.

Lamb, H. R., & Zusman, J. (1982). The seductiveness of primary prevention. In F. D. Perlmutter (Ed.). *New directions for mental health services: Mental health promotion and primary prevention* (Vol. 13, pp. 19–30). San Francisco: Jossey-Bass.

Lazar, I., Darlington, R., Murray, H., Royce, J., & Snipper, A. (1982). *The lasting effects of early education: A report from the Consortium for Longitudinal Studies, 47*(2–3; Serial No. 195).

Lorion, R. P. (Ed.). (1989). Protecting the children: Strategies for optimizing emotional and behavioral development. *Prevention in Human Services, 7,* 1–275.

Marlowe, H. A., & Weinberg, R. B. (Eds.). (1985). Is mental illness preventable? Pros and cons. *Journal of Primary Prevention, 5,* 200–313.

Maughan, B. (1988). School experiences as risk/protective factors. In M. Rutter (Ed.), *Studies of psychosocial risk: The power of longitudinal data* (pp. 200–220). New York: Cambridge University Press.

McLaughlin, M. W. (1990). The Rand Change Agent Study revisited: Macro perspectives and micro realities. *Educational Researcher, 19,* 11–16.

Mueller, D. P., & Higgins, P. S. (1988). *Funders' guide manual: A guide to prevention programs in human services—Focus on children and adolescents.* St. Paul, MN: Amherst H. Wilder Foundation.

National Advisory Mental Health Council. (1990). *National plan for research on child and adolescent mental disorders.* Washington, DC: National Institute of Mental Health.

National Commission on the Role of the School and the Community in Improving Adolescent Health. (1990). *Code Blue: Uniting for healthier youth.* Alexandria, VA: National Association of State Boards of Education.

Olds, D. L. (1988). The Prenatal/Early Infancy Project. In R. H. Price, E. L. Cowen, R. P. Lorion, & J. Ramos-McKay (Eds.), *14 ounces of prevention: A casebook for practitioners* (pp. 9–23). Washington, DC: American Psychological Association.

Pedro-Carroll, J. P., & Cowen, E. L. (1985). The Children of Divorce Intervention Program: An investigation of the efficacy of a school-based prevention program. *Journal of Consulting and Clinical Psychology, 53,* 603–611.

Pentz, M. A., Dwyer, J. H., MacKinnon, D. P., Flay, B. R., Hansen, W. B., Wang, E. Y. I., & Johnson, C. A. (1989). A multi-community trial for primary prevention of adolescent drug abuse: Effects on drug use prevalence. *Journal of the American Medical Association, 261,* 3259–3266.

Perry, C. L., & Jessor, R. (1985). The concept of health promotion and the prevention of adolescent drug abuse. *Health Education Quarterly, 12,* 169–184.

Perry, C. L., Klepp, K., & Sillers, C. (1989). Community-wide strategies for cardiovascular health: The Minnesota Heart Health Program youth program. *Health Education Research, 4,* 87–101.

Pierson, D. E. (1988). The Brookline Early Education Project. In R. H. Price, E. L. Cowen, R. P. Lorion, & J. Ramos-McKay (Eds.), *14 ounces of prevention: A casebook for practitioners* (pp. 24–31). Washington, DC: American Psychological Association.

Price, R. H., Cowen, E. L., Lorion, R. P., & Ramos-McKay, J. (Eds). (1988). *14 ounces of prevention: A casebook for practitioners.* Washington, DC: American Psychological Association.

Price, R. H., & Lorion, R. P. (1989). Prevention programming as organizational reinvention: From research to implementation. In D. Shaffer, I. Philips, & N. B. Enzer (Eds.), *Prevention of mental disorders, alcohol and other drug use in children and adolescents* (pp. 97–124). Washington, DC: Office for Substance Abuse Prevention.

Provence, S., & Naylor, A. (1983). *Working with disadvantaged parents and children: Scientific issues and practice.* New Haven, CT: Yale University Press.

Raimy, C. V. (Ed.). (1950). *Training in clinical psychology.* Englewood Cliffs, NJ: Prentice-Hall.

Report of the National Mental Health Association Commission on the Prevention of Mental-Emotional Disabilities. (1986). *The prevention of mental-emotional disabilities.* Alexandria, VA: National Mental Health Association.

Report of the Task Force on Education of Young Adolescents. (1989). *Turning points: Preparing American youth for the 21st century.* Washington, DC: Carnegie Council on Adolescent Development.

Report of the Task Panel on Prevention. (1978). *Task panel reports submitted to the President's Commission on Mental Health* (Vol. 4, pp. 1822–1863). Washington, DC: U.S. Government Printing Office.

Rotheram-Borus, M. J. (1988). Assertiveness training with children. In R. H. Price, E. L. Cowen, R. P. Lorion, & J. Ramos-McKay (Eds.), *14 ounces of prevention: A casebook for practitioners* (pp. 83–97). Washington, DC: American Psychological Association.

Royce, J. M., Darlington, R. B., & Murray, H. W. (1983). Pooled analyses: Findings across studies. In Consortium for Longitudinal Studies (Ed.), *As the twig is bent: Lasting effects of preschool programs* (pp. 411–459). Hillsdale, NJ: Erlbaum.

Rutter, M. (1982). Prevention of children's psychosocial disorders: Myth and substance. *Pediatrics, 70,* 883–894.

Rutter, M. (1987). Psychosocial resilience and protective mechanisms. *American Journal of Orthopsychiatry, 57,* 316–331.

Rutter, M., Maughan, B., Mortimore, P., & Ouston, J. (1979). *Fifteen thousand hours: Secondary schools and their effects on children.* Cambridge, MA: Harvard University Press.

Sameroff, A. J. (1991). *Prevention of developmental psychopathology using the transactional model: Perspectives on host, risk agent, and environmental interactions* (Preliminary report of the National Conference on Prevention Research). Bethesda, MD: National Institute of Mental Health.

Sarason, S. B. (1981). An asocial psychology and a misdirected clinical psychology. *American Psychologist, 36,* 827–836.

Schorr, L. B. (1988). *Within our reach: Breaking the cycle of disadvantage.* New York: Anchor Press.

Schweinhart, L. J., & Weikart, D. P. (1988). The High/Scope Perry Preschool Program. In R. H. Price, E. L. Cowen, R. P. Lorion, & J. Ramos-McKay (Eds.), *14 ounces of prevention: A casebook for practitioners* (pp. 53–65). Washington, DC: American Psychological Association.

Schweinhart, L. J., & Weikart, D. P. (1989). The High/Scope Perry Preschool Study: Implications for early childhood care and education. *Prevention in Human Services, 7,* 109–132.

Seitz, V. (1991). Intervention programs for impoverished children: A comparison of educational and family support models. *Annals of Child Development, 7,* 73–103.

Seitz, V., Rosenbaum, L. K., & Apfel, N. H. (1985). Effects of family support intervention: A 10-year follow-up. *Child Development, 56,* 376–391.

Shaffer, D. (1989). Prevention of psychiatric disorders in children and adolescents: A summary of findings and recommendations from Project Prevention. In D. Shaffer, I. Philips, & N. B. Enzer (Eds.), *Prevention of mental disorders, alcohol and other drug use in children and adolescents* (pp. 443–456). Washington, DC: Office for Substance Abuse Prevention.

Shure, M. B., & Spivack, G. (1988). Interpersonal cognitive problem solving. In R. H. Price, E. L. Cowen, R. P. Lorion, & J. Ramos-McKay (Eds.), *14 ounces of prevention: A casebook for practitioners* (pp. 69–82). Washington, DC: American Psychological Association.

Slavin, R. E. (1983). *Cooperative learning.* New York: Longman.

Slavin, R. E., Madden, N. A., Karweit, N. L., Livermon, B. J., & Dolan, L. (1990). Success for all: First-year outcomes of a comprehensive plan for reforming urban education. *American Educational Research Journal, 27,* 255–278.

Tobler, N. S. (1986). Meta-analysis of 143 adolescent drug prevention programs: Quantitative outcome results of program participants compared to a control or comparison group. *Journal of Drug Issues, 16,* 537–567.

Tuma, J. M. (1989). Mental health services for children: The state of the art. *American Psychologist, 44,* 188–199.

U.S. Department of Health and Human Services, Public Health Service. (1990). *Healthy people 2000: National health promotion and disease prevention objectives.* Washington, DC: U.S. Government Printing Office.

U.S. Department of Health, Education, and Welfare. (1967). *The story of the White House Conferences on Children and Youth.* Washington, DC: Author.

Walker, C. E., & Roberts, M. C. (Eds.). (1983). *Handbook of clinical child psychology.* New York: Wiley.

Weissberg, R. P. (1989, April). *A follow-up study of school-based social-competence promotion for young adolescents.* Symposium presentation at the Biennial Meeting for the Society for Research in Child Development, Kansas City, MO.

Weissberg, R. P. (1991). Comprehensive social-competence and health education (C-SCAHE): An urgently needed educational reform for the 1990s. *Child, Youth, and Family Services Quarterly, 14,* 10–12.

Weissberg, R. P., & Caplan, M. (1991). *Promoting social competence and preventing antisocial behavior in young urban adolescents.* Manuscript submitted for publication.

Weissberg, R. P., Caplan, M. Z., & Sivo, P. J. (1989). A new conceptual framework for establishing school-based social-competence promotion programs. In L. A. Bond & B. E. Compas (Eds.), *Primary prevention and promotion in the schools* (pp. 255–296). Newbury Park, CA: Sage.

Weissberg, R. P., Gesten, E. L., Carnrike, C. L., Toro, P. A., Rapkin, B. D., Davidson, E., & Cowen, E. L. (1981). Social problem-solving skills training: A competence building intervention with second- to fourth-grade children. *American Journal of Community Psychology, 9,* 411–423.

Zabin, L. S. (1990). Adolescent pregnancy and early sexual onset. In B. B. Lahey & A. E. Kazdin (Eds.), *Advances in clinical child psychology* (Vol. 13, pp. 247–281). New York: Plenum Press.

Zigler, E., & Berman, W. (1983). Discerning the future of early childhood intervention. *American Psychologist, 38,* 894–906.

Zigler, E., & Black, K. B. (1989). America's family support movement: Strengths and limitation. *American Journal of Orthopsychiatry, 59,* 6–19.

Zill, N., & Schoenborn, C. A. (1990). Developmental, learning, and emotional problems: Health of our nation's children, United States, 1988. *Advance data from vital and health statistics* (No. 190). Hyattsville, MD: National Center for Health Statistics.

Zins, J., & Forman, S. G. (1988). Mini-series on primary prevention: From theory to practice. *School Psychology Review, 17*(4), 539–634.

Received April 22, 1991
Revision received May 13, 1991
Accepted May 13, 1991 ■

JOURNAL OF RESEARCH ON ADOLESCENCE, 4(2), 319–345

Community Strategies for the Reduction of Youth Drinking: Theory and Application

Alexander C. Wagenaar and Cheryl L. Perry
Division of Epidemiology
School of Public Health
University of Minnesota

We review the core concepts and key propositions from several theories concerning youth alcohol use, and we integrate them into a single theory of drinking behavior. The resulting model illustrates the centrality of social interaction in influencing drinking and the critical importance of changing broader socioenvironmental conditions to achieve long-term reductions in youth drinking and associated problems. Two large-scale randomized community trials in progress (Communities Mobilizing for Change on Alcohol [CMCA] and Project Northland: Partnerships for Youth Health) are testing key components of the model of youth drinking. We conclude that effective long-term alcohol prevention programs require strategies for community and societal change.

In this article, we have four objectives. First, we briefly review several theories on alcohol consumption in young people that are particularly important for the design of community action efforts on youth drinking. Second, we present elements of an integrated meta-theory of drinking behavior, drawing on concepts from many social science theories. Third, we discuss implications of those theories for the design of community efforts to affect the use of alcohol by underage youth and

---

Requests for reprints should be sent to Alexander C. Wagenaar, Division of Epidemiology, School of Public Health, University of Minnesota, 1300 South Second Street, Suite 300, Minneapolis, MN 55454–1015.

reduce harmful consequences of youth drinking. Fourth, we summarize the objectives and implementation strategies of two large-scale randomized community trials currently in progress that are designed to reduce youth drinking.

A POPULATION-WIDE APPROACH IS REQUIRED

Youth alcohol use is a social behavior that is primarily determined by social structures, norms, and other dimensions of the social environment in which people live (Akers, 1992). Widespread patterns of alcohol use by young people are not reflective of addictive or psychopathological behavior, but, rather, are "normal" or expected results of social policies, institutional structures, and social norms concerning alcohol in our society. Prevention efforts and public action strategies must be based on an understanding of the factors that affect patterns of alcohol use across the whole population of young people rather than just the smaller sample of those identified as problem drinkers. Predicting with great sensitivity and selectivity why a given individual will drink and understanding the nature of the consequences of individual drinking may be important in a clinical setting in which a small set of individuals with alcohol-related problems is the focus of attention. Applying such an individual focus to the development of population-wide prevention efforts is, however, not fruitful.

A population-wide focus on how the social environment fosters youth drinking is necessary for several reasons (Syme, 1986). First, the magnitude of the problem is such that even if we had a perfect "cure," we most likely would not have the resources to apply it to all who are at risk. Second, because more than half of high-school seniors drink and one third become intoxicated at least once in 2 weeks (Johnston, O'Malley, & Bachman, 1991), it is evident that many youths are at significant risk for a car crash, assault, rape, injury, or another serious problem associated with drinking. Third, there is constant turnover in the high-risk population. Turnover is most obvious for youth because most high-risk, heavy-drinking youth are at substantially lower risk when they reach age 30, and new entrants replace them in the high-risk pool of teenagers. Thus, even if we cure the current incumbants of the high-risk pool, in a short period of time turnover is such that little long-term benefit is achieved.

The fourth reason a population-wide focus is necessary is that the majority of alcohol-related death and disability is attributable to moderate drinkers, not those who are alcohol dependent. The heaviest drinkers are clearly at highest risk of problems, but there are so many more people in the lower risk "moderate" drinking group that a lower individual risk still results in a larger aggregate burden to society.[1] This is the classic *population attributable risk* concept in epidemiology (A. M. Lilienfeld & D. E. Lilienfeld, 1980), which is so frequently overlooked when prevention programs are designed solely focusing on "high-risk" youth.[2]

THEORY: WHY YOUTH DRINK

We need to understand why the overwhelming majority of teenagers use alcohol on a regular basis and how the amount and frequency of such drinking can be reduced, with a consequent reduction in those social and health problems for which alcohol use is a contributing factor. To understand the many factors that may contribute to youth drinking, and to identify potential action strategies to reduce youth drinking, a broad range of theoretical approaches might be considered. Many of these theories use concepts that may have different labels but reflect conceptually similar underlying constructs.

Many etiological theories provide elements for a comprehensive meta-theory of population-wide drinking patterns: genetic theories, tension-reduction theory, psychoanalytic theory, cognitive theories, labeling theory, selective interaction/differential association theory, problem behavior theory, stage theory, economic theories, classical conditioning theory, operant conditioning theory, social learning theory, symbolic interactionism theory, social control theories, anomie theory, bonding theory, and availability theory. Dimensions of all these theories are reflected in our model of drinking behavior shown in Figure 1. A comprehensive review of all these theoretical approaches is

---

[1]Moreover, moderate-drinking youth are by no means at low risk for alcohol-related problems. At a blood alcohol concentration of .03g/dl (i.e., two drinks for most teenagers), for example, the risk of traffic crash involvement is nine times higher than for youths who have not been drinking (Farris, Malone, & Lilliefors, 1976).

[2]In a humane society, we should of course do whatever we can to assist and treat those who are identified as alcohol dependent or as being in the highest risk category. Early intervention with such individuals may well prevent further serious alcohol problems. We argue strongly, however, that primary prevention requires efforts focused on the entire population and the communities and environments that affect drinking and related behaviors. Without broader political and social change, without efforts to change the conditions that create the (high) risk in the first place, long-term success can only be limited.

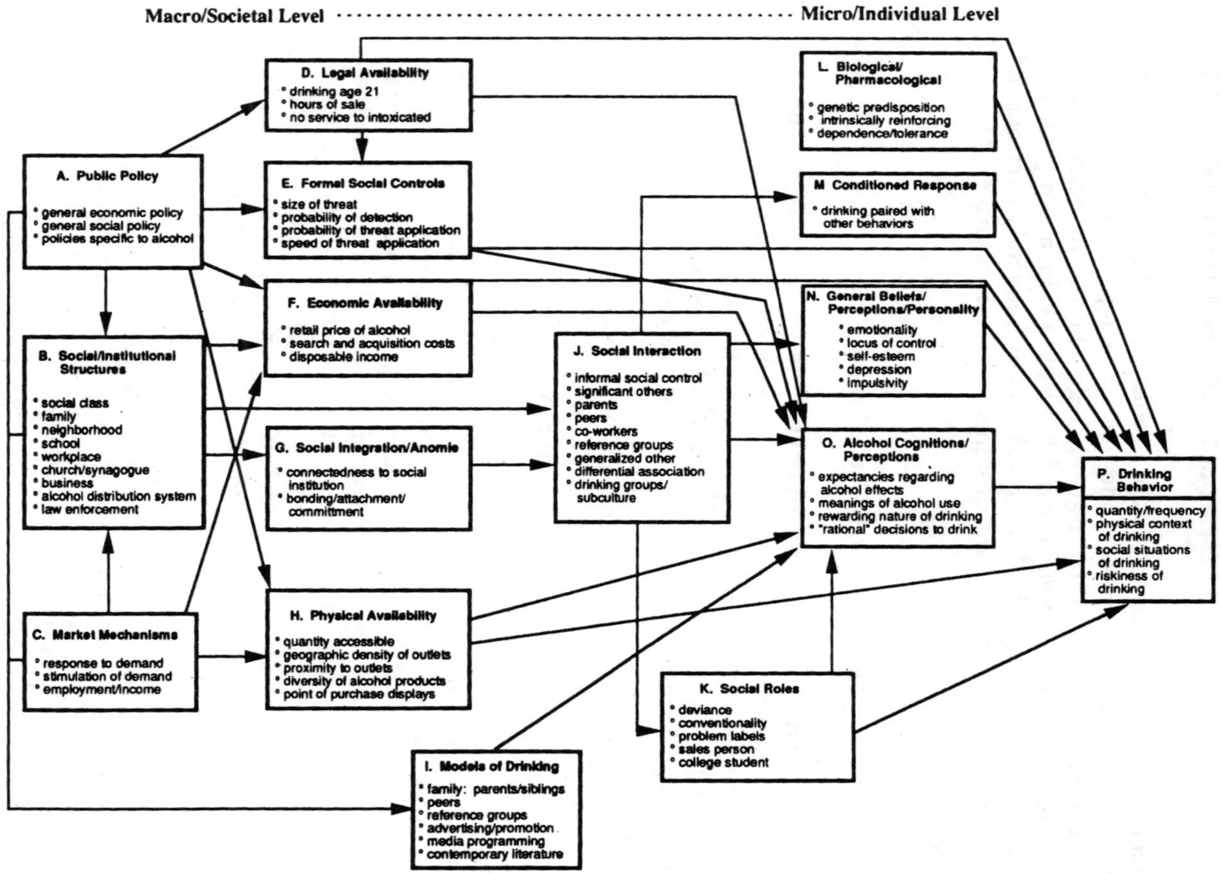

FIGURE 1 An integrated theory of drinking behavior.

beyond the scope of this article, but we briefly review the core propositions from those theories that most influence our approach to youth drinking.[3]

Cognitive theories focus on the central role of expectancies concerning the effects of alcohol (Bandura, 1977; Lewin, Dembo, Feslinger, & Sears, 1946). If one believes that consuming alcohol will give pleasure, reduce tension, make one more attractive, or achieve other positively valued states, then one is more likely to consume alcohol. The actual pharmacological effects of alcohol are therefore not as important as what one believes about those effects. Adolescents learn to expect that alcohol use is functional, helping them achieve desired ends. Advertising, promotion, television programming, parents, peers, and other dimensions of the social environment all can lead to the expectation that alcohol makes one attractive, powerful, mature, and happy. Prevention implications include cognitive "reprogramming" so that the outcomes of drinking are not perceived as positive and providing alternative methods to achieve valued states.

Problem behavior theory is a social-psychological theory of youth "problem" behavior, including alcohol use (R. Jessor, 1987; R. Jessor & S. L. Jessor, 1977). The theory postulates intercorrelations among a series of specific problem behavior areas (e.g., drug use, sexual intercourse, and other deviant behaviors) and indicators of conventional behaviors (e.g., academic achievement, church attendance) such that higher levels of problem behaviors and lower levels of conventional behaviors are associated with increased drinking. In addition, a variety of personal belief variables (e.g., values, locus of control), perceptions of parents' and friends' behaviors and support, and demographic/socialization background variables are postulated to affect youth drinking. Suggestions for prevention include the promotion of conventional behaviors and perceptions or beliefs that alcohol use is unacceptable and unsupported by significant others.

Stage theory of alcohol use focuses on the sequence of initiation of various drugs (Bailey, 1992; Kandel, 1975, 1989; Kandel, Yamaguchi, & Chen, 1992). Youth drug users typically begin with drugs that are legal for adults and for which social norms and meanings are less negative, such as tobacco and alcohol. A subset of tobacco and alcohol users then progresses to the least socially objectionable illegal drugs, such as marijuana. A further subset of the population moves on to the "hardest" drugs that have the strongest social proscriptions on use, such as heroin or crack cocaine. Adolescent alcohol use can therefore be con-

[3]For specific references for the theories cited, contact the authors.

sidered a "gateway" drug. Efforts to prevent drug problems would focus ideally on delaying or preventing the onset of alcohol use—not just because of the consequences of alcohol use alone, but also because of its potential for increasing the acceptability of other licit and illicit drugs.

Economic theories of alcohol use state that individuals make rational decisions to consume products in which they find utility (Becker & Murphy, 1988).[4] Consumers do not consume an infinite amount of alcohol, but rather they make decisions on whether to consume a drink on the basis of a balance of the expected utility from consuming it and the costs of doing so. Thus, consumption of alcohol is tied to the costs of the product in relation to the amount of disposable income available. Econometric studies have established that alcohol consumption is price elastic (Ornstein, 1980) and that young people are the most responsive to an increase in price by reducing consumption (Coate & Grossman, 1988).

Adolescents take many things into account in making decisions to drink, and many of those considerations are related to social expectations and influences concerning alcohol use, not just direct economic costs and benefits. Prevention efforts based on such an economic or decision-making model must recognize the functionality of alcohol use from an adolescent's perspective and encourage a broader awareness of the negative consequences of use and of normative expectations that not drinking has positive outcomes. Finally, an important way to reduce youth alcohol use may be to increase its direct cost through increased taxes and prices as well as to increase its indirect cost by reducing its accessibility to youths.

Operant conditioning theory postulates that people consume alcohol because it is reinforcing to do so. Behavior that is rewarded tends to be repeated (Skinner, 1953). The most direct reinforcement accrues from the pharmacological effects of ingesting alcohol. Adolescent alcohol use is notable for single sessions of overconsumption, during which these pharmacological reinforcers are learned rapidly. For young people, however, reinforcement for consuming alcohol may also be socially determined. For example, drinkers may receive more attention and enjoy more conviviality after drinking. Such rewards are a result of the socially shared meanings attached to alcohol use in various situations.

---

[4]Economic theory is related to exchange theory in sociology, which argues that exchanges are the foundation of all social behavior (I'll do *X* and you are expected to do *Y* in return).

Social learning theory builds directly on operant conditioning in postulating that alcohol use is a socially acquired, learned behavior resulting from antecedent cues to drink and reinforcements that are a consequence of drinking, with the cues and reinforcements mediated by learned cognitive beliefs and expectancies about alcohol (Bandura, 1986). In short, people base their actions on what they find rewarding. In addition, people behave like significant role models and learn reinforcements from observing the consequences of others' behaviors. What is perceived or experienced as rewarding is also, at least in part, socially learned. Thus, the position a person occupies in relevant social structures, and patterns of social interaction, influence what is rewarding for any given person. For adolescents, acquiring or learning a behavior such as alcohol use is not only a result of directly experienced cues and reinforcements but also of observing the response to cues and the reinforcements received by models, either directly observed or learned through the mass media, second-hand stories, and so forth.

Prevention implications of social learning theory include emphasis on negative social consequences of alcohol use, appropriate modeling by such key adult role models as parents, employing popular peer role models to discourage alcohol use, and limiting the presentation of drinking models in media to which youth are exposed. The depiction of inappropriate drinking models in television programming, for example, can be substantially reduced through organized efforts with the writers and producers of television programs (Breed & DeFoe, 1982, 1984; Lowery, 1980; Rychtarik, Fairbank, Allen, Foy, & Drabman, 1983; Wallack, Grube, & Madden, 1990). Exposure to drinking models in advertising can be reduced by regulating or prohibiting advertising in media with a substantial underage audience (e.g., television, outdoor billboards, in sports stadiums; Gerbner, 1990; Postman, Nystrom, Strate, & Weingartner, 1987).

Symbolic interactionism theory posits that people respond to events and objects in terms of the meanings they attribute to them (Blumer, 1969; Cooley, 1962; Mead, 1934). Socialization (both childhood and lifelong) is the process of learning the socially shared sets of meanings attached to events, objects, and language. Humans have the capacity for role taking—for imagining the attitudes and perceptions of others and being able to anticipate how they will respond to specific actions. One's behavior is directly affected by such anticipated actions on the part of others. The meanings attached to specific behaviors are acquired from society as a whole (i.e., the *generalized other*), as well as specific reference others or reference groups. Social norms affecting drinking are derived from interaction with individuals and groups in society, as well as from role models for appropriate behavior in specific settings. Role models and other dimensions of the social environment that define norms around drinking are not only reflected in interactions between individuals, they are also reflected in a wide range of community and societal structures and practices related to alcohol. The presence and active marketing of alcohol throughout the social environment experienced by youth through family, friends, advertising, and media programming therefore help define socially shared meanings that alcohol consumption is an expected behavior. This theory suggests that efforts to reduce alcohol use must involve multiple social structures and an array of agents, including the youths themselves, that are both proximal and distal to the adolescent, including the family, local community, mass media, marketing practices, and institutional and public policies related to alcohol.

Social control theories focus on nonnormative or deviant behavior, noting that deviance is a result of insufficient social controls to restrict behaviors that individuals are presumably motivated to perform (Clinard & Meier, 1989). Such controls may be informal, using social pressure as the control mechanism to discourage deviant behavior. Social controls may also be formal, using laws, public policy, organizational policies, regulations, or procedure specifications to limit deviant behavior. General deterrence theory focuses on formal social controls. Deviant behavior such as adolescent alcohol use is restricted by a threat of penalties that potential offenders perceive as swift, certain, and severe (Ross, 1992). The clear prevention implication is to enact public policies that deter alcohol use among young people rather than relying on their individual values or decisions or the operation of informal social norms.

Anomie theory suggests that social disorganization, lack of social integration, and lack of normative consensus lead to alcohol use (Merton, 1968). The core notion is that a healthy society with healthy individuals is characterized by young people who feel connected to society, feel they have a stake in society, and are active participants whose views and energies are taken seriously by others. Individuals who are integrated into society have a reciprocal relationship with that society such that they give of their energies in support of society and they receive benefits in return. The implications of anomie theory are clear, but implementation of prevention strategies is complex. Efforts should include active support for social changes that would facilitate the integration of youths into communities and society as a whole. At a minimum, prevention programs must incorporate youth as active participants and decision makers in efforts to address alcohol use, not only focusing on narrowly defined youth domains but also on broader institutional and community decision making.

Strain theory is a subset of anomie theory that states that people who do not have access to legitimate means to normatively valued aspirations (e.g., money, status, and happiness) turn to illegitimate means to achieve them. Alternatively, they retreat, dropping out of conventional society. Bonding theory is also a subset of anomie theory. The core notion is that youths who are less bonded to society are more likely to consume large amounts of alcohol (Krohn & Massey, 1980). Three dimensions of bonding are frequently discussed: (a) attachment, which is reflected in emotional and affective ties to family, peer groups, school, church, workplace, and other social institutions; (b) commitment, which is reflected in the amount of time, energy, and ambitions a person invests in conventional activities; and (c) involvement, the degree to which one is regularly engaged in conventional activities such that there is less opportunity for deviant activities, including heavy drinking. Bonding and strain theories suggest that collaborating with young people and building opportunities for them to participate actively in their families, schools, and communities would reduce alcohol use. Restructuring community institutions to increase opportunities for meaningful youth participation, rather than focusing on the needs of individuals, might strengthen social bonds and preclude tendencies to engage in deviant activities.

Availability theory points out that the degree to which alcoholic beverages are accessible to people affects the amount and pattern of alcohol use (Bruun et al., 1975; Holder, 1987). There are many dimensions of alcohol availability, which can be grouped for simplicity into three categories: physical availability, economic availability, and legal availability (Wagenaar & Farrell, 1989). Physical availability is the amount, diversity, and proximity of alcoholic beverages in the environment. Economic availability is the degree to which acquisition and consumption of alcoholic beverages requires expenditure of resources in relation to resources available (e.g., the cost of obtaining alcohol in relation to disposable income). Legal availability is the degree to which purchase and consumption of alcohol is limited by law. For example, sales are typically limited by time of day (i.e., no late night sales), age of purchaser (i.e., must be 21 or over), type of alcoholic beverage (i.e., only low-alcohol beer in grocery stores), or amount of alcohol (i.e., no sales or service to intoxicated customers). The availability of alcohol directly affects opportunities to drink and is also part of the environment that shapes normative expectations about appropriate alcohol consumption. Prevention implications include creating barriers to young people's drinking by reducing access and availability through public policies, excise taxes, and physical restraints.

PUTTING IT ALL TOGETHER: AN INTEGRATED THEORY OF DRINKING

The effort to integrate all of the diverse theories of drinking into one meta-theory is a worthwhile challenge. It serves as a start toward a broader effort of additional theory building, which examines interconnections and similarities of concepts with different labels from different theoretical traditions. Such an integrated model also points out potentially fruitful avenues for action.

In our integrated model, drinking is directly affected by personal cognitions and perceptions regarding alcohol (path O–P in Figure 1). When one expects alcohol to have reinforcing positive effects, when one understands alcohol use in terms of its socially shared positive meanings, and when one perceives the expected rewards of acquiring alcohol and consuming alcohol to be high in relation to costs, one is likely to drink alcohol. Perceptions about alcohol are a direct result of social interactions with significant others in one's environment (path J–O), observation of environmental models (path I–O), and formal social controls (path E–O).

The model points out a key reason that most educational interventions have had little effect on drinking (Moskowitz, 1989). Changing beliefs and perceptions about alcohol through such programs have little long-term effect because social structures, public policies, drinking models, and other antecedent dimensions of the environment are typically left unchanged. Specific knowledge and beliefs about alcohol might be affected, but the deeper social meanings attached to alcohol use, the patterns of social interaction affecting those socially shared meanings, the models of drinking, and the availability of alcohol remain unchanged and continue to encourage youth drinking. Furthermore, factors affecting drinking do not all operate through the mediating influence of cognitive/perceptual variables; they have direct effects as well. Legal, economic, and physical availability of alcohol therefore directly affect drinking behavior; they also operate indirectly by creating perceptions.

Social structures, modified by the degree to which people are integrated into them, affect social interaction patterns (paths B–J and B–G–J) and affect exposure to drinking models (path B–I). In addition, however, exposure to drinking models is importantly affected by: (a) public policy concerning media advertising and depiction of alcohol use in media programming (path A–I) and (b) market mechanisms that respond to and stimulate demand for alcohol (path C–I). Public policy also directly affects formal social controls (A–E), as well as the legal, economic, and physical availability of alcohol (A–D, A–F, A–H, respectively), all of which in turn affect drinking directly as well as through their influence on the meanings and perceptions of alcohol use.

Biological/pharmacological factors also play a role (L–P), although such effects are minor for the majority of drinkers. Consuming alcohol, for example, may be intrinsically rewarding because of the psychopharmacological actions of alcohol in the body. The rewarding dimensions of alcohol use, however, are largely socially learned meanings rather than solely the outcome of the intrinsic biological processes resulting from alcohol ingestion (Akers, 1992).

Social roles, including those labeled as deviant or problem, as well as other widespread social roles, such as that of salesperson or college student, affect drinking directly by offering more opportunities to drink (K–P), and they affect drinking indirectly by occupying such roles on alcohol-related cognitions and perceptions (K–O–P).

General personality characteristics, such as self-esteem and locus of control, may be correlated with drinking behavior. These personality characteristics are primarily the result of the cumulation of past and current socialization; in other words, they result from past and current experience in social interactions, which are in turn influenced by a variety of social and institutional structures. We therefore view self-esteem or locus of control not as causes of drinking but rather as correlates of drinking, because both drinking and general personality characteristics are strongly influenced by common antecedent factors in the environment.

IMPLICATIONS FOR PREVENTION

The many factors shown in Figure 1 are not independent causes of drinking, they interact in a web of social influences. They can be distinguished by their causal distance from drinking behavior and the degree to which they operate at the macro or socioenvironmental level versus the micro or individual level. Alcohol cognitions and perceptions are conceptually close or proximate to drinking behavior, and they would therefore be expected to have higher correlations with drinking than the more distal causal factors (i.e., those on the left half of Figure 1). Distal factors are more important for long-term change, however. Changing a proximate cause of drinking has, at best, a short-term effect, because without changes in the antecedent socioenvironmental conditions, the proximate factors quickly revert to their original state. If the action program that is focused on proximate causes is temporary, those exposed typically exhibit only temporary changes in attitudes and behavior. Even if those experiencing a temporary program are permanently changed, the effect on the total population is minimal because new cohorts of youths who were not exposed to the prevention program are constantly emerging. This has already been verified in smoking prevention research, in which school-based programs had effects for up to 2 or 3 years but the same programs implemented along with a broader community intervention effort demonstrated effects up to high-school graduation, 5 years after the school-based program ended (Perry, Kelder, Murray, & Klepp, 1992).

Our most intensive prevention programs that target proximate causes of drinking expose youths to program materials and no-drinking messages only a few hours a week. In contrast, young people are exposed to the broader social environment of pro-drinking messages for the remainder of their waking hours. As a result, effective efforts to reduce youth drinking require a major focus on changing the community- and societal-level factors that encourage youth alcohol use and require attention to theories of action that recognize ways all participants, including the youths themselves, can become agents in the constant re-creation of their environments.

It should be noted that etiological theories of young people's alcohol use are in some ways conceptually distinct from theories of intervention or change. Each of the theories discussed previously has specific implications for action. Each of these implications requires a theory of change to direct actual efforts, such as the systematic introduction of positive and credible role models or the process of enactment of community-wide or society-wide alcohol policies. In short, it is one thing to know that a specific dimension of the environment must be changed to reduce youth drinking, but it is another thing to know how to change that factor.

Effective intervention efforts to reduce adolescent alcohol use require simultaneous and consistent messages and actions at multiple levels in the society. If the message is that adolescent alcohol use is unacceptable, both demand and supply reduction approaches are needed. Demand reduction, such as learning to identify alcohol-use influences as well as acquiring skills to resist those influences, can be paired with actual reductions in the socioenvironmental conditions that encourage use. These conditions include peer norms around alcohol use, parental support and modeling, alcohol availability and acceptability, and alcohol advertising (Atkin, in press). The potential for success improves as more levels of the social environment provide no-use messages to young people. Because change in these influences is feasible at the personal, interpersonal, and community levels but is more difficult to achieve at the societal or global levels, the community becomes the natural unit for changing socioenvironmental conditions.

Community-change strategies can incorporate multiple objectives and multiple levels of action—through schools, parents, community ordinances, and other dimensions of public policy, institutional policies and practices, and social networks. The social world of adolescents (as represented by the norms, values, opportunities, and support provided by families, schools, and community settings) should consistently and cogently encourage reflection on the implications of alcohol use and the dimensions of social environments that encourage use. The current situation in most communities is that some elements (e.g., school health education curricula) discourage drinking whereas many other elements (e.g., low-priced alcohol readily sold or provided to youths) encourage drinking (Wagenaar et al., 1993).

Several large-scale community change projects have been implemented and carefully evaluated, including projects on alcohol (Casswell & Stewart, 1990; Ritson, 1985; Rootman & Moser, 1985; Speare & Buka, 1990; Stout, 1992; Wallack, 1985; Wallack & Barrows, 1982–1983), drinking and driving (Worden, Flynn, Merrill, Waller, & Haugh, 1989), traffic safety (Hingson, Howland, & Levenson, 1988), other drugs (Johnson et al., 1990; Pentz, Dwyer, et al., 1989), tobacco (Altman, Foster, & Rasenick-Douss Tye, 1989; Forster, Hourigan, & Weigum, 1990; Lichtenstein, Wallack, & Pechacek, 1990), and cardiovascular disease risk reduction (Blackburn, 1983; Farquhar et al., 1985; McAlister, Puska, Salonen, Tuomilehto, & Koskela, 1982; Perry, Klepp, & Shultz, 1988; Puska, Salonen, Nissinen, & Tuomilehto, 1983).

The most ambitious community-wide drug abuse prevention research program completed to date is the Midwestern Prevention Project (MPP; Pentz, Dwyer, et al, 1989). The MPP includes all communities within the Kansas City (Kansas and Missouri) and Indianapolis (Indiana) metropolitan areas. Within each of these two areas, cohorts of adolescents were assigned by school to intervention or delayed-intervention control conditions, with intervention programs targeted initially at sixth- or seventh-grade students. The intervention program consisted of a 10-session school-based social skills curriculum; 10 homework assignments to be completed with parents or guardians; mass-media coverage using television, radio, and print; community organization; and policy change. In the first 2 years of the project, 22,500 adolescents participated in the school and community intervention. Analyses from students in 42 schools (N = 5,008) indicated a lower prevalence rate of cigarette, alcohol, and marijuana use at 1-year follow-up for those exposed to the school intervention (17% vs. 24% for cigarette smoking, 11% vs. 16% for alcohol use, and 7% vs. 10% for marijuana use in the last month; Pentz, Dwyer, et al., 1989). Similar results were observed after 2 years for a longitudinal panel of students from eight schools in Kansas City (N = 1,122; Pentz, MacKinnon, et al., 1989). Third-year results demonstrated sustained impact only on tobacco and marijuana use but with equivalent reductions for adolescents at lower or higher risk (Johnson et al., 1990). The MPP is particularly important because it demonstrates the feasibility of a large-scale community-wide effort focused exclusively on youth, because of its impact on those at high risk, and because it has considerable methodological strength. The program's long-term impact on tobacco and marijuana use is still to be determined. The apparent lack of long-term impact on alcohol use is noteworthy.

Our review of previous community projects provides several insights that guide our current efforts. In previous projects, educational interventions alone were inadequate to achieve a long-term change in health behavior. Repeatedly, investigators realized they were attempting a health education and behavior change intervention within a broader environment that is generally hostile to the intervention goals. Hostility as used here does not imply intentionality, only that the natural consequence of competing community interests results in segments of the environment that are opposed to successful prevention efforts, particularly when they threaten benefits that some are accruing from the status quo. The hostile environment is particularly evident when attempting to change mass behavior in a way that threatens the interests of large industries, such as tobacco and alcohol producers, distributors, and retailers (Worden, 1979). The hostile environment is also characterized by norms supporting risky behavior—or at least ambivalence about such behavior. As a result, successful interventions must directly address the environment that is permitting or encouraging risky behaviors. Previous intervention trials that began to address broader environmental contributors to health problems have often faced controversy and political conflict (Casswell & Stewart, 1990). Addressing environmental contributors to health problems leads to a significantly higher degree of unpredictability, as political forces coalesce in favor of and in opposition to interventions that may successfully affect the consumption of commercially sold products. Despite the complexity and unpredictability of interventions focused on socioenvironmental change, it is apparent that long-term reductions in youth alcohol use will require such efforts.

It is worth noting that another major community project, the Trauma Reduction Trial, is also based on the conclusion that broader social and environmental change is needed to successfully address community alcohol problems. The Trauma Reduction Trial is a quasi-experimental study of two pairs of communities in which one community in each pair implements a package of programs designed to reduce alcohol-related injury (Holder, personal communication). The project is in progress and results are not yet available.

Two large-scale community trial projects that evolved out of the theoretical framework presented here are currently in progress. Both are designed to reduce underage drinking: Project Northland focuses on initiation into alcohol use among 10- to 14-year-olds, and Communities Mobilizing for Change on Alcohol (CMCA) focuses on alcohol use and intoxication among 15- to 20-year-olds. Northland combines school curricula with peer leader, parent, and community support components, and CMCA organizes and empowers community residents to change institutional and public policies and practices regarding the accessibility of alcohol to youth. Thus, CMCA focuses more on the left two columns in Figure 1, and Northland focuses more on the middle and right side of Figure 1. Both projects represent the integration of concepts from multiple theoretical perspectives. Both projects are randomized trials with large numbers of communities and both collect a comprehensive series of process and outcome data. The two projects are critically different, however, in the theoretical foundation for the intervention efforts and in how the intervention is implemented. Northland has a model alcohol education curriculum, developed outside the community, that is implemented through a project coordinator in schools and with parents in each community. In contrast, CMCA has a local organizer who maps the power structure of each community, organizes a local strategy team, brokers diverse interests, and works with the full range of community sectors to develop strategies for changing the community environment, institutional practices, and public policies regarding alcohol. Each project is now reviewed in more detail.[5]

CMCA PROJECT: COMMUNITIES MOBILIZING FOR CHANGE ON ALCOHOL

This 15-community, 5-year randomized trial is designed to: (a) develop community-based strategies, designed by community mem-

[5]Both the CMCA and Northland projects are in the early phase of implementation. A full range of baseline data has been collected; information on the effect of the interventions will be available in several years, after follow-up data are collected.

bers (including youth), for public action on the full range of alcohol-related social and health problems among youth; (b) reduce the availability of alcohol to young people under the legal age; (c) reduce alcohol consumption among those under age 21; and (d) reduce injury, morbidity, and other health and social problems related to alcohol use among young people.

Evaluation of intervention effectiveness will include measurement of: (a) perceived and actual degree of alcohol accessibility to youths in the study communities; (b) differential degree of access in terms of characteristics of individual purchasers, social situations, social groups, alcohol selling establishments, and communities; and (c) a range of alcohol-related behaviors and outcomes using longitudinal survey methods and time-series analyses of archival records. The project is an outgrowth of previous research demonstrating the effects of public policy and the social environment on youth alcohol use (O'Malley & Wagenaar, 1991; Wagenaar, 1983, 1986). The CMCA project is also developing new theory concerning public action on alcohol, with the participation of a broad interdisciplinary research team, including political and social theorists (Boyte, 1984, 1989). In short, the project is based on three developing streams of theory, one on the determinants of youth alcohol use, a second on the role of public and institutional policies in preventing alcohol problems, and a third on organizing communities to take collective action to alter the environment regarding alcohol, which is the subject of a forthcoming article by Wolfson et al.

Specific objectives of the CMCA organizing effort are to change community policies and procedures so as to reduce: (a) the accessibility of alcohol to youth; (b) the number and proportion of alcohol outlets selling to underage individuals; (c) accessibility of alcohol to young people, whether the source of alcohol is commercial establishments, parents, other adults, or other youths; (d) youth and adult support or tolerance of underage purchase and consumption of alcohol; (e) the prevalence, quantity, and frequency of alcohol consumption among youths 15 to 20 years of age; and (f) the incidence of alcohol-related health and social problems among young people of these ages.

The CMCA project is distinguished from most previous work in that we are collaborating with community leaders to develop locally designed strategies for action. Thus, the community is not just a site for the intervention, and it is not simply an instrument for professional manipulation or direction, but rather, it is an integral agent in project design and implementation. We are testing the effects of a theory-based process of community public action, from which new theoretical insights can be generated rather than evaluating the effects of a single intervention strategy or activity. Our objective is to enhance community capacity for public action, which should result in changes in community policies and practices, which is the focus of most previous community studies. Sample action strategies are shown in Table 1. The exact set of strategies implemented in a given community will be the result of public deliberations by residents (both youth and adults) mobilized in each community.

The communities were selected for the organizing effort randomly, not on the basis of the existence of community coalitions, other measures of readiness for action, or the extent of problems with youth drinking. Random assignment to condition is a core dimension of our research design that very few community trials implement; it dramatically improves the internal validity of the study, permitting causal inferences with a high degree of confidence. All communities within a 235-mile radius of the Twin Cities that met our size criterion and did not already have a major externally funded youth alcohol project (e.g., Center for Substance Abuse Prevention community partnership grant) were in the pool of eligible communities. After baseline surveys were completed in 15 communities, communities were randomly assigned to treatment or control condition. Thus, the project tests the ability of the organizing theory and methods to activate randomly selected communities to address dimensions of social, policy, and institutional environments that foster underage drinking.

Evaluation of the project is multidimensional, using a wide variety of process and outcome measures collected from the full set of 15 communities. We discussed the complexity of the tradeoffs between the demands of science and the demands of practice in designing such a trial in a previous article (Wagenaar & Wolfson, in press), and a comprehensive discussion of CMCA research design, data collection, and analysis issues is also available (Wagenaar, Murray, Wolfson, Forster, & Finnegan, 1994). Outcome data are being collected through school surveys of 9th and 12th graders in each community; telephone surveys of 18- to 20-year-olds; surveys of alcohol merchants; direct youth purchase attempts at on- and off-sale alcohol outlets; content analyses of print media; monitoring of governmental and organizational meeting minutes, policies, and practices; and census, police, hospital and other records on community characteristics and alcohol-related health and social problems. In addition, continuous process evaluation data are being collected by organizers and project staff in each intervention community.

TABLE 1
CMCA Project Action Strategy Examples

Community enforcement actions
Enforcement of laws prohibiting provision of alcohol to minors.
Decoy operations on outlets.
Comprehensive approach to alcohol-access laws.
Police attempt to identify source of alcohol in incidents.
Police or public safety departments notify retailers of age of sale laws and enforcement policy.
Citizen monitoring of outlets selling to youth.
Enforcement of institutional policies (school, workplace).
Enforcement of community regulations regarding alcohol.
Community institutional policies
Written policies at alcohol establishments on underage sales.
Mandatory training for new managers/servers/sellers; updated training for continuing employees.
Check IDs of all customers who appear younger than 30.
Employee rewards for identifying false ID.
All beer kegs sold have purchaser's name and address recorded.
Eliminate sales practices that encourage underage consumption (e.g., pitcher service at bars).
Alcohol-free recreational opportunities for youth.
Alcohol-free public spaces.
Eliminate alcohol ads and promotion at public events where youth are present.
Alcohol-free events and trips for youth-related associations.
Alcohol-free schools and school events.
Community-initiated regulations
Restrict sales at locations where teenagers have easy access (e.g., gas stations and convenience stores near schools).
Mandate training of all managers and servers/sellers in alcohol outlets.
Restrict sales practices that particularly encourage underage consumption (e.g., pitcher service at bars).
Zone alcohol-free public areas.
Planning and zoning ordinances.
Restrict types/numbers/placement of billboards or other advertisements.
Reduce hours of sale, early closing hours to reduce nighttime off-sale access.
Public hearings for new and renewed liquor licenses.
Restrict alcohol sales at community events.
Require outlets to have written policies and plans to prevent underage purchases.
Community information dissemination
Create social pressure against providing alcohol to youth.
Education of alcohol establishments including: management and server/seller training, identification of underage youth, and false ID.
Educate alcohol establishments and other community adults about liability laws.
Encourage news reporting of alcohol-related problems.
Media advocacy.
Speakers bureau.
Call attention to ads that appeal to youth.
Counter-ads and counter promotions.
Educate community groups (e.g., church and civic groups) on actions they can take.
Youth education.
Parent education.

PROJECT NORTHLAND: PARTNERSHIPS FOR YOUTH HEALTH

Project Northland was designed to test the efficacy of a community-wide effort to prevent alcohol use among 10- to 14-year-olds. The aim of the project is to reduce the incidence and prevalence of alcohol use among a cohort of young adolescents, the Class of 1998, who were sixth-grade students during the 1991–1992 school year. This cohort is being exposed to 3 years of school-based skills training curricula, peer leadership, parental involvement, and community-wide policy changes around the use of alcohol by adolescents. The components of the intervention are the outgrowth of previous research of the past decade that appeared both to be effective and feasible given the aims of the study (Forster et al., 1990; Pentz, Dwyer, & MacKinnon, 1989; Perry, Klepp, & Sillers, 1989; Perry, Luepker, et al., 1989).

The study sample consists of all adolescents in the Class of 1998 in 24 public-school districts from six northeastern counties of Minnesota (N = 2,419). These counties were selected because this area of Minnesota is at very high risk for alcohol-related problems. Among the 87 counties in Minnesota, for example, the number one and three counties for a composite of alcohol-related problems (morbidity and mortality) are in this region (National Institute on Alcohol Abuse and Alcoholism [NIAAA], 1991). The six Project Northland counties include a total population of about 235,000 people who are primarily of European ethnic composition. Adolescents from four Native-American (Ojibway) reservations in this region attend public schools in the 24 school districts, and they generally exhibit a higher prevalence of alcohol-related problems. Fourteen districts were randomly assigned to an immediate education program condition, with the other 10 serving as controls. The latter 10 school districts, assigned to the delayed program condition, will receive educational materials in 1994.

The 3-year intervention program includes planned parental involvement, peer-led school-based programs, peer leadership training, and community-wide policy changes in the 14 educational program communities. Adolescents in the Class of 1998 will be exposed to the intervention during their sixth, seventh, and eighth grades (1991–1994). In the sixth grade, the students took part in the Slick Tracy Home Team Program, in which they were given activity packets to complete at home with their parents. The packets included the Slick Tracy comic strip, a follow-up activity or game for parents to participate in with their child, questions for the sixth grader to consider, and Northland Notes for Parents. The students returned a card to their classrooms that indicated their participation as well as that of their parents. At the end of this program, Slick Tracy Nights were held at every school at which student alcohol-related projects and posters were shared with parents and other community members. Peer leaders were elected by their classmates and trained by University of Minnesota staff to encourage participation and to lead short activities in the classroom that complemented the themes of the comic book series. Finally, community-wide task forces were convened and took part in 2-day workshops to consider community-wide activities and policy options that would be feasible within each of their communities. Each community implemented a kickoff activity for Project Northland in the spring, 1992. Similar multilevel programs, linking students, parents, school personnel, and community representatives, are now ongoing for seventh graders in the second year of intervention. These are summarized in Table 2.

The Project Northland intervention program is unique because of the multiple levels of programs that are being implemented simultaneously and consistently in all of the communities. Each community implements the parental involvement programs, the classroom-based resistance skills curricula, alcohol-free extracurricular events for adolescents that are directed by peers, and community-wide activities and policy changes. Significant guidance is provided by the University researchers, staff, and community coordinators who represent Project Northland and yet are members of these northern Minnesota communities. The intervention program is also unique in that it explicitly links students with parents, parents with the school, students with school activities, and students and parents with the larger community. The multiple levels of intervention are therefore not distinct, but rather, they create a web of consistent ideas and messages concerning adolescent alcohol use at a time when onset is most likely to occur.

Evaluation methods for Project Northland were selected to measure change at five levels in each community. They consist of: (a) a student survey for the Class of 1998 students, (b) a parent survey for the parents of the Class of 1998, (c) a community leader survey of five specific leaders in each of the communities adjacent to the 24 school districts, (d) an observation study of potential underage buying of alcohol in all off-sale

TABLE 2
Project Northland Program Components

Years	*Program*	*Description*
School-based and peer leadership programs		
1991–1992	The Slick Tracy Program	Four sessions of peer-led activities in class to introduce Slick Tracy Home Team concepts.
1992–1993	Amazing Alternatives!	Eight sessions of peer-led activities around resisting influences to use alcohol and normative expectations.
1992–1993	Alternatives!	Multiple extracurricular social events planned by peer leaders for all seventh-grade students.
1993–1994	Shifting Gears	Eight sessions of peer-led activities around nondrinking, safe driving, and community action.
Parent involvement programs		
1991–1992	The Slick Tracy Home Team	4 weeks of activities for sixth graders and parents to complete at home regarding adolescent alcohol use issues, presented in comic book format.
1991–1992	The Slick Tracy Night	A family night for sixth graders to share health-related projects and posters with their families.
1992–1993	The Amazing Alternatives Home Program	4 weeks of activities for seventh graders and parents to complete at home.
1992–1993	The Amazing Alternatives Awesome Autumn Party	A fall-alternatives fun night for the family.
1993–1994	Shifting Gears Parents Nights	A series of forums on adolescent health issues.
Community-wide programs		
1991–1992	Task-Force Development	Community leaders are convened by Project Northland coordinators, policy options are prioritized, and community kickoff is implemented.
1992–1993	Adolescent Alcohol-Use Access	Task forces implement education and enforcement to reduce teenage access to alcohol to create alcohol-free alternative events.
1993–1994	Policy Development	Task forces develop and plan implementation of new policies regarding adolescent alcohol use.

outlets in the region, and (e) a survey of alcohol merchants. Other process measures, such as participation in activities, monitoring of local newspapers, and feedback from task force members, are being implemented so that the lessons learned through this multilevel complex study can be disseminated.

CONCLUSIONS

Effective efforts to reduce youth drinking and associated health and social problems must focus on change at multiple levels—family, social groups, community, and society. Attempting to change drinking behavior without direct attention to the socioenvironmental conditions generating alcohol use are of limited utility; at best, short-term changes in small segments of the population are achieved. In contrast, a focus on the broader environment that encourages drinking can lead to long-term reductions in drinking across the entire population of young people. Knowing that prevention efforts must focus on changing the broader environment is only the first step. The next step is learning how to change public policy, social and institutional structures, market mechanisms, alcohol availability, environmental drinking models, and lack of social integration in ways that reduce youth drinking. We need to move on to the development and testing of theories and strategies of planned social change (Chin & Benne, 1985; Zaltman & Duncan, 1977), applying lessons from that literature to youth alcohol use.

Effective prevention programs are fundamentally about changing society. Social change regarding alcohol use requires changes in public policy—facing the economic and political power of alcohol producers and sellers, who have a vested interest in encouraging alcohol use. It requires addressing the anomie, limited opportunity structure, and lack of social integration of large numbers of young people in our society. Prevention programs must now increase their efforts in this broader social environment to achieve continued success in reducing alcohol-related health and social problems among young people.

ACKNOWLEDGMENTS

Preparation of this article was supported in part by Grant R01 AA90142, to Alexander C. Wagenaar, and Grant R01 AA08596, to

Cheryl Perry, from the NIAAA.

We thank all the scientists involved in the CMCA and Northland projects at the University of Minnesota for their contributions to our thinking on these issues. This article reflects only part of the full interdisciplinary diversity of the large group of investigators on these two projects. We also thank Jan Howard and two reviewers for their insightful comments. Views expressed here remain solely our responsibility.

REFERENCES

Akers, R. L. (1992). *Drugs, alcohol, and society: Social structure, process, and policy.* Belmont, CA: Wadsworth.

Altman, D. G, Foster, L., & Rasenick-Douss Tye, J. B. (1989). Reducing the illegal sale of cigarettes to minors. *Journal of the American Medical Association, 261,* 80–83.

Atkin, C. K. (in press). Survey and experimental research on alcohol advertising effects. In S. E. Martin & P. Mail (Eds.), *Effects of mass media on the use and abuse of alcohol.* Rockville, MD: National Institute on Alcohol Abuse and Alcoholism.

Bailey, S. L. (1992). Adolescents' multisubstance use patterns: The role of heavy alcohol and cigarette use. *American Journal of Public Health, 82,* 1220–1224.

Baker, S. P., O'Neill, B., Ginsburg, M. J., & Li, G. (1992). *The injury fact book* (2nd ed.). New York: Oxford University Press.

Bandura, A. (1977). *Social learning theory.* Englewood Cliffs, NJ: Prentice-Hall.

Bandura, A. (1986). *Social foundations of thought and action: A social cognitive theory.* Englewood Cliffs, NJ: Prentice-Hall.

Becker, G. S., & Murphy, K. M. (1988). A theory of rational addiction. *Journal of Political Economy, 96,* 675–700.

Blackburn, H. (1983). Research and demonstration projects in community cardiovascular disease prevention. *Journal of Public Health Policy, 4,* 398–421.

Blumer, H. (1969). *Symbolic interactionism: Perspective and method.* Englewood Cliffs, NJ: Prentice-Hall.

Boyte, H. (1984). *Community is possible.* New York: Harper & Row.

Boyte, H. (1989). *Commonwealth: A return to citizen politics.* New York: Free Press.

Breed, W., & DeFoe, J. R. (1982). Effecting media change: The role of cooperative consultation on alcohol topics. *Journal of Communication, 32,* 88–99.

Breed, W., & DeFoe, J. R. (1984). Drinking and smoking on television, 1950–1982. *Journal of Public Health Policy, 5,* 257–270.

Bruun, K., Edwards, G., Lumio, M., Mäkelä, K., Pan, L., Popham, R. E., Room, R., Schmidt, W., Skog, O., Sulkunen, P., & Österberg, E. (1975). *Alcohol control policies in public health perspective.* Helsinki: The Finnish Foundation for Alcohol Studies.

Casswell, S., & Stewart, L. (1990). Aftermath of the community action project on alcohol. In *Research, action, and the community* (Prevention Monograph No. 4, pp. 213–224). Rockville, MD: Office for Substance Abuse Prevention.

Chin, R., & Benne, K. D. (1985). General strategies for effecting changes in human systems. In W. G. Bennis, K. D. Benne, & R. Chin (Eds.), *The planning of change* (4th ed.; pp. 22–45). New York: Holt, Rinehart & Winston.

Clinard, M. B., & Meier, R. F. (1989). *Sociology of deviant behavior* (7th ed.). New York: Holt, Rinehart & Winston.

Coate, D., & Grossman, M. (1988). Effects of alcoholic beverage prices and legal drinking ages on youth alcohol use. *Journal of Law and Economics, 31,* 145–171.

Cooley, C. H. (1962). *Human nature and the social order.* New York: Schocken.

Farquhar, J. W., Fortmann, S. P., Maccoby, N., Haskell, W. L., Williams, P. T., Flora, J. A., Taylor, C. B., Brown, B. W., Solomon, D. S., & Hulley, S. B. (1985). The Stanford Five-City Project. *American Journal of Epidemiology, 122,* 323–334.

Farris, R., Malone, T. B., & Lilliefors, H. (1976). *A comparison of alcohol involvement in exposed and injured drivers: Phases 1 and 2* (Tech. Rep. No. DOT–HS–801–826). Washington, DC: National Highway Traffic Safety Administration.

Forster, J. L., Hourigan, M., & Weigum, J. (1990, May). *The movement to restrict children's access to tobacco in Minnesota.* Paper presented at the Surgeon General's Interagency Committee on Smoking and Health, Washington, DC.

Gerbner, G. (1990). Stories that hurt: Tobacco, alcohol, and other drugs in the mass media. In H. Resnik (Ed.), *Youth and drugs: Society's mixed messages* (DHHS Publication No. ADM 90–1689, pp. 53–127). Washington, DC: Office for Substance Abuse Prevention.

Hingson, R. W., Howland, J., & Levenson, S. (1988). Effects of legislative reform to reduce drunken driving and alcohol-related traffic fatalities. *Public Health Reports, 103,* 659–666.

Holder, H. D. (Ed.). (1987). *Control issues in alcohol abuse prevention: Strategies for states and communities.* Greenwich, CT: JAI.

Jessor, R. (1987). Problem-behavior theory, psychosocial development, and adolescent problem drinking. *British Journal of Addiction, 82,* 331–342.

Jessor, R., & Jessor, S. L. (1977). *Problem behavior and psychosocial development: A longitudinal study of youth.* New York: Academic.

Johnson, C. A., Pentz, M. A., Weber, M. D., Dwyer, J. H., Baer, N., MacKinnon, D. P., & Hansen, W. B. (1990). Relative effectiveness of comprehensive community programming for drug abuse prevention with high-risk and low-risk adolescents. *Journal of Consulting and Clinical Psychology, 58,* 447–456.

Johnston, L. D., O'Malley, P. M., & Bachman, J. G. (1991). *Drug use among American high school seniors, college students and young adults, 1975–1990.* (DHHS Publication No. ADM 91–1813). Washington, DC: U.S. Government Printing Office.

Kandel, D. B. (1975). Stages in adolescent involvement in drug use. *Science, 190,* 912–914.

Kandel, D. B. (1989). Issues of sequencing of adolescent drug use and other problem behaviors. *Drugs and Society, 3,* 55–76.

Kandel, D., Yamaguchi, K., & Chen, K. (1992). Stages of progression in drug involvement from adolescence to adulthood: Further evidence for the Gateway Theory. *Journal of Studies on Alcohol, 53,* 447–457.

Krohn, M. D., & Massey, J. L. (1980). Social control and delinquent behavior: An examination of the elements of the social bond. *The Sociological Quarterly, 21,* 529–543.

Lewin, K., Dembo, T., Feslinger, L., & Sears, P. S. (1946). Level of aspiration. In

J. Hunt (Ed.), *Personality and the behavior disorders* (Vol. 1, pp. 333–378). New York: Ronald.

Lichtenstein, E., Wallack, L., & Pechacek, T. F. (1990). *Introduction to the Community Intervention Trial for Smoking Cessation (COMMIT)*. Unpublished manuscript.

Lilienfeld, A. M., & Lilienfeld, D. E. (1980). *Foundations of epidemiology* (2nd ed.). New York: Oxford University Press.

Lowery, S. A. (1980). Soap and booze in the afternoon. *Journal of Studies on Alcohol, 41*, 829–837.

McAlister, A., Puska, P., Salonen, J. T., Tuomilehto, J., & Koskela, K. (1982). Theory and action for health promotion. *American Journal of Public Health, 72*, 43–50.

Mead, G. H. (1934). *Mind, self and society from the standpoint of a social behaviorist*. Chicago: University of Chicago Press.

Merton, R. K. (1968). *Social theory and social structure*. New York: Free Press.

Moskowitz, J. M. (1989). The primary prevention of alcohol problems: A critical review of the research literature. *Journal of Studies on Alcohol, 50*, 54–88.

National Institute on Alcohol Abuse and Alcoholism. (1991). *County alcohol problem indicators, 1979–1985: Vol. 3. U.S. Alcohol epidemiologic data reference manual*. Rockville, MD: Author.

O'Malley, P., & Wagenaar, A. C. (1991). Effects of minimum drinking age laws on alcohol use, related behaviors, and traffic crash involvement among American youth 1976–1987. *Journal of Studies on Alcohol, 52*, 478–491.

Ornstein, S. I. (1980). Control of alcohol consumption through price increases. *Journal of Studies on Alcohol, 41*, 807–817.

Pentz, M. A., Dwyer, J. H., MacKinnon, D. P., Flay, B. R., Hansen, W. B., Wang, E. Y., & Johnson, C. A. (1989). A multicommunity trial for primary prevention of adolescent drug abuse: Effects on drug use prevalence. *Journal of the American Medical Association, 261*, 3259–3266.

Pentz, M. A., MacKinnon, D. P., Flay, B. R., Hansen, W. B., Johnson, C. A., & Dwyer, J. H. (1989). Primary prevention of chronic diseases in adolescence: Effects of the Midwestern Prevention Project on tobacco use. *American Journal of Epidemiology, 130*, 713–724.

Perry, C. L., Kelder, S. H., Murray, D. M., & Klepp, K-I. (1992). Communitywide smoking prevention: Long-term outcomes of the Minnesota heart health program and the class of 1989 study. *American Journal of Public Health, 82*, 1210–1216.

Perry, C. L., Klepp, K-I., & Shultz, J. (1988). Primary prevention of cardiovascular disease. *Journal of Consulting and Clinical Psychology, 56*, 358–364.

Perry, C. L., Klepp, K-I., & Sillers, C. (1989). Community-wide strategies for cardiovascular health: The Minnesota heart health youth program. *Health Education Research, 4*, 87–101.

Perry, C. L., Luepker, R. V., Murray, D. M., Hearn, M. D., Halper, A., Dudovitz, B., Maile, M. D., & Smyth, M. (1989). Parent involvement with children's health promotion: A one-year follow-up of the Minnesota Home Team. *Health Education Quarterly, 16*, 171–180.

Postman, N., Nystrom, C., Strate, L., & Weingartner, C. (1987). *Myths, men, & beer: An analysis of beer commercials on broadcast television*. Falls Church, VA: AAA Foundation for Traffic Safety.

Puska, P., Salonen, J., Nissinen, A., & Tuomilehto, J. (1983). The North Karelia

Project. *Preventive Medicine, 12,* 191–195.
Ritson, E. B. (1985). *Community response to alcohol-related problems* (Public Health Rep. No. 81). Geneva: World Health Organization.
Rootman, I., & Moser, J. (1985). *Community response to alcohol-related problems.* Washington, DC: National Institute on Alcohol Abuse and Alcoholism.
Ross, H. L. (1992). *Confronting drunk driving: Social policy for saving lives.* New Haven, CT: Yale University Press.
Rychtarik, R. G., Fairbank, J. A., Allen, C. M., Foy, D. W., & Drabman, R. S. (1983). Alcohol use in television programming: Effects on children's behavior. *Addictive Behaviors, 8,* 19–22.
Skinner, B. F. (1953). *Science and human behavior.* New York: Free Press.
Speare, M. C., & Buka, S. L. (1990, January). *The Rhode Island alcohol/injury prevention project.* Paper presented at the conference for Evaluating Community Prevention Strategies: Alcohol and Other Drugs, San Diego.
Stout R. L. (1992). Prevention experiments in the context of ongoing community processes: Opportunities or obstacles for research. In H. D. Holder & J. M. Howard (Eds.), *Community prevention trials for alcohol problems: Methodological issues* (pp. 121–136). Westport, CT: Praeger.
Syme, S. L. (1986). Social determinants of health and disease. In J. Last (Ed.), *Public health and preventive medicine* (pp. 953–970). Norwalk, CT: Appleton-Century-Crofts.
Wagenaar, A. C. (1983). *Alcohol, young drivers, and traffic accidents: Effects of minimum-age laws.* Lexington, MA: Lexington.
Wagenaar, A. C. (1986). Preventing highway crashes by raising the legal minimum age for drinking: The Michigan experience six years later. *Journal of Safety Research, 17,* 101–109.
Wagenaar, A. C., & Farrell, S. (1989). Alcohol beverage control policies: Their role in preventing alcohol-impaired driving. In U.S. Department of Health and Human Services, *Surgeon General's workshop on drunk driving, background papers* (pp. 1–14). Washington DC: Office of the Surgeon General.
Wagenaar, A. C., Finnegan, J. R., Wolfson, M., Anstine, P. S., Williams, C. L., & Perry, C. L. (1993). Where and how adolescents obtain alcoholic beverages. *Public Health Reports, 108,* 459–464.
Wagenaar, A. C., Murray, D. M., Wolfson, M., Forster, J. L., Finnegan, J. R. (1994). *Communities mobilizing for change on alcohol: Design of a randomized community trial.* Manuscript submitted for publication.
Wagenaar, A. C., & Wolfson, M. (in press). Trade-offs between science and practice in the design of a randomized community trial. *Center for Substance Abuse Prevention Proceedings of the Second International Research Symposium on Experiences with Community Action Projects, January/February, 1992, San Diego.*
Wallack, L. A. (1985). A community approach to the prevention of alcohol-related problems. *International Quarterly of Community Health Education, 5,* 85–102.
Wallack, L. A., & Barrows, D. (1982–1983). Evaluating primary prevention. *International Quarterly of Community Health Education, 3,* 307–336.
Wallack, L. A., Grube, J. W., & Madden, P. A. (1990). Portrayals of alcohol on prime-time television. *Journal of Studies on Alcohol, 51,* 428–436.
Worden, M. A. (1979). Popular and unpopular prevention. *Journal of Drug Issues, summer,* 425–433.
Worden, J. K., Flynn, B. S., Merrill, D. G., Waller, J. A., & Haugh, L. D. (1989).

Preventing alcohol-impaired driving through community self-regulation training. *American Journal of Public Health, 79,* 287–290.
Zaltman, G., & Duncan, R. (1977). *Strategies for planned change.* New York: Wiley.

Received October 30, 1992
Accepted April 30, 1993

JOURNAL OF RESEARCH ON ADOLESCENCE, 6(3), 271–284

Community Service and Political–Moral Identity in Adolescents

Miranda Yates
Brown University

James Youniss
The Catholic University of America

This article presents a theoretical framework for understanding how community service affords opportunities for stimulating identity development in adolescents. Drawing on Erikson's (1968) writings, which stressed the sociohistorical component of identity, we used Luckmann's (1991) scheme for parsing narratives into levels of transcendent identification. The narratives came from reflective essays of 132 Black parochial high school juniors who worked at a soup kitchen for the homeless as part of a school-based community service program. The majority of essays written at Time 1 (57.8%) and Time 2 (62.5%) could be scored at levels designated from "little" to "bigger" levels, and students who made transcendent statements at Time 1 and Time 2 tended to make "higher" level statements at Time 2 ($z = 2.07$, $p < .05$), thus suggesting developmental change. The results support the view that service experience can stimulate reflection on society's political organization and moral order.

Throughout U.S. history, the idea of youths serving their community has had strong appeal. From John Winthrop to Bill Clinton, government leaders have exhorted citizens, particularly youths, to become involved in bettering their communities. At several points during the 20th century, government

---

Requests for reprints should be sent to Miranda Yates, Center for the Study of Race and Ethnicity in America, Brown University, Box 1886, Providence, RI 02912. E-mail: Miranda_yates@Brown.edu sponsored initiatives to fund and administer service programs have been championed. Examples of such programs are the Civilian Conservation Corps, founded in the 1930s; Volunteers in Service to America (VISTA), established in the 1960s; and ServeAmerica, initiated in the 1990s. The most recent drive to formalize service opportunities culminated in the National and Community Service Trust Act of 1993. This act united several federal domestic volunteer organizations—including ServeAmerica, VISTA, and the new Civilian Community Corps—under the administration of the Corporation for National and Community Service. For fiscal year 1994, it allocated $30 million for the purpose of funding service programs for school-age youths (Corporation for National and Community Service, 1993, p. xv).

Advocates of the current service initiative have proposed that service programs not only provide valuable help to the community, but also have a positive impact on participants. In describing this positive impact, they submit that service can build skills and discipline, provide self-satisfaction and a sense of respect from others, and "inculcate a sense of civic responsibility" (Commission on National and Community Service, 1993). This last assertion echoes William James (1971), who, in *The Moral Equivalent of War,* written in 1910, theorized that national service forms character, encourages camaraderie, and fosters civic spirit.

This article focuses on the effect of service experience on adolescent participants and examines how service experience might encourage social development and political awareness. Our purpose is to provide insight into the process through which service is made meaningful and educationally important to youths. In doing this, we offer a theoretical framework that describes how community service by adolescents affords opportunities for stimulating identity development. We propose that community service may stimulate reflection on society's political organization and moral order and one's agency in relation to these domains. These types of reflection involve situating oneself within a social context defined by transcendent ideologies that command respect and have historical value. Community service is not the only means for such stimulation. However, in contemporary society marked by age segregation and value alternatives (Coleman, 1987), service is a concrete vehicle for connecting adolescents to institutions that symbolize and promote visions of society and ideological interpretations of right and wrong. We lay out this framework and illustrate its use with empirical data from a school-based community service program.

THEORETICAL FRAMEWORK

Researchers have tended to take a pragmatic approach to investigating the effects of service. For example, Newmann and Rutter (1983) stated explicitly that their large-scale study was not grounded in a particular developmental theory. Rather they chose to measure attitudinal changes in responsibility, competence, and anticipated future political participation because they viewed high positive levels as beneficial to individuals and society. In another example, Conrad and Hedin (1982) offered a pragmatic assessment of the effects of service programs. They measured social, psychological, and intellectual growth as outcomes with standardized instruments such as the Janis–Field Feelings of Inadequacy Scale and Owens' Career Exploration Scale. The findings from these studies indicated that community service modestly increases social responsibility and a sense of personal competence (Conrad & Hedin, 1982; Newmann & Rutter, 1983). Hamilton and Fenzel (1988) argued that these findings of modest effects may be due to the wide variety of community service programs and activities included in large-scale surveys, ceiling effects among adolescents most likely to participate, and the difficulty of producing changes in self-esteem and social responsibility over a brief duration of time.

Hamilton and Fenzel (1988) and Newmann and Rutter (1983) suggested that the analysis of the written and oral testimony of participants may be a productive alternative to measuring changes in traits due to program characteristics. The use of this approach to assessment has been fruitful. For instance, Conrad and Hedin (1989) analyzed journal entries by high school community service participants and found that through their writing students articulated fundamental questions of meaning such as "Who am I?" "Where am I going?" and "Is there any point to it all?" In designing our own research, we began with this finding and the possibility that participation in service may stimulate youths to reflect on their present condition and provide opportunities for identity development.

We developed this hypothesis by drawing on Erikson's (1968) prologue in *Identity: Youth and Crisis,* which stressed the sociohistorical component of identity. He proposed that youths need ideological guides to make sense of all that occurs around them. In having these guides, youths can evaluate and differentiate among experiences and come to weigh them as more or less worthwhile. Moreover, Erikson proposed that youths need to identify with values that have *transcendence,* that is, that supersede family and self and have historical continuity commanding respect from others who have lived and will live after them. Erikson exemplified the transcendent aspect of identity by noting that Freud defined his deepest sense of self as "my Jewish native" (p. 20).

This interpretation of Erikson differs from the more typical portrayal of his theory, which emphasizes the individual youth who looks inward to find an authentic self. In the more typical interpretation of Erikson's theory, the outside world exists mainly to give this inner self feedback; and, in the end, the quest for identity is an inward search for self that must reconcile inner feelings with outside feedback. The Erikson who wrote the 1968 prologue emphasized a different self that was situated in time and place. Youths looked outside to society to find a transcendent ideology with sociohistorical validity with which to identify. Here, society is not conceptualized as a background "factor," but as a constituting force, which individuals need as they construct a relationship with "reality" (Grotevant, 1993).

Developmental psychologists have avoided studying ideological attachments even in the simple form of institutional affiliations. Texts on the psychology of adolescence rarely deal with adolescents' religious and political beliefs, even though adolescents can be passionate about religion and politics, which give them interpretive perspectives for ordering experiences. It is not incidental that the available data indicate that community service is often institutionally mediated. Hodgkinson and Weitzman (1990) and Youniss (1993) found that the majority of participating youths became involved in service through churches, schools, charities, and local organizations, including hospitals, homes for the elderly, or sports clubs. These ideology-bearing institutions are constants in a community and mediate between youths and the people they serve.

Institutions clearly represent ideological perspectives toward society and the self's relationship to society. They play the role Erikson recognized in helping youths sort through the values put before them and in presenting clear alternatives. For example, in his study of youth organizations, Larson (1994) described them as developmental contexts for social integration. He argued that these organizations connect youths to their community by fostering relationships with adults, peers, and family, and by promoting a prosocial set of norms. Larson further proposed that this pattern of social relatedness often continues on into adulthood.

A second illustration of the significant role of social institutions is provided by Ladewig and Thomas (1987), who reported on the impact of youths' 4-H membership on later adulthood. They showed that membership in the 4-H was later associated with membership in the chamber of commerce, agricultural associations, churches, and political groups. Adults who were members as youths were 2 times more likely than were nonmembers to belong to community organizations and 4 to 5 times more likely to attend regularly and be leaders.

The findings of sociologists who studied the civil rights movement of the 1950s and 1960s also support our approach to understanding the effect of service experience from adolescence to adulthood. McAdam (1988) and Fendrich (1993), for example, found that participation in civil rights activities during the 1960s helped to define views of self–society relationships that were evident 25 years later. They found that volunteers continued to be active politically both at the local and national levels. McAdam compared participants in Mississippi Freedom Summer with applicants who were selected but unable, for a variety of reasons, to participate. Over the subsequent course of their lives, participants and no-shows manifested separate paths, which were distinguished by the participants' continuing service, political values, and activism.

Fendrich's results are more complex. No differences were evident 25 years later between Black participants and comparison nonparticipants who were officers in campus government. Both groups showed outstanding citizenship records, which Fendrich attributed to this cohort's advantage in recent racial history. White participants, however, did differ from White nonparticipants in terms of the former's continuous record of service over the years.

In both studies, continuity of service over the years was expressed through commitment to causes such as peace, women's rights, the environment, and local politics. As developmental psychologists, we interpret these results as suggesting that service during youth helped to shape not only political–moral interest, but also a sense of identity in relation to political processes and moral values.

The remainder of this article provides an example of how youths' accounts of community service support the view that service stimulates identification with and reflections on *transcendent ideologies.*

METHOD

Participants

The data for this study came from essays written by 132 parochial high school juniors participating in a mandatory school-based service program. This program required every junior to work four times at a soup kitchen as part of a yearlong course on social justice. Although we were unable to collect demographic information on individual students, we had information on the school population. The school, located in a major northeastern city, had a student population of which 40% were Catholic, 35% were Baptist, and the rest were from other Christian denominations. The students were 95% Black, 1% White, and 4% other minority groups. Parents represented a mixed socioeconomic background and selected the school for its academic reputation, discipline, athletic tradition, and Christian values. Many were government employees who valued education and set high goals for their children. Twenty percent of the students received some form of financial aid to help pay for uniforms, books, and the annual tuition of $3,500.

Essays

In September and December, 1992, the first and second times that the students worked at the soup kitchen, they were asked to write a one-page reflection on their experiences and feelings toward the work they did. We provide excerpts from these essays to show how they manifest the transcendent aspect of identity development. We do not propose that this service experience has reshaped the self in some lasting way. Rather, we propose that service is an occasion for stimulating a developmental process that can have lasting effects by directing the individual toward a potentially continuous life course (Hart, Yates, Fegley, & Wilson, in press). Service brings youths in contact with the actual workings of society by giving experience with parts of the system that are not working well. Serving the homeless may encourage questions about responsibility or the distribution of wealth. It may provoke reflection on poverty, racism, health costs, housing, or child care. Thus, serving the homeless during a course on social justice can create opportunities for reflecting on one's place in a larger sociohistorical order, which is an essential step in a lifelong identity process.

Analysis of Essays

We coded the essays using a scheme proposed by Luckmann (1991) as a tool for bringing operational clarity to the measurement of transcendence. Luckmann offered a manageable approach by parsing transcendence from little to bigger, or more concrete to more abstract levels. Luckmann described transcendent narratives as those that link everyday reality to something beyond that reality—to another reality. Such a narrative situates the present moment within a historical framework that acknowledges the past and anticipates the future. In this way, the here and now of immediate experience is incorporated within an interpretive process that allows transcendent meaning.

In relation to our data, we were interested in whether adolescents' essays would express their experiences at the soup kitchen in terms beyond the temporal and spatial here and now. This approach analyzes transcendence into levels rather than requiring an all-or-none indication of the most abstract sense of the concept. Each level is designed to denote a smaller or bigger aspect in clear behavioral terms.

In expressions of *Level I,* students *(i) see other as a person rather than as a stereotype* or *(ii) view homeless as ordinary persons who could be anyone.* In Luckmann's scheme, seeing oneself as like another in feelings or thoughts signifies little transcendence in the understanding of self and society.

Students sometimes expressed this idea by pointedly describing the homeless as people, as human beings, and as no different from themselves in their needs and aspirations.

At *Level II*, students *(iii) confront consciousness of everyday life* or *(iv) compare one's fortune to other's lot*. This bigger transcendence is expressed by reflections on how the students would feel about experiencing homelessness themselves, as well as by statements about how fortunate they are in comparison to the homeless individuals they are serving.

At *Level III*, students *(v) reflect on justice and responsibility* or *(vi) theorize about changing homelessness, society, or political processes*. This even bigger step represents the start of coming to grips with the various ideologies and values culture provides. Students exemplified this level through statements interpreting their experiences as an opportunity to reflect on homelessness as a sociohistorical issue. Often, they brought up the question of responsibility and the role they might play in ameliorating homelessness in the future.

Coding Reliability

Interrater reliability among the three coders (the first author and two graduate students in psychology) attained Cohen's κ of .88, .82, and .74. In cases of disagreement, coders discussed the essay in question and determined the final score through consensus. Coders were blind to the sex of the writer and to whether the essay was written after the first or second visit. In cases where a single statement could be scored on more than one transcendent level, the student was given a single score for the higher transcendent level. This approach is similar to Damon and Hart's (1988) method of chunking in scoring interviews on self-understanding. However, a student could receive more than one score for a single essay in cases in which units were separated by at least two sentences.

Essay Sample

All 132 juniors wrote essays after their first visit to the soup kitchen. We drew a random sample of 16 of these essays for pilot work and coder training. The remaining 116 essays (54 by male students and 62 by female students) comprised the sample of scored first essays. Forty essays (14 by males students and 26 by female students) were written after the second visit; all of these essays were scored for this analysis. The reason for the discrepancy in the number of essays written after each visit is that although the teacher required all juniors to write essays after the first visit, he did not require all sections of juniors to write essays a second time. We have no reason to believe that students who wrote second essays were different from those who did not. This conclusion is supported by the fact that sections were not divided by academic ability, and, as will be shown in the results, there was no difference on the first essay between those who wrote only one essay and those who wrote two essays.

Descriptive Design

This study utilized a descriptive design. No comparison or control group was included because all juniors were required to participate in the service program. The findings are presented to illustrate the potential of a conceptual framework linking service to transcendent reflection and identity development, rather than to evaluate experimentally the effects of service.

RESULTS

Table 1 illustrates the levels of transcendence with excerpts from the students' essays. The first pair of excerpts from Table 1 exemplifies little transcendence because the students relate direct experience to prior understandings of homeless people (stereotypes) and describe a new understanding of shared humanity. The first student (i) explicitly compares personal preconceptions about homeless people ("ignorant, course, and dirty") with the experience of serving a homeless man poor-quality food. From this experience, the student concludes "he's a human being, he should never have to worry [whether it's edible]." The next excerpt recounts how the second student's (ii) interaction with a homeless individual "made me realize that *no one* is immune to it [homelessness]." It is important to note that a student's trading one stereotype (e.g., "all homeless are dirty") for another (e.g., "the homeless are beautiful people") does not count as little transcendence. A key aspect of this category is the understanding of homeless people as individuals, not as a group.

The second pair of excerpts illustrates intermediate transcendence because the students relate direct experience to their understanding of their own lives. In stating "just imagine going through life with no friends and family," one student (iii) reveals that she is trying to "imagine" the life of a homeless person in terms of her own life experiences. In a similar way, the next student (iv) contrasts the experience of serving carrots "black with slime and dirt" to his own free access to food at home.

TABLE 1
Excerpts Representing Levels of Transcendence

I. Little transcendence

(i) See other as a person rather than as a stereotype.

"I never knew how many misconceptions I had about the poor until I had all of them proven wrong by this experience. I thought the homeless were ignorant, course, and dirty. . . . One man commented, 'I hope it's edible.' Why should he have to worry whether it's edible? He's a human being, he should never have to worry about something like this."

(ii) View homeless as ordinary persons; could be anyone.

"The best moment of the day for me was when the soup kitchen was over, and I went to the hot dog stand to get a [soda] and I saw a man, which I had served in the soup kitchen earlier, sitting on the bench. So I bought him a hot dog and we talked for about 15 minutes. He told me he was homeless for the simple fact that he was laid off. That was the first time I truly interacted with a homeless person before. He made me realize that *no one* is immune to it."

II. Intermediate transcendence

(iii) Confront consciousness of one's everyday life.

"So many people got turned down for Long Johns because their names wasn't on the list. And all [the director] could say was, 'I'm sorry, maybe next week,' but the man replied, 'there might not be a next week for me. I might freeze to death.' He had a real sad look in his eyes and he just took his plate and sat down to eat. Just imagine going through life with no friends and family."

(iv) Compare one's fortune to other's lot.

"The lady there asked us to cut open a bag of carrots. I couldn't believe the condition of these carrots. These carrots looked so bad I wouldn't give them to my worst enemy. The carrots were black with slime and dirt. . . . I thought to myself why? Why does it have to be like this? I come home every day and if I'm hungry, I'd tell my mother and in a couple of minutes I'm not hungry anymore. But it's not like that for the people I served today. If they get hungry, who are they going to tell? I felt so sorry for some of the people today because around quitting time they tried to go to sleep, but the lady threw them out. Why?"

III. Bigger transcedence

(v) Reflect on justice and responsibility.

"The director asked if anyone wanted to join the prayer [before the meal]. I wasn't surprised when only one person came to join in. The other people wouldn't want to come because what has prayer done for them? It might have kept them alive, but for what—to live on the street night and day with no friends, no food, no money, no clothes, and no place to go. Prayer for them is like asking for something they know they will never receive."

(vi) Theorize about changing homelessness, society, or political processes.

"As I was serving bowls of soup, I was called to see a four-month-old girl. Her name was C. She had come with her parents to the soup kitchen. They had been staying at different shelters every day. While I was holding her, I looked into her pleading, brown eyes. I began to grow angry, and thought, how can this be? Will this child ever have a normal life? I wanted to take her to the White House and say this is our next generation of America. Are you happy? . . .As I began serving again, I realized I could run from one homeless child, but not hide from homelessness in our society."

Finally, the third pair of excerpts exemplifies bigger transcendence because the students relate direct experience to abstract concepts such as "justice" and "society" and place their experience within a temporal framework, which allows them to theorize about change in the future. The fifth student (v) links his account of service experience to an understanding of social inequity—"with no friends, no food, no money, no clothes, and no place to go. Prayer for them is like asking for something they know they will never receive." The final student (vi) describes how playing with a homeless child led her to think about the child's opportunities ("Will this child ever have a normal life?"), government responsibility ("I wanted to take her to the White House"), and the student's own role ("I could run from one homeless child, but not hide from homelessness in our society"). The important elements of this category are a macrolevel interpretation of the experience and a vision of change. The specific content of this interpretation and vision can take a variety of forms. For example, some students emphasized government responsibility, whereas others focused on the importance of personal actions.

In our attempt to assess the soup kitchen essays according to this scheme for transcendence, we focused on two questions: How many of the first and second essays include statements of transcendence? and What is the relation between the first and second essays, specifically, would students who made transcendent statements in both essays make higher level statements in the second essay?

In answer to the first question, Table 2 shows that 57.8% of the first essays and 62.5% of the second essays contained statements that could be scored at some level of transcendence. No differences attributable to the sex of the participant were found for the two essays. It was also found that for the first essay, there were no differences in the percentage of transcendent statements between those students who wrote only one essay and those

TABLE 2
Frequency Table for First and Second Essays

Level of Transcendence	*Percentage of First Essays*	*Percentage of Second Essays*
I. (i) See other as a person	14.7 (17)	7.5 (3)
(ii) Homeless could be anyone	14.7 (17)	17.5 (7)
II. (iii) Confront consciousness of everyday life	7.8 (9)	5.0 (2)
(iv) Compare one's fortune to other's lot	15.5 (18)	7.5 (3)
III. (v) Reflect on justice	5.2 (6)	12.5 (5)
(vi) Theorize about change	0.0 (0)	12.5 (5)
No level coded	42.2 (49)	37.5 (15)
Total	100.0 (116)	110.0 (40)

Note. Frequencies are in parentheses.

who wrote two. This finding supports the comparability of the first essay sample and the second essay sample. Eleven of the first essays (9.4%) and four of the second essays (10%) included two coded statements of transcendence. Four of the first essays (3.4%) included three coded statements of transcendence. Table 2 displays the highest level scored for each essay.

A key question in applying Luckmann's scheme concerns the relation among the three levels of transcendence. Luckmann did not present these levels in a developmental manner; his purpose was to elucidate the various ways in which transcendent experiences are interpreted. Our purpose, however, was directly developmental, and, for this reason, our analyses addressed whether students who made transcendent statements in their two essays tended to make higher, rather than lower, level statements in their second essays.

Table 3 shows the cross-tabulation between the first and second essays. Of the 40 students who wrote two essays, 20 students made transcendent statements in both essays. Because of the small number of participants in the analysis, levels of transcendence were collapsed into the more general categories of *little, intermediate,* and *bigger*.

To assess the relation between the first and second essays, a modified Wilcoxon procedure was used (Zwick, Neuhoff, Marascuilo, & Levin, 1982). Intuitively, this test can be compared with a typical correlational procedure (such as τ), which one might apply in the case of ordered, discrete variables. In a correlation, the aim is to contrast the frequencies clustered near the diagonal with the frequencies dispersed away from the diagonal. However, in our approach the aim was to contrast the frequencies clustered in the upper-right region with the frequencies clustered in the lower-right region. This procedure allowed us to test the hypothesis that second essays were more likely to be on a higher level than first essays. We did not include in this analysis those students who did not make a transcendent statement in one or both of their essays because we did not interpret the absence of a transcendence statement as a 0 level of transcendence. Examining Table 3, one sees that among the 20 students with scored statements for both essays,

TABLE 3
Frequence Table of First Essay × Second Essay

	Second Essay			
First Essay	*I. Little*	*II. Intermediate*	*III. Bigger*	*No Level Coded*
I. Little	5	2	2	6
II. Intermediate	2	3	5	3
III. Bigger	0	0	1	2
No level coded	3	0	2	4

there are more scores clustered above the diagonal ($n = 9$) than below ($n = 2$).

The Wilcoxon test confirms the conclusion that students who made transcendent statements in both essays tended to make higher level statements in their second essay, $z = 2.07$, $p < .05$. This finding provides preliminary evidence for the theory that the levels of transcendence represent a developmental process.

DISCUSSION

The results indicate that Luckmann's scheme provides a useful tool for analyzing students' experience of service. A majority of the students at Times 1 and 2 expressed some level of transcendence when they could more simply have described concrete activities such as cleaning lettuce and mopping the floor. Instead, they offered interpretations that invested service experience with transcendent meaning, such as understanding that homeless are people like anyone else and theorizing about responsibility for social inequity. Furthermore, a comparison of the first and second essays indicates that if change occurs from Time 1 to Time 2, it is likely to be from smaller to bigger transcendence. This finding suggests that this scheme may measure a developmental process; with repeated experience, transcendent ideas grow from the immediate and concrete ("he's a human being") to the more general and abstract ("I realized I could ... not hide from homelessness in our society").

Our findings support Hamilton and Fenzel's (1988) and Newmann and Rutter's (1983) suggestion to study the effects of service through participants' written testimony. Just as Conrad and Hedin (1989) found, we observed that students articulated essential questions of meaning through their essays.

As we indicated earlier, this study's descriptive design precludes us from drawing causal conclusions about the effects of service on adolescents. However, the data offer preliminary support for the proposal that service activities can be a vehicle for stimulating that part of the identity process that involves situating one's self within a sociohistorical context by identifying with an ideological perspective on it. The soup kitchen essays demonstrate that service can provoke youths to think about themselves in relation to others who are less fortunate than they ("They are regular people just like you and me"). It can stimulate them to think about their own lives in comparison to the lives that differ from theirs ("I could not think how it would be to live in a car. I left there feeling much more thankful for the things I have, like an education better than most of them"). Finally, it can stimulate them to think about the political and moral dimensions of society and their role in making that order change so that it comes closer to representing an ideology that those students believe is just and achievable ("As I left, I realized that this epidemic in America is not a black, white, Indian, Chinese, man, woman, or child problem; it's a human problem. It is our responsibility to see that every individual crippled by the lack of opportunities, and that one chance, is nourished, loved, and cared for. Imagine the possibilities if every church organized a [soup kitchen] in their basement").

The theoretical framework presented in this article not only provides insight into the process of adolescent identity development, but also affords a means of evaluating youths' experience of service. Given the increasing numbers of youths who provide community service, the question of how service affects development seems worth pursuing. Our findings hint at effects in the domains of identity, moral sensitivity, and political awareness. It is important that future research efforts determine the kinds of service that stimulate such reflectivity and identity processes.

ACKNOWLEDGMENTS

This work was supported in part by the William T. Grant Foundation. We are grateful for their support. We also thank Robert Hoderny, Mary Jo Pugh, and Michelle Khajavi for their assistance.

REFERENCES

Coleman, J. S. (1987). Families and schools. *Educational Researcher, 16*, 32–38.

Commission on National and Community Service. (1993). *What you can do for your country.* Washington, DC: Author.

Conrad, D., & Hedin, D. (1982). The impact of experiential education on adolescent development. *Child & Youth Services, 4*, 57–76.

Conrad, D., & Hedin, D. (1989). *High school community service: A review of research and programs.* Madison: National Center on Effective Secondary Schools.

Corporation for National and Community Service. (1993, October). *Americorps.* Washington, DC: Author.

Damon, W., & Hart, D. (1988). *Self-understanding in childhood and adolescence.* Cambridge, England: Cambridge University Press.

Erikson, E. (1968). *Identity: Youth and crisis.* New York: Norton.

Fendrich, J. (1993). *Ideal citizens.* Albany: State University of New York Press.

Grotevant, H. D. (1993). The integrative nature of identity: Bringing the soloist to the choir. In J. Kroger (Ed.), *Discussions on ego identity* (pp. 121–147). Hillsdale, NJ: Lawrence Erlbaum Associates, Inc.

Hamilton, S., & Fenzel, M. (1988). The impact of volunteer experience on adolescent social development. *Journal of Adolescent Research, 3,* 65–80.

Hart, D., Yates, M., Fegley, S., & Wilson, G. (1995). Moral commitment among inner city adolescents. In D. Hart & M. Killen (Eds.), *Morality in everyday life* (pp. 317–341). New York: Cambridge University Press.

Hodgkinson, V. A., & Weitzman, M. S. (1990). *Volunteering and giving among American teenagers 14 to 17 years of age.* Washington, DC: Independent Sector.

James, W. (1971). *The moral equivalent of war and other writings.* New York: Harper & Row.

Ladewig, H., & Thomas, J. K. (1987). *Assessing the impact of 4-H on former members* (Res. Rep.). College Station: Texas A & M University.

Larson, R. (1994). Youth organizations, hobbies, and sports as developmental contexts. In R. K. Silbereisen & E. Todt (Eds.), *Adolescence in context: The interplay of family, school, peers, and work in adjustment* (pp. 46–65). New York: Springer-Verlag.

Luckmann, T. (1991). The new and old in religion. In P. Bourdieu & J. S. Coleman (Eds.), *Social theory for a changing society* (pp. 167–188). Boulder, CO: Westview Press.

McAdam, D. (1988). *Freedom summer.* New York: Oxford University Press.

Newmann, F., & Rutter, R. A. (1983). *The effects of high school and community service programs on students' social development.* Madison: Wisconsin Center for Education Research.

Youniss, J. (1993). Integrating culture and religion into developmental psychology. *Family Perspective, 26,* 171–188.

Zwick, R., Neuhoff, V., Marascuilo, L. A., & Levin, J. R. (1982). Statistical tests for correlated proportions: Some extensions. *Psychological Bulletin, 92,* 258–271.

Received July 5, 1994
Revision received October 31, 1994
Accepted November 4, 1994

Acknowledgments

Hartup, Willard W. "The Company They Keep: Friendships and Their Developmental Significance." *Child Development* 67 (1996): 1–13. Reprinted with the permission of the Society for Research in Child Development.

Cairns, Robert B., Man-Chi Leung, Lisa Buchanan, and Beverley D. Cairns. "Friendships and Social Networks in Childhood and Adolescence: Fluidity, Reliability, and Interrelations." *Child Development* 66 (1995): 1330–45. Reprinted with the permission of the Society for Research in Child Development.

Larson, Reed, and Maryse H. Richards. "Daily Companionship in Late Childhood and Early Adolescence: Changing Developmental Contexts." *Child Development* 62 (1991): 284–300. Reprinted with the permission of the Society for Research in Child Development.

Brown, B. Bradford, Nina Mounts, Susie D. Lamborn, and Laurence Steinberg. "Parenting Practices and Peer Group Affiliation in Adolescence." *Child Development* 64 (1993): 467–82. Reprinted with the permission of the Society for Research in Child Development.

Cauce, Ana Mari, Keith Hannan, and Marion Sargeant. "Life Stress, Social Support, and Locus of Control During Early Adolescence: Interactive Effects." *American Journal of Community Adolescence* 20 (1992): 787–98. Reprinted with the permission of Plenum Publishing Corp.

Feiring, Candice. "Concepts of Romance in 15-Year-Old Adolescents." *Journal of Research on Adolescence* 6 (1996): 181–200. Reprinted with the permission of Lawrence Erlbaum Associates, Inc.

Silbereisen, Rainer K., Peter Noack, and Alexander von Eye. "Adolescents' Development of Romantic Friendship and Change in Favorite Leisure Contexts." *Journal of Adolescent Research* 7 (1992): 80–93. Reprinted with the permission of Sage Publications, Inc.

East, Patricia L., Marianne E. Felice, and Maria C. Morgan. "Sisters' and Girlfriends' Sexual and Childbearing Behavior: Effects on Early Adolescent Girls' Sexual Outcomes." *Journal of Marriage and the Family* 55 (1993): 953–63. Copyright 1993 by the National Council of Family Relations, 3989 Central Avenue, NE, Suite 550, Minneapolis, MN 55421. Reprinted by permission.

Bingham, C. Raymond, and Lisa J. Crockett. "Longitudinal Adjustment Patterns of Boys and Girls Experiencing Early, Middle, and Late Sexual Intercourse." *Developmental Psychology* 32 (1996): 647–58. Copyright 1996 by the American Psychological Association. Reprinted by permission.

Hamilton, Stephen F., and Wolfgang Lempert. "The Impact of Apprenticeship on Youth: A Prospective Analysis." *Journal of Research on Adolescence* 6 (1996): 427–55. Reprinted with the permission of Lawrence Erlbaum Associates, Inc.

Earls, Felton, Lee N. Robins, Arlene R. Stiffman, and Jack Powell. "Comprehensive Health Care for High-Risk Adolescents: An Evaluation Study." *American Journal of Public Health* 79 (1989): 999–1005. Reprinted with the permission of the American Public Health Association.

Hamburg, Beatrix A., and Barbara B. Varenhorst. "Peer Counseling in the Secondary Schools: A Community Mental Health Project for Youth." *American Journal of Orthopsychiatry* 42 (1972): 566–81. Copyright 1972 by the American Orthopsychiatric Association, Inc. Reprinted by permission.

Masten, Ann S., Jennifer Neemann, and Signe Andenas. "Life Events and Adjustment in Adolescents: The Significance of Event Independence, Desirability, and Chronicity." *Journal of Research on Adolescence* 4 (1994): 71–97. Reprinted with the permission of Lawrence Erlbaum Associates, Inc.

Hamburg, David A., and Ruby Takanishi. "Great Transitions: Preparing American Youth for the 21st Century — The Role of Research." *Journal of Research on Adolescence* 6 (1996): 379–96. Reprinted with the permission of Lawrence Erlbaum Associates, Inc.

Hurrelmann, Klaus. "Health Promotion for Adolescents: Preventive and Corrective Strategies Against Problem Behavior." *Journal of Adolescence* 13 (1990): 231–50. Reprinted with the permission of Academic Press Ltd.

Lerner, Richard M. "Features and Principles of Effective Youth Programs: Promoting Positive Youth Development Through the Integrative Vision of Family and Consumer Sciences." *Journal of Family and Consumer Sciences* 87 (1995): 16–21. Reprinted with the permission of the American Association of Family and Consumer Sciences.

Weissberg, Roger P., Marlene Caplan, and Robin L. Harwood. "Promoting Competent Young People in Competence-Enhancing Environments: A Systems-Based Perspective on Primary Prevention." *Journal of Consulting and Clinical Psychology* 59 (1991): 830–41. Copyright 1991 by the American Psychological Association. Reprinted by permission.

Wagenaar, Alexander C., and Cheryl L. Perry. "Community Strategies for the Reduction of Youth Drinking: Theory and Application." *Journal of Research on Adolescence* 4 (1994): 319–45. Reprinted with the permission of Lawrence Erlbaum Associates, Inc.

Yates, Miranda, and James Youniss. "Community Service and Political-Moral Identity in Adolescents." *Journal of Research on Adolescence* 6 (1996): 271–84. Reprinted with the permission of Lawrence Erlbaum Associates, Inc.